109

HATE CRIMES

HATE CRIMES

VOLUME 5

Responding to Hate Crime

Barbara Perry, General Editor
Frederick M. Lawrence, Volume Editor

PRAEGER PERSPECTIVES

Westport, Connecticut
London

Library of Congress Cataloging-in-Publication Data

Hate crimes / Barbara Perry, general editor.

  p. cm.

 Includes bibliographical references and index.

 ISBN 978–0–275–99569–0 (set : alk. paper) — 978–0–275–99571–3
(vol. 1 : alk. paper) — 978–0–275–99573–7 (vol. 2 : alk. paper) — 978–0–275–99575–1
(vol. 3 : alk. paper) — 978–0–275–99577–5 (vol. 4 : alk. paper) — 978–0–275–99579–9
(vol. 5 : alk. paper)

 1. Offenses against the person. 2. Hate crimes. 3. Violent crimes. 4. Genocide.
I. Perry, Barbara, 1962–

 K5170.H38 2009

  364.15—dc22 2008052727

British Library Cataloguing in Publication Data is available.

Library of Congress Catalog Card Number: 2008052727
ISBN: 978–0–275–99569–0 (set)
   978–0–275–99571–3 (vol. 1)
   978–0–275–99573–7 (vol. 2)
   978–0–275–99575–1 (vol. 3)
   978–0–275–99577–5 (vol. 4)
   978–0–275–99579–9 (vol. 5)

First published in 2009

Praeger Publishers, 88 Post Road West, Westport, CT 06881
An imprint of Greenwood Publishing Group, Inc.
www.praeger.com

Printed in the United States of America

The paper used in this book complies with the
Permanent Paper Standard issued by the National
Information Standards Organization (Z39.48–1984).

10 9 8 7 6 5 4 3 2 1

CONTENTS

Set Introduction

Barbara Perry
General Editor

The twentieth century appeared to close much as it had opened—with sprees of violence directed against the Other. The murder of Matthew Shepard, the lynching of James Byrd, the murderous rampage of Benjamin Smith, and post-9/11 anti-Muslim violence all stand as reminders that the bigotry that kills is much more than an unfortunate chapter in U.S. history. Racial, gender, ethnic, and religious violence persist. It is a sad commentary on the cultural and social life of the United States that a series such as this remains timely as we enter the twenty-first century. The dramatic cases cited earlier are but extreme illustrations of widespread, daily acts of aggression directed toward an array of minority communities. I use the term *communities* purposefully here since these acts are less about any one victim than about the cultural group they represent. Hate crime is, in fact, an assault against all members of stigmatized and marginalized communities.

Clearly this is not a new phenomenon, even in the United States. It is important to keep in mind that what we currently refer to as hate crime has a long historical lineage. The contemporary dynamics of hate-motivated violence have their origins in historical conditions. With respect to hate crime, at least, history does repeat itself, as similar patterns of motivation, sentiment, and victimization recur over time. Just as immigrants in the 1890s were subject to institutional and public forms of discrimination and violence, so, too, were those of the 1990s; likewise, former black slaves risked the wrath of the Ku Klux Klan (KKK) when they exercised their newfound rights in the antebellum period, just as their descendants risked violent reprisal for their efforts to win and exercise additional rights and freedoms in the civil rights era; and women who demanded the right to vote on the eve of the twentieth century suffered the same ridicule and harassment as those who demanded equal rights in the workplace later in the century. While the politics of difference that underlie these periods of animosity may lie latent for short periods of time, they nonetheless seem to remain on the simmer, ready to resurface whenever a new threat is perceived—when immigration levels increase; or when relationships between groups shift for other political, economic, or cultural reasons; or in the aftermath of attacks like those on 9/11. Consequently, hate crime remains a crucial indicator of cultural fissures in the United States and around the globe. This set, then, remains similarly relevant in the current era.

Hate Crimes offers interested readers a comprehensive collection of original chapters surveying this phenomenon we have come to know as hate crime. Interestingly, the field of hate crime studies is interdisciplinary, so the contributors here represent a variety of disciplines, including law, sociology, criminology, psychology, and even public health. Moreover, since it is also a global phenomenon, we have invited not just American scholars, but international contributors as well. This comparative/cross-cultural approach adds an important element to the set. It reminds readers that hate crime is a universal problem and that approaches taken elsewhere might be of use to North Americans.

The volumes included in this set have been divided into five distinct focal areas. Volume 1, *Understanding and Defining Hate Crime*, is edited by Brian Levin of California State University, San Bernardino. He has collected a series of chapters that lay a strong foundation for the volumes that follow. The pieces here provide an introduction to what it is we mean by the term *hate crime*. There is ongoing debate about such things as whether the term is even appropriate, what behaviors ought to be included in our understanding of hate crime, and what classes of victims should be included. The relevant chapters, then, offer diverse definitions, ranging from legal to sociological approaches.

One consequence of the varied and divergent definitions used to conceptualize bias-motivated crime is that the confusion also complicates the process of gathering data on hate crime. Berk, Boyd, and Hamner (1992) astutely observe that "much of the available data on hate motivated crime rests on unclear definitions; it is difficult to know what is being counted as hate motivated and what is not" (p. 125). As a result, while both academic and media reports make the claim that ethnoviolence represents a "rising tide," the truth is that we don't know whether in fact this is the case or not (Jacobs & Potter, 1998). Thus Levin also includes a number of chapters that attempt to address the issue of data collection and measurement of hate crime.

The limitations of definition and measurement highlighted previously help to explain the limited attempts thus far to theorize hate crime. In the absence of empirical information about bias-motivated violence, it is difficult to construct conceptual frameworks. Without the raw materials, there is no foundation for theorizing. Additionally, the relatively recent recognition of hate crime as a social problem (Jenness & Broad, 1998) also contributes to the lack of theoretical accounts. This volume, however, includes chapters that begin to offer compelling models to help us make sense of hate crime.

The second volume, *The Consequences of Hate Crime*, is a particularly valuable contribution to the literature on hate crime. Editor Paul Iganski of Lancaster University in the United Kingdom has brought together a unique collection of chapters that explore both the individual and the social impacts associated with this form of violence. Running through much of the literature—even through court decisions on hate crime—is the assumption that such offences are qualitatively different in their effects, as compared to their non-bias-motivated counterparts. Specifically, Iganski (2001) contends that there are five distinct types of consequences associated with hate crime: harm to the initial victim; harm to the victim's group; harm to the victim's group (outside the neighborhood); harm to other targeted communities; and harm to societal norms and values. The first of these has been the subject of considerable scholarly attention. Research suggests that first and foremost among the impacts on the individual is the physical harm: bias-motivated crimes are often characterized by extreme brutality (Levin & McDevitt, 1993). Violent personal crimes motivated by bias are more likely to involve extraordinary levels of violence. Additionally, the empirical findings of studies of the emotional, psychological, and behavioral impacts of hate crime are beginning to establish a solid pattern of more severe impact on bias crime victims, as compared to nonbias victims (see, e.g., Herek, Cogan, & Gillis, 2002; McDevitt et al., 2001). Several chapters in this volume explore these individual effects.

Additionally, however, this volume includes a number of chapters that begin to offer insights into other often overlooked consequences of hate crime: community effects. Many scholars point to the "fact" that hate crimes are "message crimes" that emit a distinct warning to all members of the victim's community: step out of line, cross invisible boundaries, and you, too, could be lying on the ground, beaten and bloodied (Iganski, 2001). Consequently, the individual fear noted previously is thought to be accompanied by the collective fear of the victim's cultural group, possibly even of other minority groups likely to be victims. Weinstein (as cited by Iganski, 2001) refers to this as an *in terrorem* effect: intimidation of the group by the victimization of one or a few members of that group. It is these effects that contributors such as Monique Noelle and Helen Ahn Lim address.

Barbara Perry, editor of volume 3, *The Victims of Hate Crime*, introduces this volume with the caveat that little empirical work has been done on the distinct experiences of different groups of hate crime victims. Much of the literature has more or less assumed a homogeneous group known as "victims." However, this occludes the fact that the frequency, dynamics, motives, and impacts of bias-motivated violence differ across target communities. Thus the volume draws on emerging theoretical and empirical work that explores manifestations of hate crime within diverse communities. Especially novel here is the inclusion of pieces that address hate-motivated crime directed toward women and the homeless community. Consideration of these groups, in particular, forces us to expand our traditional characterization of hate crime victims, which is often restricted to race, religion, ethnicity, or sexual orientation.

Volume 4, *Hate Crime Offenders*, brings us to a consideration of the second half of the equation: perpetrators of hate crime. Randy Blazak from Portland State University has gathered an intriguing collection of chapters. The authors here have been set the task of responding to Blazak's opening question, Who are the hate mongers? Many would respond to this question by reference to members of the KKK or a skinhead group, for example. This is a very common myth. In fact, fewer than 5 percent of identifiable offenders are members of organized hate groups. Recognizing this, Blazak has asked his contributors to explore both individual perpetrators and those involved in hate groups. Thus this is an engaging and diverse collection of chapters, which explore issues ranging from women's involvement in hate crime, to typologies of hate crime offenders, to white power music. He even includes an interview with a hate offender.

Frederick Lawrence, editor of volume 5, *Responding to Hate Crime*, has solicited work from his contributors that gives us food for thought with respect to how we might respond to hate crime. Clearly there are diverse approaches available: legislation, social policy, community organizing, or education, to name just a few. In the extant scholarship, there have been relatively few concentrated analyses of such efforts to respond to or prevent bias-motivated crimes. In large part, such recommendations come by way of a conclusion and are thus not fully developed. Hence the chapters in Lawrence's volume explicitly present interventions intended to ameliorate the incidence or impact of hate crime. While the emphasis is on criminal justice responses (legislation, policing, prosecution), Lawrence also includes chapters that explore preventative measures, restorative justice initiatives, and the role of organizations like the Southern Poverty Law Center.

I speak for all of the editors when I say that we are very pleased to have been asked to develop this collection of hate crime literature. It was a unique opportunity to share emerging perspectives and analyses with a diverse audience. It is hoped that what we offer here will provide the insights that readers are seeking, but also inspiration for further explorations and interventions into this disturbing class of violence.

REFERENCES

Berk, R., Boyd, E., & Hamner, K. (1992). Thinking more clearly about hate-motivated crimes. In G. Herek & K. Berrill (Eds.), *Hate crimes: Confronting violence against lesbians and gay men* (pp. 123–143). Newbury Park, CA: Sage.

Herek, G., Cogan, J., & Gillis, R. (2002). Victim experiences in hate crimes based on sexual orientation. *Journal of Social Issues, 58,* 319–339.

Iganski, P. (2001). Hate crimes hurt more. *American Behavioral Scientist, 45,* 626–638.

Jacobs, J., & Potter, K. (1998). *Hate crimes: Criminal law and identity politics.* New York: Oxford University Press.

Jenness, V., & Broad, K. (1998). *Hate crimes: New social movements and the politics of violence.* New York: Aldine de Gruyter.

Levin, J., & McDevitt, J. (1993). *Hate crimes: The rising tide of bigotry and bloodshed.* New York: Plenum.

McDevitt, J., Balboni, J., Garcia, L., and Gu, J. (2001). Consequences for victims: A comparison of bias- and non-bias motivated assaults. *American Behavioral Scientist, 45,* 697–713.

INTRODUCTION

Frederick M. Lawrence

The Hate Crimes Project in the United States, the expanded use of criminal legislation creating enhanced punishment for bias-motivated crimes, is now nearly 30 years old. Prior to 1980, only the state of Connecticut criminalized bias-motivated violence as a particularized crime. Today, virtually every state expressly criminalizes bias crimes. Over these three decades, states have employed different forms of bias crime laws, some focusing on the animus exhibited by the perpetrator of a crime against a member (actual or perceived) of a racial, ethnic, religious, or other included group, others focusing on the perpetrator's discriminatory selection of his or her victim. Although numerous court challenges have been brought challenging bias crime laws, the constitutionality of these statutes has been largely resolved in favor of these laws, with limitations.[1]

Now is therefore a propitious time to begin to evaluate the full scope of the Hate Crimes Project, along with the societal gains and risks associated with bias crime law enforcement. This volume sets out a framework from which to understand bias crime law, and then considers and addresses many of the issues raised by the range of legal responses to bias-motivated crimes. The chapters use bias crime law enforcement as a touchstone, but many go beyond the use of the criminal law to consider creative uses of civil law and private law to respond to hate crimes. This volume thus represents not only a summary of the lessons of the past 30 years, but also an examination of potential future legal responses to hate crimes, from our vantage point at the end of the first decade of the twenty-first century.

The context for this volume is set out in the first chapter, on hate crime laws and legislation, in which Michael Lieberman and Steven Freeman of the Anti-Defamation League set out the policy rationale for enactment of these laws, discuss the significance of widespread support for these measures, and argue for the constitutionality of well-crafted bias crime laws. The chapter includes descriptions of existing federal hate crime laws, including the most recent proposed legislation that was pending at the time of drafting, and the various types of state antibias crime penalty enhancement and data collection and reporting statutes.

This next set of chapters considers issues of investigation and police conduct in the context of bias crime law. Professor Jeannine Bell addresses the impact of police officers and others in the criminal justice system charged with the investigation and enforcement of hate crime law. Her chapter details the distinctive procedures and means of police investigation for hate crimes and the legal guidelines that encourage police departments to place special emphasis on the investigation of bias-motivated crimes. The normative aspects of this chapter proceed to evaluate which procedures are best suited for the tasks they seek to accomplish. In chapter 3, Robin Parker explores the challenges of police hate crime training in the face of divisive issues of race, religion, ethnicity, and sexual orientation that are inherent in hate crime policies. Parker reviews a wide range of issues raised in training police and argues that to improve training, there must be community and prosecutorial support for hate crime initiatives, and education programs to develop trainee cross-cultural skills and engender an appreciation for the moral foundations of hate crime legislation. Finally, Professor James Nolan and his coauthors, Susie Bennett and Paul Goldenberg, consider the special challenges that hate crime investigations create for law enforcement officers. These challenges play a role in improving both the quality of criminal prosecutions and the quality of the data that become available for intelligence purposes, crime analysis, and criminological research. The unique challenges of hate crime investigations are discussed, including the organizational climate for hate crime investigations, the inherent ambiguity of the term *hate crime*, and special considerations for investigators as they work to provide the support that will lead to a successful prosecution of a bias criminal.

Chapter 5 moves from the investigatory process to the prosecutorial role. Richard Devine and Alan Spellberg, both of the Cook County, Illinois, State's Attorney's Office, examine the special considerations that prosecutors in bias crime law enforcement face. Issues include victims and their reluctance to believe that they were purposefully targeted because of a core characteristic such as race or religion, police officers who may be unfamiliar with the particular requirements of the hate crime law, and community advocates who may believe a hate crime should be charged even if the evidence does not support such a classification. Devine and Spellberg argue that prosecutors must not only work closely with the victims once hate crime charges are approved, but should forge productive relationships with both the other law enforcement agencies and diverse community groups even before a hate crime occurs in their jurisdiction. Prosecutors must also account for special constitutional and sentencing issues related to hate crime cases.

Richard W. Cole, a leading civil rights attorney and the former chief of the Civil Rights Division of the Massachusetts Attorney General's Office, moves the discussion beyond the specific criminal law context and considers the role of civil rights injunctions to protect victims and safeguard communities from perpetrators of hate crimes and related civil rights violations. His essay focuses on the use of the Massachusetts civil rights injunction law as a valuable supplement to its state and federal criminal hate crime laws, but at times the most effective legal tool for combating hate crimes. He suggests that the Massachusetts law provides a model for other states and national jurisdictions looking to adopt successful, innovative approaches for deterring bias-motivated harassment and violence.

The balance of the chapters in this volume explores a range of broader themes implicated by the legal responses to hate crimes. In chapter 7 Professor Cynthia Lee examines the special issues concerning hate crimes in an age of terrorism. She situates the private acts of hate violence committed against Arab Americans, Muslim Americans, Sikh Americans, and South Asian Americans in the aftermath of 9/11 into the broader context of the war on terror. Professor Lee suggests that government action in the war on terror has been influenced by and reinforced anti-Arab and anti-Muslim stereotypes.

School-based antihate initiatives are the subject of chapter 8. Lindsay J. Friedman and Esther Hurh of the Anti-Defamation League and Stephen Wessler and Nicole Manganelli of the Center for the Prevention of Hate Violence review the current state of bias and harassment in schools and their potential to escalate into hate incidents and hate crimes, and review models of intervention and training for students, educators, and administrators that have been found to create an inclusive, safe school community.

In chapter 9, Dr. Kellina Craig-Henderson discusses the services that are most likely to assist victims of hate crime. She analyzes the alternatives available to hate crime victims and suggests the best practices for the victim service providers, including police, social workers, and attorneys.

The context for chapter 10 is hate speech on the Internet. Christopher Wolf demonstrates that legal responses to hate speech on the Internet are limited in light of the permissive rules in the United States under the First Amendment. Wolf also considers the role of the Internet business community in controlling hate speech, but concludes that their efforts, unless coordinated, may have limited impact. He concludes with Justice Brandeis that "sunlight" may be "the best disinfectant" to counter the harmful effects of hate speech.[2]

In the final chapter in this volume, Mark Potok and Dr. Heidi Beirich, of the Southern Poverty Law Center, review another means of combating hate crimes through the use of private litigation against hate groups with the intention of bankrupting the groups by holding them responsible for the illegal actions of their members. They also address additional antihate strategies, many of which use investigative journalism techniques to achieve the goal of destroying hate groups.

It has been 40 years since Gordon Allport asked whether America would continue to make progress toward tolerance and stand as a "staunch defender of the right to be the same or different," or whether "a fatal retrogression will set in."[3] The legal response to hate crimes, reviewed in the essays in this volume, are only one set of means of answering Allport's call, but they do constitute a critical element in the defense of the "right to be the same or different." Legal responses to bias crimes, including criminal law enforcement, civil injunctions, private civil suits, and a range of efforts to address the needs of bias crime victims will not by themselves end bigotry in society. If, however, we are to be "staunch defender[s] of the right to be the same or different," we cannot desist from this task. The essays in this volume are part of that great effort to address this vital task.

NOTES

1. See *Virginia v. Black*, 538 U.S. 343 (2003) (upholding a construction of the Virginia cross-burning statute that limits its reach to cases of intended racial intimidation); *Wisconsin v. Mitchell*, 508 U.S. 476 (1993) (upholding Wisconsin penalty enhancement bias crime law).

2. Louis D. Brandeis, *Other People's Money* (Washington, DC: National Home Library Foundation, 1933), 62.

3. Gordon Allport, *The Nature of Prejudice* (Cambridge, MA: Addison Wesley, 1954), 480.

CHAPTER 1

CONFRONTING VIOLENT BIGOTRY: HATE CRIME LAWS AND LEGISLATION

Michael Lieberman and Steven M. Freeman

HATE CRIME STATUTES: A MESSAGE TO VICTIMS AND PERPETRATORS

All Americans have a stake in effective response to violent bigotry. These crimes merit a priority response because of their special impact on the victim and the victim's community. Failure to address this unique type of crime could cause an isolated incident to explode into widespread community tension. The damage done by hate crimes cannot be measured solely in terms of physical injury or dollars and cents. Hate crimes may effectively intimidate other members of the victim's community, leaving them feeling isolated, vulnerable, and unprotected by the law. By making members of minority communities fearful, angry, and suspicious of other groups—and of the power structure that is supposed to protect them—these incidents can damage the fabric of our society and fragment communities.

Punishing Bias-Motivated Violence: Public Policy Implications

Before turning to a description of existing state and federal hate crime laws, it is useful to set out the policy rationale for enactment of these laws. The starting point for our analysis is that criminal activity motivated by bias is distinct and different from other criminal conduct. These crimes occur because of the perpetrator's bias or animus against the victim on the basis of actual or perceived status—the victim's race, religion, national origin, gender, gender identity, or disability is the *reason* for the crime. In the vast majority of these crimes, but for the victim's personal characteristic, no crime would occur at all.

Analogous to antidiscrimination civil rights laws. Hate crime laws are best viewed as a criminal justice system parallel to the thousands of federal, state, and local laws that prohibit invidious discrimination because of race or other identifying characteristic. In language, structure, and application, the majority of the nation's hate crime laws are directly analogous to antidiscrimination civil rights laws.[1] Under our nation's workplace civil rights laws, for example, an employer can refuse to hire, or may fire or promote employees for virtually any reason. It is only when that decision is made "by reason of" race, religion, national origin, gender, or disability that the conduct becomes unlawful. Like workplace and housing civil rights laws, the prohibited conduct under hate crime laws is the intentional selection of the victim for targeted, discriminatory behavior on the basis of the victim's personal characteristics.

Comparable to other status crimes. Many federal and state criminal laws provide different penalties for crimes depending on the victim's special status. Virtually every criminal code provides enhanced penalties for crimes directed at the elderly, or the very young, or teachers on school grounds, or law enforcement officials. Legislators have legitimate and neutral justifications for selective protection of certain categories of victims—and enhanced criminal penalties—based on their judgment of the social harm these crimes cause.

Consistent with the First Amendment. The First Amendment does not protect violence—and it does not prevent the government from imposing criminal penalties for violent discriminatory conduct directed against victims on the basis of their personal characteristics. Hate crime laws do not punish speech. Americans are free to think and believe whatever they want. It is only when an individual commits a crime because of those biased beliefs and intentionally targets another for violence or vandalism that a hate crime statute can be triggered.

Deterrent impact. Law enforcement officials have come to recognize that strong enforcement of these laws can have a deterrent impact and can limit the potential for a hate crime incident to explode into a cycle of violence and widespread community disturbances. In partnership with human rights groups, civic leaders and law enforcement officials have found they can advance police-community relations by demonstrating a commitment to be both tough on hate crime perpetrators and sensitive to the special needs of hate crime victims.

Punishment to fit the crime. Laws shape attitudes. Bigotry cannot be outlawed, but hate crime laws demonstrate an important commitment to confront and deter criminal activity motivated by prejudice. Hate crime laws—like antidiscrimination laws in the workplace—are color-blind mechanisms that allow society to redress a unique type of wrongful conduct in a manner that reflects that conduct's seriousness. Since hate violence has a uniquely serious impact on the community, it is entirely appropriate for legislators to acknowledge that this form of criminal conduct merits more substantial punishment.

Hate Crimes Defined: State Laws

The vast majority of hate crimes are investigated and prosecuted by state and local law enforcement officials. Hate crimes are generally not separate and distinct criminal offenses. Each state defines the criminal activity that constitutes a hate crime differently—and the breadth of coverage of these laws varies from state to state, as well. In general, a hate crime is a criminal offense intentionally directed at an individual or property in whole or in part because of the victim's actual or perceived race, religion, national origin, gender, gender identity, sexual orientation, or disability.[2]

Penalty Enhancement Laws

At present, 45 states and the District of Columbia have enacted hate crime penalty enhancement laws,[3] many based on a model statute drafted by the Anti-Defamation League in 1981.[4] Under these laws, a perpetrator can face more severe penalties if the prosecutor can demonstrate, beyond a reasonable doubt, for the trier of fact that the victim was intentionally targeted on the basis of his personal characteristics because of the perpetrator's bias against the victim.[5]

Almost every state penalty enhancement hate crime law explicitly includes crimes directed against an individual on the basis of race, religion, and national origin/ethnicity. Currently, however, only 31 states and the District of Columbia include sexual orientation-based crimes in these hate crimes statutes;[6] only 26 states and the District of Columbia include coverage of gender-based crimes;[7] only 9 states and the District of Columbia include coverage of gender identity-based crimes;[8] and only 30 states and the District of Columbia include coverage for disability-based crimes.[9] For additional details see Table 1.1, which shows existing state hate crime laws.

Institutional Vandalism Statutes

Forty-three states and the District of Columbia now have institutional vandalism laws, that is, statutes designed to specifically punish bias-motivated defacement, desecration, or destruction of houses of worship, religious schools and institutions, and cemeteries.[10]

Data Collection and Law Enforcement Training Mandates

Hate crime data collection mandates provide an essential baseline for understanding the nature and magnitude of the problem of hate violence.

Table 1.1 Comparison of FBI Hate Crime Statistics 2007–1991

	2007	2006	2005	2004	2003	2002	2001	2000	1999	1998	1997	1996	1995	1994	1993	1992	1991
Participating Agencies	13,241	12,620	12,417	12,711	11,909	12,073	11,987	11,690	12,122	10,730	11,211	11,354	9,584	7,356	6,865	6,181	2,771
Total Hate Crime Incidents Reported	7,624	7,722	7,163	7,649	7,489	7,462	9,730	8,063	7,876	7,755	8,049	8,759	7,947	5,932	7,587	7,466	4,558
Number of States, including D.C.	50	50	50	50	50	50	50	49	49	47	49	50	46	44	47	42	32
Percentage of U.S. Population Agencies Represented	85.7%	85.20%	82.7%	86.6%	82.8%	85.7%	85.0%	84.2%	85.0%	80.0%	83.0%	84.0%	75.0%	58.0%	58.0%	51.0%	N/A
Offenders' Reported Motivations in Percentages of Incidents																	
Racial Bias	3,870/ 50.8	4,000/ 51.8	3,919/ 54.7	4,402/ 57.5	3,844/ 51.3	3,642/ 48.8	4,367/ 44.9	4,337/ 53.8	4,295/ 54.5	4,321/ 55.7	4,710/ 58.5	5,396/ 61.6	4,831/ 60.8	3,545/ 59.8	4,732/ 62.4	4,025/ 60.7	2,963/ 62.3
Antiblack	2,658/ 34.9	2,640/ 34.2	2,630/ 36.7	2,731/ 35.7	2,548/ 34.0	2,486/ 33.3	2,899/ 30	3,884/ 35.8	2,486/ 33.3	2,901/ 37.4	3,120/ 38.8	3,674/ 41.9	2,988/ 37.6	2,174/ 36.6	2,815/ 37.1	2,296/ 34.7	1,689/ 35.5
Antiwhite	749/ 9.8	890/ 11.5	828/ 11.6	829/ 10.8	830/ 11.1	719/ 9.6	891/ 9.1	875/ 10.9	781/ 9.9	792/ 10.2	993/ 12.3	1,106/ 12.6	1,277/ 16.1	1,010/ 17	1,471/ 19.4	1,342/ 20.2	888/ 18.7

Anti-Asian/Pacific Islander	188/ 2.5	181/ 2.3	199/ 2.8	217/ 2.8	231/ 3.1	217/ 2.9	280/ 2.9	281/ 3.5	298/ 3.8	293/ 3.8	347/ 4.3	355/ 4.1	355/ 4.5	211/ 3.6	258/ 3.4	275/ 3.4	287/ 6.0
Religious Bias	1,400/ 18.4	1,462/ 18.9	1,227/ 17.1	1,374/ 18.0	1,343/ 17.9	1,426/ 19.1	1,828/ 18.8	1,472/ 18.3	1,411/ 17.9	1,390/ 17.9	1,385/ 17.2	1,401/ 15.9	1,277/ 16.1	1,062/ 17.9	1,298/ 17.1	1,162/ 17.5	917/ 20.1
Anti-Semitic	969/ 12.7	967/ 12.5	848/ 11.8	954/ 12.5	927/ 12.4	931/ 12.5	1,043/ 10.7	1,109/ 13.8	1,109/ 14.1	1,081/ 13.9	1,087/ 13.5	1,109/ 12.7	1,058/ 13.3	915/ 15.4	1,143/ 15.1	1,017/ 15.4	792/ 16.7
Anti-Semitic as Percentage of Religious Bias	69	66	69	69	69	65	57	75	79	78	79	79	83	86	88	88	86
Anti-Islamic	115/ 1.5	156/ 2.0	128/ 1.8	156/ 2.0	149/ 2.0	155/ 2.1	481/ 4.9	28/ 0.35	32/ 0.40	21/ 0.27	28/ 0.35	27/ 0.30	29/ 0.36	17/ 0.29	13/ 0.17	17/ 0.20	10/ 0.20
Ethnicity/National Origin	1,007/ 13.2	984/ 12.7	944/ 13.2	972/ 12.7	1026/ 13.7	1,102/ 14.8	2,098/ 21.6	911/ 11.3	829/ 10.5	754/ 9.7	836/ 10.4	940/ 10.7	814/ 10.2	638/ 10.8	697/ 9.2	669/ 10.1	450/ 8.5
Anti-Hispanic	595/ 7.8	576/ 7.5	522/ 7.3	475/ 6.2	426/ 5.7	480/ 6.4	597/ 6.1	557/ 6.9	466/ 5.9	482/ 6.2	491/ 6.1	564/ 6.4	516/ 6.5	337/ 5.7	472/ 6.2	498/ 6.2	242/ 5.1
Sexual Orientation	1,265/ 16.6	1,195/ 15.5	1,017/ 14.2	1,197/ 15.6	1,239/ 16.5	1,244/ 16.7	1,393/ 14.3	1,299/ 16.1	1,317/ 16.7	1,206/ 16.2	1,102/ 13.7	1,016/ 11.6	1,019/ 12.8	685/ 11.5	860/ 11.3	767/ 11.6	425/ 8.9
Disability	79/ 1.0	79/ 1.0	53/ 0.74	57/ 0.74	33/ 0.44	45/ 0.59	35/ 0.36	36/ 0.45	19/ 0.24	25/ 0.32	12/ 0.15	NA	NA	NA	NA	NA	NA

Note: Compiled by the Anti-Defamation League's Washington Office from information collected by the FBI. More information about ADL's resources on response to hate violence can be found at the league's Web site, www.adl.org. Updated October, 2008.

Studies have demonstrated that victims are more likely to report a hate crime if they know a special reporting system is in place.[11] Twenty-seven states and the District of Columbia now require their police agencies to collect and report hate crime data[12] and 14 states require training for law enforcement officials in how to identify, report, and respond to bias-motivated criminal activity.[13] Data collection efforts have also increased public awareness of the problem and prompted improvements in the local response of police and the criminal justice system to these crimes.

Hate Crimes Defined: Federal Criminal Civil Rights and Hate Crime Statutes

There is no general federal statute that addresses bias-motivated criminal activity. The vast majority of hate crime prosecutions are handled by the states. Federal officials investigate and prosecute a limited range of bias-motivated crimes as criminal civil rights violations. This jurisdiction is necessary to permit joint state and federal investigations and to authorize federal prosecution in those cases in which state and local officials are either unable or unwilling to act. These Justice Department enforcement efforts provide an important backstop for state and local authorities.

18 U.S.C. § 241 Conspiracy against Rights/Civil Rights Conspiracy

Section 241 makes it unlawful for two or more persons to agree together to injure, threaten, or intimidate a person in any state in the free exercise or enjoyment of any right or privilege secured by the Constitution or the laws of the Unites States. This Civil War–era anti-Klan statute provided the basis for federal involvement in the murders of civil rights workers Andrew Goodman, Mickey Schwerner, and James Chaney in Philadelphia, Mississippi, in June 1964.[14]

18 U.S.C. § 245 Bias-Motivated Interference with Federally Protected Rights

Enacted in 1968 in the aftermath of the ineffective and inadequate state and local response to the murders of Goodman, Schwerner, and Chaney, this statute prohibits intentional interference, by force or threat of force, with the enjoyment of a federal right or benefit (such as voting, going to school, or serving on a jury) on the basis of race, color, religion, or national origin. Under the statute, it is unlawful to willfully injure, intimidate, or interfere with any person, or to attempt to do so, by force or threat of force, because of that person's race, color, religion, or national origin *and* because the victim was engaged in one of the enumerated federally protected activities.[15] The utility of the statute is limited by both the double layer motivation required and the fact that prosecutions require written certification by the attorney general or certain designees that "a prosecution by the United States is in the public interest and necessary to secure substantial justice."[16]

18 U.S.C. § 247 Interference with the Exercise of Religious Beliefs/Destruction of Religious Property

Originally enacted in 1988, this statute provided federal jurisdiction for religious vandalism cases in which the destruction exceeded $10,000. The statute's restrictive interstate commerce requirement and its relatively high damages threshold limited federal prosecutions.

In 1996, in response to a disturbing series of attacks against houses of worship, federal agencies responded with unusually integrated and coordinated action focused on prevention, enforcement, and rebuilding. According to Justice Department officials, from January 1995 to September 2000, over 945 investigations were initiated under the specially convened National Church Arson initiative. Over 430 persons were arrested and charged with federal or state crimes in connection with over 225 church arsons or bombings.[17]

In response, Congress enacted the Church Arson Prevention Act,[18] which prohibits anyone from intentionally defacing, damaging, or destroying any religious real property because of the religious nature of the property where the crime is committed in, or affects, interstate commerce. The statute also prohibits the intentional obstruction, by force or threat of force, of any person in the enjoyment of that person's free exercise of religious beliefs so long as the crime is committed in, or affects, interstate commerce. In addition, the statute prohibits anyone from intentionally defacing, damaging, or destroying any religious real property because of the race, color, or ethnic characteristics of any individual associated with the property.[19]

42 U.S.C. § 3631 Interference with Right to Fair Housing

This statute, enacted in 1968 as part of the Fair Housing Act, makes it unlawful for an individual to use force or threaten to use force to injure, intimidate, or interfere with, or attempt to injure, intimidate, or interfere with, any person's housing rights because of that person's race, color, religion, sex, handicap, family status, or national origin. In addition, the statute makes it unlawful to, by use of force or threatened use of force, injure, intimidate, or interfere with any person who is assisting an individual or class of person in the exercise of their housing rights. Included within the statute is protection for the sale, rental, or occupation of a dwelling, or for its financing.[20]

18 U.S.C. § 844 (h)(1) Federal Explosives Control Statute

This statute provides criminal penalties for anyone who (1) uses fire or an explosive to commit any felony that may be prosecuted in a court of the United States, or (2) carries an explosive during the commission of any felony that may be prosecuted in a court of the United States. This statute is frequently used by the Justice Department to prosecute cross burning.[21]

28 U.S.C. § 534 Hate Crime Statistics Act (HCSA)

Enacted in 1990,[22] the HCSA requires the Justice Department to acquire data on crimes that "manifest prejudice based on race, religion, sexual orientation, or ethnicity" from law enforcement agencies across the country and to publish an annual summary of the findings. Congress expanded coverage of the HCSA to require FBI reporting on crimes based on "disability" in the Violent Crime Control and Law Enforcement Act of 1994.[23]

The FBI's annual HCSA report, though clearly incomplete, provides the best snapshot of the magnitude of the hate violence problem in America. As documented by the FBI in its 2007 HCSA report, violence directed at individuals, houses of worship, and community institutions because of prejudice based on race, religion, sexual orientation, national origin, and disability is far too prevalent. The bureau's 2007 report documented:

- Approximately 51 percent of the reported hate crimes were race-based, with 18.4 percent on the basis of religion, 16.6 percent on the basis of sexual orientation, and 13.2 percent on the basis of ethnicity.
- Approximately 69 percent of the reported race-based crimes were anti-black, 19 percent of the crimes were antiwhite, and 4.9 percent of the crimes were anti-Asian/Pacific Islander. The number of hate crimes directed at individuals on the basis of their national origin/ethnicity increased to 1,007 in 2007 from 984 in 2006.
- The 969 crimes against Jews and Jewish institutions comprised 12.7 percent of all hate crimes reported in 2007—and 69 percent of the reported hate crimes based on religion. The report states that 115 anti-Islamic crimes were reported in 2007, 8.2 percent of the religion-based crimes and a decrease from 156 reported anti-Islamic crimes in 2006.
- Of the 13,241 police and sheriffs departments that reported HCSA data to the FBI in 2007 (an increase over the 12,620 agencies that participated in 2006), more than 84 percent affirmatively reported to the FBI that that they had *zero* hate crimes. Only 2,025 agencies reported one or more hate crimes to the Bureau. Even more troublesome, more than 4,000 agencies did not participate in this hate crime data collection effort at all. These figures strongly suggest a serious undercounting of hate crimes in the United States.

However, there is no doubt that police officials have come to appreciate the law enforcement and community benefits of tracking hate crime and responding to it in a priority fashion. By compiling statistics and charting the geographic distribution of these crimes, police officials may be in a position to discern patterns and anticipate an increase in racial tensions in a given jurisdiction. See Table 1.1.

28 U.S.C § 994 Note Hate Crime Sentencing Enhancement Act

Congress enacted a federal complement to state hate crime penalty enhancement statutes in the 1994 Violent Crime Control and Law Enforcement Act.[24] This provision required the United States Sentencing Commission to increase the penalties for crimes in which the victim was selected "because of the actual or perceived race, color, religion, national origin, ethnicity, gender, disability, or sexual orientation of any person." Although important, this measure has limited utility—it applies only to federal crimes, such as the federal criminal civil rights statutes and other federal crimes, such as attacks and vandalism that occur in national parks and on federal property.

Federal Campus Hate Crime Data Collection Requirements

In 1998, to increase awareness of hate violence on college campuses, Congress enacted an amendment to the Higher Education Act (HEA) requiring all colleges and universities that receive federal aid to collect and report hate crime statistics to the Office of Postsecondary Education (OPE) of the Department of Education. Colleges must report hate crime statistics for all campus crime categories, as well as for crimes in which the victim was targeted because of race, gender, religion, sexual orientation, ethnicity, or disability.

In the past, the Department of Education's hate crime statistics reflected very substantial underreporting. Even worse, the limited data reported conflicted with campus hate crime information collected by the Federal Bureau of Investigation under the HCSA. Although the Department of Education has always used the FBI HCSA hate crime definition[25] of hate crime, the categories of hate crimes collected by the Department of Education were different from those collected by the Department of Justice. With the support of a broad coalition of religious, civil rights, civic, and law enforcement organizations, Congress recently corrected this discrepancy with a simple, straightforward amendment expanding the Department of Education's hate crime data collection mandate in the Higher Education Opportunity Act, enacted into law as Public Law 110-315 on August 14.[26] Now the Department

of Education's campus hate crime data collection efforts can parallel those of
the FBI and the Department of Justice under the HCSA.

PENDING FEDERAL LEGISLATION

The Local Law Enforcement Hate Crime Prevention Act (LLEHCPA)

This legislation would establish a new federal criminal code provision,
18 U.S.C. § 249.[27] This new section would complement and expand existing
law to provide additional tools for the federal government to combat bias-
motivated violence. The legislation would also facilitate federal investigations and prosecutions when local authorities are unwilling or unable to
achieve a just result. Finally, the LLEHCPA would also mandate additional
reporting requirements for hate crimes directed at individuals on the basis
of their gender or gender identity—as well as for crimes committed by and
against juveniles.

As previously noted, under 18 U.S.C. § 245, the government must prove
that the crime occurred *both* because of a person's membership in a protected
group, such as race or religion, *and because* (not *while*) the victim was engaging in a federally protected activity. At a series of House and Senate hearings
on this pending legislation in 1998[28] and 1999,[29] Justice Department officials
identified a number of significant racial violence cases in which federal prosecutions had been stymied by these unwieldy dual jurisdictional requirements.
In addition, federal authorities are currently unable to involve themselves in
cases involving death or serious bodily injury resulting from crimes directed
at individuals because of their sexual orientation, gender, gender identity, or
disability.

The LLEHCPA would complement existing law in three main ways.
First, the legislation would remove the overly restrictive obstacles to federal involvement by permitting prosecutions without having to prove that
the victim was attacked because she was engaged in a federally protected
activity. Second, the new law would provide authority for federal officials to
investigate and prosecute cases in which the bias violence occurs because of
the victim's real or perceived sexual orientation, gender, gender identity, or
disability, provided that prosecutors could demonstrate a commerce clause
nexus as an element of the offense.

Third, the measure would provide authority for the Department of Justice to render technical, forensic, or any other form of assistance to state and
law enforcement agencies to aid in the investigation of and prosecution of
crimes motivated by prejudice based upon the actual or perceived race, color,
religion, national origin, gender, sexual orientation, gender identity or disability of the victim or crime that is a violation of state or local hate crime

law.[30] The bill would also create a grant program under the authority of the Department of Justice to assist state and local law enforcement agencies in funding the extraordinary expenses associated with the investigation and prosecution of these hate crimes.

Neither the sponsors nor the supporters of this measure expect that enactment of the LLEHCPA would significantly expand the number of bias crimes prosecuted as federal criminal civil rights violations.[31] State and local authorities currently investigate and prosecute the overwhelming majority of hate crime cases—and would continue to do so after the LLEHCPA is enacted. From 1991 to 2006, for example, the FBI documented almost 121,000 hate crimes. During that period, however, the Justice Department brought fewer than 100 cases under 18 U.S.C. § 245.

EMMETT TILL UNSOLVED CIVIL RIGHTS CRIME ACT

This legislation would establish an Unsolved Crimes Section in the Civil Rights Division of the Justice Department, and an Unsolved Civil Rights Crime Investigative Office in the Civil Rights Unit of the Federal Bureau of Investigation.[32] The bill authorizes funds for these federal initiatives, as well as grants for state and local law enforcement agencies for expenses incurred in investigating and prosecuting these cases. The measure is intended to provide for an urgent, well-coordinated effort to investigate and prosecute Civil Rights–era racially motivated murders. While the exact number of unsolved racially motivated murder cases that occurred before the 1970s is unknown, the Southern Poverty Law Center has estimated that 114 race-related killings occurred between 1952 and 1968.[33] The House of Representative approved its version of this legislation on June 20, 2007, by a vote of 422–2.[34] The Senate approved the bill by unanimous consent on September 24, 2008, and President Bush signed it into law as Public Law 110-344 on October 7, 2008.[35]

OTHER LAWS DIRECTED AT BIAS-MOTIVATED CONDUCT

In addition to penalty enhancement hate crime laws and institutional vandalism statutes, about half of the states have specifically outlawed cross burning with intent to intimidate.[36] The burning cross is inextricably associated with the Ku Klux Klan—it is an unmistakable symbol designed to intimidate and terrorize. As Justice O'Connor wrote in her majority opinion affirming, in part, the Virginia cross burning statute in *Virginia v. Black*, "[T]he history of violence associated with the Klan shows that the possibility of injury or death is not just hypothetical. The person who burns a cross directed at a particular person often is making a serious threat, meant to coerce the victim to comply with the Klan's wishes unless the victim is willing to risk the wrath of the Klan."[37]

A CONTINUING PRIORITY

The punishment of hate crimes alone will not end bigotry in our society. That great goal requires the work not only of the criminal justice system but of all aspects of civil life, public and private. Criminal punishment is indeed a crude tool and a blunt instrument. But our inability to solve the entire problem should not dissuade us from dealing with parts of the problem. If we are to be staunch defenders of the right to be the same or different in a diverse society, we cannot desist from this task.[38]

The attempt to eliminate prejudice requires that Americans develop respect and acceptance of cultural differences and begin to establish dialogue across ethnic, cultural, and religious boundaries. Education and exposure are the cornerstones of a long-term solution to prejudice, discrimination, bigotry, and anti-Semitism. Hate crime laws and effective responses to hate violence by public officials and law enforcement authorities can play an essential role in deterring and preventing these crimes.

HATE CRIME JURISPRUDENCE

Hate crime laws have been challenged on a variety of constitutional bases, focused on First Amendment, equal protection, and due process grounds. The defining court decision in the body of case law governing hate crimes is *Wisconsin v. Mitchell*, 508 U.S. 476 (1993). In this landmark ruling, the United States Supreme Court spoke with one voice, unanimously upholding a Wisconsin penalty enhancement hate crime statute against a constitutional First Amendment challenge.

This discussion will focus on the *Mitchell* case and its enduring importance. First, it will provide background on some of the earlier rulings from both the Supreme Court and state courts that laid the foundation on which *Mitchell* was built. Second, it will focus on *Mitchell* itself—the facts of the case, the lower court decision, some of the arguments made by the many *amici* who filed briefs with the Court, and finally then-Chief Justice William Rehnquist's reasoning in his ruling upholding the Wisconsin statute. Finally, this section will examine challenges raised to penalty enhancement hate crime laws on other grounds, both before and after *Mitchell*, as well as key court decisions addressing cross-burning and mask-wearing with an intent to intimidate or threaten.

ANALYZING LEGISLATIVE INTENT: THE LEGAL LANDSCAPE PRE-*MITCHELL*

In evaluating hate crime laws, the judicial branch has understood and re-spected the legislative intent behind such laws. As previously noted, legisla-tors have always had a variety of policy reasons for enacting criminal laws and establishing the appropriate punishment. First and foremost, criminal laws provide for retribution—the perpetrator has misbehaved and the in-terests of justice demand that he or she be punished. Under this theory, the more serious the crime, the more serious the punishment should be.

Crimes can be considered more serious because of their consequences. An arson attack that destroys a significant portion of a city, for example, would be considered more serious than one that does minimal harm to one building. This factor has clearly been relevant to legislatures considering hate crime laws. Indeed, concern about the broader harm that such crimes can pose to a society has always been a legislative reason for enhancing the sentences for bias crimes. When Oregon was considering a state hate crime law in 1983, then-governor Vic Atiyeh supported the legislation out of a belief that bias-motivated assaults were more likely than other assaults "to result in retalia-tory violence and to threaten social order."[39] In its decision upholding the Oregon law, that state's supreme court determined that "causing physical injury to a victim because of the perception that the victim belongs to one of the specified groups creates a harm to society distinct from and greater than the harm caused by the assault alone."[40] The court continued: "Such crimes—because they are directed not only toward the victim but, in essence, toward an entire group of which the victim is perceived to be a member—invite imi-tation, retaliation, and insecurity."[41] Their harm is even greater, according to this court, when the victim belongs to a group that has "historically been targeted for wrongs."[42]

Crimes can also be considered more serious because of the perpetrator's intent. Legislatures have determined, for example, that intentional murder is more serious—and deserving of a harsher sentence—than reckless or negli-gent homicide, even though in both cases the perpetrator bears responsibility for the victim's death. The Supreme Court has acknowledged this, observing in the 1987 case *Tison v. Arizona* that "deeply ingrained in our legal tradition is the idea that the more purposeful is the criminal conduct, the more serious is the offense, and, therefore, the more severely it ought to be punished."[43] The concept is, of course, directly relevant to statutes that enhance penalties for vandalism, assault, and similar crimes when the victim has been inten-tionally selected because of his status.

Retribution, however, has never been the only reason for criminal laws. Legislators frequently consider several other factors—including taking mea-sures to ensure that the perpetrator is not at liberty to harm others, and to

deter others from committing similar crimes. These factors are relevant in the
hate crimes context as well, and courts prior to *Mitchell* also endorsed them.

In *Barclay v. Florida*, for example, the Supreme Court upheld a death sentence for an extremist convicted of murdering a white hitchhiker. The sentencing judge in the case, noting that the defendant was a member of the
Black Liberation Army, a group whose purpose was "to indiscriminately kill
white persons and to start a revolution and a racial war,"[44] had observed
in his sentencing statement that one of the aggravating circumstances sup-
porting the death sentence he had pronounced was that the defendant represented "a great risk of death to many persons."[45] The Court upheld the death
sentence in the case, specifically allowing the sentencing judge to take into
account the defendant's racial animus towards his victim and the threat he
posed to society.[46]

Courts have also recognized the element of deterrence in criminal laws
prior to *Mitchell*. Here, an analogy to antidiscrimination laws is relevant.
Numerous state and federal antidiscrimination laws were upheld against
First Amendment challenges prior to *Mitchell*. In cases like *Roberts v. United
States Jaycees*,[47] *Hishon v. King & Spalding*,[48] and *Runyon v. McCrary*,[49] all cited
in *Mitchell*, the Court made a distinction between hateful views—which are
constitutionally protected—and conduct motivated by those views, which is
not protected.[50] One of the major aims of the nation's landmark employment
and housing civil rights laws of the 1960s and 1970s was to deter individuals
from acting on their biases and prejudices in a discriminatory way. Such laws,
consistently acknowledged as constitutionally sound by the courts, have
compelled employers not to discriminate in their hiring practices, schools
not to discriminate in admissions practices, and public accommodations not
to discriminate in who they serve for fear of legal sanction. In other words,
the laws sought to deter—and have deterred—individuals from acting on
their prejudices. The precedent was important when it came time for the
Court to consider laws that prohibit individuals from engaging in criminal
activity motivated by their prejudices.

In addition, the well-established legal status of the federal and state criminal civil rights laws was another important precedent established prior to
Mitchell. As previously mentioned, federal law prohibits interference with an
individual's civil rights—such as the right to vote, the right to attend public
school, the right to travel in interstate commerce, and many other federally
protected activities—on the basis of race, color, religion, or national origin.
These laws have been upheld by the courts, both before and after *Mitchell*.[51]
Parallel state laws have also been upheld. For example, in 1991, a California
appellate court applied one of that state's civil rights statutes in upholding a
conviction for a racially motivated shooting in *People v. Lashley*.[52]

By 1992, the legal groundwork appeared to be in place to support the
judgment of several state legislatures that hate crimes could be punished

more seriously than other crimes because of the serious threat to American society they posed and because the perpetrator(s) typically intend(s) to cause harm to a broader community and not just an individual victim. The precedents also seemed to suggest that such crimes did not violate the free speech clause of the First Amendment, because there would be no sanction for bias or prejudice unless that bias or prejudice prompted a perpetrator to commit a crime targeting a specific victim because of his status.

Before the Court confronted the facts of *Mitchell*, however, it altered the landscape by striking down a local St. Paul, Minnesota, cross burning ordinance that prohibited "bias-motivated" messages because the ordinance only prohibited one class of "fighting words."[53] In *R.A.V. v. St. Paul*, the Court ruled that the local ordinance was a form of "content-based discrimination" because it only addressed "fighting words" characterized by prejudice.[54] This decision—now widely regarded by many as anomalous—sowed considerable confusion when it was announced, puzzling advocates of hate crime laws and leaving them concerned about what the ruling might mean for penalty enhancement statutes.[55] As it turned out, these advocates did not have long to wait for welcome clarification. One year after *R.A.V.* was handed down, in June 1993, the Court resolved the confusion by speaking clearly and definitively in *Mitchell*.

WISCONSIN V. MITCHELL

This landmark case decided in 1993 involved a vicious racial assault by a group of young black men against a white boy. The Supreme Court summarized the facts as follows:

> On the evening of October 7, 1989, a group of young black men and boys, including Mitchell, gathered at an apartment complex in Kenosha, Wisconsin. Several members of the group discussed a scene from the motion picture "Mississippi Burning," in which a white man beat a young black boy who was praying. The group moved outside and Mitchell asked them: "Do you all feel hyped up to move on some white people?" Shortly thereafter, a young boy approached the group on the opposite side of the street where they were standing. As the boy walked by, Mitchell said: "You all want to fuck somebody up? There goes a white boy; go get him." Mitchell counted to three and pointed in the boy's direction. The group ran toward the boy, beat him severely, and stole his tennis shoes. The boy was rendered unconscious and remained in a coma for four days.[56]

A jury convicted Mitchell of aggravated battery, and also found that he had intentionally selected the victim because of his race. Under Wisconsin's hate crime law, the maximum sentence for a felony such as aggravated battery is enhanced by five years (in this case, from two to seven years) when the defendant "intentionally selects" the victim "because of the race, religion, color, disability, sexual orientation, national origin or ancestry of that person." Mitchell was sentenced to four years in prison.

Appealing his conviction and sentence, Mitchell challenged the constitutionality of the Wisconsin law, contending that it violated his First Amendment rights. The Wisconsin Court of Appeals upheld his sentence, but the Wisconsin Supreme Court overturned it, finding that the penalty enhancement statute punished his offensive thoughts.[57] The state's highest court had an additional problem with the statute, reasoning that it was "overbroad" because it would invite the state to introduce evidence of racial epithets a defendant might have uttered at an earlier time in his life—and thus have a "chilling effect" on anyone who feared some future prosecution.[58]

The Wisconsin court was not persuaded by the state's effort to compare the hate crime law to antidiscrimination laws. Distinguishing the two, the court said that "the Wisconsin statute punishes the subjective mental process of selecting a victim because of his protected status, whereas antidiscrimination laws prohibit objective acts of discrimination."[59] The state of Wisconsin appealed this ruling, and the Supreme Court granted *certiorari*.

When the Supreme Court agreed to hear the *Mitchell* case, many interested parties weighed in by filing friend-of-the-court briefs. Mitchell's supporters included groups of defense lawyers, several nonprofits, and constitutional scholars. On Wisconsin's side, a much larger number of *amici* included the United States; 35 members of Congress; the cities of Atlanta, Baltimore, Boston, Chicago, Cleveland, Los Angeles, New York, Philadelphia, and San Francisco; several law enforcement agencies; and many of the major civil rights organizations including the Anti-Defamation League, the NAACP Legal Defense and Educational Fund, the National Gay and Lesbian Task Force, the National Asian Pacific American Legal Consortium, the Southern Poverty Law Center, and the national ACLU. One of the more remarkable *amicus* briefs—filed by the attorney general of Ohio—was submitted in support of Wisconsin by the other 49 states and the District of Columbia.

The primary theme running through the briefs filed by Mitchell's supporters was that the Wisconsin statute punished thoughts. As the Wisconsin Association of Criminal Defense Lawyers asserted in their brief,

> the right of all people to assert their opinions, regardless of how unpopular or odious, must be preserved—even if this means sentencing a hate criminal under the same guidelines as one who committed the offense for a more acceptable motive . . . the Wisconsin enhancement provision does not even attempt to punish one for the harm caused by a physical act. Rather, it targets only the harm caused by the expression of hurtful opinions. Such expression, however, is absolutely protected by the First Amendment, regardless of the pain or fear it may engender.[60]

Wisconsin's supporters emphasized the devastating impact of hate crimes on American society, and rejected the contention that the statute violated the First Amendment. According to the brief filed on behalf of Wisconsin's sister states, mentioned above:

> Citizens of the Amici States have been criminally intimidated, harassed and assaulted solely because of their race, ethnicity, religion or other discriminatory distinction. Furthermore, the incidence of hate crime is increasing. The Amici States have a compelling interest—indeed a duty—to combat the pernicious effects of such crime on victims and on society as a whole. . . . By enhancing penalties for crimes committed by reason of the victim's status, Amici are adopting responsive and responsible measures to ensure that their citizens' civil rights are protected.[61]

As for Mitchell's First Amendment argument, the national ACLU provided a rebuttal in its *amicus* brief: "Respondent is facing an additional two years in prison because he deliberately chose the victim of his assault on the basis of race. Until he engaged in this discriminatory behavior, respondent was free to think and say whatever he wished. . . . Once he engaged in this discriminatory behavior, respondent crossed a crucial constitutional line."[62] As to the possible chilling effect of the statute, another *amicus* brief, submitted by the Anti-Defamation League on behalf of itself and 15 other civil rights and law enforcement agencies, pointed to built-in safeguards in the Wisconsin law, asserting that "to prove intentional selection of the victim, the state cannot use evidence that the defendant has bigoted beliefs or has made bigoted statements unrelated to the particular crime. . . . The statute requires the state to show evidence of bigotry relating directly to the defendant's intentional selection of this particular victim."[63]

In June 1993, the U.S. Supreme Court issued its decision unanimously reversing the Wisconsin Supreme Court and finding Wisconsin's hate crimes law constitutionally sound. Writing for the Court, Chief Justice William Rehnquist distinguished the Wisconsin law from the ordinance at issue in *R.A.V.*, observing that the Wisconsin law was aimed at and punished criminal conduct, and "a physical assault is not by any stretch of the imagination expressive conduct protected by the First Amendment."[64] He acknowledged that "the only reason for the enhancement is the defendant's discriminatory motive for selecting his victim," but added that "motive plays the same role under the Wisconsin statute as it does under federal and state antidiscrimination laws" that the Court had previously upheld.[65]

The Chief Justice asserted that the Wisconsin statute was intended to address conduct that the Wisconsin legislature thought would "inflict greater individual and societal harm."[66] He accepted that legislative judgment, citing several *amicus* briefs that underscored how "bias-motivated crimes are more likely to provoke retaliatory crimes, inflict distinct emotional harms on their victims, and incite community unrest."[67] The state's desire to redress these perceived harms, he said, "provides an adequate explanation for its penalty enhancement provision over and above mere disagreement with offenders' beliefs or biases."[68]

The Court opinion also acknowledged the relevance of intent in criminal law, citing by way of example its significance for judges attempting to decide on an appropriate criminal sentence—"the defendant's motive for committing the offense is one important factor."[69] Adding the caveat that a defendant's beliefs *alone*, "however obnoxious to most people," cannot be considered by a sentencing judge, the Court observed that there was no "per se" barrier to the admission of evidence concerning a defendant's previous statements, subject to "evidentiary rules dealing with relevancy, reliability and the like."[70] The Court emphatically rejected Mitchell's contention that the law would have a chilling effect, calling that notion "too speculative a hypothesis" and refusing to "conjure up a vision of a Wisconsin citizen suppressing his unpopular bigoted opinions for fear that if he later commits an offense covered by the statute, these opinions would be offered at trial to establish that he selected his victim on account of the victim's protected status."[71]

The Court's resounding endorsement of hate crime laws in the *Mitchell* case reflected a reaffirmation of several key concepts of criminal law. First and foremost, it stood for the proposition that the punishment should fit the crime, and legislatures are justified in prescribing harsher sentences for crimes whose impact transcends individual victims. Second, it reaffirmed that—as in the case of different degrees of homicide—intent is relevant in addressing bias-motivated crimes, and legislatures can mandate tougher sentences for perpetrators who target their victims because of an immutable characteristic such as race or ethnicity. Finally, the Court determined that hate crime laws, like antidiscrimination laws, do not violate a perpetrator's free speech rights, because even if bias is present, absent the prohibited conduct there would be no legal sanction.

PENALTY ENHANCEMENT HATE CRIME CASE LAW POST-*MITCHELL*

In the years since the Supreme Court issued its decision in *Mitchell*, defendants prosecuted in courts in various states have sought to challenge hate crimes laws. These challenges have not been based only on First Amendment grounds, but also on grounds that the laws violate the equal protection clause and/or the due process clause, because not everyone who commits the same criminal act is punished similarly. Sometimes the laws have also been challenged on grounds of vagueness or over-breadth. For the most part, the laws have been consistently upheld.[72]

One noteworthy exception came in Georgia in 2004. The Georgia hate crimes law, enacted after Wisconsin's, was phrased differently—providing for an enhancement when the perpetrator "intentionally selected any victim or any property of the victim as the object of the offense because of bias or prejudice." When this statute was challenged, the Georgia Supreme Court found it unconstitutionally vague and struck it down as a violation of the due process clauses of both the United States and Georgia Constitutions.[73]

Another interesting legal issue was raised in a case out of Brooklyn, New York, in 2007. In this case, a grand jury found that the defendants used an Internet chat room to intentionally lure a gay man to a particular location in order to rob him. In an effort to escape, the victim fled onto a parkway, where he was hit by a car and killed. The defendants contended that their actions were not bias-motivated because they did not harbor any animosity toward gays, but the judge in the case ruled that under the New York hate crime law, intentional selection was sufficient and proof of animus was unnecessary.[74]

Finally, courts considering penalty enhancement hate crimes laws post-*Mitchell* must take cognizance of another important Supreme Court decision—a decision that actually has had an impact across a broad spectrum of criminal laws. In 2000, the Supreme Court ruled in *Apprendi v. New Jersey* that any factor that increases the penalty for a crime beyond the prescribed statutory maximum must be submitted to a jury and proved beyond a reasonable doubt.[75] The *Apprendi* case did not reject the penalty enhancement concept for hate crimes. However, the Court did reject New Jersey's approach, which involved a judge looking at a case following a conviction and pronouncing a tougher sentence if he or she found that the defendant committed the crime with a purpose to intimidate an individual or group of individuals because of their status. Following *Apprendi*, the intentional targeting that forms the basis of a hate crimes charge must be established, beyond a reasonable doubt, at trial, and not afterwards.

CROSS BURNING AND ANTIMASK LAWS

Statutes prohibiting cross burning and wearing masks with the intent to threaten or intimidate could also be termed hate crime laws, although they obviously differ in approach from penalty enhancement laws. This section provides a brief summary of the separate case law that has developed regarding cross-burning and antimask statutes.

The major Supreme Court ruling on cross burning was not the *R.A.V.* case, mentioned earlier, but rather a 2003 decision in *Virginia v. Black*.[76] The latter involved a constitutional challenge to a Virginia statute that made it a crime for "any person or persons, with the intent of intimidating any person or group of persons, to burn, or cause to be burned, a cross on the property of another, a highway, or a public place."[77] The statute added that "any such

burning of a cross shall be prima facie evidence of an intent to intimidate a
person or group of persons."[78]

Setting the context for its ruling, the Court first discussed the history of
Ku Klux Klan cross burnings at some length, noting that "from the incep-
tion of the second Klan, cross burnings have been used to communicate both
threats of violence and messages of shared ideology . . . while a burning
cross does not inevitably convey a message of intimidation, often the cross
burner intends that the recipients of the message fear for their lives. And
when a cross burning is used to intimidate, few if any messages are more
powerful."[79]

While acknowledging the symbolic significance of the burning cross, a
plurality of the Court decided, in a series of splintered opinions, that "a State,
consistent with the First Amendment, may ban cross burning carried out
with the intent to intimidate," but the "prima facie evidence" provision of the
Virginia law rendered it unconstitutional.[80] "It may be true," the Court said,
"that a cross burning, even at a political rally, arouses a sense of anger or
hatred among the vast majority of citizens who see a burning cross. But this
sense of anger or hatred is not sufficient to ban all cross burnings. . . . The
prima facie evidence provision in this case ignores all of the contextual factors
that are necessary to decide whether a particular cross burning is intended to
intimidate. The First Amendment does not permit such a shortcut."[81]

This conclusion prompted the Court to reverse the conviction of one of
the defendants, Barry Black, because in his case the jury was told that it could
infer the required intent just from the cross burning act itself. However, in
the case of a second defendant, Richard Elliott, there was no comparable jury
instruction, and the Supreme Court left open the possibility of a retrial. The
following year, Elliott's case came back before the Virginia Supreme Court,
which determined that the unconstitutional prima facie provision was sever-
able from the rest of the statute, and a retrial was therefore not required.[82]
A third defendant, Jonathan O'Mara, had entered a plea agreement, and the
Virginia Supreme Court found that he had "waived any claim of error based
upon the unconstitutionality of the prima facie evidence provision."[83]

Cross burning laws are commonly associated with efforts to combat the Ku
Klux Klan. So are antimask laws—efforts to "unmask the Klan"—that date
back to the late 1940s.[84] While the Supreme Court has not addressed the constitutionality of antimask laws, several court decisions have found that such
laws are also constitutionally sound so long as the prosecution can prove that
the mask-wearer knew or reasonably should have known that the conduct
would provoke a reasonable apprehension of intimidation, threats, or violence.
In a key 1990 case, the Georgia Supreme Court upheld that state's antimask
law against challenges premised on the freedom of speech, freedom of association, vagueness, and over-breadth.[85] The Georgia Court found that "the
statute is intended to protect the citizens of Georgia from intimidation, vio-

lence, and actual and implied threats; it is also designed to assist law enforcement in apprehending criminals, and to restore confidence in law enforcement by removing any possible illusion of government complicity with masked vigilantes."[86] The Court added that "the state's interests furthered by the Anti-Mask Act lie at the very heart of the realm of legitimate government activity."[87] Moreover, the statute did not prevent the Klansman from publicly proclaiming his message.[88]

Examples of other courts that have addressed antimask laws include the Supreme Court of West Virginia and the U.S. Court of Appeals for the Second Circuit. The West Virginia court upheld that state's antimask law against a constitutional challenge in 1996,[89] and the Second Circuit reached a similar conclusion several years later, upholding New York's antimask law as a proper exercise of the state's police power to prevent and detect crime.[90]

LOOKING FORWARD

The Supreme Court's decision in *Mitchell* has foreclosed most First Amendment challenges to penalty enhancement statutes similar to Wisconsin's. However, as New Jersey learned in 2000, the intentional selection must be proven to the jury. And as Georgia learned in 2004, these laws still must be crafted carefully to avoid vagueness problems. As long as states follow the Wisconsin model, they will be on solid ground in enacting and enforcing hate crimes laws.

In addition, courts are likely to continue to distinguish between constitutionally protected hate speech and hate crimes. For hateful expressive activity to be subject to criminal sanction, as in the case of cross burning or mask wearing, the prosecution must be able to prove that the perpetrator engaged in that activity with an intent to threaten or intimidate.

Finally, the Supreme Court has made it clear that it recognizes the prerogative of the legislative branch to determine the relative seriousness of different kinds of crimes based upon the impact they have on our broader society, and to establish sentences accordingly. Legislatures across the country have exercised this judgment when it comes to hate crimes. They have decided, consistently, that Justice John Paul Stevens was on target when he wrote, with regard to hate crimes, "conduct that creates special risks or causes special harms may be prohibited by special rules."[91]

NOTES

1. For example, Title VII of the Civil Rights Act of 1964, as amended, prohibits various discriminatory employment actions *"because of* the employee or prospective employee's race, color, religion, sex, or national origin." One relevant section of Fair Housing Act, 42 U.S.C. § 3604 (a), prohibits interference with housing choices *"because of* [the

victim's] race, color, religion, sex, familial status, or national origin." Further, a number of federal criminal laws punish intentional discrimination on the basis of race, religion, or other characteristic. For example, by enacting 18 U.S.C. § 242, the Reconstruction Era Congress made it a crime to deprive a person of constitutional rights "by reason of his color, or race."

2.   The International Association of Chiefs of Police defines hate crimes in this way: "criminal offenses committed against persons, property, or society, which are motivated in whole or in part by offenders' bias against an individual's or a group's actual or perceived race, religion, ethnicity/national origin, disability, sexual orientation, or gender." 1998 IACP Hate Crime in America Summit. http://www.theiacp.org/documents/index.cfm?fuseac tion= document&document_id=160

3.   Alabama *Code of Ala. § 13A-5-13* (1993); Alaska *Alaska Stat. § 12.55.155* (1996); Arizona *Ariz. Rev. Stat. §13-702* (1997); California *Cal. Pen. Code §§ 422.7, 422.75* (1995); Colorado *C.R.S. 18-9-121* (1988); Connecticut *Conn. Gen. Stat. §§ 53a-181j- 53a-181l* (1990); Delaware *11 Del. C. § 1304* (1997); District of Columbia *D.C. Code §§ 22-3703 and 22-3704* (1990); Florida *Fla. Stat. § 775.085* (1992); Hawaii *HRS § 706-662* (2001); Idaho *Idaho Code § 18-7902* (1983); Illinois *720 ILCS 5/12-7.1* (1996); Iowa *Iowa Code § 729.A* (1992); Kansas *K.S.A. Supp. § 21-4716* (1994); Kentucky *KRS § 532.031* (1996); Louisiana *La. R.S. 14:107.2* (1997); Maine *17-A M.R.S. § 1151* (1995); Maryland *MD. ANN. Code [Crim.Law] §10-305 through 10-306* (1994); Massachusetts *Mass. Ann. Laws ch. 265, § 39* (1982); Michigan *MCL § 750.147b* (1989); Minnesota *Minn. Stat. §§ 609.2231, 609.749* (1995); Mississippi *Miss. Code Ann. § 99-19-301* (1994); Missouri *§ 557.035 R.S.Mo.* (1988); Montana *Mont. Code Anno. § 45-5-221 -222* (1989); Nebraska *R.R.S. Neb. § 28-111* (1997); Nevada *Nev. Rev. Stat. Ann. § 207.185* (1997); New Hampshire *RSA 651:6* (1995); New Jersey *N.J. Stat. §§ 2C:44-3, 2C:16-1* (1995); New Mexico *NMSA § 31-18b* (2003); New York *NY CLS Penal § 485.05* (2000); North Carolina *N.C. Gen. Stat. § 14-3* (1993); North Dakota *NDCC §12.1-14-04* ; Ohio *ORC Ann. § 2927.12* (1987); Oklahoma *21 Okl. St. § 850* (1992); Oregon *ORS § 166.155; §166.165* (1989); Pennsylvania *18 Pa.C.S. §2710* (1982); Rhode Island *R.I. Gen. Laws § 12-19-38* (1994); South Dakota *S.D. Codified Laws § 22-19B-1* (1993); Tennessee *Tenn. Code Ann. § 40-35-114* (1990); Texas *Tex. Penal Code § 12.47; Tex. Code Crim. Proc. Art. § 42.014* (1993); Utah *U.C. § 76-3-203.3* (1992); Vermont *13 V.S.A. § 1455* (1990); Virginia *Va. Code Ann. § 18.2-57* (1997); Washington *Rev. Code Wash. (ARCW) § 9A.36.080* (1993); West Virginia *W.Va. Code § 61-6-21* (1998); Wisconsin *Wis. Stat. § 939.645* (1996).

In addition, many states have laws that provide for civil remedies for victims of hate violence and provide for other additional forms of relief—including injunctive relief, recovery of general and punitive damages, attorney's fees, and, in some cases, parental liability for minor children's actions.

4.   In 1981, the Anti-Defamation League's Legal Affairs Department drafted a model hate crime bill for state legislatures. The core of the proposed legislation provided for enhanced penalties for crimes directed at an individual because of the actual or perceived race, color, religion, national origin, sexual orientation, or gender of the victim. The ADL model statute also includes an institutional vandalism section that increases the criminal penalties for vandalism aimed at houses of worship, cemeteries, schools, and community centers.

5.   "Motivation is a critical part of the definition of bias crimes because it is the bias-motivation of the perpetrator that caused the unique harm of the bias crime." Statement by Frederick M. Lawrence, dean and Robert Kramer Research Professor of Law, George Washington University Law School, before the Committee on the Judiciary House of Representatives Subcommittee on Crime, Terrorism, and Homeland Security Concern-

ing H.R. 1592, April 17, 2007. http://judiciary.house.gov/hearings/April2007/Law-rence070417.pdf (accessed October 27, 2008).

For an excellent, comprehensive discussion of the nature of bias crimes, their causes, and their resulting harms, see Frederick M. Lawrence, *Punishing Hate: Bias Crimes Under American Law*, Harvard University Press, 1999.

6.   Arizona *Ariz. Rev. Stat. § 13–702* (1997); California *Cal. Pen. Code §§ 422.7, 422.75* (1995); Colorado *C.R.S. 18–9-121* (1988); Connecticut *Conn. Gen. Stat. §§ 53a-181j-53a-181l* (1990); Delaware *11 Del. C. § 1304* (1997); District of Columbia *D.C. Code § 22–3701* (1990); Delaware *11 Del. C. § 1304* (1997); Florida *Fla. Stat. § 775.085* (1992); Hawaii *HRS § 846–51* (2001); Illinois *720 ILCS 5/12-7.1* (1996); Iowa *Iowa Code § 729.A* (1992); Kansas *K.S.A. Supp. § 21–4716* (1994); Kentucky *KRS § 532.031* (1996); Louisiana *La. R.S. 14:107.2* (1997); Maine *17-A M.R.S. § 1151* (1995); Maryland *MD. ANN. Code [Crim.Law] §10–301 through 10–306* (1994); Massachusetts *Mass. Ann. Laws ch. 265, § 39* (1982); Minnesota *Minn. Stat. § 609.2231* (1995); Missouri *§ 557.035 R.S.Mo.* (1988); Nebraska *R.R.S. Neb. § 28–111* (1997); Nevada *Nev. Rev. Stat. Ann. § 207.185* (1997); New Hampshire *RSA 651:6* (1995); New Jersey *N.J. Stat. § 2C:16–1* (1995); New Mexico *NMSA § 31–18b* (2003); New York *NY CLS Penal § 485.05* (2000); Oregon, ORS Chapter 166.165 (2003); Rhode Island *R.I. Gen. Laws § 12–19–38* (1994); Tennessee *Tenn. Code Ann. § 40–35–114* (1990); Texas *Tex. Penal Code § 12.47; Tex. Code Crim. Proc. Art. § 42.014* (1993); Vermont *13 V.S.A. § 1455* (1990); Washington *Rev. Code Wash. (ARCW) § 9A.36.080* (1993); Wisconsin *Wis. Stat. § 939.645* (1996).

7.   Alaska *Alaska Stat. § 12.55.155* (1996); Arizona *Ariz. Rev. Stat. § 13–702* (1997); California *Cal. Pen. Code §§ 422.7, 422.75* (1995); Connecticut *Conn. Gen. Stat. §§ 53a-181j-53a-181l* (1990); District of Columbia *D.C. Code § 22–3701* (1990); Hawaii *HRS § 846–51* (2001); Illinois *720 ILCS 5/12-7.1* (1996); Iowa *Iowa Code § 729.A* (1992); Louisiana *La. R.S. 14:107.2* (1997); Maine *17-A M.R.S. § 1151* (1995); Michigan *MCL § 750.147b* (1989); Minnesota *Minn. Stat. § 609.2231* (1995); Mississippi *Miss. Code Ann. § 99–19–301* (1994); Missouri *§ 557.035 R.S.Mo.* (1988); Nebraska *R.R.S. Neb. § 28–111* (1997); New Hampshire *RSA 651:6* (1995); New Jersey *N.J. Stat. § 2C:16–1* (1995); New Mexico *NMSA § 31–18b* (2003); New York *NY CLS Penal § 485.05* (2000); North Carolina *N.C. Gen. Stat. § 99D-1;* North Dakota *NDCC § 12.1–14–04* (1973); Rhode Island *R.I. Gen. Laws § 12–19–38* (1994); Tennessee *Tenn. Code Ann. § 40–35–114* (1990); Texas *Tex. Penal Code § 12.47; Tex. Code Crim. Proc. Art. § 42.014* (1993); Vermont *13 V.S.A. § 1455* (1990); Washington *Rev. Code Wash. (ARCW) § 9A.36.080* (1993); West Virginia *W.Va. Code § 61–6-21* (1998).

8.   California *Cal. Pen. Code §§ 422.7, 422.75* (1995); Colorado *C.R.S. 18–9-121* (1988); Connecticut *Conn. Gen. Stat. §§ 53a-181j- 53a-181l* (1990); District of Columbia *D.C. Code § 22–3701* (1990); Hawaii *HRS § 846–51* (2003); Maryland *MD. ANN. Code [Crim. Law] §10–301 through 10–306* (1994); Minnesota *Minn. Stat. § 609.2231* (1995); Missouri *§ 557.035 R.S.Mo.* (1988); New Mexico *NMSA § 31–18b* (2003); Vermont *13 V.S.A. § 1455* (1990).

9.   Alabama *Code of Ala. § 13A-5–13* (1993); Alaska *Alaska Stat. § 12.55.155* (1996); Arizona *Ariz. Rev. Stat. § 13–702* (1997); California *Cal. Pen. Code §§ 422.7, 422.75* (1995); Colorado *C.R.S. 18–9-121* (1988); Connecticut *Conn. Gen. Stat. §§ 53a-181j- 53a-181l* (1990); District of Columbia *D.C. Code § 22–3701* (1990); Delaware *11 Del. C. § 1304* (1997); Florida *Fla. Stat. § 775.085* (1992); Hawaii *HRS § 846–51* (2001); Illinois *720 ILCS 5/12-7.1* (1996); Iowa *Iowa Code § 729.A* (1992); Kansas *K.S.A. Supp. § 21–4716* (1994); Louisiana *La. R.S. 14:107.2* (1997); Maine *17-A M.R.S. § 1151* (1995); Massachusetts *Mass. Ann. Laws ch. 265, § 39* (1982); Minnesota *Minn. Stat. § 609.2231* (1995);

Missouri § *557.035 R.S.Mo.* (1988); Nebraska *R.R.S. Neb.* § *28–111* (1997); Nevada *Nev. Rev. Stat. Ann.* § *207.185* (1997); New Hampshire *RSA 651:6* (1995); New Jersey *N.J. Stat.* § *2C:16–1* (1995); New Mexico *NMSA* § *31–18b* (2003); New York *NY CLS Penal* § *485.05* (2000); Oklahoma *21 Okl. St.* § *850* (1992); Rhode Island *R.I. Gen. Laws* § *12–19–38* (1994); Tennessee *Tenn. Code Ann.* § *40–35–114* (1990); Texas *Tex. Penal Code* § *12.47; Tex. Code Crim. Proc. Art.* § *42.014* (1993); Vermont *13 V.S.A.* § *1455* (1990); Washington *Rev. Code Wash. (ARCW)* § *9A.36.080* (1993); Wisconsin *Wis. Stat.* § *939.645* (1996).

    10.   Alabama *Ala. Code* § *13A-11–12* (1977); Arizona *Ariz. Rev. Stat. Ann.* § *13–1604* (1994); Arkansas *Ark. Code Ann.* § *5–71–215* (1993); California *Cal. Pen. Code* § *594.3* (1983); Colorado *Colo. Rev. Stat.* § *18–9-113* (1991); Connecticut *Conn. Gen. Stat.* § *53a-181b* (1990); Delaware *11 Del. C.* § *1331;* District of Columbia *D.C. Code* § *22–3312.02* (1983); Florida *Fla. Stat. Ann.* § *806.13* (1995); Hawaii *Haw. Rev. Stat.* § *711–1107* (1993); Georgia *Ga. Code Ann.* § *16–7-26* (1968); Hawaii *Haw. Rev. Stat.* § *711–1107* (1993); Idaho *Idaho Code* § *18–7902* (1983); Illinois *720 Ill. Comp. Stat. 5/21–1.2* (1994); Indiana *Ind. Code Ann.* § *35–43–1-2* (1996); Kansas *An. Stat. Ann.* § *21–4111* (1994); Kentucky *Ky. Rev. Stat. Ann.* §§ *525.110, 525.113* (1992, 1998); Louisiana *La. Rev. Stat. Ann.* § *14:225* (1984); Maine *Me. Rev. Stat. Ann. tit. 17-A,* § *507* (1976); Maryland *MD. ANN. Code [Crim.Law]* § *10–301 through 10–304* (1994); Massachusetts *Mass. Gen. Laws Ann. ch. 266,* §§ *126A, 127* (1989); Michigan *Mich. Comp. Laws Ann.* § *750.147b* (1989); Minnesota *Minn. Stat. Ann.* § *609.595* (1989); Mississippi *Miss. Code Ann.* § *97–17–39* (1993); Missouri *Mo. Ann. Stat.* § *574.085* (1997); Montana *Mont. Code Ann.* § *45–5-221* (1989); Nebraska *Neb. Stat. Ann.* § *28–111;* Nevada *Nev. Rev. Stat. Ann.* § *206.125* (1995); New Jersey *N.J. Stat. Ann.* § *2C:33–11* (1995); New Mexico *N.M. Stat. Ann.* § *30–15–4* (1965); New York *NY CLS Penal* § *240.31;* North Carolina *N.C. Gen. Stat.* § *14–49* (1993); Ohio *Ohio Rev. Code Ann.* § *2927.11* (1986); Oklahoma *Okla. Stat. Ann. tit. 21,* § *1765* (1921); Oregon *Or. Rev. Stat.* § *166.075* (1971); Pennsylvania *Pa. Cons. Stat., tit. 18,* § *3307* (1994); Rhode Island *R.I. Gen. Laws* § *11–44–31* (1986); South Carolina *S.C. Code Ann.* § *16–11–535* (2003); South Dakota *S.D. Codified Laws Ann.* § *22–19B-1* (1993); Tennessee *Tenn. Code Ann.* § *39–17–309* (1990); Texas *Tex. Penal Code Ann.* § *28.03* (1994); Virginia *Va. Code Ann.* § *18.2–138* (1990); Washington *Wash. Rev. Code Ann.* § *9A.36.080* (1993); Wisconsin *Wis. Stat. Ann.* § *943.012* (1996).

    11.   National Organization of Black Law Enforcement Executives (NOBLE), "Racial and Religious Violence: A Model Law Enforcement Response," September 1985.

    12.   Arizona *Stat. Ann.* § *41–1750* (1991); California *Cal. Pen. Code* § *13023* (1992); Connecticut *Conn. Gen. Stat.* § *29–7m* (1987); District of Columbia *D.C. Code* § *22–3702* (1990); Florida *Fla. Stat.* § *877.19* (1996); Hawaii *Haw. Rev. Stat.* §§§§ *846–51, 846–52, 846–53, 846–54* (2003); Idaho *Idaho Code* § *67–2915* (1995); Illinois *20 ILCS 2605/2605-390* (1995); Iowa *Iowa Code* § *692.15* (1996); Kentucky *KRS* § *17.1523* (1992); Louisiana *La. Rev. Stat. Ann.* § *15:1204.2(B)(4) and 1204.4* (1997); Maine *Me. Rev. Stat. Ann. tit. 25,* § *1544* (1991); Maryland *Md. Code Ann. art. 88B,* § *9* (1992); Massachusetts *Mass. Gen. Laws Ann. ch. 22C,* §§ *33 to 35* (1991); Michigan *Executive Order* (1996 and 1997); Minnesota *Minn. Stat. Ann.* § *626.5531* (1997); Nebraska *R.R.S. Neb.* § *28–114* (1997); Nevada *NRS 179A.175* (1995); New Jersey *Attorney General Directive No. 1987–3* (1987); New Mexico *NMSA* § *31–18b-4* (1978); Oklahoma *21 Okl. St.* § *850* (2001); Oregon *ORS* § *181.550* (1989); Pennsylvania *71 P.S.* § *250* (1987); Rhode Island *R.I. Gen. Laws* § *42–28–46* (1994); Texas *Tex. Gov. Code Ann.* § *411.046* (1991); Virginia *Va. Code Ann.* § *52–8.5* (1988); Washington *Wash. Rev. Code Ann.* § *36.28A.030* (1993); West Virginia *W.Va. Code* § *15–2-24(I) (1977)*

    13.   Arizona *Stat. Ann.* § *41–1822* (1991); California *Cal. Pen. Code* § *13515.25* (1992); Connecticut *Conn. Gen. Stat.* § *7–294n* (2001); Illinois *20 ILCS 2605/2605-390* (1995); Iowa *Iowa Code* § *729A.4* (1992); Kentucky *Ky. Rev. Stat. Ann.* § *15.334* (2005); Louisiana *La.*

Rev. Stat. Ann. § 40:2403(H) (1997); Massachusetts *Mass. Ann. Laws ch. 6, § 116B* (1991); Minnesota *Minn. Stat. Ann. § 626.8451* (1993); New Jersey *N.J. Bias Incident Investigation Standards* (1991); New Mexico *NMSA § 31–18b-5* (2003); Oregon *ORS § 181.642* (2003) Rhode Island *R.I. Gen. Laws § 42–28.2–8.1* (1993); Washington *Wash. Rev. Code Ann. § 43.101.290* (1993).

14. *U.S. v. Price, et al.* 383 U.S. 787 (1966). When the three civil rights workers went missing, their colleagues immediately reported their disappearance. President Johnson ordered dozens of FBI agents to Mississippi. Following an extensive search, the remains of the young men were discovered on August 4, 1964. A grand jury returned indictments in January, 1965, charging three law enforcement officials (including Cecil Price, Deputy Sheriff of Neshoba County) and 15 private citizens who were members of the White Knights of the Ku Klux Klan, with conspiring to deprive the three men of their Fourteenth Amendment rights. After a series of procedural delays, in October 1968 a trial was held, ending with an all-white jury convicting Price and six of his codefendants and acquitting eight others.

More recently, in *United States v. Saldana*, four members of a violent Latino street gang in Los Angeles were convicted of participating in a conspiracy aimed at threatening, assaulting, and murdering African-Americans in a neighborhood claimed by the defendants' gang. *United States v. Saldana, et al.* (C.D. California 2006).

15. The six enumerated "federally protected activities" are: "(A) enrolling in or attending any public school or public college; (B) participating in or enjoying any benefit, service, privilege, program, facility or activity provided or administered by any State or subdivision thereof; (C) applying for or enjoying employment, . . . ; (D) serving . . . as grand or petit juror; (E) traveling in or using any facility of interstate commerce, . . . ; (F) enjoying the goods [or] services [of certain places of public accommodation]." 18 U.S.C. § 245(b)(2).

16. 18 U.S.C. § 245 (a) (1). On August 10, 1999, Buford Furrow, Jr., an avowed racist and former security guard for the white supremacist group Aryan Nations, walked into the North Valley Jewish Community Center in Los Angeles and shot three young children, a teenager, and an elderly woman with a modified semiautomatic, Uzi-style rifle. Furrow fled the scene in a hijacked car. As he drove, Furrow came upon Joseph Ileto, a Filipino-American postal worker who was delivering mail. Furrow shot and killed Ileto because Ileto was non-white and was working for the federal government. The following morning, after seeing his picture broadcast over the national news media, Furrow surrendered himself to FBI agents in Las Vegas, Nevada. Furrow was charged with murder of a federal employee, six counts of 18 U.S.C. § 245, and a number of other federal crimes. On January 24, 2001, Furrow pled guilty to all charges and was sentenced to two consecutive life terms followed by 110 years in prison on March 26, 2001.

17. National Church Arson Task Force, *Fourth Report to the President,* http://www.atf. treas.gov/pub/gen_pub/report2000/fullrpt.pdf (September, 2000).

18. Church Arson Prevention Act of 1996, Pub. L. No. 104–155, 110 Stat. 1392, amending 18 U.S.C. § 247, July 3, 1996.

19. Between 1994 and 1999, Jay Scott Ballinger and his girlfriend, Angela Wood, set fire to more than 30 churches—mostly isolated, rural churches, including 13 in Indiana, 5 in Georgia, 4 in Kentucky, 3 in Ohio, and 1 each in Alabama, California, South Carolina, and Tennessee. A 27-year-old volunteer firefighter was killed while fighting one of the Georgia fires. The defendants, who identified themselves as "Luciferians" (Satanworshipers), burned the churches for religious reasons. On July 11, 2000, Ballinger pled guilty to 20 counts of church arson, in violation of 18 U.S.C. § 247 and a variety of other

federal crimes. Angela Wood was sentenced to serve 16 years and 8 months in prison after she admitted that she helped Ballinger burn 4 churches in Indiana. On April 13, 2001, Ballinger pled guilty to 5 more counts of church arson and admitted that his offense caused the death of a firefighter. On August 17, 2001, Ballinger was sentenced to life in prison without parole. The constitutionality of the statute was upheld in *United States v. Ballinger*, 395 F.3d 1218 (2005).

20.   In October and November 2006, defendants Joseph Kuzlik and David Fredericy pled guilty to conspiracy, interference with housing rights, and making false statements to federal investigators. *United States v. Fredericy and Kuzlik* (Northern District of Ohio). In February 2005, these defendants poured mercury on the front porch and driveway of a biracial couple in an attempt to force them and their child out of their Cleveland, Ohio, home.

21.   On September 27, 2007, Defendant Kyle Shroyer pled guilty to conspiring to violate the civil rights of a woman and her three biracial children, and admitted having burned a cross at the family's home in Muncie, Indiana. In March 2006, Shroyer built an eight-foot wooden cross with another individual and then erected the cross in front of the victims' home. The two men then doused the cross with gasoline and set it on fire. On January 4, 2008, Shroyer was sentenced to serve 15 months in prison. A recent case held that it was not a First Amendment violation to enhance a sentence under 18 U.S.C. § 844(h)(1) based on the use of fire, even if it was used as a symbol. *U.S. v. Magleby*, 2005 WL 1995581 (8/19/05).

22.   Public Law 102–275, April 23, 1990. President George H. W. Bush's signing statement for the act from April 23, 1990 is eloquent:

> Enacting this law today helps move us toward our dream: a society blind to prejudice, a society open to all. Until we reach that day when the bigotry and hate of mail bombings, and the vandalisms of the Yeshiva school and the Catholic churches we've seen recently, and so many other sad, sad incidents are no more—until that day, we must remember: For America to continue to be a good place for any of us to live, it must be a good place for all of us to live. (http://bushlibrary.tamu.edu/research/public_papers.php?id=1791&year=1990&month=all [accessed October 27, 2008])

23.   Public Law 103–322, September 13, 1994.

24.   The Violent Crime Control and Law Enforcement Act of 1994, Pub. L. No. 103–322 (1994). Section 280003a of this act provides:

> (a) DEFINITION: In this section, "hate crime" means a crime in which the defendant intentionally selects a victim, or in the case of a property crime, the property that is the object of the crime, because of the actual or perceived race, color, religion, national origin, ethnicity, gender, disability, or sexual orientation of any person.
>
>   (b) SENTENCING ENHANCEMENT: Pursuant to section 994 of title 28, United States Code, the United States Sentencing Commission shall promulgate guidelines or amend existing guidelines to provide sentencing enhancements of not less than 3 offense levels for offenses that the finder of fact at trial determines beyond a reasonable doubt are hate crimes. . . .

25.   34 CFR 668.46 (c) (7) provides: "UCR definitions. An institution must compile the crime statistics required under paragraphs (c)(1) and (3) of this section using the definitions of crimes provided in appendix A to this subpart and the Federal Bureau of Investigation's Uniform Crime Reporting (UCR) Hate Crime Data Collection Guidelines and Training Guide for Hate Crime Data Collection."

26.   For more information on Public Law 110-315 see http://frwebgate.ac cess.gpo. gov/cgi-bin/getdoc.cgi?dbname=110_cong_public_laws&docid=f:publ315.110.pdf (accessed October 27, 2008).

27.   In the 110th Congress, this legislation is H.R. 1592 and S. 1105. The House of Representatives approved its version of this legislation by a vote of 237–180 on May 3, 2007. See http://clerk.house.gov/evs/2007/roll299.xml (accessed October 27, 2008).

Facing a veto threat from President Bush, the Senate added the text of S. 1105 as an amendment to the Department of Defense Authorization legislation on September 27. The key vote, 60–39 (http://www.senate.gov/legis lative/LIS/roll_call_lists/roll_call_ vote_cfm.cfm?congress=110&session=1&vote=00350 [accessed October 27, 2008]) was on a motion to limit debate on the bill, as policy opponents tried to kill the measure through the use of a filibuster. The House version of the Department of Defense Authorization bill, H.R. 1585, had been approved on May 17, without hate crime provisions. Despite concerted lobbying efforts, the hate crime provisions were ultimately stripped from the defense bill in conference because of a sustained veto threat, conservative opposition to the hate crime provisions, and unrelated opposition among Democrats to the larger Pentagon policy bill.

28.   Hearings on H.R. 3081, House Judiciary Committee, July 22, 1998. Hearings on S. 1529, Senate Judiciary Committee, July 8, 1998.

29.   Hearings on S. 622, Senate Judiciary Committee, May 11, 1999.

30.   "[T]he Federal Government's resources, forensic expertise, and experience in the identification and proof of bias-motivated violence and criminal networks have often provided an invaluable investigative complement to the familiarity of local investigators with the local community and its people and customs. Through this cooperation, State and Federal law enforcement officials have been able to bring the perpetrators of hate crimes swiftly to justice." House report 110–113 Local Law Enforcement Hate Crime Prevention Act, House Judiciary Committee, April 30, 2007. See http://thomas.loc.gov/cgi-bin/ cpquery/R?cp110:FLD010:@1(hr113): (accessed October 27, 2008).

31.   Indeed, Bill Lann Lee, then acting Assistant Attorney General for Civil Rights, testified about the important, but limited, use contemplated by the Department of Justice at House Judiciary Committee hearings on the Hate Crime Prevention Act on July 22, 1998:

From 1992 through 1997, the Department of Justice brought a total of only 33 Federal hate crimes prosecutions under 18 USC § 245, an average of fewer than 6 per year. We predict that the enactment of the Hate Crimes Prevention Act of 1997 would result in only a modest increase in the number of hate crimes prosecutions brought each year by the federal government. Our partnership with state and local law enforcement would continue with state and local prosecutors continuing to take the lead in the great majority of cases. Concurrent federal jurisdiction is necessary only to permit joint state-federal investigations and to authorize federal prosecutions in rare circumstances. Although the increase in the number of federal prosecutions we would bring pursuant to an amended section 245 would likely be modest, the increase in our ability to work effectively as partners with state and local law enforcement would be great. (Hearings on H.R. 3081, The Hate Crimes Prevention Act of 1997, House Committee on the Judiciary, July 22, 1998, http://commdocs.house.gov/committees/judiciary/hju57839.000/hju57839_0.HTM [accessed October 27, 2008])

32.   In the 110th Congress, this legislation is H.R. 923 and S. 535. In the summer of 1955, a 14-year-old African-American teenager from Chicago named Emmett Till traveled to Mississippi to visit relatives. Four days after a nonchalant encounter with a white female shopkeeper, he was abducted from his relatives' house. His body was later found in the Tallahatchie River, with a 70-pound gin-mill fan tied to his neck with barbed wire. Till's mother, Mamie Bradley, insisted that his body be shipped back to Chicago, where it was displayed in an open coffin for four days. Two individuals were tried for Till's murder, but were acquitted by an all-white jury after only an hour of deliberation. The murder of Emmett Till was one of the most infamous acts of racial violence in American history, yet his killers have never been punished (see http://clerk.house.gov/evs/2007/roll512.xml [accessed October 27, 2008]).

33.   Statement of Richard Cohen, president and CEO of the Southern Poverty Law Center, at joint hearings before the House Judiciary Subcommittee on the Constitution, Civil Rights, and Civil Liberties and Subcommittee on Crime, Terrorism, and Homeland Security, June 12, 2007. (See http://judiciary.house.gov/hearings/June2007/061207cohen.pdf [accessed October 27, 2008].)

34.   http://clerk.house.gov/evs/2007/roll512.xml (accessed October 27, 2008).

35.   For more information see http://frwebgate.access.gpo.gov/cgi-bin/getdoc.cgi?dbname=110_cong_bills&docid=f:h923enr.txt.pdf (accessed October 27, 2008).

36.   Alabama *Ala. Code § 13a-6-28;* Arizona *Ariz.Rev.Stat.Ann. § 13–1707;* California *Cal. Pen. Code § 11411;* Connecticut *Conn. Gen. Stat. Ann. § 46a-58;* Delaware *Del. Code Ann. Tit.11 § 805;* Florida *Fla. Stat. Ann. § 876.17;* Georgia *Ga. Code § 16–11–37;* Idaho *Idaho Code § 18–7902;* Illinois *Ill. Comp. Laws Ann. Ch.720 ¶5, § 12–7.6;* Louisiana *La. Rev. Stat. Ann. § 14:40.4;* Maryland *Md. Code Ann.,Crim. Law § 10–304;* Missouri *Mo. Ann. Stat. § 565.095;* Montana *Mont. Code Ann. § 45–5-221;* New Hampshire *N.H.Rev. Stat.Ann. § 631:4;* New Jersey *N.J. Stat. Ann. § 2c:33–10;* North Carolina *N.C. Gen. Stat. § 14–12.13;* Oklahoma *Okla. Stat. Ann. Tit. 21 § 1174;* South Carolina *S.C. Code Ann. § 16–7-120;* South Dakota *S.D. Cod. Laws Ann. § 22–19b-1;* Vermont *Vt. Stat. Ann. Tit.13 § 1456;* Virginia *Va. Code Ann. § 18.2–423;* Washington *Wash. Rev. Code Ann.*

37.   538 U.S. 343, 357 (2003).

38.   Statement by Frederick M. Lawrence, dean and Robert Kramer Research Professor of Law, George Washington University Law School, before the Committee on the Judiciary House of Representatives Subcommittee on Crime, Terrorism, and Homeland Security Concerning H.R. 1592, April 17, 2007. (See http://judiciary.house.gov/hearings/April2007/Lawrence070417.pdf [accessed October 27, 2008]).

39.   *State v. Plowman,* 838 P.2d 558, 564, 314 Or. 157, 166 (Or. 1992).

40.   Id.

41.   Id.

42.   Id.

43.   *Tison v. Arizona,* 481 U.S. 137, 156, 107 S.Ct. 1676, 1687 (1987).

44.   *Barclay v. Florida,* 463 U.S. 939, 942, 103 S.Ct. 3418, 3421, (1983).

45.   *Barclay,* 463 U.S. at 978, 103 S.Ct. at 3439.

46.   *See Barclay,* 463 U.S. at 949, 103 S.Ct. at 3424–5.

47.   468 U.S. 609 (1984).

48. 467 U.S. 69 (1984).

49. 427 U.S. 160 (1976).

50. *Wisconsin v. Mitchell*, 508 U.S. at 487, 113 S.Ct. at 2200.

51. See, for example, *People v. Lashley*, 1 Cal. App.4th 938, 951 (Cal. Ct. App. 1991) (enforcing civil rights laws prohibiting interference with an individual's state or federal rights because of race, color, religion, ancestry, national origin, or sexual orientation); *U.S. v. Nelson*, 68 F.3d 583 (2d Cir. 1995) (upholding criminal penalties for civil rights violations involving interference with federally protected activities).

52. *People v. Lashley*, 1 Cal. App. 4th at 951.

53. *R.A.V. v. City of St. Paul, Minn*, 505 U.S. 377, 378, 112 S.Ct. 2538, 2540 (1992).

54. Id.

55. Indeed, *New York Times* Supreme Court reporter Linda Greenhouse commented, "The majority's approach would appear not only to have invalidated ordinances of the St. Paul type, in which activities are defined as hate crimes and added to a city or state's criminal code, but also to have dealt what was probably a fatal constitutional blow at another popular legislative approach to the hate crime issue. Under the second approach, existing crimes like vandalism or harassment are punished more severely if the prosecution can show that bias was a factor in the crime." *New York Times*, June 23, 1992.

56. *Wisconsin v. Mitchell*, 508 U.S. at 480, 113 S.Ct. at 2197.

57. *Mitchell*, 508 U.S. at 481–2, 113 S.Ct. at 2197.

58. *Mitchell*, 508 U.S. at 482, 113 S.Ct. at 2198.

59. Id.

60. Brief Amicus Curiae of the Wisconsin Association of Criminal Defense Lawyers (WACDL) in Support of Respondent, 1992 U.S. Briefs 515, 1993 U.S. S. Ct. Briefs LEXIS 196 (1993).

61. Brief of Amici Curiae States in Support of Petitioner, 1992 U.S. Briefs 515, 1993 U.S.S. Ct. Briefs LEXIS 175 (1993).

62. Brief Amicus Curiae of the American Civil Liberties Union in Support of Petitioner, 1992 U.S. Briefs 515, 1993 U.S. S. Ct. Briefs LEXIS 178 (1993).

63. Brief of Amici Curiae the Anti-Defamation League et al., 1992 U.S. Briefs 515, 1993 U.S. S. Ct. Briefs LEXIS 162 (1993).

64. *Mitchell*, 508 U.S. at 484, 113 S.Ct. at 2199.

65. *Mitchell*, 508 U.S. at 487, 113 S.Ct. at 2200.

66. *Mitchell*, 508 U.S. at 488, 113 S.Ct. at 2201.

67. Id.

68. Id.

69. *Mitchell*, 508 U.S. at 485, 113 S.Ct. at 2199.

70. *Mitchell*, 508 U.S. at 489, 113 S.Ct. at 2201.

71. *Mitchell*, 508 U.S. at 488, 113 S.Ct. at 2201.

72. See, for example, *People v. Aishman*, 10 Cal. 4th 735, 42 Cal. Rptr. 2d 377 (Cal. 1995) (upholding a penalty-enhancement statute in the face of First Amendment and due process arguments); *People v. Fox*, 17 Misc.3d 281, 2007 NY Slip Op 27317, (N.Y. Sup. Ct. 2007) (interpreting a statute to only require the intentional selection of a victim because of race, color, national origin, ancestry, gender, religion, religious practice, age, disability or sexual orientation; proof did not require animus toward people belonging to such groups).

73. *Otts v. State*, 604 S.E.2d 512, 513, 278 Ga. 538, 538 (Ga. 2004).

74. *People v. Fox*, 17 Misc.3d at 284, 2007 NY Slip Op at 3.

75. *Apprendi v. New Jersey*, 530 U.S. 466, 490, 120 S.Ct. 2348, 2362–3 (2000).

76. *See Virginia v. Black*, 538 U.S. 343, 123 S.Ct. 1536 (2003).

77. *Va Code Ann.* § 18.2–423 (1996).

78. *Virginia v. Black*, 538 U.S. at 363, 123 S.Ct. at 1550.

79. *Black*, 538 U.S. at 357, 123 S.Ct. at 1547.

80. *Black*, 538 U.S. at 347, 123 S.Ct. at 1541.

81. *Black*, 538 U.S. at 363, 123 S.Ct. at 1552 (demonstrating a marked difference of opinion from dissenting Justice Thomas, who argues that cross burning should constitute a First Amendment exception even without looking to context as the majority does here, and dissenting Justice Souter, arguing that even with intent to intimidate, cross burning should not be a crime).

82. *Elliott v Virginia*, 593 S.E.2d 270, 290, 267 Va. 396, 427–8 (Va. 2004).

83. *Elliott v Virginia*, 593 S.E.2d at 270, 267 Va. at 475.

84. *State v. Miller*, 398 S.E.2d. 547, 260 Ga. 669, at 671–672 (Ga. 1990).

85. *State v. Miller*, 398 S.E.2d 547, 549, 260 Ga. 669, at 669–70.

86. *State v. Miller*, 398 S.E.2d at 550, 260 Ga. at 672.

87. *Miller*, 398 S.E.2d at 551, 260 Ga. at 672.

88. *Miller*, 398 S.E.2d at 551, 260 Ga. at 673.

89. *West Virginia v. Berrill*, 196 W.Va. 578, 474 S.E. 2d. 508 (W.Va. June 14, 1996).

90. *Church of American Knights of the Ku Klux Klan v. Kerik*, 356 F.3d 197, 205 (2d Cir., N.Y. 2004).

91. *R.A.V. v. City of St. Paul, Minn*, 505 U.S. at 416, 112 S.Ct. at 2561 (Stevens, J., dissenting).

CHAPTER 2

POLICING AND SURVEILLANCE

Jeannine Bell

The Jones family awoke in the predawn hours one day in June 1990 to a cross burning on their front lawn. The Joneses were black and three months before had moved to a working-class white neighborhood in St. Paul, Minnesota. There had been a few other incidents. Within the first few months of living in the neighborhood their tires were slashed. A month later the tailgate in their new station wagon was broken.

After each of these incidents, the Joneses called the police. After the cross burning, the police responded quickly. The officers seemed shocked, but didn't really know what to do, Mr. Jones later reported. After asking the usual questions the police prepared to leave, telling Mr. Jones that they didn't have any suspects because there were no witnesses. Mr. Jones reported that they hadn't taken the cross so he was forced to place the smoldering pieces in the trash (Lederer, 1995).

The vandalism of their property and the cross burning the Joneses endured fit the typical patterns for hate crimes that occur in the neighborhood context. Hate crime—crimes motivated by bias on the basis of race, religion, sexual orientation, ethnicity, or color—may be punished under a variety of federal, state, or local laws. In the case of hate crime, despite the fact that they are often not considered legal actors, police officers may play a critical role in the crime's identification as a hate crime and also, if it ends up being prosecuted, its prosecution.

Some of what officers do in incidents suspected of being bias crimes is similar to what they do with other cases that are not believed to be bias-motivated. For instance, if the crime is reported to the police, as the first responders, police patrol officers may need to secure the crime scene, collect evidence, and/or arrest any perpetrators remaining on the scene. As an additional matter, the patrol officer who responds may also need to provide assistance to victims and/or call for medical assistance. It is at this point—when interacting with the victim—that the role played by officers responding to a hate crime call begins to diverge. Research has shown that in hate crime cases, victims are often especially destabilized and, as first responders, law enforcement officers have a significant role to play in comforting the victims and reassuring them that the attacker will not return (Herek, Gillis, & Cogan, 1999; Kelly, 1993; Levin, 1992–1993; McDevitt, Balboni, Garcia, & Gu, 2001).

After the victim has been tended to, in many jurisdictions the responding officer may also have the discretion to decide whether to file a report. If no report is filed, the criminal justice inquiry will end at this point, as the existence of a police report is crucial to later investigation. If a report is filed, police detectives who are often charged with crime investigation have the discretion to decide whether the crime is worthy of investigation. In cases that are considered worthy of investigation, police investigators are charged with gathering evidence to support criminal charges. In jurisdictions with hate crime statutes, police may also be required to identify or classify particular crimes as hate crimes. Because of the peculiarities attendant to hate crime, the task of responding to, classifying, and investigating this type of crime is distinct from the police role in other areas. The peculiarities of the demands on the police, and officers' resulting responses, are the subject of this chapter.

THE SPECIAL CHALLENGES OF RESPONDING TO BIAS-MOTIVATED CRIME

Policing bias-motivated crime poses many challenges particularly that relate to bias crimes' distinctive effect—the impact of such attacks on victims and their communities. Hate crimes tend to be more brutal, for instance. In a study of 452 hate crimes reported to the Boston police, half were personal attacks, compared to 7 percent of all crimes reported to the police (Levin & McDevitt, 2002, p. 17). Thirty percent of hate crime victims are sent to the emergency room as a result of injuries suffered in the attack. Even if there is no physical injury there may be additional emotional difficulties that hate crime victims must overcome. Responding to bias-motivated crime may require additional victim-oriented skills. Several studies show that bias crime victims face more depression, anger, and difficulty coming to terms with their attack than victims of non–bias-motivated assaults, even in cases with similar levels of physical injury and financial loss (Garofalo & Martin, 1993b; Herek et al., 1999; McDevitt et al., 2001; Rose, 2002).

Because bias-motivated attacks on individuals are prompted by the victim's characteristics—for example, race, religion, or sexual orientation—bias-motivated attacks can also affect a community, causing anyone with the same characteristics as the victim to fear a similar attack. In other words, if a black person is attacked because of his or her race, other blacks who live in the neighborhood might also worry that they might be similarly victimized. The community effects of bias crimes do not simply relate to fears victims may have. Police must also be attuned to the spillover effects of bias-motivated attacks as groups retaliate for attacks made on individual members. For instance, in New York City, well-publicized hate crimes in Howard Beach and Bensonhurst were followed by other incidents—harassment, vandalisms, and assaults—that the offenders indicated were motivated by bias crimes in Howard Beach and Bensonhurst that had occurred earlier (Garofalo & Martin, 1993b, p. 65).

Police enforcement of hate crime law may also be complicated by the over-representation of minority hate crime victims and their relationship with the police. According to FBI statistics, the majority of all hate crime victims are racial, religious, and sexual minorities. Crimes directed at racial and ethnic minorities comprise 47 percent of hate crimes reported to the FBI by police departments; crimes against gays, lesbians, and individuals who are bisexual comprise 14 percent of reported hate crimes (FBI, 2005). Victim advocates from the minority and GLBT communities have accused the police of ignoring crimes committed against them, and in many contexts neglecting their duties of care toward these communities (Kelly, 1993, p. 28). Members of both the GLBT and racial minority communities have claimed that the police have been complacent in handling bias crimes in which they are victims.

Police officers' interaction with minority victims and victims' willingness to trust the police are directly related to officers' ability to investigate crime in this area. A history of poor interaction with the police in other contexts may make victims of color leery of reporting hate crimes to the police (McDevitt et al., 2001). Hate crimes require significant investigation. If victims are wary of interaction with the police, they may shy away from in-depth investigative interviews. If the police do not have an opportunity to interact with victims, such crimes may remain unsolved. A related issue is the equal enforcement of hate crime law across racial lines. Drawing on the long history of poor minority/police relations resulting in the mistreatment of minority criminal suspects, a number of scholars have hypothesized that police officers may disproportionately use hate crime law to prosecute racial and ethnic minorities (Franklin, 2002; Gellman, 1991; Jacobs & Potter, 1998).

LEGISLATIVE SOLUTIONS AND POLICE RESPONSE

Hate Crime Statistics Act of 1990

The special problems outlined above have prompted legislative response. These legislative responses have in turn led to changes in policing structure.

Many state and local police departments began to develop targeted responses in the form of hate crime policies and hate crime general orders mandating changes in departmental policy after the Hate Crime Statistics Act (HCSA) was passed in 1990. The HCSA requires the Justice Department to conduct annual nationwide surveys of law enforcement agencies to obtain data on

> crimes that manifest evidence of prejudice based on race, religion, disability, sexual orientation, or ethnicity, including where appropriate the crimes of murder, not negligent manslaughter, forcible rape; aggravated assault, simple assault, intimidation; arson and destruction, damage or vandalism of property. (Public Law 101–275)[1]

One of the purposes of the HCSA was to spur law enforcement efforts aimed at crime prevention and victim service. In order to help local law enforcement efforts the FBI, in partnership with law enforcement organizations, hate crime victim advocacy groups, and academics, developed publications detailing collection methods. Two publications created out of that effort, *Hate Crime Data Collection Guideline* and *Training Guide for Hate Crime Data Collection*, have been used by law enforcement agencies around the country to train personnel and develop investigative procedures for dealing with bias-motivated incidents (Nolan & Akiyama, 1999).

The HCSA also requires the U.S. Attorney General to publish a summary of the data collected on a yearly basis. Despite the fact that participation in the data collection efforts is voluntary, increasing numbers of law enforcement agencies participate. The 1991 report, for instance, included figures from some 3,000 agencies from 32 states, covering less than 50 percent of the U.S. population. By 2000, 11,000 agencies were participating. Though the dramatic increase in participation has slowed, in 2005, the latest year for which figures are available, approximately 12,400 agencies participated in data collection efforts (FBI, 2005).

Despite increasing numbers of agencies participating, the degree to which agencies actually report hate crimes is widely uneven. For instance in 2005, though 12,417 agencies participated, the vast majority (some 84 percent) of those agencies did not report a single bias-motivated incident. Only 2,037 agencies, just 16 percent, submitted data showing that *any* bias-motivated crimes had occurred in their jurisdiction during the year of the survey. Policing agencies in the South and Midwest were less likely to participate than those in the Northeast and West (McVeigh, Welch, & Bjarnson, 2003). The Deep South is especially plagued by scanty reporting, with only *one* hate crime law enforcement agency in Alabama and Mississippi combined submitting any reports of hate crime in 2000 (King, 2007, p. 190).

Research has suggested that a variety of factors both at the level of the department or agency and at the individual officer level affect whether a department will report hate crimes. Different levels of organizational procedure exist around hate crimes. In order to be reported, hate crimes must be recognized, counted, and eventually reported. There are vast differences between police departments in the degree to which, and in what way officers are trained. Training specifically focused on hate crime factors often leads to increased hate crime reporting. Other institutional factors that increase hate crime reporting include the level of supervision in crime investigations and whether there is departmental policy regarding hate crimes. Forces that have led to higher levels of hate crime reporting at the agency level include a belief by agency superiors that crime reporting will improve police/community relations and a belief that hate crime victims will get help (McDevitt et al., 2001; Nolan & Akiyama, 1999).

In a similar vein, a nationwide survey of 705 law enforcement agencies revealed that the officers' preconceived ideas about minorities, the department's preparation with respect to hate crimes, and departmental training all impact hate crime reporting. Having policies in place that send clearer messages about the department's priorities with respect to hate crime, and providing adequate supervision regarding hate crime identification, both encourage reporting. In addition, the police officers' negative view of minorities and hate crime may discourage reporting (McDevitt et al., 2001).

There are individual-level factors that may discourage hate crime reporting, as well. One analysis of a sample of police departments that report and do not report hate crimes divided departments into *good reporting* and *nonreporting* agencies. Good reporting agencies that had departmental hate crime policies in place, and that were given procedures to facilitate hate crime identification, were more likely to participate in crime reporting. At the same time, those departments that did not provide hate crime training for officers were less likely to participate in hate crime reporting (Nolan, Akiyama, & Berhanu, 2002).

In addition to whether a department will report any hate crimes to the FBI, there is also the issue of the accuracy of each department's hate crime report. Research has revealed that reporting no hate crimes may stem not just from lack of will in the department but rather from the lack of proper institutional infrastructures. Infrastructures that encouraged reporting included those that train patrol and other responding officers to apply a broad inclusive definition of bias crime (Cronin, McDevitt, Farrell, & Nolan, 2007). This may require a structure in which patrol officers are trained to identify bias-motivated crimes, but are not allowed the final decision of whether a crime is bias-motivated or not. In addition, in order for departments to effectively identify and report bias crimes, higher officers must also be trained and participate in some type of bias crime classification review.

Even if a department is fully committed to reporting and does indeed report all hate crimes of which it has knowledge to the FBI, the annual survey may still not be an accurate picture of hate crimes in that particular community. Even before the police are involved, individuals who have been attacked must recognize themselves as victims of hate crimes and decide to report the incident. Bias crimes are greatly underreported. According to the National Crime Victimization Survey on bias victimization, only 44 percent of hate crimes were reported to the police. The survey indicated that roughly a third of victims report bias crimes to "get the offender." Approximately 30 percent may report in order to "get help with the incident." Another survey revealed that among high school victims of bias crimes, fewer than 5 percent of incidents were reported to police (Cronin et al., 2007).

In the end, hate crime reporting statutes only capture the level of hate crimes in the particular jurisdiction. While this is good for raising awareness in this area, documenting hate crimes as reporting statutes do is only a partial solution to the problem of bias-motivated violence. Such statutes count rather than punish bias-motivated crimes. This is a problem not just for issues of deterrence and retribution but also for policing. Empirical work that has been conducted in this area demonstrates that officers may lack enthusiasm to enforce bias-motivated crime because of the low penalties (Bell, 2002a; Martin, 1996). This is especially true in the context of reporting statutes, where officers are documenting incidents that may not violate the criminal law. The solution to the lack of enthusiasm that can be caused by reporting statutes are hate crime statutes, described in the next section.

Hate Crime Statutes

A second legislative response to the problem of bias-motivated crime is to create laws designed to punish bias-motivated conduct. Hate crime laws exist in many different jurisdictions in a variety of forms at the federal, state, and local levels. Laws of this type include federal criminal rights statutes, state and local bias-motivated violence and intimidation statutes, and other criminal and civil statutes (Wolfe, 2008). Prosecution under hate crime statutes often requires the perpetrator to have committed an underlying offense identified in the statute with the requisite motivation. The key issue for police is gathering evidence to support the perpetrator having committed the crime because of a bias on the basis of race, religion, sexual orientation, gender, or any other prohibited motivation delineated in the statute.

Though laws prohibiting bias-motivated conduct may be better at addressing the problem of hate crime, they also require a much more involved response from the entire criminal justice system. In addition to requiring that the police gather evidence to support hate crime charges, prosecutors must be committed to prosecuting hate crime cases. Prosecutors may be reluctant to bring hate crime charges for a variety of reasons. First, prosecutors acknowledge that hate crime cases are more difficult because, unlike most other types of crimes, they require that motivation be proven. Prosecutors may feel that it is easier to bring ordinary criminal charges than to gather evidence of motivation. Second, because hate crimes are relatively rare, it is difficult for prosecutors to build the experience required to prosecute them successfully. Even in jurisdictions where hate crimes are frequently prosecuted, if the jurisdiction is large judges may be unfamiliar with the type of case. All of this means that the prosecutor has a lower likelihood of winning the case and therefore may be reluctant to bring hate crime charges.

Jurisdictions may increase the chance of winning hate crime cases by increasing coordination between police detectives responsible for investigating hate crime and prosecutors. Prosecutors must communicate to police the type of evidence they need in order to clearly demonstrate that bias motivated the crime. If, for instance, the judge or jury believes that the perpetrator was motivated by something else (revenge, drugs, or anger), then they may acquit the defendant. Prosecutors believe that several factors may indicate bias including: (1) The absence of a prior history between the suspect and the victim that might have created a reason for the attack; (2) the absence of any reason for the attack; and (3) the attack having occurred near a salient location, such as outside a gay bar (Bell, 2002a).

Police Responsibility under Traditional Hate Crime Statutes

Even though a hate crime might be charged under federal law and could be investigated by the FBI, local police are often the first responders when a hate crime occurs (Levin & McDevitt, 1993, p. 159). State and local law enforcement agencies provide not only the first response but also shoulder the lion's share of the burden for hate crime law enforcement, as most prosecutions of hate crimes occur at state and local levels. These units must overcome a variety of enforcement challenges posed by the very nature of bias crime. First, hate crimes may be hard to identify, requiring the police to develop strategies for identifying the crime's motivation, something that police are not often required to do. Empirical studies of hate crime investigation reveal that this may require police to devote significant resources to what may be a small number of crimes. Second, the majority of hate crimes are low-level assaults and vandalism (FBI, 2005; Wilson & Ruback, 2003). In many cases, incidents reported as hate crimes may not even constitute criminal behavior. Crimes of such a low-offense level do not normally get investigated by the police. Thus, when a jurisdiction passes hate crime legislation, police must reorient many of their normal priorities.

Law enforcement agencies around the country have responded in a variety of ways to the difficulty that enforcing hate crime legislation poses. In 1999, the U.S. Department of Justice created a variety of protocols for combating hate crime and distributed them to police departments around the nation. Prosecutors' offices in a few large cities created hate crime units devoted to prosecuting hate crime. Police departments began to devote more resources to hate crime. The 1990 Law Enforcement Management and Administrative Statistics (LEMAS) survey showed that 35 percent of all municipal departments reported having either a bias crime unit or procedures for dealing with bias crime (Martin, 1996, p. 307).

The mere passage of hate crime laws does not ensure that the law will be enforced. Hate crimes often require detailed investigation. Law enforcement agencies may create formal policies setting forth the agency's understanding of and commitment to hate crime, and protocols for dealing with the specialized investigations required. An individual law enforcement agency's adoption of a hate crime policy is not necessarily contingent on the existence of a crime law. One study of California found that 44 percent of the responding police agencies did not have a hate crime policy, despite the California's hate crime statute (Jenness & Grattet, 2005). When asked about differences, law enforcement agencies indicated that the lack of a hate crime policy stemmed from a variety of reasons, including the absence of hate crimes in the jurisdiction, administrative error, or other difficulty (p. 351). The authors found that organizational factors like size of the police department and environmental factors such as being located in a high-crime neighborhood contribute to the development of hate crime policies (Jenness & Grattet, 2005).

INSTITUTIONAL ARRANGEMENTS FOR HATE CRIME INVESTIGATION

Once law enforcement agencies have committed themselves to hate crime by promulgating a hate crime order and a hate crime policy, they are committing to undertake investigation in some form. Law enforcement agencies have developed a variety of approaches to the investigation of hate crime. These approaches reflect the institutional structures currently at work in police departments. Police departments are commonly organized by geographic districts or divisions that split the jurisdiction into areas. The least expensive way of dealing with hate crime, at least in terms of agency resources, is a decentralized approach. Slightly less resource-consuming than establishing some sort of centralized unit, this option involves sending a group of officers representing every geographic unit or division in the department to specialized hate crime training. Once trained, the officers are not organized in a centralized unit but rather they are dispersed. Each officer is given responsibility for the investigation and report of all hate crimes that occur in his or her area. Because there are likely to be few hate crimes, this officer may have other responsibilities—responding to other specialized crimes, working as a community services officer, or performing other community functions.

The use of the decentralized approach is similar to that used in the community policing context and other community-based crimes. One study of this approach applied to hate crime examined the process in Baltimore County, Maryland, for investigating and otherwise dealing with racial, religious, or ethnic hate crimes, or "RRE incidents" (Martin, 1996). In Baltimore County, responsibility for investigating RRE incidents fell to community service officers, who received reports of the incident from the beat officer. Generally officers in the precinct in which the incident occurred conducted the follow-up investigation, which in most cases consisted of a single telephone call (Martin, 1996).

Similar to Baltimore County, another police department, the Metropolitan Police Department (MPD), was organized into 18 administratively distinct units, which separately administered the department hate crime policy. The department's policy required that responding patrol officers note potentially bias-motivated crimes on the incident report. Incidents suspected of being hate crimes were assigned to a designated hate crime detective in each division. The new policies also required commanding officers or hate crime detectives to contact the victims of hate crimes and to notify the chief of police if unusual circumstances were noticed (Boyd, Berk, & Hamner, 1996, p. 825). The divisions were also required to individually track crimes and report on a quarterly and an annual basis the hate crimes that had occurred in their geographic area.

The decentralized approach contrasts quite strongly with the creation of specialized hate crime units. Specialized hate crime units with full-time personnel solely responsible for the investigation of hate crime are often located in large urban police departments—Boston, Chicago, Los Angeles, New York. A survey of police departments in 2000 revealed that only 7 percent of police agencies had specialized bias crime units with full-time personnel (Bureau of Justice Statistics, 2004). Such specialized units may widely vary in size and function, and can be quite large; the police bias crime unit in Los Angeles has 90 full-time sworn officers (Jenness & Grattet, 2001, p. 128; Walker & Katz, 1995).

Specialized bias crime units are often composed of officers specially trained in the investigation of hate crime (Bell, 2002a; Garofalo & Martin; 1993a). If the process of a crime investigation is to begin from within the police department it will begin when the unit receives a crime report written by the patrol officers. Thus, unless procedures are created to circumvent the discretion of patrol officers, the street-level officers will have the ability to limit enforcement of hate crime law simply by neglecting to file reports.

One of the reasons that departments create specialized units is not just to develop expertise through training but also to focus resources, especially investigative resources, on bias-motivated crime. One early study analyzed the Bias Incident Investigating Unit (BIIU), New York City's specialized hate crime unit that operated based on referrals received from the patrol officers who reported to the scene of the crime. This 23-officer unit was focused on a very small number of crimes. The authors indicate that the *yearly* caseload of a detective in BIIU was estimated to be roughly the same as the *monthly* caseload of a neighborhood detective investigating nonhate crimes (Garofalo & Martin, 1993a).

To get a sense of whether there was actually more activity in the BIIU, Garofalo and Martin compared a selection of bias crimes referred to the unit with a comparison group of non–bias-motivated crimes dealt with outside the BIIU. Most of the crimes in both groups were misdemeanors, the researchers indicated, and would normally have received little if any attention. The researchers found vast differences in the treatment of bias and nonbias crimes. They looked at reports of investigative activity that were supposed to be filed documenting the detectives' work. The police department's general approach to nonbias cases was characterized as "file and forget it" (Garofalo & Martin, 1993a). In a sample of nonbias crimes, 80 percent of case folders had zero follow-up reports. By contrast, 94 percent of the bias case folders had three or four reports. Follow-up activities in which the detectives engaged included interviews with the victim after that initial crime report, canvassing the area for witnesses, taking photos of the crime scene, and having victims or witnesses view photos of suspects. The different rates at which the detectives engaged in these activities are startling. For instance, a subsequent interview after the follow up interview was found in 73 percent of bias cases but only 4 percent of nonbias cases (Garofalo & Martin, 1993a).

Similar intensity of investigative activity was found in a more recent study of the Anti-Bias Task Force (ABTF), a specialized hate crime detective unit in Center City, a large city. In Center City the vast majority of cases referred to the bias crime unit (92 percent) received at least minimal investigation (Bell, 2002a). Like the unit in New York City, the ABTF received reports from patrol officers and followed through on the investigation. The unit was notified about cases when patrol officers checked a box on the police report indicating that the incident was bias-motivated. The ABTF's practices suggest how it is possible to limit the street-level discretion exercised by patrol officers. Patrol officers, even if trained, may fail to identify hate crime. A study of a sample of more than 400 bias-motivated incidents in the late 1980s revealed that only 4.2 percent were correctly identified by reporting officers (Levin, 1992–1993). The ABTF employed several mechanisms ranging from routinely checking reports in areas in which bias-motivated crimes had occurred in the past, to having the department's central administrative body send all crime reports with a difference in race between the victim and perpetrator to the unit (Bell, 2002a).

For the most involved specialized hate crime units, being charged with the duty to investigate hate crime creates myriad related tasks, which may be very time intensive. The initial contact with the victim may take several attempts. Next, there is the initial victim interview, which may take several hours and involve reassuring the victim of his or her safety. If the officer remains committed to the investigation, his or her next task centers on finding suspects— often a difficult task because hate crime victims and perpetrators are often unknown to each other. If suspects are found, detectives must interview them and then sort through versions of the suspect's and victim's stories. If the case goes to trial, the detectives may be responsible for testifying, and also for making sure the victim is available to offer testimony.

The task-oriented ambiguity attendant to hate crimes creates a wide variety of jobs that police officers must perform. Officers must act as victim service providers, as well as investigators. Because few hate crimes may be reported in the entire city, the decentralized approach has significant disadvantages. If the hate crime policy allocates responsibility by giving it to a single officer in a particular geographic area, the hate crime detective or officer may not see enough hate crimes to develop routines necessary to effectively investigate. Moreover, the absence of other, more experienced officers also grappling with similar issues may interfere with the officers' learning in this regard. Specialized hate crime units, while more resource-consuming, at minimum provide interaction between officers on cases. In addition to grappling with difficult issues as a group, the city's hate crimes are concentrated among the officers in a single unit, thereby providing repeat encounters with the complexity of hate crimes that may allow officers to develop routines for dealing with this type of crime.

PROCEDURES FOR IDENTIFYING BIAS MOTIVATION

Whether law enforcement is acting as a single officer investigating a crime or as a large specialized unit, one of the crucial issues in crime investigation is the manner in which bias motivation is identified. Many law enforcement agencies are trained in hate crime identification training modules created by the FBI. Since the Hate Crime Statistics Act was first passed in 1990, the FBI has put forth several training guides intended to assist law enforcement agencies in hate crime identification. The FBI guidelines, in addition to providing background on the definition of bias crimes, put forth procedures for handling hate crime collection, and as a result, the identification of bias motivation. The FBI training guidelines recommend a two-tier process in which the officer on the scene makes an initial determination of bias motivation and the second officer with more expertise in bias crimes makes a final determination of whether a hate crime has actually occurred (FBI, 1997, 1999).

According to the FBI model guidelines, the two-step procedure allows issues of bias to be evaluated by two layers of decision makers—the patrol officer, and the second judgment officer or detective unit (FBI, 1997). For the patrol officer, identification of the incident as possibly bias-motivated will stem from obvious factors—the absence of other motivation; the offender's stated motivation; whether the incident occurred on a holiday of particular significance; any indications that the demographics of the area may have led to the event; or the use of offensive words or symbols that may constitute evidence of bias against the victim. At the next stage, the reviewing officer is cautioned that the offender's prejudice or bias does not mean that the incident is a hate crime, "rather, the offender's criminal act must have been motivated, in whole or in part, by his/her bias" (FBI, 1997, p. 19). In reviewing whether the perpetrator was actually motivated by bias, FBI guidelines counsel investigators to evaluate factors such as the difference in background, especially differences with regard to race, religion, disability, ethnicity/national origin, or sexual orientation between the victim and the perpetrator; the use of biased comments, statements, or epithets used by the perpetrator; the extent to which the victim is a member of a group that is overwhelmingly outnumbered by other residents in the neighborhood where the victim lives or where the incident took place (FBI, 1997).

Police procedures in cities around the country indicate that departments have largely followed FBI guidelines by implementing two-step procedures for the identification of bias (Cronin et al., 2007). For instance, the Police Department of Glendale, California, uses a special policy for crimes motivated by race, religion, ethnicity, and sexual orientation. In the police department's order describing the new policy, the department describes the two-step process in which responding officers are to identify particular actions as bias crimes and make a report. If identified as bias-motivated, special procedures are activated: the field supervisor and others—the watch commander or operations supervisor—are notified to ensure that evidence of bias motivation is documented and it is communicated to the victim that the investigation of the crime will be actively pursued. The second-level procedure is forwarded to the Criminal Intelligence Unit, which provides follow-up investigation and confirmation of bias (Freeman & Lieberman, 1999).

Examining the criteria for determining whether a hate crime has occurred, police procedures often require that bias motivated the attack. For instance, the Burbank, California, Police Department criteria for determining hate crimes specified that in addition to the crime involving a specific target, "bigotry must be the central motive for the attack, rather than economics, revenge, etc., as in other kinds of crime" (Freeman & Lieberman, 1999, p. 61). Though motivation is the central factor in identifying crimes as bias-motivated, it doesn't mean that proof of bias is required. The same order, which was also used in Los Angeles, indicates that there are particular cases—such as those in which there is no motivation, or when the crime is carried out against particular targets—wherein motivation is to be assumed. The order directs officers attention to:

1. Any assault against a person in the absence of other apparent motivation, when initiated with racial, ethnic, religious, or homophobic epithets, will be considered to be a hate crime.
2. Vandalism to a house of worship, or ethnic, religious, or gay or lesbian organization will be considered to be a hate crime in the absence of evidence or other motives.
3. Obscene or threatening phone calls, when containing racial, ethnic, religious or homophobic slurs, are considered hate crimes (Freeman & Lieberman, 61).

IDENTIFYING BIAS MOTIVATION

Having a hate crime policy in place, however, may not be sufficient to ensure that police officers are properly identifying bias motivation. Because discerning bias motivation may present such difficulties, an agency's overall ability to identify bias-motivated incidents may be strongly linked to institutional mechanisms that create incentives for thorough investigation of hate crimes. If an agency with a hate crime policy lacks institutional incentives to investigate hate crime, those officers charged with dealing with a crime have the discretion to pursue a variety of different options including: (1) do nothing, and close the case without investigation; (2) conduct a cursory investigation; (3) conduct an extensive investigation without classifying the incident; and (4) conduct an extensive investigation, requesting hate crime charges if warranted.

In some cases, the process of investigation and the number of incidents referred to the hate crime investigators help investigators narrow their focus to motivation. Studies of hate crime investigation suggest that officers receive large numbers of crimes that are potentially bias-motivated (Bell, 2002a; Boyd et al., 1996; Martin, 1996). These may be incidents involving perpetrators and victims who have different races, or incidents in which racial, ethnic, or homophobic slurs are used. Police officers readily accept that not all of these incidents are bias-motivated. Thus, the process of investigation requires a certain amount of ordinary detective work.

Often investigators of hate crimes will first have to sort through the victim's and perpetrator's stories, interviewing the victim and the alleged perpetrator to make sure there is a true victim, and a perpetrator. For instance, incidents that present as assaults in the initial report may actually be fistfights between individuals who disagreed over other matters. These aren't the only incidents that may appear as a hate crime on the initial report and later get rejected for absence of bias motivation. One study of a specialized detective unit revealed that in order to sort through incidents, officers developed a shorthand for several different types of incidents that the unit received that were in actuality not hate crimes. In addition to fights these "typical non hate crimes" included traffic accidents, neighbor disputes, and failed drug deals (Bell, 2002b).

Once detectives eliminated situations involving traffic accidents, drug disputes, and assaults, they turned their attention to motivation, examining specifically why an individual committed the crime. Evidence of the perpetrator's motivation came from the circumstances of the crime—how the perpetrator behaved while committing the crime, where and when the incident occurred, and the victim and perpetrator's history. These issues were examined by questioning the victim, the victim's family members and neighbors, the perpetrator(s), and anyone else who might know about the crime. Such thorough investigations were quite detailed and time-consuming, but allowed detectives to carefully examine incidents for evidence of bias motivation.

Police departments that adopt a decentralized approach to carry out their hate crime policy may be unable to provide incentives that allow for a detailed examination of motivation. This was found in one study of a large urban police department which had adopted a decentralized approach to hate crime investigation. As in specialized units, in this department patrol officers had the initial job of identifying bias crimes. After patrol officers flagged the incident as bias-motivated, it was assigned to a designated detective in the geographic division in which it occurred. Under a decentralized approach, the secondary step was not as useful as might have been predicted. Several detectives resented the demands placed on them by the new policy. Hate crimes, in their view, were not real crimes. These detectives maintained the belief that true hate crimes were rare, and therefore attempted to deflate summary statistics by adopting a heightened definition for bias motivation. In some cases, this stringent approach meant rejecting all other possible explanations before categorizing an incident as bias-motivated. In the end, cases most likely to be identified as hate crimes were those that had the clearest markers of bias: no provocation by victim, no prior encounters between the victim and the perpetrator, and slurs or epithets used during the crime (Boyd et al., 1996).

Specialized hate crime units that focus entirely on hate crime with formal procedures for screening possibly bias-motivated incidents provide the best locus for an examination of motivation. In specialized units, there is space for a much more detailed approach to examining motivation. If such units are composed of officers who are trained in the identification and in the investigation of hate crime and the unit contains procedures that appropriately encourage and support full investigation, officers in such units will be able to negotiate the complexity of hate crime identification.

The intensified investigative activities in hate crime cases in which motivation has been identified may have a significant impact on whether perpetrators are arrested. For example, in New York City one study found that in comparing bias cases with a similar type of nonbias case, for the bias cases the arrest rate was double that of the nonbias cases (Martin, 1996). The authors attributed this dramatic difference in outcomes to two main factors: the important differences in the laws, and departmental priorities centered on hate crime. With respect to the law, non–bias-motivated harassment is only a violation, while harassment targeting an individual's "race, color, religion, or national origin," may subject the perpetrator to aggravated harassment, a Class A misdemeanor, or Class E felony (Martin, 1996). Departmental priorities encouraged officers to pursue increased investigation in potentially bias-motivated crime, and also to make more arrests in these crimes, than those in nonbias crimes at the same offense level. A comparison study in Baltimore County, Maryland, found special incentive to make arrests, and thus produce a difference in arrest rates, between cases involving bias-motivated violence and nonbias cases (Martin, 1996, p. 473).

Police enforcement of hate crime laws may be related to individual and community level influences. There is significant support for the contention that making hate crime a serious offense creates an incentive for police to be involved. Research conducted in multiple jurisdictions across time reveals that the severity of offense is a significant predictor of police involvement (Martin, 1996; Wilson & Ruback, 2003). Incidents involving property or personal crimes rather than noncriminal offenses increase the likelihood that the police will become involved. One study found also the community's characteristics were significantly related to whether or not the police respond to hate incidents. Comparing a variety of communities, both urban and rural, the research revealed that police were more likely to become involved in incidents in counties with large Jewish populations than in incidents in counties with large black populations. The researchers suggested that police involvement may in part have been motivated by hate crime victim advocacy organizations that exist in the Jewish community but were absent in the black community (Wilson & Ruback, 2003).

ADDRESSING POTENTIAL PROBLEMS WITH HATE CRIME LAW ENFORCEMENT

There are also several issues with discerning motivation. Research has indicated that motivation in hate crimes may be ambiguous (Bell, 2002a; Cronin et al., 2007; Martin, 1996). Confronted with this ambiguity, officers may identify several different motivations for hate crime. For instance, the robbery and assault of a lesbian who just left a gay bar might be attributed to a variety of motives. The crime might be considered a bias-motivated attack or rather, some sort of opportunistic crime. Patrol officers may not have much chance to develop routines to help them cope with ambiguity because of the relative infrequency of bias-motivated crimes (Cronin et al., 2007). Finally, the ambiguity of motivation in these crimes is magnified by the fact that victims may be reluctant to identify particular crimes as bias-motivated (Levin & McDevitt, 1993).

There is concern with how officers may cope with crimes in which motivation is not clear. Some scholars have complained that the law enforcement officers will use protected hate speech as the sole evidence that one has committed a hate crime (Gellman, 1991; Gerstenfeld, 1998; Jacobs & Potter, 1998). In other words, individuals will be arrested for having violated hate crime law primarily on the basis of having referred to the victim using a slur or epithet. If this is the case, such behavior is problematic because in *R.A.V. v. St. Paul* the Supreme Court held that the use of hate speech is protected by the First Amendment. Legally, police are allowed to take slurs and epithets used in the commission of a hate crime into account since the Supreme Court has also held that the use of such language as evidence of motivation of does not violate the First Amendment. In other words, enforcing hate crime law requires police to strike a difficult balance—they must respect citizens' constitutionally protected right to free speech while at the same time they must protect individuals' right to be free from attacks based on their racial, ethnic, and other identities (Martin, 1996, p. 47).

Walking the fine line between policing free speech and enforcing hate crime law is difficult for police. The complexity of their task is compounded by the fact that many crimes that come to their attention may involve situations in which there is a difference in race between the victim and the perpetrator and there is evidence that the perpetrator used slurs and epithets while committing the crime. Police readily acknowledge that not all of the cases involving perpetrators and victims of different races in which racial or other slurs have been used are hate crimes. Frequently encountering such cases allows police officers to use fine-tuned analysis. Rather than just focusing on the words used during the crime, the officers' detailed approach requires them to look to the crime's larger context to distill motive. Hate speech used during the crime may be relevant to the detectives' determination that bias motivated the crime, but it does not constitute the whole analysis. In other words, to properly respect the First Amendment the detectives may look to factors such as the crime's location, the relationship between the victim and perpetrator, and other potential explanations for the crime.

Detailed examinations of the procedure the police use to identify motivation suggest that when enforcing hate crime law, police may tend to err on the side of protecting the First Amendment. Detectives who are reluctant to enforce hate crime law may characterize hate speech as "jokes" or "pranks"

(Boyd et al., 1996). Even those who are more committed to enforcing hate crime law may have been found to exercise restraint when it comes to policing free speech. Even detectives committed to hate crime victims and to enforcing hate crime law possessed a healthy respect of the First Amendment issues involved in their jobs (Bell, 2002b).

In addition to these doctrinal issues there is the extent to which difficult relations between the police and racial and ethnic minorities may disrupt the hate crime investigation process. Though there is significant research documenting police brutality and insensitivity toward racial and sexual minorities in other contexts, there is some data suggesting that police may operate differently when they are investigating hate crimes. First, on the issue of the over-enforcement of hate crime law, empirical studies show no evidence of the disproportionate use of hate crime law against racial and ethnic minorities. On the related issue of police interaction with hate crime victims, one study supports the idea that the proper environment may foster the creation of detectives who become committed victim advocates devoted to the job of hate crime investigation. This occurred through a process of conversion during which ordinary detectives were transformed into victim advocates by repeatedly watching victims undergo traumatizing circumstances. One hate crime detective described the connection between seeing what happened and developing understanding and commitment to the job.

> You can read all the case reports you want to but you never get what's really happening out there until you what see the victims are going through. You have to go out there and see what is happening and see what effect it has on them. . . . "Mike" has seen it. He's seen what hate can do. (Bell, 2002a, p. 128)

The close contact with victims—created in part through the more intensive investigation required in bias crime cases—may lead to increased victims' satisfaction with the police, in stark contrast to the poorer minority police relations that frequently characterize nonbias cases. Other research has surveyed bias crime victims in two jurisdictions (New York City and Baltimore County) on the issue of police response. The study found a great majority of bias crime victims, some 73 percent, claim to be very satisfied with police behavior. In New York City the satisfaction of bias crime victims was significantly greater even than victims of non–bias-motivated crimes of a similar offense level (Martin, 1996).

CONCLUSION

As the first responders to acts of bias-motivated violence, local police officers set the stage for the state's response to hate crime. Because of this, law enforcement officers charged with enforcement of hate crime law have the power to use their discretion to limit the cases that appear downstream, on the desk of prosecutors and in front of judges. Depending on a variety of environmental and institutional factors, officers' behavior in bias-motivated crime cases can greatly affect the services hate crime victims receive. At minimum, the best environment for enforcement of bias crime laws by the police includes some sort of hate crime statute that requires the police to do more than simply collect data on hate crime. In addition to an actual hate crime criminal or civil statute, best practices in this area would include a district attorney committed to enforcing violations of the law. These factors provide essential support to allow police departments to develop procedures like officer training, specialized hate crime units, and dual-stage hate crime classification. Training, standardized hate crime procedures, and mechanisms for officer supervision help demonstrate a department's commitment to hate crime law and create significant incentives encouraging officers to fully and properly investigate hate crime.

NOTE

1. The original HCSA did not include crimes motivated by bias on the basis of disability. Disability was added as part of the Violent Crime and Law Enforcement Act of 1994.

REFERENCES

Bell, J. (2002a). *Policing hatred: Law enforcement, civil rights and hate crime.* New York: New York University Press.

Bell, J. (2002b). Deciding when hate is a crime: The First Amendment, police detectives and hate crime. *Rutgers Race & the Law Review, 4,* 33–76.

Boyd, E., Berk, R. A., & Hamner, K. M. (1996). "Motivated by hatred or prejudice": Categorization of hate-motivated crimes in two police divisions. *Law & Society Review, 30,* 819–849.

Bureau of Justice Statistics. (2004). *Law enforcement management and administrative statistics, 2000: Data for individual state and local agencies with one hundred or more officers.* Washington DC: Government Printing Office.

Cronin, S. W., McDevitt, J., Farrell, A., & Nolan, J. J., III. (2007). Bias-crime reporting: Organizational responses to ambiguity, uncertainty, and infrequency in eight police departments. *American Behavioral Scientist, 51,* 213–231.

Federal Bureau of Investigation. (1997). *Training guide for hate crime data collection.* Washington, DC: U.S. Government Printing Office.

Federal Bureau of Investigation. (1999). *Hate crime data collection guidelines.* Washington, DC: U.S. Government Printing Office.

Federal Bureau of Investigation. (2005). *Hate crime report: 2005.* Washington, DC: U.S. Government Printing Office.

Franklin, K. (2002). Good intentions: The enforcement of hate crime penalty-enhancement statutes. *American Behavioral Scientist, 46,* 154–172.

Freeman, S. M., & Lieberman, M. (1988). *Hate crimes policies and procedures for law enforcement agencies.* New York: Anti-Defamation League of B'nai B'rith.

Garofalo, J., & Martin, S. E. (1993a). *Bias-motivated crimes: Their characteristics and the law enforcement response.* Illinois: Southern Illinois University at Carbondale.

Garofalo, J., & Martin, S. E. (1993b). The law enforcement response to bias motivated crime. In Kelly, Robert J. (Ed.), *Bias crime: American law enforcement and legal responses.* Chicago: Office of International Criminal Justice, at the University of Illinois at Chicago.

Gellman, S. (1991). Sticks and stones can put you in jail, but can words increase your sentence? Constitutional and policy dilemmas of ethnic intimidation laws. *UCLA Law Review, 39,* 333–396.

Gerstenfeld, P. B. (1992). Smile when you call me that!: The problems with punishing hate motivated behavior. *Behavioral Science & Law, 10,* 259–285.

Herek, G. M., Gillis, J. R., & Cogan, J. C. (1999). Psychological sequelae of hate-crime victimization among lesbian, gay, and bisexual adults. *Journal of Consulting and Clinical Psychology, 67,* 945–951.

Jacobs, J., & Potter, K. (1998). *Hate crimes: Criminal law and identity politics.* New York: Oxford University Press.

Jenness, V., & Grattet, R. (2001). *Making hate a crime: From social movement to law enforcement.* New York: Russell Sage.

Jenness, V., & Grattet, R. (2005). The law-in-between: The effects of organizational perviousness on the policing of hate crime. *Social Problems 52,* 337–359.

Kelly, R. J. (Ed.). (1993). *Bias crime: American law enforcement and legal responses.* Chicago: Office of International Criminal Justice, at the University of Illinois at Chicago.

King, R. D. (2007). The context of minority group threat: Race, institutions, and complying with hate crime law. *Law & Society Review, 41,* 189–224.

Lederer, L. J. (1995). The case of the cross burning: An interview with Russ and Laura Jones. In L. J. Lederer & R. Delgado (Eds.), *The price we pay: The case against racist speech, hate propaganda, and pornography.* New York: Hill & Wang.

Levin, B. (1992–1993). Bias crimes: A theoretical and practical overview. *Stanford Law and Policy Review, 4,* 165–182.

Levin, J., & McDevitt, J. (1993). *Hate crimes: The rising tide of bigotry and bloodshed.* New York: Plenum Press.

Levin, J., & McDevitt, J. (2002). *Hate crimes revisited: America's war on those who are different.* Boulder, CO: Westview Press.

McDevitt, J., Balboni, J., Garcia, L., & Gu, J. (2001). Consequences for victims: A comparison between bias and non-bias assaults. *The American Behavioral Scientist, 45,* 697–713.

McVeigh, R. Welch, M., & Bjarnson, T. (2003) . Hate crime reporting as successful movement outcome. *American Sociological Review, 68,* 843–847.

Martin, S. E. (1996). Investigating hate crimes: Case characteristics and law enforcement responses. *Justice Quarterly, 13,* 455–480.

Nolan, J. J., III, & Akiyama, Y. (1999). An analysis of factors that affect law enforcement participation in hate crime reporting. *Journal of Contemporary Criminal Justice, 15,* 111–127.

Nolan, J. J., III, Akiyama, Y., & Berhanu, S. 2002. The Hate Crime Statistics Act of 1990. *American Behavioral Scientist, 46,* 136–153.

Walker, S., & Katz, C. M. (1995). Less than meets the eye: Police department bias-crime units. *American Journal of Police, 14,* 29–48.

Wilson, M. S., Ruback, R. B. (2003). Hate crimes in Pennsylvania, 1984–1999: Case characteristics and police responses. *Justice Quarterly, 20,* 373–398.

Wolfe, Z. J. (2008). *Hate crimes law.* Minneapolis: Thomson Reuters/West.

CHAPTER 3

POLICE TRAINING

Robin Parker

NEED FOR HATE CRIME TRAINING

A number of factors point to the need for effective hate crime training for law enforcement officers. Most state legislatures have enacted laws to address hate crime within their jurisdictions (Thompson/West, 2006, p. 246). Many, like the New York legislature, agree that hate crimes are particularly heinous and warrant enhanced punishment, distinct from what the criminal law otherwise provides for crimes against persons or property:

> The legislature finds and determines as follows: criminal acts involving violence, intimidation and destruction of property based upon bias and prejudice have become more prevalent in New York state in recent years. The intolerable truth is that in these crimes, commonly and justly referred to as "hate crimes", victims are intentionally selected, in whole or in part, because of their race, color, national origin, ancestry, gender, religion, religious practice, age, disability or sexual orientation. Hate crimes do more than threaten the safety and welfare of all citizens. They inflict on victims incalculable physical and emotional damage and tear at the very fabric of free society. Crimes motivated by invidious hatred toward particular groups not only harm individual victims but send a powerful message of intolerance and discrimination to all members of the group to which the victim belongs. Hate crimes can and do intimidate and disrupt entire communities and vitiate the civility that is essential to healthy democratic processes. In a democratic society, citizens cannot be required to approve of the beliefs and practices of others, but must never commit criminal acts on account of them. Current law does

not adequately recognize the harm to public order and individual safety that hate crimes cause. Therefore, our laws must be strengthened to provide clear recognition of the gravity of hate crimes and the compelling importance of preventing their recurrence.

Accordingly, the legislature finds and declares that hate crimes should be prosecuted and punished with appropriate severity. (N.Y. Penal Law § 485.00 [McKinney Supp. 2006])

It is noteworthy that the New York legislature found that hate crimes are increasing, that such crimes tear at the fabric of society, that they inflict special harm on victims and communities, and that they must be deterred through criminal penalties that specifically address hate crimes. The criminal justice engine is being used not just to enforce the law, but also to address a very particular social problem that has its genesis in bigotry and prejudice.

The goal is laudable, but certainly one fraught with difficulties that must be addressed through law enforcement training. For example, law enforcement officers would need to understand the legal distinctions the courts have made between individual freedom of expression guaranteed in the Constitution, and the state's power to curtail hate crime, which may spring from prejudice or bigotry. Thus, it would be important for law enforcement officers to know when they investigate hate crimes or make hate crime arrests that they are neither treading on the First Amendment guarantees nor coming so close to those guarantees that they will lose the respect of the public that they serve.

Allied with this need for understanding the legal, constitutional, and moral situs of hate crime law is an understanding of the individuals and communities that have unique interests in hate crime enforcement. Although any individual can be a hate crime victim, African Americans, Jews, and gay men and lesbians are especially frequent hate crime victims who have a history of marginalization (Federal Bureau of Investigation, 2003, p. 6). Hate crime training that makes officers aware of the cultural backgrounds, histories, needs, and concerns of these and other groups, and how officers' own cultural conditioning affects their interactions with others, will likely make the relationship between the police and the citizenry more amicable, and also make the interdiction of hate crime easier. Ultimately, improved relationships between the police and historically marginalized groups redound to everyone's benefit: the police force becomes more responsive to its citizenry, and the citizenry becomes more cooperative with the police force.

Understanding how to investigate hate crime is a fundamental need that can be addressed through training. The range of activities that may constitute hate crime is striking:

- Two Vermont sisters spray painted antigay slogans and slashed the tires of the automobiles of two men joined in a civil union (Rathke, 2007).
- A Houston, Texas, man was beaten and sodomized with a patio umbrella pole by two men who shouted "white power" during the attack. He underwent more than 20 operations ("Texas: Young Victim," 2007).
- A teenager forced his high school classmate, a Sikh, into a restroom, tore off his turban, and cut off his waist-length hair to the neckline. The attack, which was one in a spike of hate crimes that occurred after September 11, 2001, was especially vicious because Sikh men do not cut their hair as a matter of religious faith (Buckley, 2007).
- A Jewish professor at Teachers College found a swastika painted on her door. The hate crime was one in a series that included hanging a noose on the office door of an African American professor ("Swastika Found," 2007).
- A white supremacist sprayed a Jewish community center in California with bullets from an Uzi submachine gun. After hitting five people, he left the scene and murdered a letter carrier because he was Filipino (Sterngold, 2001).

Knowing who are the more frequent perpetrators of hate crime, when hate crimes are more likely to occur, what attributes are covered under applicable hate crime statutes (race, ethnicity, religion, sexual orientation, etc.), and whether organized hate groups have played a role in a specific hate crime all lends to efficient investigation and ultimate prosecution. Similarly, training can impart useful strategies that officers can use to aid hate crime victims and to help communities prevent hate crimes before they occur.

Although organized hate groups commit only a small percentage of hate crimes in the United States (Bradley, 2007; McDevitt, Levin, & Bennett, 2002), law enforcement officers need to understand the nature, beliefs, and operations of such groups because of the potential they have, not only to commit hate crimes, but to cause community anxiety and unrest. Training may be especially useful in helping a police agency identify hate group activity, and work with a community and its leadership to ensure that the violence that might arise during a demonstration, march, or rally is avoided.

The 1996 Ku Klux Klan march in Ann Arbor, Michigan, is an illustration of this issue. On June 22 of that year, 15 Klan members spoke from a balcony of the city hall building. Hundreds of anti-Klan protesters appeared on the scene chanting. "No free speech for KKK—let's shut them down—let's do it today." Those same demonstrators began hurling objects at the Klan members and police. In the melee, police used mace, tear gas, and pepper spray to scatter the protesters. The wife of the Imperial Wizard was injured, one protester suffered a broken leg, 30 police officers were treated for exposure to chemical irritants, 8 persons were arrested, and buildings were damaged. The security and police enforcement costs of the rally were over \$55,000. Although the police were doing what they had to do—protect the constitutional rights of Klan members to voice their opinions in a public forum—some viewed their dispersing of the protesters as harassment, violence, or support for the Klan (Baybik, 1996). Training on ways to work with community leaders in advance of such hate group protests can focus counter-protests so that violence is avoided. Two years later, for example, more than 600 counter-protesters in Ann Arbor held a peace rally away from Klan speeches at the city hall without major incident (Holmes, 1998a, 1998b).

There is a wide array of factors that a law enforcement officer must consider in determining whether a crime is a hate crime. Those offered as part of the Federal Law Enforcement Training Center's train-the-trainer program include the following (Federal Law Enforcement Training Center, 2005):

- The offender and the victim were of a different race, religion, disability, sexual orientation, ethnicity, or national origin.
- Bias-related drawings, markings, symbols, or graffiti were left at the scene.
- Certain objects, items, or things that indicate bias.
- The victim is a member of a racial, religious, disability, sexual orientation, ethnic, or national origin group that is overwhelmingly outnumbered.
- The victim was visiting a neighborhood where previous hate crimes were committed against other members of his or her group and where tensions against his or her group remain high.
- A substantial portion of the community where the crime occurred perceived that the incident was motivated by bias.
- The victim was promoting his or her cultural group when the crime occurred.
- The crime occurred on a date of special significance to a racial, ethnic, religious, or cultural group.
- The offender was previously involved in a similar hate crime.
- The offender was a member of a hate group.
- A historical animosity existed between the victim's and offender's group.

Hate crime training must explain these factors, but also explain that none of the factors is alone sufficient to show that a hate crime has occurred. For example, persons whose races, religions, and ethnicities are different from their victims' commit many crimes. That alone does not create a hate crime. Instead, an officer must look at the factors in both the immediate context of the criminal activity and in the historical context of the motivations that individuals bring to bear when they interact with one another. The officer must then make a commonsense, but culturally well-informed determination of whether, given all the factors involved, the person who committed a crime did so because of the victim's cultural background, gender, or some other factor that makes a crime a hate crime under applicable law.

Training helps sort out these factors so that officers understand when the elements of proof for a hate crime are satisfied and when they are not. Thus, the letters "KKK" painted on a building are not simply graffiti, but a symbol that can be recognized as evincing racial animosity if an officer understands United States history, culture, and the legacy of organized hate groups. An assault committed by a person of one race against a person of another race is, without more motivation, simply an assault; whereas an assault committed by a person of one race who expressed prior racial animosity toward his different-race victim may be a hate crime.

Another factor that strongly militates in favor of hate crime training is the need for the accurate collection of data on hate crime. The Hate Crime Statistics Act mandates that the Justice Department collect and annually publish data about hate crimes in the United States. The act does not obligate state and local law enforcement agencies to report hate crimes to the Justice Department, however (Hate Crime Statistics Act, 28 U.S.C.A. § 534 note [West, 2006]). Instead, the Justice Department, through the FBI, depends on the cooperation of state and local agencies to fulfill the act's reporting mandate (FBI, 1999). Accurate data helps police, policy makers, and community groups better focus their efforts to address hate crime. It also raises public awareness about the problem of hate crime. Training not only ensures that the proper mechanisms are used for hate crime reporting, but provides a springboard for better assuring that hate crime is seen as important enough to be pursued, and that the most complete body of information about hate crime is collected.

HATE CRIME TRAINING TODAY

Crimes committed with a "bias motivation," that is, because of animus toward an individual's race, ethnicity, religion, gender, sexual orientation, or disability, are not new to America; but hate crime was not part of American criminal jurisprudence until 1981 when Oregon and Washington enacted the first criminal laws that had bias motivation as an element (Or. Rev. Stat. Ann. § 166.165 [West, 2003]; Wash. Rev. Code Ann. § 9A.36.080 [West, 2000]). Training for law enforcement officers on the nature, impact, investigation, and prevention of hate crime is therefore relatively recent. A few states like Iowa and New Mexico have mandatory hate crime training requirements for law enforcement officers (Iowa Code Ann. § 80B.11.3 [West, 1996]; New Mexico Stat. Ann. § 31–18B-5 [Michie Supp. 2006]), but in most jurisdictions, hate crime training is neither mandated by statute or regulation. Such training is widely available, however. The Federal Law Enforcement Training Center, for example, offers a three-and-one-half-day hate crime training program for state and local law enforcement officers with no tuition charge (Federal Law Enforcement Training Center,

2007, p. 155; Federal Law Enforcement Training Center, n.d.). On its Web site, the FBI states that it annually "provides hate crimes training for new agents, hundreds of current agents, and thousands of police officers worldwide" (FBI, n.d.). Indeed, even persons in the private sector, such as retired police officers, make hate crime training available to law enforcement agencies (Bouman & Holland, n.d.).

Models for hate crime training curricula are also widely available. Generally, the components include the following modules:

- History—provides a historical, social, and political backdrop for hate crime laws and includes a discussion of societal inequities, bigotry, and hate crime statistics
- Definitions—provides key definitions including those for hate crime, organized hate groups, and the classes of persons protected under hate crime laws
- Legal considerations—identifies the elements of hate crime laws, discusses the constitutionality of such laws, and explains state and federal laws that may otherwise be applicable in the prosecution of hate crime offenders
- Hate groups—identifies major hate groups, their categories, history, beliefs, and interdiction strategies
- Initial response—identifies the unique characteristics of hate crime and the role of the first responding law enforcement officer in investigations, reporting, and victim support
- Investigative strategies—provides insight into the factors that ensure a competent hate crime investigation
- Supervisory role—identifies the initial and ongoing responsibilities of supervisory personnel in hate crime investigations
- Community relations—provides an overview of key community relations strategies that help in the reporting, investigation, and prevention of hate crime
- Victim/witness considerations—focuses on strategies for interacting with the victims of hate crime, and the governmental and social service agencies that can be resources for victims

The Federal Law Enforcement Training Center's curriculum contains these or similar modules, and is typical of programs used as vehicles to train officers to train others within their departments (Federal Law Enforcement Training Center, 2005).

With training so widely available, curricula so comprehensive, and a cadre of trained officers so large, it would be tempting to conclude that generally speaking, hate crime training meets its desired goal: the preparation of police officers to investigate and prevent hate crime, to apprehend hate crime offenders, and to offer assistance to hate crime victims. The FBI's *Hate Crime Statistics* offers some support for the idea that hate crime training is effective. According to those reports, from 2000 to 2005 hate crimes reported annually by law enforcement agencies across the nation ranged from a year 2005 low of 7,163 incidents to a year 2001 high of 9,730 incidents, and the five-year trend has been decreasing (FBI, 2000, 2001, 2002, 2003, 2004, 2005a). Furthermore, hate crimes constitute only a small fraction of the more than 11 million violent and property crimes reported in 2005 (FBI, 2005b).

Other statistics, however, point to factors that show the need for better law enforcement and thus better law enforcement training. The Bureau of Justice Statistics reports that an average of 191,000 hate crime incidents occurred annually between 2000 and 2003 in which the victims believed the offenders selected them because of race, ethnicity, religion, sexual orientation, or disability (U.S. Department of Justice, 2005, pp. 1–2). That the FBI's hate crime statistics amount to as little as 4 percent of those captured by the Bureau of Justice Statistics is striking. Some of the disparity can be accounted for in the way that the statistics are collected. The Bureau of Justice Statistics figures are based on victim perception of whether a crime has a bias motive, whereas the FBI figures are based on a police department's determination of that fact. Nevertheless, the gulf between the 191,000 *perceived-by-victim* hate crimes and a maximum of 9,730 *confirmed-by-police* hate crimes raises the question of whether the inconsistency can be attributed largely to victim misperception or instead attributed to law enforcement failures.

One reason appears to be that victims do not report the majority of hate crimes to state and local law enforcement agencies (U.S. Department of Justice, 2005, p. 4). Additionally, 41 percent of victims who did not report hate crimes said they handled the matters in "another way," such as reporting the crimes to officials other than police, or keeping the matters private. Fourteen percent did not report because they felt the police would not help, and 8 percent believed the police could do nothing (U.S. Department of Justice, 2005, p. 5). With regard to violent hate crimes, police were less likely to arrive on the scene within 10 minutes, and less likely to take a report (U.S. Department of Justice, 2005, p. 4).

Another cause of disparity is poor reporting of hate crime by law enforcement agencies. For example, according to the more conservative FBI statistics, in 2005 there was a reported national total of 7,160 hate crimes. During that year California and New Jersey reported 1,379 and 738 hate crimes respectively, but Alabama and Mississippi reported none. Similarly, in 2003 and 2004 Alabama and Mississippi reported no more than 3 hate crimes each, a maximum of 0.04 percent of the national total (FBI, 2003, 2004, 2005). The apparent lack of reporting by those states and others realistically cannot be attributed to an absence of hate crimes.

Why would victims report so few hate crimes to police, and why would police apparently report even fewer hate crimes officially? Inadequate training may be part of the answer. The foreword to the 2000 FBI *Hate Crimes Statistics* report begins as follows:

Sterilized from emotion, hate crime . . . is those offenses motivated in part or singularly by personal prejudice against others because of diversity—race, sexual orientation, religion, ethnicity/national origin, or disability. The FBI Uniform Crime Reporting (UCR) Program's responsibility regarding hate crime is to provide a reliable set of statistics through the Hate Crime Data Collection Program. Through this program, law enforcement agencies nationwide voluntarily submit data about hate crimes within their jurisdictions . . . for publication in the annual report, *Hate Crime Statistics.* Though law enforcement agencies need only report data for one month of a year to be included in this publication, most agencies that participate in the Program submit four quarters of data. . . . *All data reported by law enforcement agencies are presented in this publication, free of the nuances that many factions of society impose upon the subject.* (emphasis added)

The foreword does not suggest a neutral point of view. The reader is immediately alerted that the agency feels a need to sterilize or clean up hate crime by distancing it from any emotional tether. This leaves a puzzle: Because a statistical report is expected to contain statistics, why does the FBI feel the need to announce that fact? The reader is left to conclude that perhaps some of the "many factions of society" to which the FBI refers have been too emotional or opinionated on the subject of hate crime. The foreword begs those who have been the victims of hate crime, or who have been emotionally moved in some way by the subject, to be held at a distance, and even insulted. Indeed, the foreword stumbles over so many cultural tripwires—making an apparent reference to people of color and marginalized groups as "factions"; saying that those factions "impose" "nuances" on hate crime; and implying that the foreword is itself neutral—that it invites an examination of the kinds of education and training needed so that law enforcement personnel would not so easily dash any hope of relating to many of their constituents.

It would be a mistake to generalize too broadly from one law enforcement publication. Nevertheless, the publication does point to a problem of public relations that could be addressed through hate crime training. Likewise, inadequate reporting of hate crime by law enforcement, and reticence of victims to report such crimes, are both problems that are susceptible to positive change. Why the current hate crime training, though available, may not adequately address these and other needs can be understood best in the context of the barriers, both internal and external, to law enforcement agencies, that make hate crime training difficult or less effective.

BARRIERS TO EFFECTIVE HATE CRIME TRAINING

To understand how hate crime training is perceived by law enforcement, one must first understand the history of law enforcement training in the

United States and how it has shaped group and individual attitudes. That history may be surprising to the layperson.

It is not well known that police training in the United States is a relatively new development. In the 1800s and early 1900s, working as a police officer was not seen as a profession, but as a kind of "casual labor" for which special training was unnecessary (Walker, 1977, pp. 3, 11). In Chicago, for example, there was no police training in 1900 although the city had over 3,000 officers. New members of the force simply received a "speech from a high-ranking officer, . . . a hickory club, a whistle, and a key to the call box" (Haller, 1976, p. 303). Because it was thought that anyone of decent moral background could be a police officer, training was superfluous. One commentator (Gammage, 1963, pp. 5–6) notes that "until 1915, any suggestion that a policeman needed formal training would have been received with amazement and doubt." It was perceived that a brief period of training on the streets was all that was needed. A chief, in recounting his advice to a new recruit, would say as follows:

> I say to him that now he is a policeman, I hope he will be a credit to the force. I tell him he doesn't need anybody to tell him how to enforce the law, that all he needs to do is to go out on the street and keep his eyes open. I say: "(Y)ou know the ten commandments, and you go out on your beat, and you see somebody violating one of those ten commandments, you can be pretty sure he is violating some law." (National Commission on Law Observance and Enforcement, 1931, p. 66)

In some cities, police training became institutionalized in the 1920s, and consisted of military-style drills, firearms training, and education on department rules and applicable laws. Yet the training was often inadequate, and outside of a few major cities, the view remained that police training was unimportant (Fosdick, 1920, p. 298; Haller, 1976, p. 306).

Social unrest of the 1960s changed this view. The civil disorder of the time and police mishandling of a myriad of incidents on university campuses, urban centers, and elsewhere brought law enforcement into a "crisis of legitimacy" that was attributed in part to "abrasive relationships" between the police and various groups (Rumbaut & Bittner, 1979, p. 241). As a consequence, nationwide efforts were undertaken to professionalize police and enable them to effectively dispose of the "sensitive human relations" obligations that were part of their work (Richardson, 1974, p. 154).

Although police training is more ubiquitous and routine today, old attitudes regarding training still persist. The idea that the best training is often on-the-job training in which a junior officer learns from a more senior one is still a common sentiment. This presents a special challenge for hate crime training because much of it is centered on understanding the histories and experiences of groups that have been historically marginalized and who are the primary victims of hate crime—African Americans, Jews, gay men and lesbians, and so forth (FBI, 2003, p. 6). With a reticence for training in general, and a cadre of officers in smaller departments that is often mostly white and male (U.S. Department of Justice, 2003), hate crime training may not be welcomed, and incomplete information about race, ethnicity, sexual orientation, and other features may be difficult to address. Hate crime pointedly brings to the fore cultural conflicts that have been a part of the American experience.

Cultural issues are often complex and nuanced. In an October 2007 *Philadelphia Inquirer* interview (Maykuth, 2007), former Philadelphia Police Commissioner Sylvester M. Johnson referred to persons who participated in community patrols as "Afro-American men," and praised them for their willingness to work with police. The term "Afro-American" is not used by African Americans or blacks in the United States to describe themselves, however, and indeed has fallen from any common usage since 1982 (Smith, 1974, p. 504). Such racial, ethnic, and cultural labels carry great importance to the referent groups, including those affected by hate crime. (It is worth noting that Commissioner Johnson is himself an African American, and made the obsolete reference about his own racial group.) A general unwillingness to learn about such issues through training puts officers at a disadvantage in working with individuals or groups who are "different," especially when they have been traumatized through hate crime. It can also create antipathy toward the police.

Training unwillingness, especially around important cultural issues, may be due to the defensiveness that is inherent in police institutions. There are constant tensions in a democratic society among the values of freedom, the need to enforce public order through agencies like the police force, and the desire to constrain the police force so that freedom and order are balanced in light of societal conceptions of fairness. As Harris (1973, pp. 29–30) states:

> Finding themselves barraged by a steady onslaught of criticisms from many segments of the community—all of whom the policeman is supposed to be serving—police officers try to protect themselves by curling up individually and organizationally, like the vulnerable porcupine . . . a "defensive bureaucracy."

An unfortunate consequence of this defensiveness is that marginalized groups, especially to the extent that their members are perceived to exert pressure on the police through media criticism, may be seen as hostile outgroups (Harris, 1973, pp. 47–58). As a result, hate crime training may be seen as education—and even bellyaching—in the service of groups not supportive of the law enforcement community. This explains why the previously mentioned Foreword in the FBI's year 2000 *Hate Crime Statistics* took a hostile tone toward the so-called "factions" that had interest in the data. Of course, such hostility towards the training makes learning especially difficult.

A closely linked attribute of defensiveness is what Harris (1973) calls "depersonalization." The phenomenon is one in which police officers objectify groups and individuals, and in which society in turn objectifies the police officers themselves. It is typified by the "just-the-facts-ma'am" attitude of *Dragnet*'s Detective Joe Friday—that of a detached, deadpan professional who remains aloof from the social and emotional polemics that are a part of his job. The expectations put on officers like Detective Friday, though usually unstated, are familiar:

- Always be tough
- Always be in control and able to handle any situation
- Be emotionally stable
- Keep your mouth shut and do your job
- Don't get too involved
- Don't be enthusiastic
- Keep a low profile
- Adapt to peer pressure
- Don't get too educated
- Be strong and protective
- Always be "right" (make no mistakes)
- Never be tired, or upset, or "fed-up" (Dufford, 1986, p. 9)

The expectations are engendered by a circular process: the public calls upon the police to do the sometimes dangerous and distasteful job of law enforcement, but often fails to support officers by treating them as individuals with feelings and normal fallibilities. Occupational necessity also demands that police maintain emotional detachment for the performance of various tasks. (For example, officers who investigate homicides cannot afford to be emotionally incapacitated by the very criminal activity to which they have been assigned.) As a consequence of job necessity and being depersonalized by the public, police depersonalize others (Harris, pp. 113–132). If not checked, the process makes it difficult for officers to empathize with individuals who are different from themselves, and to treat individuals as other than objects to be manipulated (Harris, p. 114).

Depersonalization, an entrenched factor in law enforcement work, presents a special barrier to hate crime training. To be effective, that training must convey the importance of empathy skills for hate crime victims, and teach officers how to use those skills to support victims and to get the best information possible about the nature of the criminal activity. Yet if entrenched depersonalization means that for officers a swastika painted on a synagogue carries the same emotional impact as any random graffiti, then that officer will be unable to understand the congregants' fear and outrage except as a purely intellectual fact. Hate crime training must push against this predisposition.

In one sense, hate crime laws are not complex legal creations. New York's hate crime statute is typical of many across the nation:

1. A person commits a hate crime when he or she commits a specified offense and either:

    a. intentionally selects the person against whom the offense is committed or intended to be committed in whole or in substantial part because of a belief or perception regarding the race, color, national origin, ancestry, gender, religion, religious practice, age, disability or sexual orientation of a person, regardless of whether the belief or perception is correct, or
    b. intentionally commits the act or acts constituting the offense in whole or in substantial part because of a belief or perception regarding the race, color, national origin, ancestry, gender, religion, religious practice, age, disability or sexual orientation of a person, regardless of whether the belief or perception is correct (N.Y. Penal Law § 485.05(1) [McKinney Supp. 2006]).

"Specified offenses" in the statute include assault and aggravated assault, manslaughter, murder, criminal mischief, burglary, harassment, arson, rape, and other crimes (N.Y. Penal Law § 485.05(3) [McKinney Supp., 2006]). Under the law, the punishment for those offenses is increased above what would be the punishment if the additional elements for a hate crime were not proved (N.Y. Penal Law § 485.10 [McKinney Supp., 2006]).

Viewed most simplistically, the law adds new elements to existing criminal statutes to create a new offense with enhanced penalties. Yet, closer scrutiny shows that the law is more than just a criminal statute with extra elements. It is based not only on the premise that individuals should not be victims of crime, but more specifically that it is *especially bad* for individuals to be singled out as victims of crime based on their racial, ancestral, gender, religious, or other specified characteristics. Title VII of the Civil Rights Act of 1964 similarly prohibits discrimination in employment, taking into account the ways in which groups of individuals have been historically excluded from employment because of race, color, religion, gender, or national origin. This is the same type of reasoning that is inherent in the Supreme Court's adjudication of the equal protection clause of the Fourteenth Amendment. There, legislative classifications that disadvantage individuals based on nationality, alienage, or race are inherently suspect, and usually invalid because they are aimed at groups "relegated to such a position of . . . powerlessness as to command extraordinary protection" (*San Antonio Independent School Dist. v. Rodriguez*, 411 U.S. 1, 28 [1973]). Hate crime laws operate in the same way by prohibiting crimes committed against individuals because of their membership in these same marginalized groups.

Problems arise in hate crime training because of this strong social and moral emphasis. Law enforcement training has generally turned away from educating officers on the higher moral issues inherent in the laws they enforce. This arose because the training too often focused on the mere mechanics of the law rather than the ethical values inherent in law (Das, 1987, p. 45). Thus, officers may be taught not to violate the strictures of *Miranda v. Arizona* (1966) (requiring that persons in custody be told of their rights against self-incrimination and their right to consult an attorney), so that an offender will not go free, but they are often not taught that the *Miranda* decision is rooted in America's abhorrence for the unjust process of inquisition in Europe, which was explained over a century ago in *Brown v. Walker*, 161 U.S. 591, 596–597 (1896). No doubt, this tendency arises in part because lawyers—the persons responsible for decisions like *Miranda* and often responsible for teaching about such decisions—are considered members of out-groups (Harris, 1973, p. 98); also, it may be that it has too long been perceived that it is better to lay out a series of rules that officers should follow rather than burdening them with the "complexities" inherent in the values of the law (Delattre, 1989, pp. 141–142).

Additionally, there is a public viewpoint that hate crime laws are unnecessary because they overprotect persons of color and others. The reasoning goes that crimes are crimes, and that as a matter of public policy, there is no need to enhance criminal penalties simply because an actor chose his or her victim on the basis of race, religion, and the like. Indeed, hate crimes are seen as a device to divide rather than unite the society (*Combating Hate Crimes*, 1999; Gellman, 1991). The arguments are, in short, that the moral history upon which hate crime law is based is irrelevant, invalid, or misplaced. Although the wide passage of state hate crime legislation and public opinion polls show that the majority of Americans favor hate crime legislation, many do not, and support for such legislation drops when groups like gay men and lesbians are added ("Study: Hoosiers Favor Sentence-Enhancing," 2001). Law enforcement officers, like the public at large, hold varying personal views on the value of hate crime, and to the extent that officers do not share positive sentiments on the subject, training presents a greater challenge.

A final barrier to training lies not with the police, but with outside forces in the community and in the prosecutor's office. Community members may dislike the negative publicity that comes when a hate crime happens in their town, and may feel that it unfairly casts a stigma on them. This problem is exacerbated because hate crime typology shows that most hate crimes are committed not by hate group members, but by ordinary people who do not harbor entrenched cultural hatred toward others (McDevitt et al., 2002). Juveniles (persons aged 17 or younger) commit more hate crimes than any other age group (Nolan, Mencken, & McDevitt, n.d., Table 1.2, Table 2.1).

The majority of these hate crime offenses are relatively minor ones involving simple assault, intimidation or harassment, and vandalism (FBI, 2005a). In other words, rather unexceptional teens committing otherwise petty offenses and low-level crimes are the most frequent hate crime problem. This sometimes does not sit well either with prosecutors or communities who see the label of hate crime and the enhanced punishment that accompanies it as most appropriate for hate group members with racial animus. Law enforcement agencies may find themselves unsupported in their efforts to curb hate crime against those persons—youth—who are the most frequent perpetrators, and may well not wish to investigate such crimes with vigor if prosecutorial agencies will not take such offenses seriously. The problem is especially compounded because law enforcement, like any other profession, is competitive, and working on the petty offenses and minor crimes that make up most hate crime investigations may not be viewed as especially prestigious work. Training on matters of hate crime will consequently receive little interest.

IMPROVING HATE CRIME TRAINING

Not all barriers to quality hate crime training originate with law enforcement. Certainly, community support that makes hate crime a priority even when the perpetrators are unexceptional teens has to come from a public that is willing to face the realities of hate crime and stand behind those whom they have asked to enforce hate crime laws. Similarly, prosecutorial agencies must accord priority to hate crimes so that the investigative work that accompanies such offenses mirrors high community concern.

Community and prosecutorial support must then be coupled with training that will address the pressing cultural issues inherent in hate crime that were previously discussed. Fortunately, American law enforcement has a strong values tradition from which to harvest the necessary elements of such training in what Das (1987) calls the "historical model" of American police. In this model, police are envisioned as (1) embodying the values in the Bill of Rights, which promote individual freedom, but recognize the need for the maintenance of an orderly society; (2) referencing the London Metropolitan Police Department, which is seen as a polestar for creating a nonadversarial, consensual police force of citizen officers; and (3) maintaining a service tradition in which police officers are an integral part of the societal support system and act not only as enforcers of the law, but as advisors, mediators, guides, and friends (Das, 1987, pp. 1–17).

This model strikes at important factors in the building of an excellent hate crime training program. It offers a springboard for discussing the values inherent in the U.S. Constitution and how those values are addressed through hate crime laws with the cooperation of law enforcement and other agencies. This view enhances hate crime training by insisting that, although applicable laws and investigative strategies are important, effective training must include an in-depth discussion of the moral situs of hate crimes and the role a law enforcement officer plays in this value-laden area of the criminal law. Such an approach does not presume that every law enforcement officer is favorably disposed to hate crime as a matter of public policy, but it does require that the training challenge officers to examine their own principles and those of others so that their understanding about the underlying moral values is clear. As Fuller stated in *The Morality of Law*, "Even if a man is answerable only to his own conscience, he will answer more responsibly if he is compelled to articulate the principles on which he acts" (1964/1975, p. 159). Good hate crime training must prompt officers to discuss and question the moral values in hate crime and in turn instructors must answer back with responses based in ethics, not merely regulations or policies.

The historical model, as it harkens to the Metropolitan Police Model, also aids hate crime training. The model presupposes community policing (Tobias, 1975, p. 96), and police that are as actively engaged in preventing crime as in apprehending criminals (Rubinstein, 1973, p. 10). Because hate crime is so disproportionately driven by juvenile offenders who commit minor offenses, but who do not have a mission to hurt others because of their status as different, hate crime may be particularly amenable to prevention through school and other education programs. Additionally, outreach to cultural advocacy groups, and programs that raise community awareness about the impact of hate crime, may be particularly useful. These are, so to speak, soft policing and training issues that work only if the value of proactive hate crime reduction and building better community relations is understood and emphasized.

Another essential part of the hate crime curriculum must be diversity education that emphasizes the use of cross-cultural skills in building better communication and relationships with persons of diverse backgrounds. To best help officers interact with hate crime victims and the community from which they come, those skills should include the following:

- Awareness of the officer's own culture and how it shapes worldview
- Empathy (the ability to see the world as others see it)
- Respect for other cultures
- A tolerance for the ambiguity that arises in cross-cultural interactions
- Awareness of one's own prejudices and use of stereotypes
- Ability to relate to individuals who are different from the officer
- Willingness to be a continual learner about new cultural information (Lynch & Hanson, 1992; Thomas, 1999)

This training is enhanced with the greater police contact with diverse citizenry affected by hate crime. According to the "contact hypothesis" of Allport (1954/1979, pp. 261–281), prejudice is reduced by greater contact between members of different groups. To put the matter simply, officers cannot effectively investigate and prevent crimes rooted in prejudice unless they understand the causes of prejudice in themselves and others. Hate crime training must make this principle well understood and, of course, employ trainers who exemplify how to integrate cultural competence and sensitivity into the lessons taught to participants. There is no room for a trainer who says, "Well, I don't like 'those people,' and you might not either, but you have to do your job."

The service tradition of the historical model also provides a useful framework for hate crime training. As a victim-centered crime in which the emotional toll on the individual and community often far outweighs the economic costs of resulting property damage, hate crime provides an opportunity for law enforcement officers to show their best characteristics as individuals who care about the community and how individuals in the community are treated. The extra effort that needs to be expended to offer support to hate crime victims is often minimal. For example, a referral to state, county, or local offices for victim advocacy, and adopting a style of listening that conveys a sense of empathy, will require small effort from law enforcement officers and will not interfere with other investigative priorities. Hate crime training must emphasize this service tradition and the opportunities for greater cooperation and better community relations that arise from the unique, close contact officers have with the hate crime victims they serve. Indeed, to be most effective the training must view the tradition of service as central—not exceptional—to competent police work in hate crime.

CONCLUSION

At its core, hate crime takes law enforcement to the crucible of the moral dilemmas of bigotry, prejudice, and intolerance and their consequences, which have been a long part of the American experience. Effective hate crime training must address these issues directly and overcome internal and external barriers that divert the training away from a focus on values, cultural diversity, and victim needs. If hate crime training fails, it will fail not because the participants disagreed about the value of hate crime interdiction, but because the training did not explore fully *why* the participants hold their individual views, and what traditions of police service make hate crime such a worthy law enforcement focus.

REFERENCES

Allport, G. W. (1979). *The nature of prejudice* (25th ann. ed.). Reading, MA: Addison-Wesley. (Original work published 1954.)

Baybik, E. (1996, July 3). The rally: Protesters march against KKK demonstration. *The Michigan Daily Online*. Retrieved November 10, 2007, from http://www.pub.umich.edu/daily/1996/jul/07–03–96/news/news16.html

Bouman, W. P., & Holland, J. T. (n.d.). *Fighting hate crimes.* Retrieved November 1, 2007, from http://www.hatecrimestraining.com/index.htm

Bradley, M. S. (2007). Symbolizing hate: The extent and influence of organized hate group indicators. *Journal of Crime and Justice, 30,* 1–15.

Brown v. Walker, 161 U.S. 591 (1896).

Buckley, C. (2007, March 26). Hate crime is charged in attack on Sikh boy. *The New York Times.* Retrieved November 8, 2007 from http://www.nytimes.com/2007/05/26/nyregion/26bias.html

Civil Rights Act of 1964, Title VII, 42 U.S.C. 2000e-2 (West 2003).

Combating hate crimes: Promoting a responsive and responsible role for the federal government: Hearing before the Committee on the Judiciary, United States Senate, 106th Cong., 1st Sess. 60 (1999) (prepared statement of Timothy Lynch).

Das, D. K. (1987). *Understanding police human relations.* Metuchen, NJ: Scarecrow Press.

Delattre, E. J. (1989). *Character and cops: Ethics in policing.* Washington, DC: American Enterprise Institute for Public Policy Research.

Dufford, P. (1986). *Police personal behavior and human relations: For police, deputy, jail, corrections and security personnel.* Springfield, IL: Charles C. Thompson.

Federal Bureau of Investigation [FBI]. (n.d.). *Hate crime—overview.* Retrieved November 1, 2007, from http://www.fbi.gov/hq/cid/civilrights/overview.htm

FBI. (1999). *Hate crime data collection guidelines.* Washington, DC: Author.

FBI. (2000). *Hate crime statistics 2000.* Washington, DC: Author.

FBI. (2001). *Hate crime statistics 2001.* Washington, DC: Author.

FBI. (2002). *Hate crime statistics 2002.* Washington, DC: Author.

FBI. (2003). *Hate crime statistics 2003.* Washington, DC: Author.

FBI. (2004). *Hate crime statistics 2004.* Washington, DC: Author.

FBI. (2005a). *Hate crime statistics 2005.* Washington, DC: Author.

FBI. (2005b). *Crime in the United States 2005.* Washington, DC: U.S. Government Printing Office.

Federal Law Enforcement Training Center. (n.d.). *Domestic terrorism and hate crime training program (DTHCTP).* Retrieved on November 24, 2007, from http://www.fletc.gov/training/programs/state-local/training-opportunities/domestic-terrorism-hate-crimes-training-program-dthctp/

Federal Law Enforcement Training Center. (2005). *Hate and bias crimes train-the-trainer program.* Glynco, GA: Author.

Federal Law Enforcement Training Center. (2007). *Catalog of training programs 2007 and 2008.* Glynco, GA: Author.

Fosdick, R. B. (1920). *American police systems.* New York: The Century Company.

Fuller, L. L. (1975). *The morality of law.* New Haven, CT: Yale University Press. (Original work published 1964.)

Gammage, A. Z. (1963). *Police training in the United States.* Springfield, IL: Charles C. Thomas.

Gellman, S. (1991). Sticks and stones can put you in jail, but can words increase your sentence? Constitutional and policy dilemmas of ethnic intimidation laws. *U.C.L.A. Law Review, 39,* 333–396.

Haller, M. (1976). Historical roots of police behavior: Chicago, 1980–1925. *Law & Society Review, 10*(2), 303–325.

Harris, R. N. (1973). *The police academy: An inside view.* New York: Wiley.

Hate Crime Statistics Act, 28 U.S.C.A. § 534 note (West, 2006).

Holmes, E. (1998a, May 11). Rally gives community a peaceful alternative. *The Michigan Daily.* Retrieved November 10, 2007, from http://www.pub.umich.edu/daily/1998/may/05–11–98/news/news9.html

Holmes, E. (1998b, May 11). Ann Arbor remembers violence, pain of '96 KKK demonstration. *The Michigan Daily.* Retrieved November 10, 2007, from http://www.pub.umich.edu/daily/1998/may/05–11–98/news/news10.html

Iowa Code Ann. § 80B.11.3 (West, 1996).

Lynch, E. W., & Hanson, M. J. (1992). *Developing cross-cultural competence: A guide for working with young children and their families.* Baltimore: Paul H. Brookes.

Maykuth, A. (2007, October 29). Johnson knocks Nutter's "stop and frisk" policy. *The Philadelphia Inquirer.* Retrieved November 10, 2007, from http://www.philly.com/inquirer/home_top_left_story/20071029_Johnson_knocks_Nutters_stop_and_frisk_policy.html

McDevitt, J., Levin, J., & Bennett, S. (2002). Hate crime offenders: An expanded typology. *Journal of Social Issues, 58*(2), 303–317.

Miranda v. Arizona, 384 U.S. 436 (1966).

National Commission on Law Observance and Enforcement. (1931). *No. 14: Report on police.* Washington, DC: U.S. Government Printing Office.

New Mexico Stat. Ann. § 31–18B-5 (Michie Supp. 2006).

Nolan, J., Mencken, F. C., & McDevitt, J. (n.d.). *NIBRS hate crimes 1995–2000: Juvenile victims and offenders.* Retrieved November 12, 2007, from http://www.as.wvu.edu/~jnolan/incav.htm; and from http://www.as.wvu.edu/~jnolan/offasr.htm

N.Y. Penal Law § 485.00 (McKinney Supp. 2006).

N.Y. Penal Law § 485.05(1) (McKinney Supp. 2006).

N.Y. Penal Law § 485.05(3) (McKinney Supp. 2006).

N.Y. Penal Law § 485.10 (McKinney Supp. 2006).

Or. Rev. Stat. § 166.165 (West 2003).

Rathke, L. (2007, October 4). 2 sisters charged in Vt. hate crimes: Gays targeted in two incidents. *The Boston Globe.* Retrieved November 3, 2007, from http://www.boston.com/news/local/articles/2007/10/04/2_sisters_charged_in_vt_hate_crimes/

Richardson, J. F. (1974). *Urban police in the United States.* Port Washington, NY: Kennikat Press.

Rubinstein, J. (1973). *City police.* New York: Farrar, Straus and Giroux.

Rumbaut, R. G., & Bittner, E. (1979). Changing conceptions of the police role: A sociological review. *Crime and Justice: Annual Review of Research, 1,* 239–288.

San Antonio Independent School Dist. v. Rodriguez, 411 U.S. 1 (1973).

Smith, T. W. (1992). Changing racial labels: From "Colored" to "Negro" to "Black" to "African American." *The Public Opinion Quarterly, 56*(4), 496–514.

Sterngold, J. (2001, January 24). Supremacist who killed postal worker avoids death sentence. *The New York Times.* Retrieved November 1, 2007, from http://query.nytimes.com/gst/fullpage.html?res=9F0CEED61E3CF937A15752C0A9679C8B63&sec=&spon=&pagewanted=1

Study: Hoosiers favor sentence-enhancing hate crime law. (2001, February 26). *Newscenter, Ball State University.* Retrieved November 12, 2007, from http://www.bsu.edu/news/article/0,1370,-1019–2118,00.html

Swastika found on Columbia prof's door. (2007, November 1). *The Washington Post.* Retrieved November 5, 2007, from http://www.washingtonpost.com/wp-dyn/content/article/2007/10/31/AR2007103103242.html

Texas: Young victim of hate crime kills himself. (2007, July 3). *The New York Times.* Retrieved November 5, 2007, from http://www.nytimes.com/2007/07/03/us/03brfs-YOUNGVICTIMO_BRF.html

Thomas, R. R. (1999). *Building a house for diversity: How a fable about a giraffe and elephant offers new strategies for today's workforce.* New York: American Management Association.

Thompson/West. (2006). *Hate crime law.* St. Paul, MN: Author.

Tobias, J. J. (1975). Police and public in the United Kingdom. In G. L. Mosse (Ed.), *Police forces in history* (pp. 95–113). Beverly Hills: Sage Publications.

U.S. Department of Justice, Office of Justice Programs, Bureau of Justice Statistics. (2005). *Hate crime reported by victims and police.* Washington, DC: Author.

U.S. Department of Justice, Office of Justice Programs, Bureau of Justice Statistics. (2003). *Local police departments, 2003.* Washington, DC: Author.

Walker, S. (1977). *A critical history of police reform: The emergence of professionalization.* Lexington, MA: Lexington Books.

Wash. Rev. Code Ann. § 9A.36.080 (West 2000).

CHAPTER 4

HATE CRIME INVESTIGATIONS

James J. Nolan, Susie Bennett, and Paul Goldenberg

Hate crime investigations offer special challenges to law enforcement officers. In most police agencies there are basic protocols for all criminal investigations, such as securing the crime scene, locating witnesses, collecting evidence, interrogating suspects, and much more. In this chapter we do not enumerate or expound on these fundamental investigative techniques. Rather, we take a look at the unique challenges law enforcement officers experience when addressing hate crimes.

As chief of the first statewide bias crime unit in the state of New Jersey (1990–1995), the third author has had many firsthand experiences conducting hate crime investigations. Goldenberg speaks from personal experience that police culture and organizational policies and practices often get in the way of successful hate crime investigations. For instance, many hate crimes are actually low-level crimes, such as destruction of property or harassment, and therefore, not viewed as *serious* by police officers. Traditional police culture, which is influenced and reinforced by training and organizational policies, leads police officers to respond to crimes based on a level of seriousness that parallels the Uniform Crime Report (UCR) crime hierarchy. Committing resources to protracted investigations for misdemeanor crimes may seem absurd to police commanders. In addition, police officers themselves sometimes may not want to invest extensive time and energy investigating hate crimes because of personal prejudices, lack of training, or organizational policies and practices that reward and promote officers for serious in-progress felony arrests or life-saving heroics rather than their ability to mediate or prevent intergroup conflict. So, why is it important to investigate hate crime?

WHY INVESTIGATE HATE CRIMES?

Proponents of hate crime legislation argue that a bias motivation makes ordinary criminal offenses worse and, therefore, penalties for these crimes should be more severe than those for similar crimes without bias. The arguments suggest that victims are harmed more physically, psychologically, and emotionally (Lawrence, 1999; B. Levin, 1999; Levin and McDevitt, 1993), that the impact of hate crimes extends beyond the victim to others in the victims' group and community (Lawrence, 1994; B. Levin, 1999), and that the members of the victim's group present an increased risk of violent retaliatory action against the offenders or members of the offenders' group (Lawrence, 1994). In a similar vein, proponents argue that enhanced penalties may deter future hate crimes and send a message to others that hate crimes will not be tolerated (Gerstenfeld, 2004). Although it is important for police to conduct skillful investigations for the purpose of criminal prosecution, Nolan, McDevitt, Cronin, and Farrell (2004) suggest that investigations are also important for data collection purposes. Their argument is that in order for police to truly understand the nature of the crimes that are occurring in local communities, they must investigate and record *all* suspected bias crime. With more accurate data, police will be better able to conduct crime and intelligence analyses to better target prevention and victim service activities.

WHAT WE KNOW ABOUT HATE CRIMES FROM POLICE INVESTIGATIVE REPORTS

Police investigative reports not only help with gaining convictions in court, but are also the source of information for criminological studies of hate crime. Investigative reports are the source of information for the National Incident-Based Reporting System (NIBRS), which is managed by the Federal Bureau of Investigation (FBI) and accessible to anyone interested in studying crime. They are also the source of information for local, qualitative studies of crime. In this section, we will describe some of the information derived from police reports regarding hate crimes.

Findings from the National Incident-Based Reporting System (NIBRS)

The National Incident-Based Reporting System (NIBRS) is an incident-level crime reporting program that is available to local, state, and federal law enforcement agencies. It is considered an update to the UCR and captures more detailed information about offenses, victims, offenders, property, and persons arrested within each criminal incident. As a more in-depth source of information, it is an improvement over the existing UCR program but it also provides an estimated reliability check for UCR hate crime figures.

Between the years 1995 through 2000, 5,855 hate crime incidents were reported via NIBRS. The police agencies that reported these crimes covered approximately 14 percent of the U.S. population. Of the 5,855 incidents, fully 40 percent ($n = 2,342$) were serious or violent in nature, including offenses such as murder, kidnapping, forcible rape, sodomy, forcible fondling, robbery, aggravated assault, and simple assault. Sixty percent ($n = 3,513$) are arguably less serious and include offenses such as intimidation, weapons violations, burglary, theft, larceny, counterfeiting, swindling, vandalism, destruction of property, and shoplifting. Similar to figures reported by the UCR, 62 percent ($n = 3,640$) were motivated by race, 13 percent ($n = 747$) were motivated by religion, 13 percent ($n = 752$) were motivated by sexual orientation, and 1 percent ($n = 47$) were motivated by disability. Of the crimes where race was the motivating factor, 42 percent ($n = 1,536$) are considered serious or violent, with intimidation reported as the modal category ($n = 921$). Nearly 16 percent of those hate crimes motivated by religion were serious or violent while destruction of property and vandalism comprised over half (52%). Again, similar to figures reported by the UCR program and advocacy groups, 44% ($n = 331$) of hate crimes motivated by sexual orientation tended to be serious or violent, with simple assault being the modal category ($n = 205$) followed by destruction of property ($n = 203$). Patterns of the NIBRS hate crime data are similar to those of the UCR, but in addition, NIBRS captures more detailed information about the hate crime incident.

Other types of information captured by NIBRS provide a level of detail about hate crime offenders, victims, and contexts that moves beyond the UCR level of analysis. For example, in 83 percent ($n = 4,881$) of the 5,855 hate crime incidents reported by NIBRS, a person was the victim of the crime, that is, not a business or school. The offender of the hate crime was known in approximately 74 percent ($n = 4,313$) of incidents and the age could be identified in 77 percent ($n = 3,330$) of these. Where the offender was known, they were identified as juveniles under 18 years of age in approximately 22 percent ($n = 969$) of cases, young adults between the ages of 18 and 24 in approximately 20 percent ($n = 867$) of cases, and adults over the age of 25 in approximately 35 percent ($n = 1,494$) of hate crime cases. Where the age of both the hate crime offender and victim were known, one-third (33 percent) involved juvenile or youthful offenders attacking other juveniles or youthful offenders, and approximately 28 percent were adults attacking other adults. Juvenile or youthful offenders perpetrated attacks on adults in approximately 16 percent of these cases, and adults victimized juveniles or youths in about 10 percent. Personal weapons such as hands, feet, or teeth were identified as the primary type of weapon used ($n = 1,588$) while weapons such as guns, knives, blunt objects, explosives, motor vehicles, or other types of incendiary weapons were identified in 706 cases. The NIBRS data also reveals that hate incidents begin to escalate around three o'clock in the afternoon and continue to rise, hitting their maximum around midnight and dropping thereafter. These are just a few examples of the type of details captured by NIBRS. It should be noted that any of these variables can be cross tabulated to examine much finer levels of detail.

Local Studies of Hate Crime

As our coauthor (Goldenberg) describes it, the demographics of some of New Jersey's most established towns and cities in the late 1980s shifted virtually overnight. While this type of change may not have been unique to New Jersey, their response to it certainly was. With the rapid influx of an estimated 30,000 Asian Indians within 30 square blocks of an area best described as blue collar, working class, and a mix of European, Jewish, and African American residents, the sights and sounds of the area changed quickly and dramatically. Within one year the violent crime rate soared and the police found themselves ill-equipped to handle the changes. The overt language often used by perpetrators of the violence and destruction was, "Dot heads, get out." Based on the high victimization rate of Asian Indians in these areas, New Jersey prosecutors formed what some consider to be the first anti-bias unit in the country. The task force was a multi-police unit effort to stop what was then considered a form of terrorism. Within three months of assembling the team, headed by Goldenberg, the task force built cases on several gangs of local male youth ranging in age from approximately 13 to 21. Surprisingly, the youth were made up of Filipino, Jewish, Irish American, Italian American, and African American males.

Based on some of the lessons we have learned through hate crime research since the mid to late 1980s we can more clearly understand what was occurring in places like New Jersey. Research has shown that competition between groups for scarce resources, even when the scarcity and competition is only imagined and the resource is cultural identity, creates a unifying dynamic or alliance between the more established groups and a hostile stance toward those considered the new group (McDevitt, Levin, & Bennett, 2001). This early example can be categorized as what McDevitt and colleagues refer to in their typology of hate crime offenders as "defensive" offenders. The New Jersey residents in the example above, though comprising an unlikely mix of ethnicities, were defensive toward the new immigrants and their strange customs and felt forthright in using violence and intimidation to preserve what they, the residents, felt was their own way of life. Unfortunately, what was demonstrated in the New Jersey example is that the level of violence associated with defensive hate crime can be very serious. Consistent with defensive offenders described by Levin and colleagues, the offenders in the New Jersey cases were found to be groups of teens or young adults, involved in several previous acts of intimidation, with a moderate level of commitment to bias, and a low likelihood of deterrence.

In addition to the defensive hate crime offender, other types of offenders within the typology include thrill, retaliatory, and mission. Thrill-seeking offenders are characterized as groups of teens and young adults who engage in low levels of violence, and who have no history of bias, little commitment to bias, and a high likelihood of deterrence. The retaliatory offender is characterized as a single youthful offender, employing a higher level of violence, no history of bias against the victim, a moderate commitment to bias, and low likelihood of deterrence. Finally, mission offenders are characterized as groups of young adults and adults who are willing to employ extreme violence, who have no history with their victims, who have a full commitment to violence, and who have a very low likelihood of deterrence. While the New Jersey hate crime investigations above confirm some of the Levin and colleagues typology, investigative reports in other jurisdictions should be analyzed to test the generalizability of the model.

THE LAW ENFORCEMENT RESPONSE TO HATE CRIMES

The conceptual emergence of hate crime within the political arena reflects the diligent work and support of various interest groups (Haider-Markel, 2006). The development of hate crime as a unique policy domain developed out of the convergence of the civil rights movement, the crime victim's movement, the women's movement, and the gay and lesbian movement (Grattet & Jenness, 2001). These forces culminated in the development of the Hate Crime Statistics Act—a mandate created by Congress in 1990 that charged the U.S. attorney general with collecting data regarding hate crime. The attorney general appointed the task to the director of the FBI, who designated responsibility to the Uniform Crime Reporting (UCR) Program. In response to the congressional mandate, the UCR program developed and implemented the hate crime reporting program. The FBI defines a hate crime as "a criminal offense committed against a person, property or society which is motivated, in whole or in part, by the offender's bias against a race, religion, disability, sexual orientation, or ethnicity/national origin" (Federal Bureau of Investigation [FBI], 1997). The act was amended in 1994 to include bias against persons with disabilities, for which data collection commenced in 1997. Today, law enforcement agencies struggle to apply the FBI definition and other legal definitions of hate crime to their own real-world experiences and to document these crimes in their police reports. It is from these police reports that investigations are initiated and documented.

As depicted in Figure 4.1, the flow of hate crime reports through a *typical* law enforcement agency might go something like this: For the process to begin, someone must recognize that he or she was the victim of a crime and decide to report it to the police (step 1 in Figure 4.1). Sometimes victims might suspect that the motivation was bias or that they were selected simply because of their group status. However, if victims miss or deny this

Figure 4.1 The Hate Crime Reporting Process

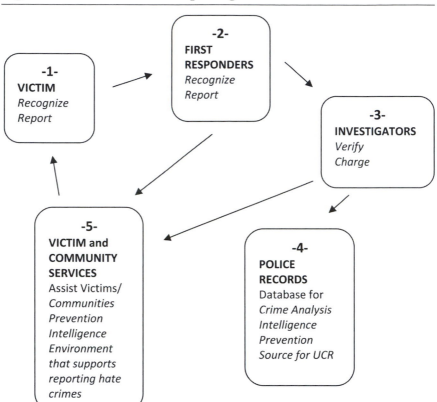

motivation, the first responding police officers may pick it up. In any event the crime must be reported to a *first responder*, that is, a police officer who is assigned to a unit responsible for responding to calls for service. Once the victim relays this information to the first responding officer, that officer must also recognize the nature of the offense as a possible hate crime and report it as such in an incident report (step 2 in Figure 4.1). Once recorded, this incident may be assigned to a follow-up investigator who will work to apprehend the offender(s) (step 3 in Figure 4.1). These follow-up investigators work with prosecutors to file formal charges on the offender(s) if apprehended. The first responders and follow-up investigators may forward their initial reports to victim and community services units so that they will be able to take appropriate actions (step 5 in Figure 4.1). The incident and follow-up reports are filed in a designated area for police records and often entered into a database (step 4 in Figure 4.1). The police reports provide one source of data for intelligence and crime analysis.

In this chapter on hate crime investigations, we focus on steps 3 and 4 (first responders and follow-up investigators), but acknowledge the significance of all steps in the process on the investigation.

In the following section we describe the unique challenges for first responders and follow-up investigators whose responsibility it is to investigate and arrest those who perpetrate hate crimes.

UNIQUE CHALLENGES IN HATE CRIME INVESTIGATIONS

The complex nature of police work and its organizational structures makes police investigations of all sorts difficult at times. In this section we focus on the specific challenges relating to hate crime investigations.

An Organizational Climate for Hate Crime Investigations

As Bell (2002) learned in her study of hate crime investigations in a large metropolitan police department, being assigned to a special bias crimes unit was not always a welcomed change. She once found a sign hanging in one of the police precincts, supposedly hung by a member of the community, which described that community member's dislike for the bias crime unit known by the initials ABTF.

> ABTF: These are the initials of the Anti-Bias Task Force of the (name of city) Police Dept. This unit is made up of the dregs of the . . . police department. Most normal cops don't want anything to do with this unit, and we don't blame them. They must have been trained in (area of the city), because all they do is follow young White boys around and then pick them up every chance they get. Their boss used to be called "Ben Dover" in (an area of the city with a large gay and lesbian population) for obvious reasons. Not one member of this unit has any balls, and instead of preying on young White boys in (name of section of city), they should be guarding a harem for some rich sheik, where they couldn't get into any trouble. (p. 115)

Bell found that the disdain for hate crime investigations and investigators affected the level of cooperation the officers assigned to do hate crime investigations received from fellow officers. In another precinct she found that officers would even tip off the haters about investigations.

Much less pronounced than in Bell's study, but still indicative of an organizational climate that impedes hate crime investigations, Nolan and Akiyama (2002) discovered in four jurisdictions a dissonance in officers' beliefs and perceptions regarding hate crime policies and practices, which also may help to understand some of the broader structural impediments to hate crime investigations (see Table 4.1).

**Table 4.1   Dissonance in Officer Responses Regarding Hate Crime
Initiatives in Their Organizations**

RATED *HIGH* BY OFFICERS		RATED *LOW* BY OFFICERS
Investigating hate crimes is important in this department	→	The department recognizes and rewards officers for investigating hate crimes
My department wants to support the community in reporting hate crime	→	Citizens appreciate the department's efforts to report hate crimes
My department policy mandates hate crime reporting	→	Internal checks are in place to make sure officers don't misidentify hate crimes
My department policy mandates hate crime reporting	→	The department trains officers to identify and respond to hate crimes
I want to be a "good officer"	→	I will be recognized as a "good officer" for identifying and reporting hate crimes
I want to comply with department policies	→	There is a clear hate crime policy in this department
I am concerned for gay and minority victims of crime	→	I support for gay and minority political agendas
I am concerned for gay and minority victims of crime	→	I believe gay and minority citizens have problems in the community
Investigating hate crimes is important in this department	→	There is sufficient staff to support hate crime reporting

A row-by-row examination of Table 4.1 reveals that on one hand police
officers believed that investigating hate crimes was viewed as important by
department officials, but on the other hand these investigations were not re-
warded or recognized. Similarly, officers indicated with high scores that policies were in place that mandated the reporting of hate crimes, but they scored
much lower in their assessment that training and internal checks were in place
to make sure these policies were implemented correctly. Also, the officers indicated with high scores that they believed their departments wanted to support
their diverse communities by investigating hate crimes, but indicated with

significantly lower scores their beliefs that residents appreciated their efforts. Additionally, the police officers in the study indicated with high scores their desire to be "good officers," but indicated with significantly lower scores that the investigations of hate crime were not a way to be viewed as a "good officer." Finally, police respondents registered high concern for gay and minority victims of crimes, but indicated to a much lesser degree a belief that these citizens really experience problems in the community. The respondents also rated much lower their support for gay and minority political agendas.

DEALING WITH AMBIGUITY: *SEEING* HATE CRIMES AMID A PLETHORA OF "OTHER" CRIMES

In addition to the broader organizational issues, police officers sometimes find the term *hate crime* to be somewhat ambiguous, particularly when the bias is not the primary motivation for the crime or when there is a mixture of motivations. Unambiguous hate crimes are those in which the sole or primary motivation is bias, such as when a cross is burned on the lawn of a black family who recently moved into an all-white neighborhood. Ambiguous hate crimes are those in which the primary motivation for a crime is something other than bias, but where bias is a secondary motivation. (See Table 4.2.) The problem arises in part because of the definition of hate crime. A hate crime is defined by the FBI as a "criminal offense committed against a person or property which is motivated, *in whole or in part*, by the offender's bias

Table 4.2   Distinction between "Unambiguous" and "Ambiguous" Hate Crimes

	Primary Motivation	**Secondary Motivation**
Unambiguous Hate Crime	Hate or bias toward victim's group	Can be something other than bias or hate
Ambiguous Hate Crime	Something other than bias or hate, such as greed or revenge.	**Target Section** – Victim chosen because of group status, either a) *rational choice* or b) *bias* **Response/Retaliation** for some triggering event

against race, religion, disability, ethic/national origin group, or sexual orientation group" (FBI, 1997 p. 4—emphasis added by authors). Although this
definition seems clear in black-and-white text, hate crimes are more often
gray in real life.

Consider, for example, the case of J. R. Warren, a 26-year-old gay black
man from rural Grant Town, West Virginia. On July 3, 2000, Warren met
with three white teens at a vacant house in this predominately white rural
town. The teens had been painting a vacant house that day and, prior to their
meeting with Warren, had also been "drinking beer, huffing gasoline, and
snorting tranquilizers" according to official sources (Smith, 2000). Shortly
after he arrived at the house, Warren became engaged in an altercation with
the group. The three teens took $20 from Warren, and then beat him until he
was unconscious—and believed dead. Two of the youths put Warren's body
into the trunk of a Camaro and drove to a remote area to dump it. While en
route to the dump site, the teens discovered that Warren was still alive. They
stopped the car in a secluded spot alongside a remote rural road, dragged his
body out of the trunk, and while Warren was still conscious, the teens repeatedly drove their vehicle over his slender body, crushing him to death (Nolan,
McDevitt, Cronin, & Farrell, 2004).

The murder of J. R. Warren was popularly considered a hate crime in the
minority communities of West Virginia and by the local media because it had
all the right elements: the victim was black, slightly built, and openly gay
while the offenders were young white males from a rural southern town. Immediately following the crime the community held peace vigils, while advocacy groups like the Marion County NAACP and the West Virginia Lesbian
and Gay coalition called on the police to investigate the incident as a hate
crime (Fischer, 2000; Smith, 2000). The police refused to recognize the incident as a hate crime because they claimed to have uncovered an alternative
explanation for the crime: as the result of a "drug- and alcohol-fueled rage,"
that was brought on by the belief on the part of one of the defendants that
Warren had told others of a "long-standing sexual relationship that the two
had shared" (Smith, 2000).

Contemporary research on hate crime investigations seems to indicate
that the ambiguity present in the J. R. Warren murder case was more the
norm than the exception (Cronin, McDevitt, Farrell, & Nolan, 2007; Martin,
1999; Nolan et al., 2004). This is especially true when bias or hate is not the
sole motivation for the crime. Consider the following two examples from a
national study of hate crime investigations:

> While driving on a state highway, a white male cut in front of a car driven
> by a Hispanic male. In response the Hispanic male pursued the car driven by
> the white male and followed it to a local fast food restaurant. The Hispanic
> male exited his car and approached the white male driver and his female

passenger while yelling, "You shouldn't mess with Mexicans." He then proceeded to assault the white male.

While playing in a local neighborhood, a young white child acciden-
tally knocked over the soda can of an African American child, spilling its
contents. The mother of the white child approached the mother of the
African American child to explain the incident and apologize for the mis-
hap. The African American woman yelled at the white woman, "Get your
white ass out" and "I will kick your white ass." The white women said she
did not want any trouble and would not fight back. The African American
woman then proceeded to assault the white woman. The investigating officers reported that the African American woman had a history of "causing
trouble" in the neighborhood. (Nolan et al., 2004)

In both of these incidents, the police recognized that indicators of bias
motivation were present, that is, the victims and offenders were from different groups and their differences were highlighted in the aggressive language
used by the offenders. However, the police were also able to explain both of
these crimes in another way: as violent *responses* to some other "triggering"
event. In the first incident described above, the violent behavior was triggered by an unexpected traffic maneuver. In the second incident, the violent
act was initiated by the accidental spilling of a drink. Because these crimes
could be explained as a response to or retaliation for some other event, the
police did consider them to be bias crimes.

McDevitt and colleagues (2003) found that the definition of hate crime,
specifically "motivated in whole or in part" (FBI, 1997) created problems for
some officers in terms of recognizing and investigating hate crimes. They
identified two primary types of bias crimes that were motivated in part by
bias: response/retaliation and target selection.

Response/retaliation crimes are defined as situations in which the offender's
actions are prompted by some other triggering incident. The descriptions of
the two ambiguous bias crimes at the beginning of this section are examples
of response/retaliation crimes. The actions of the offender in response to or
retaliation for some other triggering event may or may not be exacerbated by
the victim and offender difference. In some cases a criminal response to some
triggering event might occur even when the victim and offender are from the
same group. Also, there are situations where response or retaliation actions of
the offender may not even constitute a crime, as in the case of a person giving
an obscene hand gesture in response to some unexpected traffic maneuver.
But there are instances in which the offender's bias against the victim's group
does in fact become a motivating factor in his or her actions. When these actions become criminal, they may be considered hate crimes.

In target-selection hate crimes, offenders are motivated to commit a crime
for reasons other than bias. However, the offender(s) select their victims because of their group membership. In other words, the motivation for the

behavior is considered separate from the motivation for selecting the victim. Target-selection hate crimes are different from response/retaliation hate crimes in that they are not actions in direct response to some other triggering incident. Instead, they result from some rational process by the offender. There are two types of target-selection crimes: (1) rational choice and (2) bias motivation. In rational choice crimes the victim may be chosen because he or she is a member of a particular group. This choice seems to indicate a hate crime. For example, Cronin and colleagues (2007) described a situation in a large Midwestern city where patrons of gay bars were being targeted for robbery. When detectives apprehended the suspects they found that the choice of victims was made based on the stereotype of gay men having lots of money and being unlikely to call the police. In this same study, researchers uncovered crimes that were being committed against East African immigrants because the offenders were aware that this population of people was unlikely to contact the police for cultural reasons. Bias-motivated target selection events are those situations in which the target of the action is selected because of the offender's bias. As an example of this type of event, consider the situation described by McDevitt and colleagues (2003). The police reported that several intoxicated white males went out looking for a fight one night in order to demonstrate their physical prowess. While driving around the community in their vehicle, the group noticed a black male pumping gas and decided to attack him. The police determined that although the primary motivation for this incident was simply to get into a fight, the offenders selected a black male target because of their hatred for African Americans. Secondary or partial motivations make identifying hate crimes difficult for police (Martin, 1999).

THE FIRST RESPONDING OFFICER

Important to the investigation of all crimes is the quality of the investigation conducted by the first responding officers. This is particularly true for hate crimes. In order for follow-up investigators to even begin a hate crime investigation, the first responding officers must have recognized the crime as a possible hate crime and recorded it as such in their incident reports.

In her study of a hate crime investigation unit in a large metropolitan police department, Bell (2002) found that hate crime investigators worried that first responders would only recognize and, therefore, send them cases that were unambiguously hate crimes, such as a cross burning. She also found that some first responders didn't agree with hate crime laws and therefore failed to indicate on the initial report that bias was a possible motive. By periodically reading the narratives of a sample of incident reports, hate crime investigators may uncover and correct situations like the one described above.

In a policy paper on hate crime investigations by the International Association of Chiefs of Police (IACP), the unique aspects of hate crime investigations for the first responding officers are described in some detail so that
officers will be better able to conduct sound preliminary investigations. Some
of these aspects are briefly described below:

1. Stabilizing the crime scene may be more difficult as sympathetic friends
   and neighbors may congregate at the scene of the crime. These individuals may also talk of retaliation, causing tensions to run high.
2. Victims of hate crime often suffer deep emotional distress. They fear for
   their safety and the safety of their family and others in their identity
   group. Victims may be particularly fearful of revenge for cooperating with
   the police.
3. The collection and preservation of evidence is important and can be
   jeopardized if there are large crowds at the scene. The initial responding
   officer should make sure photographs of the scene are taken, paying particular attention to hate graffiti and literature, and symbols of hate such
   as swastikas.
4. Hate symbols should be moved or covered up as soon as possible, to prevent prolonged exposure to the message of hate.
5. Since words and symbols are the evidence of the hate motivation, officers should take statements from witnesses and the victims as soon as
   it is practical to do so. The first responder should be prepared to ask
   probing questions about the exact wording of statements made by the
   perpetrator(s). They should also try to find out if there have been hate
   crimes or hate incidents in the community in the recent past. Officers
   should recognize that the anxiety caused by crime may cloud the victim's
   memory and should be prepared to let the victim express emotions of
   anger and frustration and have time to calm down.
6. First responders should look for indicators of hate crime that include the
   following:

   a. perceptions of the victim or witnesses about the nature of the crime
   b. perpetrator's comments or gestures that reflect bias, including sym-
      bols left at the scene
   c. differences between the offender and the victim, such as race, ethnicity,
      or other group identification, either actual or perceived
   d. whether a similar incident had occurred in the area
   e. whether the victim was involved in activities that promoted his or her
      group identity
   f. whether the incident occurred on or near a holiday that may be signifi-
      cant, such as Adolf Hitler's birthday
   g. whether it can be confirmed that a hate group or groups were involved
   h. whether the crime can be explained by another motivation, such as
      revenge or economic gain (International Association of Chiefs of Police
      [IACP], 2008).

FOLLOWING UP: FINDING OBJECTIVE EVIDENCE TO SUPPORT A HATE CRIME DESIGNATION

The FBI recommends a second-level review of all suspected hate crimes (FBI, 1997). This review of the facts of the case can be conducted by a supervisor who is charged with reviewing all incident reports, or it could be forwarded to a special investigative unit with training and expertise in hate crime investigation. The IACP recommends that officers consider multiple factors before verifying that a crime is a hate crime. Its published list of questions for follow-up investigators includes the following (IACP, 2008, p. 6):

- Is the victim a member of a target racial, religious, ethnic or national origin, sexual orientation, gender, gender identity, or disability group?
- Were the offender and the victim of different groups?
- Would the incident have taken place if the victim and offender were from the same group?
- Were comments, written statements, or gestures made that indicate a bias on the part of the offender?
- Were drawings, symbols, or graffiti that indicate a bias left at the scene?
- Did the victim's personal characteristics make him or her a minority in the location where the offense occurred?
- Was the victim visiting a location where hate crimes have occurred against his or her group?
- Did the crime occur around a significant holiday, such as Martin Luther King's birthday?
- Were there indicators of hate group involvement or did the offender have a prior arrest or conviction for hate crime?
- Are there other explanations for the incident?

These are just some of the questions a follow-up investigator might ask to confirm whether the crime was in fact a hate crime.

In her study of hate crime investigations, Bell (2002) found how public opinion and politics can play a role in how much support police received in a hate crime investigation. For, example, in a community that does not want to become integrated, current residents benefit from crimes that send a message to new members that they are not welcome. On the other hand, advocacy groups can also interfere with police investigations by publicly criticizing a department's claim that a crime was not a hate crime despite its appearance.

Bell (2002) also found that cases forwarded to the follow-up investigators were subjected to an initial screening. First, the case must be solvable—as perceived by the reviewing detective. If not, it was excluded from the unit's case files. The detectives also checked on the credibility of the victims and took this into account when trying to decide whether to believe a victim's account as told. The follow-up detectives also had the freedom to change the initial framing of the situation by the patrol officers and replace it with their own. This reframing often occurred based on the detective's own personal experiences or stock stories from previous cases. In sum, investigative routines are established in detective units in order to process all the information that comes in. These routines provide the freedom to investigate only a portion of the cases that are forwarded to them, allowing some to fall through the cracks.

In order to improve the law enforcement response to hate crimes, the U.S. Department of Justice (DOJ) published a comprehensive training curriculum for police investigators, including procedures for interviewing witnesses and interrogating suspects. In the following section we review some of this material (U.S. Department of Justice [DOJ], 1998).

Interviewing Victims

DOJ training material suggests that only one officer should conduct an interview with the victim of a hate crime. This investigator should allow the victims to tell their stories in their own words without interruption. The investigator should not ask the victim directly, "Was this a hate crime?" Investigators should also avoid making assumptions about the victims that may be inappropriate such as the assumption about sexual orientation; for example, do not ask, "Are you gay?"

Investigators should not "blame the victim" by making personal value judgments about the victim's lifestyle or about the victim's having placed himself or herself in an unsafe situation. This training material makes the point to ask the victims to recall the exact language used by the offender(s) since this may be important to determining motivation. The words that were used may be offensive but it is important to know for court purposes. Finally, it is recommended that the officers refer victims to organizations that can provide assistance and stay in touch with the victims to provide updates regarding the status of the case.

In Bell's 2002 study, officers did as the DOJ training suggested. They let the victims tell the story in their own words. The detectives asked broad probing questions such as, "Why do you think this happened to you?" rather than, "Was this a hate crime?" They also followed up with questions about specific details of the case. Bell also found that the detectives in her study used a list of objective criteria as established in the DOJ and IACP training. However, the detectives used this information more as a reminder to consider broadly what might indicate bias rather than a list to be systematically checked.

In addition, Bell (2002) made an important observation about victim interviews in hate crime cases versus other criminal cases: she found that in hate crime cases, interviews with victims were important for making the case against suspects. She cites previous research on detectives that suggest victim interviews are more often used to confirm the identification of the suspect who had already been identified.

Interrogating Suspects

The DOJ training manual reminds investigating officers that many hate crime suspects mistakenly assume that others—even in law enforcement—share their biased perceptions (DOJ, 1998). Therefore, by simply being asked to describe his or her feelings about a particular minority group, a suspect may express his or her bias motivation for the crime. The DOJ material also suggests that investigators look for things beyond the content of the suspect's statements for clues as to motivation, such as tattoos, bumper stickers, or other symbols that might indicate the bias motivation of the suspect.

Investigators in Bell's 2002 study used interrogation tactics that were aimed at trying to establish the suspect's bias toward the victim's group. The following is an excerpt from the interview of a white suspect accused of spraying mace in the face of a Puerto Rican man at a bus stop (Bell, 2002, pp. 79–80):

Detective: I think . . . he was sprayed because he was a Puerto Rican, right?
Suspect: Because he bothered my friend.
Detective: You don't even know for sure whether he was the one who bothered your friend. So there were two reasons, he was Puerto Rican and he bothered your friend?
Suspect: MMM
Detective: Is that a yes?
Suspect: Yes.
Detective: And he was a Puerto Rican and he was in [white area of the city]. Is that a yes?
Suspect: Yes.
Detective: And neither Puerto Ricans nor blacks should be in [white area of the city] at night, is that the golden rule? . . .
Suspect: You wouldn't have a white walking through [a black area of the city].

In this case example the suspect admitted that the assault was motivated, at least in part, by a bias against Puerto Ricans. He also established his views about the safety of different groups in his neighborhood and the safety of whites in minority neighborhoods. In addition to the roles that interviews and interrogations have in hate crime investigations, the DOJ training also emphasizes the need for investigators to collect evidence such as photographs of symbols and property damage along with statements from witnesses who may be able to remember exact words and phrases that can be used to establish a bias motivation.

SUMMARY AND CONCLUSIONS

Hate crimes are traditional crimes, but with a unique dimension: they terrorize victims and send a message to the victim and the broader community that people like the victim are not wanted. This fact makes even minor underlying crimes more significant.

The investigation of hate crimes and the filing of investigative reports are important for criminal prosecution, but they are also important for data collection, intelligence gathering, crime analyses, hate crime prevention activities, and victim services. Typically, police investigators only work to apprehend the offender and get a conviction in court. However, due to the nature of hate crimes, it may be just as important to simply have a record of the incident so police and others will understand the nature of crimes committed in various locations in the jurisdiction. This information can be used for criminological research, crime analysis, and intelligence gathering, among other more proactive initiatives. This point is especially important as technology becomes more sophisticated and police record keeping systems improve.

There are unique challenges to investigators of hate crimes. At the organizational level, a climate may exist where hate crime investigations are viewed as not being real police work.` In extreme cases, police officers may refuse to comply with requirements to report hate crimes. In more subtle ways, police administrators can point to policies that reflect a commitment to hate crime investigations, but these policies are not supported by organizational structures and rewards systems that would encourage officers to fully participate.

In addition to organizational climate, the term *hate crime* can be ambiguous and cause problems in the consistency and accuracy with which these crimes get reported to and recorded by police. Through training, police officers may be better able to work through this ambiguity, especially in cases where there is a mix of motivations for the crimes.

The federal government and police professional organizations have established training for police investigators to deal with the unique challenges provided by hate crime investigations. By participating in this training and by implementing model hate crime policies, like the one proposed by IACP (2008), police agencies will surely improve the quality of their hate crime investigations.

REFERENCES

Bell, J. (2002). *Policing hatred: Law enforcement, civil rights, and hate crime*. New York: New York University Press.

Cronin, S., McDevitt, J., Farrell, A., & Nolan, J. J. (2007). Bias-crime reporting: Organizational responses to ambiguity, uncertainty, and infrequency in eight police departments. *American Behavioral Scientist 51*(2), 213–231.

Federal Bureau of Investigations. (1997). *Hate Crime Statistics 1996.* Washington, DC: U.S. Government Printing Office.

Fischer, K. (2000, July 20). Parents request action: Washington vigil set to remember slain Marion man. *Charleston Daily Mail,* 1A.

Gerstenfeld, P. B. (2004). *Hate crimes: Causes, controls, and controversies.* Thousand Oaks, CA: Sage.

Grattet, R., & Jenness, V. (2001). The birth and maturation of hate crime policy in the United States. *American Behavioral Scientist, 45,* 668–696.

Haider-Markel, D. P. (2006). Acting as fire alarm with law enforcement? Interest group and bureaucratic activity on hate crime. *American Politics Research, 347*(1), 30–62.

International Association of Chiefs of Police. (2008). *Investigation of hate crimes: Concept and issues paper.* Alexandria, VA: IACP National Law Enforcement Center.

Lawrence, F. M. (1994). The punishment of hate: Toward a normative theory of bias-motivated crime. *Michigan Law Review, 93,* 320–381.

Lawrence, F. M. (1999). *Punishing hate: Bias crimes under American law.* Cambridge, MA: Harvard University Press.

Levin, B. (1999). Hate crimes: Worse by definition. *Journal of Contemporary Criminal Justice, 15,* 1–21.

Levin, J., & McDevitt, J. (1993). *Hate crime: The rising tide of bigotry and bloodshed.* New York: Plenum.

Martin, S. (1999). Police and the production of hate crimes: Continuity and change in one jurisdiction. *Police Quarterly, 2*(4), 417–437.

McDevitt, J., Cronin, S., Balboni, J., Farrell, A., Nolan, J. J., & Weiss, J. (2003). *Bridging the information disconnect in national bias crime reporting.* Washington, DC: U.S. Department of Justice.

McDevitt, J., Levin, J., & Bennett, S. (2001). Hate crime offenders: An expanded typology. *Journal of Social Issues, 58,* 303–317.

Nolan, J. J., & Akiyama, Y. (2002). Assessing the climate for hate crime reporting in law enforcement organizations. *The Justice Professional, 15*(2), 87–103.

Nolan, J. J., McDevitt, J., Cronin, S., & Farrell, A. (2004). Learning to see hate crime: A framework for understanding and clarifying ambiguities in bias crime classification. *Criminal Justice Studies, 17*(1), 91–105.

Smith, V. (2000, July 8). Groups want answers on death: Gay-rights activists demand to know if case is hate crime. *Charleston Daily Mail,* 1A.

U.S. Department of Justice (DOJ). (1998). *Hate crime training: Core curriculum for patrol officers, detectives, and command officers.* Washington, DC: Bureau of Justice Assistance.

CHAPTER 5

HATE CRIME PROSECUTION

Richard A. Devine and Alan J. Spellberg

Stories of violence and other crimes committed because of bigotry permeate the history of mankind and continue to occur in every continent, country, state, and city. Such "hate crimes" have two victims: the individual involved in the specific incident and the community to which that individual belongs. Hate crimes subject victims to a sense of violation and powerlessness that results from knowing that the perpetrator acted out of feelings of hatred or bigotry. Hate crimes affect communities where they occurred because they leave group members feeling vulnerable and fearful that they may be victims as well simply because of who they are. Moreover, society as a whole suffers because the feelings that hate crimes cause—humiliation, inequality, distrust, and the lack of security—decrease the opportunities of group members to participate freely in the greater community.

Prosecutors have a unique role in our criminal justice system. They have the responsibility of protecting society by convicting the guilty, but also seeking redress for the victim while, at the same time, protecting the rights of the accused. While hate crimes are no different from other crimes in this regard, special considerations arise at every stage of a hate crime prosecution. Beginning with the investigation and the decision to file charges in hate crime cases, prosecutors must be familiar not only with the particular statutes and applicable judicial decisions, but also be aware of the special considerations affecting victims of hate crimes. Prosecutors must coordinate their efforts with other law enforcement agencies to ensure that each hate crime is properly identified and can be successfully prosecuted. At the same time, prosecutors must reach out and forge relationships with the various, diverse communities within our greater society to help alleviate the harm caused by the offender and restore the well-being of both the individual and the victimized community.

CASE INVESTIGATION AND INITIATION

Although prosecutors are considered the gatekeepers of the judicial system,[1] the decision to charge a hate crime is greatly affected by the victims and the investigating police officers. Specifically, victims may be reluctant to believe that they were purposefully targeted because of a core characteristic such as race or religion, or may be afraid of further attacks by the offender's cohorts. Similarly, police officers may be unfamiliar with the particular requirements of the hate crime statutes or might believe that the criminal act was motivated by something other than a bias against one of the protected classifications. On the other hand, victims, community advocates, and others may believe a hate crime should be charged even if the evidence does not support such a classification. Thus, the prosecutor's screening process is critical in these cases.

Any screening or review of potential hate crime cases must begin with a thorough knowledge of the particular statutes and the judicial decisions interpreting those statutes. Because the adoption of hate crime statutes is a relatively recent phenomenon, it is important to understand the context in which they came about.

In the early 1980s, statistics indicated that crimes motivated by hatred or bias were increasing nationwide.[2] Although federal antibias crime laws were already in existence, those statutes were considered inadequate due to limited federal resources and because they were drafted to confront bias crimes by organized hate groups like the Ku Klux Klan and neo-Nazi organizations.[3] Because these statutes had no application to hate-motivated crimes unless they were committed during the course of conspiracies, and because research demonstrated that individuals rather than organized groups committed the majority of such crimes, several states adopted new statutes to specifically address these problems. These "ethnic intimidation" statutes provided for slightly enhanced penalties for certain misdemeanors committed because of race or ethnicity.[4]

As the rate of hate crime and the recognition of the diversity of its victims increased, prosecutors across the nation called on state legislatures to either replace or improve their ethnic intimidation statutes. Legislators quickly responded by adapting the model hate crime legislation drafted by the Anti-Defamation League (ADL). In addition to providing greater penalties than generally found in the ethnic intimidation statutes, these laws often expanded coverage to include individuals attacked because of their gender, sexual orientation, disabilities, or national origin.[5]

As of 2007, 49 states and the District of Columbia have passed some form of legislation designed to combat hate crimes.[6] Forty-six states have enacted laws against bias-motivated violence and intimidation. Most legislative attempts at punishing bias-motivated offenses have taken the form of sentence-enhancement statutes, whereby an offender who acts out of hate or bias is subject to a significantly greater penalty for the crime. For example, Wisconsin law currently provides for an increased penalty of up to five additional years for any felony offense, if the offender

[i]ntentionally selects the person against whom the crime . . . is committed or selects the property that is damaged or otherwise affected by the crime . . . in whole or in part because of the actor's belief or perception regarding the race, religion, color, disability, sexual orientation, national origin or ancestry of that person or the owner or occupant of that property, whether or not the actor's belief or perception was correct.[7]

A few states have created a separate felony offense that enhances certain enumerated misdemeanor offenses, such as battery or criminal trespass, when they are committed out of hate or bias toward the victim. For example, Illinois law currently provides that

[a] person commits hate crime when, by reason of the actual or perceived race, color, creed, religion, ancestry, gender, sexual orientation, physical or mental disability, or national origin of another individual or group of individuals, regardless of the existence of any other motivating factor or factors, he commits assault, battery, aggravated assault, misdemeanor theft, criminal trespass to residence, misdemeanor criminal damage to property, criminal trespass to vehicle, criminal trespass to real property, mob action or disorderly conduct . . . or harassment by telephone . . . or harassment through electronic communications.[8]

Moreover, 42 states and the District of Columbia have adopted "institutional vandalism" statutes, which increase the penalty for criminal damage to property of specific types of property associated with particular groups, such as churches, synagogues, and mosques, as well as cemeteries and schools.[9] Also, Illinois has recently enacted a "Conspiracy against Civil Rights" provision in order to ensure that hate group members and their leaders can be prosecuted when they agree that violence should be used against a certain group (such as African Americans or Jews), but do not necessarily agree on the specifics of a particular crime and are purposefully vague as to what will occur.[10]

In addition to the specifics of the statutes in their jurisdictions, prosecutors must also be aware of the judicial decisions interpreting those statutes because police officers and victims may not realize that a particular crime falls within the scope of the hate crime laws. For example, it is commonly believed that a hate crime cannot be charged unless the offender's sole motivation was one of bias or hatred towards the victim. However, courts across the country have held that hate crimes can be committed even if the offender is acting out of a mixed or dual motive.

In *People v. Aishman* the California Supreme Court held that the term "because of" in California's hate crime statute means that "when multiple concurrent causes exist, the bias motivation must have been a substantial factor in bringing about the offense."[11] Similarly, the Illinois Appellate Court in *People v. Nitz* stated: "In terms of common understanding, the phrase 'by reason of' means 'because of.' There is no requirement that the statute specify whether, for instance, racism must be the main motivation, or one motivation among many, for the statute to apply."[12]

Also, police officers and victims may not realize that a hate crime can be charged even if the victim was not a member of the targeted classification. Specifically, in *In re B.C.*, the Illinois Supreme Court held that two juveniles were properly charged with a hate crime predicated upon disorderly conduct after they displayed materials containing white supremacist symbols and depictions of extreme violence toward African Americans to a group of other students, including some African American children.[13] The trial court dismissed the charges because, rather than identifying the African American children as the victims in the charging instrument, the school principal who confiscated the materials was named even though he was not African American or perceived by the boys to be African American.

The Illinois Supreme Court reversed the trial court's ruling and remanded the matter for further proceedings. The court held that Illinois's hate crime statute "does not require as an element [of the offense] that the victim be an individual or of the group of individuals whose class provides reason for the underlying criminal offense."[14] The Supreme Court further explained that:

> Accepting the respondents' interpretation results, for example, in the inability of a Caucasian person who is not perceived as, but associates or socializes with, African-Americans to maintain a charge against a defendant who admittedly burns a cross on that person's property because of racial animosity directed against the person's associates. Similarly, a defendant professing hatred against homosexuals might bomb a "gay" bar which causes injury, by happenstance, to only heterosexual patrons of the bar as well as the bar's heterosexual owner, and avoid prosecution under the hate crime statute. Likewise, a defendant professing hatred against Jewish persons might physically assault a person who, though not Jewish or perceived to be Jewish by the defendant, is engaged in demonstrating against the desecration of synagogues. This defendant, also, would avoid prosecution under respondents' interpretation of the hate crime statute.
>
> In each of these instances, individual persons, but more importantly our entire community, are harmed by a defendant's bias-motivated criminal

conduct. We conclude that the legislature, aware of this fact, intended that improper bias which motivates certain criminal acts be the component which elevates the conduct to the level of hate crime, rather than merely the status of a particular victim.[15]

Because judicial decisions interpreting the statutes can greatly affect the ability to charge a hate crime, prosecutors should maintain a close working relationship with the various law enforcement agencies in their jurisdiction and keep them apprised of new developments.

Moreover, while prosecutors are expected to be fully conversant with the law before making any charging decisions, they must also recognize that hate crime victims are often more reluctant to come forward than victims of other crimes. Studies have shown that some of the most likely targets of hate violence, such as African Americans, gays and lesbians, and immigrants, are the least likely to report these crimes to the police.[16] Some African Americans are distrustful of the police. Gay and lesbian victims may hesitate in reporting these crimes due to fear of hostility and discrimination based on their sexual orientation. Finally, some immigrant victims may be concerned about deportation if they go to the police.

Prosecutors can often overcome much of this reluctance by carefully interviewing any hate crime victim in order to determine the reasons for the reluctance or refusal. Frequently, a reluctance to prosecute can be surmounted by a prosecutor who expresses appropriate concern for the victim, provides reassurance that the criminal justice system can serve the victim's interests, and makes arrangements to provide for the protection of the victim. Prosecutors may also turn to community groups to help guide reluctant victims and witnesses through the criminal justice system.

Of course, victims and witnesses are sometimes also reluctant due to a fear of reprisal from the offender or his cohorts. Thankfully, such concerns are usually unwarranted, but can be addressed with a visible police presence. Prosecutors should try to arrange for increased protection for victims of hate crime whenever there is a legitimate safety concern. In extreme cases, such as when the offender is a member of an organized hate group or a street gang, it may be necessary to relocate the victim or witness to protect them from retaliation or intimidation.

Ultimately, when deciding whether or not to charge a hate crime, the prosecutor must carefully analyze all the facts to determine if the burden of proof can be met at trial. In making this determination, the following "Textbook Indicators of Hate Crime" are considered:

1. Did the offender(s) use words, symbols, or acts that are or may be offensive to an identifiable group?
2. Are the victim and offender members of different racial or ethnic groups? If so, has there been past hostility or tension between these two groups?

Has the victim's group been subject to prior similar criminal acts or harassment?

3. Is the victim the sole member of his or her group, or one of a small number of members living or present in the neighborhood where the crime occurred?

4. Has the victim recently moved to the area in which the incident took place?

5. Does the incident appear timed to coincide with any holiday or observance of significance to a certain group or community, such as a religious holiday or ethnic celebration?

6. Has the victim or the victim's group been involved in recent public or political activity that makes the group a likely victim of hate-motivated violence?

7. Does the offender appear to belong to or does the manner of the commission of the crime appear to involve an organized hate group such as the Ku Klux Klan or a neo-Nazi organization? When the offender is wearing clothing that indicates membership in such a group, the arresting agency should seize the clothing as evidence. If the offender has tattoos indicating such an affiliation, photos of the tattoos should be taken at the time of charging.

8. Does the defendant, in a postarrest interview or in statements made before or during the commission of the crime, recognize the victim to be a member of a potential "target" group?

9. Has there been recent news coverage or media exposure of similar events?

10. Does the defendant have a prior history involving hate-motivated conduct?

11. Is the attack particularly vicious?[17]

Each of these factors goes directly to the question of whether the offender's bias or hatred can be proven beyond a reasonable doubt. Of course, even if an examination of these factors indicates that a hate crime should not be charged, the offender's conduct could still be considered a crime, possibly even a more serious offense than hate crime. If so, the prosecutor will typically charge the offender with the appropriate offense and explain to the victim why a hate crime charge was not made against the offender.

BOND HEARINGS

As in any case, once the decision to charge is made, the next step in the prosecution is usually the bond hearing. At that hearing, a judge will decide whether the defendant should remain in custody or if he should be released on bond. Prosecutors may argue against releasing the defendant, reminding the judge that "although bail serves several functions, its primary function is protection of the public, not merely whether or not the defendant will return to court."[18]

If the judge decides to set a bond, however, the judge must decide not only what amount is sufficient to guarantee the defendant's appearance in court, but also whether any special conditions of bond should be imposed. In a hate crime case, the prosecutor should bring the defendant's hate motivation to the attention of the court and ask the judge to impose those conditions of bond which are necessary to ensure not only the protection of the victim and witnesses, but also the safety of other members of the group targeted by the offender.[19] "This may be accomplished either by specifying that the defendant refrain from approaching or communicating with particular persons or classes of persons, or by geographical restrictions that keep the defendant out of areas that are identified as potential target areas for the offender."[20] Of course, the prosecutor should always seek conditions that are appropriate for the specific case.

The prosecutor should give the victim a copy of any special conditions of bond ordered by the court, and should explain to the victim what to do if the defendant violates any of the conditions. "The victim should be encouraged to report any threats, contacts or other violations immediately to either the police or the prosecutor's office."[21] In an extreme case, the prosecutor may also contact the local police commander directly and inform him about the case and the special conditions of the defendant's bond.[22]

PRETRIAL PROCEEDINGS

In addition to the typical pretrial proceedings in criminal cases, such as the exchange of discovery and the filing of motions to suppress evidence, it is common for defendants charged with hate crimes to also file various motions seeking to have the charges dismissed. In particular, such defendants often file motions claiming that the hate crime statutes are unconstitutional because they violate the First Amendment as well as the due process and equal protection clauses of the U.S. Constitution. However, courts across the country, including the U.S. Supreme Court, have repeatedly rejected these arguments.

First Amendment

Defendants charged with hate crimes often claim that such laws improperly infringe the right to free expression because they impose greater punishment simply based upon what the offender believes rather than what he does. However, in 1993, the U.S. Supreme Court expressly held otherwise in *Wisconsin v. Mitchell*.[23]

Mitchell arose from a 1989 Kenosha, Wisconsin, incident involving a group of young black men and boys who attacked a 14-year-old white boy. In addition to stealing his tennis shoes, the group beat the boy until he was unconscious.

The boy remained in the beating-induced coma for four days. Prior to the beating, some group members discussed a particularly brutal scene in the movie *Mississippi Burning* that depicted a group of white men beating a little black boy who was praying. Fueling the already heightened emotions of the group, the defendant asked the others if they "all fe[lt] hyped up to move on some white people." The defendant further incited the others to use violence toward the victim who was walking opposite them on the street, saying, "There goes a white boy; go get him." The defendant then counted to three and pointed in the boy's direction. The group ran toward the boy, beat him severely, and stole his shoes.

The defendant was convicted of aggravated battery. In addition to the ordinary elements of the offense, the jury also found, pursuant to Wisconsin's hate crime statute, that the defendant intentionally selected his victim because of his race. As a result of that finding, the maximum possible sentence the defendant could receive was increased from two years to seven years. The trial court sentenced the defendant to four years' imprisonment.

The Wisconsin Supreme Court affirmed the defendant's conviction but reversed his enhanced sentence on three grounds. First, the court held that the hate crime statute authorizing the five-year increase in the maximum possible sentence violated the First Amendment because the statute punished the defendant for his beliefs, motives, and reasons for choosing the victim. Second, the court found that the statute was unconstitutionally overbroad because the prosecution would have to admit evidence of the defendant's prior statements, and the use of that possibly protected speech may have a "chilling effect" on those who fear the prospect of future prosecution for offenses that could be subject to penalty enhancement. Third, the court differentiated between the hate crime penalty enhancement statute and constitutional antidiscrimination statutes, determining that the enhancement statute punished the "subjective mental process" of choosing a victim as opposed to punishing "objective displays of discrimination."[24]

The U.S. Supreme Court reversed that decision in a unanimous ruling. The Court expressly held that a defendant's First Amendment rights are not violated when a penalty-enhancement statute, specifically designed to deter bias-related crimes, is applied at sentencing. The Court further rejected the defendant's argument that enhancing a penalty because of bias-related victim selection punished the defendant's beliefs.

The Court first recognized that sentencing judges have a great deal of discretion in considering information to determine a sentence. The Court emphasized that evidence concerning a person's beliefs and associations are not necessarily barred from consideration, even though those beliefs and associations are protected by the First Amendment. The Court explained that in *Barclay v. Florida*,[25] the defendant's racial animus toward his victim, as shown by his membership in the Black Liberation Army and his desire to provoke a "race war," were held to be properly considered by the sentencing judge during death penalty sentencing because the hatred was particularly relevant. The Court reasoned that if a sentencing court is allowed to consider the defendant's hatred and bias in determining whether or not to impose the death penalty, the Wisconsin statute's use of the defendant's motives to enhance the maximum penalty is entirely appropriate.

The *Mitchell* Court distinguished its earlier decision in *R.A.V. v. City of St. Paul*, which struck down an ordinance making it a misdemeanor to "place on public or private property a symbol, object, appellation, characterization, or graffiti, including, but not limited to, a burning cross or Nazi swastika, which one knows or has reasonable grounds to know arouses anger, alarm or resentment in others on the basis of race, color, creed, religion or gender."[26] In *Mitchell* the Court explained that, unlike the ordinance in *R.A.V.*, which violated the First Amendment because it amounted to content-based discrimination (i.e., it prohibited certain types of expression that the city deemed offensive), the Wisconsin statute was "aimed at conduct unprotected by the First Amendment."[27]

The *Mitchell* Court further noted that the "bias-inspired conduct" targeted by the Wisconsin statute is thought to "inflict greater individual and societal harm," because "bias-motivated crimes are more likely to provoke retaliatory crimes, inflict distinct emotional harms on their victims, and incite community unrest."[28]

Finally, the Court rejected the defendant's argument that the statute was "overbroad" because it would have a "chilling effect" on free expression, since evidence of a defendant's prior statements or associations could be used to prove that the defendant intentionally selected his victim because of the victim's protected status. The Court dismissed the claim as "too speculative" since it would require "a citizen suppressing his bigoted beliefs for fear that evidence of such beliefs will be introduced against him at trial if he commits a . . . serious offense against person or property." Instead, the Court explained that the best available evidence of intent often comes from what the offender said. The Court stated:

> The First Amendment . . . does not prohibit the evidentiary use of speech to establish the elements of a crime or to prove motive or intent. Evidence of a defendant's previous declarations or statements is commonly admitted in criminal trials subject to evidentiary rules dealing with relevancy, reliability and the like.[29]

Following *Mitchell*, courts across the country have upheld hate crime statutes in the face of challenges based upon the First Amendment or state constitutional provisions guaranteeing free expression. Each court has recognized that a defendant's right to free expression is not infringed by a statute that punishes illegal conduct more severely when it is accompanied by hatred or bias against another person or group.[30] As the Montana Supreme Court stated in *State v. Nye*, "free speech does not include the right to cause substantial emotional distress by harassment or intimidation. Activities which are intended to embarrass, annoy or harass, as was the case here, are not protected by the First Amendment."[31]

Due Process

Defendants charged with committing hate crimes also typically challenge the statutes on due process grounds. Specifically, they claim that the statutes are "void for vagueness" because they do not adequately identify what behavior is prohibited. Like the First Amendment claims, courts have repeatedly rejected such arguments. For example, in *State v. Plowman*, the Oregon Supreme Court rejected the defendant's claim that the term in the Oregon intimidation statute, "because of their perception of [the victims'] race, color, religion, national origin or sexual orientation"[32] was "inherently nebulous and imprecise" and invited a "standardless prosecution."[33] The court held that the crime was defined in sufficiently clear and explicit terms to apprise defendants and others of what conduct is prohibited, noting that

> the statute prohibits two or more assailants, acting together, from causing physical injury to another because the assailants perceive the victim to belong to one of the specified groups. The challenged phrase means simply that the assailants' perception need not be accurate for them to have committed the crime of intimidation in the first degree.[34]

The *Plowman* court further rejected the argument that the statute failed to give sufficient guidance to police and prosecutors when it held that the statute "expressly and unambiguously requires the state to prove a causal connection between the infliction of injury and the assailants' perception of the group to which the victim belongs."[35]

Similarly, in *In re M.S. & A.G.*, the California Supreme Court rejected the defendants' arguments that that state's hate crime statutes were unconstitutionally vague when it held that the statutory term "because of" connotes a causal link between the victim's characteristic and the defendant's conduct.[36]

Finally, in *Nye* the Montana Supreme Court rejected a vagueness challenge to its "malicious intimidation" statute, based upon the language that prohibits "damaging, destroying or defacing the property of another with the intent to harass, annoy or offend because of another's race, religion or national origin."[37] The court rebuffed the defendant's arguments and explained that the statute "does not punish a defendant for offending or annoying another individual because of that individual's race, religion or national origin.

The statute punishes a defendant for assaults and damage to property when that conduct is done *with the intent to annoy or offend* another individual because of that individual's race, religion or national origin."[38]

However, in *Botts v. State* the Georgia Supreme Court ruled that the statutory language "that the defendant intentionally selected any victim or any property of the victim as the object of the offense because of bias or prejudice" in the Georgia hate crime penalty enhancement statute was unconstitutionally vague.[39] The *Botts* Court stated that because the statute was not limited to specifics types of "bias or prejudice," such as racial or religious, it could apply to situations involving

> [a] rabid sports fan convicted of uttering terroristic threats to a victim selected for wearing a competing team's baseball cap; a campaign worker convicted of trespassing for defacing a political opponent's yard signs; a performance car fanatic convicted of stealing a Ferrari—any "bias or prejudice" for or against the selected victim or property, no matter how obscure, whimsical or unrelated to the victim it may be, but for which proof beyond a reasonable doubt might exist, can serve to enhance a sentence.[40]

Equal Protection

Finally, some defendants have challenged the hate crime statutes under equal protection grounds, arguing that the statues allow the prosecution to charge a defendant with either the hate crime or a lesser, non–bias-motivated offense based upon the same conduct, depending on whether the prosecution approves of the defendant's beliefs. In other words, the defendants claim that under the statutes, they are treated differently based on their beliefs.

Such arguments have been rejected on the grounds that offenders who purposefully select their victims out of an animus toward an individual or a group are not similarly situated to those offenders who select their victims for other reasons.[41] Legislatures may reasonably determine that bias-motivated crimes have a greater and more harmful effect on the safety and welfare of their citizens than do ordinary crimes.[42] Thus, courts have held that the increased punishment for hate crimes bears a rational relationship to the legislative purpose since it is "justified by the additional element of victim selection and its associated greater harm."[43]

TRIAL: JURY ISSUES

When preparing for trial, prosecutors must account for certain aspects of cases unique to hate crime. In particular, even though the courts have repeatedly upheld the propriety of hate crime statutes, some people, including police officers and prospective jurors, continue to harbor a hostility toward them. For example, because hate crime cases usually involve an enhanced version of an otherwise less serious crime, some police witnesses may not consider these cases to be as important as the prosecutor does. This is mainly true in situations where the victim suffered minimal physical harm or property damage. In these cases, police witnesses should be reminded prior to trial of the importance of the case to both the victim and the community.[44]

Similarly, because some prospective jurors may have the impression that hate crime statutes improperly infringe First Amendment rights, they would be considered more likely to acquit the defendant. Accordingly, prosecutors must sometimes make strategic decisions as to how, or even if, the evidence of the defendant's hate or bias will be presented to the jury. For example, if the evidence of the defendant's bias or motive is not as strong as the evidence establishing his unlawful conduct, and the defendant is also charged with other serious offenses, the prosecutor may choose to forgo the hate crime charges and simply seek a conviction for the other, non–bias-motivated offenses. This is because the jury must find beyond a reasonable doubt that the defendant acted out of hate or bias before he can be convicted of a hate crime or given an enhanced penalty.[45] Prosecutors have a concern that jurors who have indicated a hostility to hate crime laws could vote to acquit based solely upon the bias-motivation element. Of course, the prosecutor should consult with the victim and explain her decision before dismissing a hate crime charge.

Prosecutors can avoid some of these problems if they are allowed to conduct an extensive jury selection, or voir dire, process. Prosecutors will typically ask prospective jurors questions that probe not only their feelings regarding hate crime laws and the precise charges in the case, but also any bias or prejudice the prospective jurors themselves might have regarding the victim's actual or perceived group. Prosecutors may also inquire into a potential juror's background to distinguish between those jurors with an isolated, narrow background from those with broader experience. Some questions that prosecutors might ask in a typical hate crime case are:

1. Residence—length—where raised—where lived?
2. Marital status—family—children?
3. Current job/occupation/profession—spouse's—adult children—past jobs?
4. Education and training?
5. Military service—government service?
6. Decision-making in life?
7. Organizational memberships?
8. Hobbies—sports—outside interests?
9. Any experience in life with protected class, for example, relevant race, gender, age, religion, and so forth?
10. Feelings toward protected class, for example, relevant race, gender, age, religion, and so forth.
11. Any personal, religious, moral, philosophical, or political belief that would make it difficult to serve as juror in the case?[46]

Moreover, if a case involves a hate crime committed against a person who is a member of a frequently targeted group, such as Arab Americans in the aftermath of September 11, 2001, the prosecutor should ask specific questions to each prospective juror regarding any ill feelings or prejudice the juror might have about that group. Otherwise, the prosecutor risks seating a juror who sympathizes more with the defendant than the victim.

TRIAL: EVIDENCE

Because hate crimes require proof of motive and bias, prosecutors may seek to introduce "prior act" evidence to establish that the defendant's conduct was motivated by reason of the victim's actual or perceived membership in a protected group. In *State v. Davidson* the court ruled that evidence of prior acts by the defendant and prior disparaging remarks made by the defendant were admissible to show defendant's state of mind at the time he committed the hate crime by spray painting racial slurs on the victim's house.[47] Evidence that the defendant had previously poured rice or sugar into the victim's gas tank and that he had made racially derogatory remarks were properly admitted to show racial motivation.

If the defendants are members of organized hate groups, prosecutors may seek to introduce expert testimony on the hate groups and their ideologies. Expert testimony can also explain the significance of tattoos, symbols, and historic dates. For example, in *People v. Slavin*, the New York Court of Appeals affirmed the defendant's hate crime conviction where the prosecution relied upon expert testimony to explain the meaning of the letters, symbols, and pictures represented in the defendant's tattoos.[48]

TRIAL: ARGUMENT

When giving her closing argument in a hate crime case, the prosecutor should remind the jury that the defendant is not being prosecuted for possession of any particular literature or for harboring an unpopular belief. This will help negate any defense theory that the defendant is being punished for his beliefs and will refocus the jury on the defendant's criminal conduct, which was motivated by his own hate and bias toward the protected group. The prosecutor should stress that the defendant's possession of the literature or espousal of a belief demonstrates the defendant's motivation for committing those crimes.

SENTENCING

Although hate crime statutes typically enhance the penalties for offenses, not every convicted hate crime offender is sentenced to prison. Recognizing

that some hate crime offenders, particularly juvenile offenders, might be amenable to rehabilitation and education, some prosecutors have developed alternative sentencing programs that combine educational components with
intensive probation services.[49] In addition, some hate crime statutes expressly
provide that if the convicted offender is not imprisoned, he must perform a
significant number of hours of community service. For example, the Illinois
statute provides in pertinent part:

> In addition, any order of probation or conditional discharge entered fol-
> lowing a conviction or an adjudication of delinquency shall include a con-
> dition that the offender perform public or community service of no less
> than 200 hours if that service is established in the county where the of-
> fender was convicted of hate crime. The court may also impose any other
> condition of probation or conditional discharge under this Section[50]

In an attempt to provide a meaningful experience and hopefully prevent
additional hate crimes, prosecutors in Illinois work with courts and community groups to ensure that hate crime offenders actually serve their
community service hours in the targeted community.

COMMUNITY OUTREACH

In order to ensure effective cooperation and coordination after a hate
crime occurs, prosecutors must cultivate and maintain productive and trusting relationships with the diverse community organizations in their jurisdiction. These relationships not only build mutual trust, but often furnish an
indispensable service in the prosecution of hate crime cases. It can make the
difference between winning or losing the trial, and between serving or alien-
ating the community victimized by the hate crime.

Community-based prosecution programs are also an important tool in
establishing a trusting relationship. By building on the community-based
approach, prosecutors are able to educate a diverse community to ensure that
hate crime incidents are reported. Building an effective line of communication with community groups in the local police district is an important step
in establishing trust.

CONCLUSION

Prosecuting hate crimes is a challenging, but rewarding responsibility.
Prosecutors across the country are willing to accept these challenges because they recognize that "aggressive enforcement of hate crime statutes . . .
sends the clear message that hate violence is a law enforcement priority and
that each hate crime—and each hate crime victim—is important."[51]

Cases Rejecting Free Speech Challenges to Hate Crime Statutes

California—*In re M.S. & A.G.*, 10 Cal. 4th 698, 896 P.2d 1365 (Calif. 1995) (Court held that sections 422.6 & 422.7 require proof of a specific intent to interfere with a person's right protected under state or federal law, and therefore do not regulate protected speech. Thus, neither statute violates the First Amendment pursuant to *Mitchell*.)

Florida—*State v. Stalder*, 630 So.2d 1072 (Fla. 1994) (Sec.775.085, Fla. Stat. 1989) (This statute requires penalty enhancement where the commission of a felony or misdemeanor evidences prejudice based on the race, color, ancestry, ethnicity, religion or national origin of the victim, is a bias-motivated provision, and therefore does not violate the First Amendment pursuant to *Mitchell*.)

Kansas—*City of Wichita v. Edwards*, 23 Kan. App. 2d 962, 939 P.2d 942 (Kan. App. 1997) (Relying on *Mitchell*, Court held that the ethnic intimidation ordinance, Sec. 5.01.010 of the Wichita City Code, is not aimed at regulating speech, but rather is intended to penalize conduct undertaken by reason of a specific motivation or intent, and therefore does not violate the First Amendment.)

Michigan—*People v. Richards*, 202 Mich. App. 377, 509 N.W.2d 528 (Mich. App. 1993) (Relying entirely on *Mitchell*, Court concludes that the offense of ethnic intimidation, MCL 750.147b; MSA 28.344(2), was not aimed at regulating speech protected by the First Amendment.)

Missouri—*State v. Vanatter*, 869 S.W.2d 754 (Mo. 1994) (The offense of ethnic intimidation in the second degree, Sec. 574.093 does not violate the First Amendment because it is aimed at, and expressly requires, conduct that independently is subject to criminal sanction and is not afforded First Amendment protection.)

Montana—*State v. Nye*, 283 Mont. 505, 943 P.2d 96 (Mont. 1997) (Section 45–5–221, MCA, does not violate defendant's right to freedom of speech under the First Amendment of the U.S. Constitution *or* Article II, Section 7, of the Montana Constitution.)

New Jersey—*State v. Mortimer*, 135 N.J. 517, 641 A.2d 257 (N.J. 1994) (Court examined the offense of fourth-degree harassment, N.J.S.A. 2C:33–4, subsection d, which increases certain offenses from disorderly offenses to fourth-degree offenses when a person acts "at least in part, with ill will, hatred or bias toward, and with a purpose to intimidate . . . because of race, color, religion, sexual orientation or ethnicity." Relying on *Mitchell*, Court held that subsection d did not violate the First Amendment or the New Jersey Constitution, because it neither regulates speech nor impermissibly punishes motive.)[52]

New York—*People v. Miccio*, 155 Misc. 2d 697, 589 N.Y.S.2d 762 (Crim. Cr. 1992) (Court examined the aggravated harassment and antidiscrimination statutes, Penal law Sec. 240.3 [3]; and Civil Rights law Sec. 40-c, which both make it illegal to strike, shove, kick, or otherwise subject another person to physical contact or attempt to threaten to do the same because of the "race, color, religion or national origin of such person." Court found that the provisions do not punish a person for biased thought or expression, but rather prohibit violence and physical intimidation based on bigotry, and therefore do not violate the First Amendment and are a valid exercise of police power.)

Oregon—*State v. Plowman*, 314 Ore. 157, 838 P.2d 558 (Ore. 1992) (Court held that offense of intimidation, ORS 166.165(a)(a)(A), does not proscribe speech or target conduct on the basis of its expressive intent, and therefore does not offend the First Amendment or Article I, section 8, of the Oregon Constitution.)

Ohio—*State v. Wyant*, 68 Ohio St. 3d 162, 624 N.E.2d 722 (Ohio 1994) (Pursuant to *Mitchell*, this decision upheld the constitutionality of R.C. 2927.12, the ethnic intimidation law under both the First Amendment of the U.S. Constitution and Section II, Article I of the Ohio Constitution.)

Vermont—*State v. Ladue*, 160 Vt. 630, 631 A.2d 236 (Vt. 1993) (Relying entirely on *Mitchell*, the Court held that Vermont's hate-motivated crime statute, 13 V.S.A. Sec. 1455, does not violate the First Amendment.)

Washington—*State v. Talley*, 122 Wash. 2d 192, 858 P.2d 217 (Wash. 1993) (RCW 9A.36.080 subsection (1) does not violate the First Amendment because it is aimed at criminal conduct where the defendant chooses his victim because of perceived membership in a protected category, and therefore only incidentally affects speech. However, RCW 9A.36.080 subsection (2), which makes it a per se violation to burn a cross or deface the property of the victim or third person with symbols when the symbols or words historically or traditionally connote hatred or threats toward a person, inhibits free speech on the basis of its content.)

Cases Rejecting Voidness Challenges to Hate Crime Statutes

Florida—*State v. Stalder*, 630 So.2d 1072 (Fla. 1994) (Sec. 775.085, Fla. Stat. (1989), which requires penalty enhancement where the commission of a felony or misdemeanor evidences prejudice based on the race, color, ancestry, ethnicity, religion, or national origin of the victim, is not vague.)

Iowa—*State v. McKnight*, 511 N.W.2d 389 (Iowa 1994) (Iowa Code Sec. 729.5(3)(a)(1991), an enhancement provision, is not vague.)

Kansas—*City of Wichita v. Edwards*, 23 Kan. App. 2d 962, 939 P.2d 942 (Kan. App. 1997) (Court held that Sec. 5.01.010 of the Wichita City Code, which provides that any person who commits or attempts to commit one of the specified crimes "by reason of any motive or intent relating to, or any antipathy, animosity or hostility based upon, the race, color or gender" is guilty of ethnic intimidation, is not vague.)

Michigan—*People v. Richards*, 202 Mich. App. 377, 509 N.W.2d 528 (Mich. App. 1993) (Court held that the offense of ethnic intimidation, MCL 750.147b; MSA 28.344(2) was not vague, because the elements are "very clear and definite." The statute is satisfied only when there is evidence of an underlying predicate criminal act committed because of racial animosity.)

New Jersey—*State v. Mortimer*, 135 N.J. 517, 641 A.2d 257 (N.J. 1994) (Court examined the offense of fourth-degree harassment, N.J.S.A. 2C:33–4, subsection d, which increases certain offenses from disorderly offenses to fourth-degree offenses when a person acts "at least in part, with ill will, hatred or bias toward, and with a purpose to intimidate . . . because of race, color, religion, sexual orientation or ethnicity." Although the Court found subsection d to be vague, it sustained it with a limiting construction. The Court held that when construed to exclude the words, "at least in part with ill will, hatred or bias toward," subsection d survives a constitutional vagueness challenge.)

Washington—*State v. Talley*, 122 Wash. 2d 192, 858 P.2d 217 (Wash. 1993) (RCW 9A.36080 subsection (1) is not vague. This section provides adequate notice and sufficient standards to prevent arbitrary enforcement because the average citizen can understand the phrase, "in a way that is reasonably related to, associated with, or directed toward," as well as the phrase "reasonable fear.")

NOTES

1.   American Prosecutor's Research Institute, *A Local Prosecutor's Guide for Responding to Hate Crimes* (Alexandria, VA: APRI, 2000), p. 21 [hereinafter APRI].

2.   Cook County State's Attorney Office, *Hate Crime: A Prosecutor's Guide* (1998), pp. II-2 [hereinafter Cook County].

3.   Jack Levin and Jack McDevitt, *Hate Crimes: The Rising Tide of Bloodshed and Bigotry* (New York: Plenum Press, 1993), pp. 182–183.

4.   For example, Illinois Revised Statutes, ch. 38, par. 12–7.1 (1983).

5.   For example, Missouri Revised Statutes, Section 557.035 (enhancing the penalty for crimes "because of race, color, religion, national origin, sex, sexual orientation or disability of the victim or victims").

6.   Wyoming is the only state that does not have any hate crime statutes.

7.   Wisconsin Statutes Annotated § 939.645.

8.   720 Illinois Complied Statutes 5/12–7.1(a) (2006).

9.   For example, California Penal Code § 594.3 (authorizing an increased penalty for "[a]ny person who knowingly commits any act of vandalism to a church, synagogue, mosque, temple, building owned and occupied by a religious educational institution").

10.   720 Illinois Complied Statutes 5/8–2.1. This statute was drafted and proposed by the Cook County State's Attorney's Office in response to Benjamin Smith's July 4, 1999, rampage when he killed two people and injured nine others after learning that World Church of the Creator leader, Matthew Hale, had been denied a law license by the Illinois Supreme Court.

11.   10 Cal. 4th 735, 741, 896 P.2d 1387, 1390 (1995).

12.   285 Ill. App. 3d 364, 370, 674 N.E.2d 802, 806 (1996). Subsequent to the decision in *Nitz*, the Illinois General Assembly amended the hate crime statute to specifically include language that it applies "regardless of the existence of any other motivating factor or factors." See 720 Illinois Complied Statutes 5/12–7.1(a) (2006).

13.   176 Ill. 2d 536, 680 N.E.2d 1355 (1997).

14.   176 Ill. 2d at 551, 680 N.E.2d at 1363.

15.   176 Ill. 2d at 550–51, 680 N.E.2d at 1362–63.

16.   APRI, pp. 2–3.

17.   Cook County, p. V-2.

18.   APRI, p. 33.

19.   APRI, p. 33.

20.   Cook County, p. V-7.

21.   Cook County, p. V-9.

22.   APRI, p. 33.

23.   508 U.S. 476, 113 S.Ct. 2194 (1993)

24.   *State v. Mitchell*, 169 Wis. 2d 153, 174–176, 485 N.W.2d 807, 816–17 (1992).

25.   463 U.S. 939, 103 S.Ct. 3418 (1983).

26.   05 U.S. 377, 112 S. Ct. 2538 (1992) (citing St. Paul, Minn. Legis. Code sec. 292.02 (1990)).

27.   508 U.S. at 487, 103 S.Ct. at 2201. In *Virginia v. Black*, 538 U.S. 343, 363, 123 S. Ct. 1536, 1549 (2003), the Court further distinguished *R.A.V.* and upheld a Virginia statute prohibiting cross burning when done with the intent to intimidate, holding that "[i]nstead of prohibiting all intimidating messages, Virginia may choose to regulate this subset of intimidating messages in light of cross burning's long and pernicious history as a signal of impending violence."

28.   508 U.S. at 488, 103 S.Ct. at 2201.

29.   508 U.S. at 489, 103 S.Ct. at 2201.

30.   *State v. Vanatter*, 869 S.W.2d 754, 757 (Mo. 1994) ("[w]hile [the statute] admittedly creates a new motive-based crime, its practical effect is to provide additional punishment for conduct that is illegal but is seen as especially harmful because it is motivated by group hatred").

31.   283 Mont. 505, 513, 943 P.2d 96, 101 (Mont. 1997).

32.   Oregon Revised Statutes 166.165(1)(a)(A).

33.   314 Ore. 157, 161, 838 P.2d 558, 561 (1992).

34.   314 Ore. At 161, 838 P.2d at 561. The *Plowman* court then illustrated the point by stating, "if the assailants, acting together, intentionally cause physical injury to a victim because they perceive the victim to be Catholic, the assailants have committed the crime of intimidation in the first degree even if the victim is not in fact Catholic, but is instead Episcopalian."

35.   314 Ore. At 161, 838 P.2d at 561.

36.   10 Cal. 4th 698,718–19, 896 P.2d 1365, 1375–77 (Calif. 1995).

37.   § 45–5-221, Montana Code Annotated.

38.   283 Mont. at 514, 943 P.2d at 102 (emphasis in original). See also attached chart for additional cases.

39.   278 Ga. 538, 538–39, 604 S.E.2d 512, 514 (2004).

40.   278 Ga. at 540, 604 S.E.2d at 514–15.

41.   *People v. MacKenzie*, 34 Cal. App. 4th 1256, 1269–72, 40 Cal. Rptr. 2d 793, 800–01 (Cal. App. 1995).

42.   *State v. Mortimer*, 135 N.J. 517, 536–37, 641 A.2d 257, 267 (N.J. 1994).

43.   *State v. Talley*, 122 Wn.2d 192, 215, 858 P.2d 217, 230 (Wash. 1993).

44.   Cook County, p. VI-2.

45.   *Apprendi v. New Jersey*, 530 U.S. 466, 120 S. Ct. 2348 (2000) (holding that a hate crime penalty enhancement that raises the maximum possible sentence for the crime cannot be imposed unless the factor is proven to the jury beyond a reasonable doubt).

46.   APRI, p. 46.

47.   225 N.J. Super 1, 12–14, 541 A.2d 700, 706–07 (1988).

48.   1 N.Y.3d 392, 807 N.E.2d 259 (2004).

49.   APRI, p. 51–52.

50.   720 ILCS 5/12–7.1(b-10).

51.   APRI, p. 3.

52.   In *State v. Vawter & Kearns*, 136 N.J. 56, 642 A.2d 349 (N.J.1994), the Court held that different provisions (N.J.S.A. 2C:33–10 [section 10] and –11 [section 11]) which prohibit "put[ting] or attempt[ing] to put another in fear of bodily violence by placing on . . . property a symbol . . . that exposes another to threats of violence, contempt or hatred on the basis of race, color, creed or religion, including, but not limited to[,] a burning cross or Nazi swastika," or "damag[ing private premises or property] . . . by placing thereon a symbol . . . that exposes another to threats of violence, contempt or hatred on the basis of race, color, creed or religion, including, but not limited to, a burning cross or Nazi swastika," violate First Amendment under *R.A.V.* However, this decision seems erroneous in light of *Virginia v. Black*. See note 28, supra.

CHAPTER 6

CIVIL HATE CRIME INJUNCTIONS: A VITAL WEAPON IN COMBATING HATE CRIMES

Richard W. Cole, Esq.

In the past few decades states are increasingly recognizing the substantial benefits of civil enforcement authority to help combat the scourge of crimes of bigotry and prejudice that often devastate victims and inflame communities where they occur. These states provide their leading law enforcement officials with the power to obtain civil rights injunction orders prohibiting hate crime perpetrators from engaging in future bias-motivated activities against the victim or others based on their race, color, ethnicity, national origin, religion, sexual orientation, gender, or disability, with the threat of serious criminal sanctions if disobeyed.

When reviewing federal and state efforts at addressing hate-motivated violence and intimidation in the United States, however, commentators most frequently focus on the criminal enforcement tools provided to law enforcement under both federal and state criminal hate crime laws. Rarely, if ever, do commentators examine the innovative use by states of civil hate crime injunction orders that effectively supplement criminal hate crime laws in addressing the serious challenge of bias-motivated violence and related civil rights violations in our schools, neighborhoods, and communities.

Some law enforcement officials contend that violent and threatening forms of discrimination are better dealt with through the criminal courts and that they cannot identify circumstances where law enforcement could appropriately use a civil injunction in response to a criminal act involving bigotry. They assert that criminal laws are sufficient to deter and respond to hate crimes and their risks of retaliatory violence. They maintain that community members would clamor for an arrest under the criminal laws if an injunction

were sought as a substitute for criminal prosecution. Some also maintain that
civil hate crime injunctions are inappropriate for use against juveniles, whom
they suggest, unlike adults, generally do not commit true hate crimes.

The compelling record from states, such as the Commonwealth of Massachusetts, that have regularly used civil hate crime injunctions against both
adults and juveniles, however, demonstrates that they are an extraordinarily
effective weapon in preventing hate crimes and protecting civil rights. Granting law enforcement leaders the authority to obtain civil hate crime injunctions also reaffirms our fundamental commitment to protecting civil rights
and applying all effective enforcement strategies in combating acts of hate-
motivated intimidation and terror.

As discussed in more detail below, these special civil hate crime orders
strengthen the legal protections for victims of incidents of violent and
threatening forms of hate, harassment, and discrimination. For example, on
many occasions hate crime prosecutions do not result in convictions. When
prosecutions are successful, hate crime offenders, particularly juveniles, are
often not incarcerated, or subject to more than a brief imprisonment. At
other times, a crime is prosecuted, but not as a hate crime, even where the
incident is motivated by bigotry and bias. For example, in making charging
decisions, some prosecutors will not include a hate crime charge in their case,
even where appropriate, believing it will complicate the criminal trial, or is
unnecessary because it will not change the nature or extent of the punishment imposed. Community members, however, often interpret the failure to
charge a hate crime as a sign of disrespect for the victim and disregard for
the special impact a hate crime has on the community.

For some hate crimes offenders, prosecutors cannot marshal sufficient evidence to charge a hate crime, or any crime, concluding that they are unable to
establish the perpetrator's criminal culpability or bias motivation "beyond a
reasonable doubt." For example, because of investigatory or evidentiary limitations, prosecutors are often unable to prosecute more marginal hate crime
participants who, for example, implicitly or explicitly encourage or provide
support to the primary perpetrator.

Additionally, criminal trials are often delayed, sometimes for extended periods, with most defendants free on bail or on personal recognizance pending trial. Courts may issue a stay-away order to prohibit the defendant from
communicating with or approaching the victim pending the criminal trial,
but in general, violation will result at most in the court ordering the defendant into custody pending trial. Furthermore, juvenile criminal proceedings
and its sanctions are often insufficient to serve as an effective deterrent for
juvenile hate crime offenders.

Many hate crime victims live in intense fear of further victimization. Civil
hate crime injunctions provide these vulnerable and terrorized victims additional guarantees of security and support. They are applied, for example, to

those who participate or play any role in the hate crime but are not charged criminally. They are particularly effective in preventing intimidation while a criminal case is pending or when the victim and offender live, work, walk, or drive near one another. Civil hate crime injunction proceedings also often provide a more rapid law enforcement response to bias-motivated crimes than criminal proceedings.

Hate crime injunctions also help meet the specific needs of communities, by helping reduce the risk of escalating or retaliatory violence. They not only subject defendants to serious criminal penalties if they retarget the same victim, but they criminalize future civil rights-related violations by the defendants against any other person (who lives, works, or travels in the same community or state) who shares a common racial, ethnic, religious, or other legally protected characteristic of the victim. They can also assist communities in defusing simmering racial and ethnic conflicts and intergroup tensions and polarization. For example, they often have a calming effect on groups of juvenile perpetrators who are followers rather than leaders, by providing them with an excuse for resisting peer pressure for further involvement in bias-related activities against the victim or others.

Hate crime injunctions also have many legal advantages over criminal prosecutions, from a lower burden of proof, its ready application to juveniles, the use of victim and witness affidavits rather than live testimony for preliminary relief, and the flexibility of crafting a civil order that is individualized to the victim's actual needs and the specific facts and circumstances presented.

Finally, hate crime injunction orders may also include provisions that require participation in programs or activities that encourage perpetrators to better understand the harm they have caused and modify the hateful attitudes that motivated their unlawful behavior.

STATE CIVIL HATE CRIME INJUNCTION LAWS

State civil rights injunction laws commonly grant the state attorney general, the state's chief law enforcement officer, and at times also district attorneys, the authority to obtain "hate crime injunctions" where necessary to prevent future bias-motivated crimes and related civil rights violations in their jurisdictions. Ten states (California, Florida, Maine, Massachusetts, New Hampshire, New Jersey, Oregon, Pennsylvania, Vermont, and West Virginia) grant their leading state law enforcement officials similar or related civil hate crime enforcement authority.[1]

For example, the Commonwealth of Massachusetts grants its attorney general the authority to obtain civil rights injunctions under a law known as the Massachusetts Civil Rights Act (MCRA).[2] The MCRA was enacted in 1979 to help Massachusetts law enforcement address more effectively the rising racial polarization and racially motivated harassment and violence, particularly in the City of Boston, in the aftermath of federal court-ordered desegregation of its public schools.[3] "These acts of violence continued into 1979, culminating in September with the shooting of a black high school student on a [Boston] playing field by white youths from a neighboring housing project."[4] The MCRA was enacted amid growing recognition that Massachusetts needed to supplement its criminal laws by providing its law enforcement with both a criminal civil rights law and new civil enforcement tools to help deter and prevent hate crimes that were tearing apart the fabric of Massachusetts neighborhoods, communities, and schools.[5]

Through the MCRA, the Massachusetts Attorney General is granted broad authority to obtain civil rights injunctions against persons who violate the rights of others, secured by federal or state law or constitution, through threats, intimidation, or coercion.[6] A violation of the attorney general's civil rights injunctive order constitutes a separate criminal offense, with enhanced criminal penalties imposed where bodily injury occurs.[7]

Similarly, California authorizes hate crime injunctions as part of its broad scheme of civil rights legislation written into both the California civil code and its penal code.[8] In enacting the civil injunction law, California's goal was to fill in the gaps left in its civil rights laws, by giving its law enforcement officials "clear effective authority to prevent acts of hate violence, and to deter such conduct by establishing serious criminal penalties." It empowers "the Attorney General, district attorney, or city attorney, to bring an action to enjoin crimes of hate violence when they are threatened."[9] Under the California law, civil rights injunctions may be enforced by criminal sanctions for violations.[10]

In New Hampshire, the attorney general may seek a civil hate crimes injunction or other form of equitable relief against a person where there is "probable cause to believe" that a person or persons, by some unlawful act, has interfered with or attempted to interfere with another person's rights under state or federal law because of the "race, color, religion, national origin, ancestry, sexual orientation, gender or disability" of the victim(s).[11] The law requires proof of "actual or threatened physical force or violence" or "actual or threatened damage to or trespass on property."[12] Violation of the injunction is a criminal offense.[13]

Pennsylvania's hate crime injunction statute empowers its district attorneys, or its attorney general, after consultation with a district attorney, to institute a civil action for injunctive or other equitable relief to protect persons or property, for conduct "relating to ethnic intimidation," based on the race, color, religion, or national origin of another, or to "institutional vandalism."[14] The circumstances permitting these injunction actions, however, are quite limited. Before seeking a hate crime injunction the offender must already have been convicted of the criminal offense of ethnic intimidation under Pennsylvania's criminal ethnic intimidation statute.[15] Generally, the hate crime injunction law enhances the penalty for persons who have already been convicted of committing specified offenses with "malicious intention toward the race, color, religion, or national origin" of the victim.[16] Violation of the injunction is a criminal offense.[17]

In Vermont, its legislature granted its state attorney general the authority to obtain an injunction when a "hate motivated crime" occurs based on the victim's "race, color, religion, national origin, sex, ancestry, age, service in the armed forces of the United States, handicap . . . , sexual orientation and gender identity, and perceived membership in any such group."[18] A violation of the hate crime injunction is a criminal offense.[19]

THE MASSACHUSETTS CIVIL RIGHTS ACT

The Massachusetts Civil Rights Act, through its broad enforcement authority, practical applicability, and compelling record of effectiveness, provides a model for state and national jurisdictions committed to adopting innovative laws for protecting civil rights and combating bias-motivated crimes.

Broad Enforcement Powers and Applicability

Although initially enacted by the Massachusetts legislature to respond to racially motivated violence, harassment, and intimidation, the civil sections of the MCRA were written as a law of broad applicability. The MCRA provides for the state attorney general, and, in a separate section, for private parties, to obtain injunctive relief for a violation of any right secured by the U.S. or Massachusetts state constitution or law, through threats, intimidation, or coercion.[20] The statutory grant of authority to the Massachusetts attorney general, who is the state's chief law enforcement officer, constituted an important symbol of the state's strong and unwavering commitment to justice and the civil rights of all individuals.

The civil component of the MCRA is the Massachusetts counterpart to 42 U.S.C. § 1983, the federal civil rights law. In contrast to the federal civil rights law, however, the MCRA addresses civil rights violations perpetrated by both private parties and individuals acting with governmental authority.[21] By omitting the state action requirement found in 42 U.S.C. § 1983, Massachusetts "greatly expand[ed] the reach" of the MCRA.[22] Importantly, for enforcement purposes, the MCRA is remedial in nature and therefore interpreted liberally to achieve its goals.[23] Additionally, unlike the federal civil rights law, the MCRA provides that when the Massachusetts attorney general obtains a civil rights injunction, a violation constitutes a criminal offense.[24]

Rather than punishing a person for past behavior, as occurs when violating a criminal law, civil rights injunctions provide perpetrators a warning, specifically informing them about the criminal consequences of engaging in the same or similar conduct in the future. For first-time offenders, agreeing to a hate crime injunction may also help them avoid criminal prosecution and a criminal record (that includes a civil rights violation). The written judicial warning (through the provisions of the injunctive order), along with the oral admonition from the court about the importance of compliance with the judge's order, helps perpetrators, particularly juveniles, resist peer pressure to continue to target others, and helps them refrain from further involvement in bias-related activities against the victim or others.

Enforcing Public Rights

When bringing an MCRA claim, the Massachusetts attorney general acts in accordance with broad common law and statutory powers to represent the public interest and enforce public rights.[25] Whenever the Massachusetts attorney general brings an MCRA case, the court will presume that the civil rights injunction action is brought in the public interest.[26] The attorney general often enforces the MCRA in circumstances where individual plaintiffs are unlikely or unwilling to come forward and seek judicial relief.[27] The attorney general also employs the MCRA to protect persons "not currently identifiable" from future unlawful conduct.[28] Through this law, the attorney general represents the public interest "in guarding against future violations of the MCRA."[29]

In order to establish a claim for preliminary relief under the MCRA, the attorney general must prove by a preponderance of the evidence that there is a likelihood there has been an MCRA violation and that a civil rights injunction will promote the public interest, or alternatively, that such relief will not adversely affect the public.[30] To obtain a permanent civil rights injunction, the Massachusetts attorney general must demonstrate a statutory violation by a preponderance of the evidence.[31] Additionally, to obtain either preliminary or permanent injunction relief, the attorney general needs to demonstrate the likelihood of repetition of the conduct, absent an injunction.[32] Unlike private litigants, however, the Massachusetts attorney general is not required to demonstrate irreparable harm absent an injunction, as private parties must establish.[33]

Because the MCRA is civil in nature and does not involve criminal penalties, the MCRA applies to minors.[34] The attorney general has obtained MCRA hate crime injunctions against juveniles as young as age 13. For offenders younger than 13, the attorney general has chosen to pursue nonjudicial remedies. Additionally, trial by jury is inapplicable, where the legal action filed by the attorney general is civil, not criminal, and only seeks to enjoin future violations of the MCRA, and not monetary damages on behalf of victims of civil rights violations.[35]

Protecting Victims and Communities

Since 1980, the Massachusetts attorney general has obtained many hundreds of civil rights injunctions to protect victims of bias-motivated crimes or civil rights violations where they are targeted, at least in part, based on their race, color, ethnicity, national origin, ancestry, gender, sexual orientation, disability, age, or religion. For example, since 1980, the Massachusetts Office of Attorney General, through its Civil Rights Division,[36] has protected, through MCRA injunctions, many hundreds, if not thousands, of residents of and visitors to Massachusetts victimized because of their race or ethnicity, including, for example, African Americans,[37] Asians, Hispanics, and whites, interracial couples and their friends, and Cape Verdean, Haitian, Arab, Greek, Portuguese, Italian, and Native Americans; persons targeted because of their religion, including Jews, Christians, Muslims, and Sikhs; and persons victimized because they are gay or lesbian, individuals with disabilities, AIDS victims, elderly persons, and women who have been victims of an alleged pattern of repeated verbal and physical abuse and harassment in dating or marital relationships, motivated by bias against women as a class.[38]

For example, in a precedent-setting case successfully defended on appeal in the Massachusetts Supreme Judicial Court, the attorney general successfully obtained a civil rights injunction against white juveniles allegedly engaged in two separate incidents of racially motivated threats and intimidation, including rock throwing, racial slurs, and chasing their young African American victims on public streets and at a public beach.[39]

After the tragic events of September 11, 2001, some perpetrators targeted members of the Arab, Muslim, Sikh, and South Asian communities for no other reason than they were, or were perceived to be, of the same ethnicity or religion as the terrorists. For example, the Civil Rights Division obtained a civil rights injunction against four women who, two days after September 11, allegedly threatened and attacked a young American woman of Iranian descent in her home. The four women allegedly shouted racial slurs and spit at her, and repeatedly punched and kicked her while screaming that she should leave the United States.[40] The Civil Rights Division also obtained a civil rights injunction in July 2002 against three teenagers who allegedly threw a Molotov cocktail onto the roof of a convenience store owned and occupied by a man of Indian descent who they believed was Arab or Muslim, for the express purpose of getting revenge for the September 11 attacks.[41] Similarly, in April 2003, the division obtained a civil rights injunction on behalf of two Indian students attending the University of Massachusetts at Lowell who, while walking home, were allegedly attacked by one white female and two white male teenagers. The white teens allegedly shouted obscenities at the Indian students and kicked and punched them in the face while shouting derogatory remarks about Osama Bin Laden.[42]

Additionally, based on the broad language of the MCRA, the Massachusetts attorney general has obtained MCRA injunctions against offenders who violate fundamental, constitutionally protected rights unrelated to bias-motivated conduct.[43]

In general, both because of its civil rights enforcement priorities, and because of limited resources, the Massachusetts Office of the Attorney General has historically not applied the MCRA to circumstances unrelated either to bias-motivated conduct or a violation of a fundamental federal or state protected constitutional right.[44]

Protecting Secured Rights

To obtain a MCRA civil rights injunction, the attorney general must demonstrate that a "secured" federal or state law or constitutional right was abridged through threats, intimidation, or coercion. Secured rights involve a broad array of state and federally protected rights.

In cases pursued by the attorney general or by private parties, Massachusetts courts have recognized various secured rights in finding a violation under the civil provisions of the MCRA.[45] They include the right to free speech and protected political activity;[46] freedom from retaliation for petitioning about prison conditions;[47] bodily integrity and freedom from police use of excessive force;[48] access to abortion services;[49] political leafleting and ballot access;[50] freedom from sexual harassment in employment;[51] to safely attend K-12 schools, to walk the sidewalks and public streets and parks (free from racially motivated threats and intimidation);[52] to contract without interference;[53] and as homeowners to use, build on, and enjoy their property;[54] freedom from unlawful arrests and from self-help evictions without due process;[55] and freedom of parents to educate their children by home schooling.[56]

Other secured rights protected by the MCRA identified in civil rights injunction cases brought by the Massachusetts attorney general[57] include the right to purchase, rent, and enjoy housing accommodations free from discrimination;[58] the right to live where one chooses;[59] access to and enjoyment of public accommodations such as public streets, parks, restaurants, businesses, and public transportation stations and facilities free from discrimination;[60] the right to attend public schools and institutions for higher education free from discrimination;[61] and to contract and to work and perform employment duties free from discrimination.[62]

Broad Definition of Violations

To violate the MCRA, the Massachusetts attorney general must establish that the offender engaged in "threats," "intimidation," or "coercion" when interfering or attempting to interfere with a federal or state secured right. Proof of threats, intimidation, or coercion constitute separate and independent bases for issuance of civil rights injunctive relief.[63]

To achieve the MCRA's important remedial goals, the proscribed conduct "may take on many forms" and refers to many types of conduct and activities.[64] Although the courts have not adopted a comprehensive definition, they have provided almost three decades of guidance as to the meaning of "threats, intimidation, or coercion" under the MCRA.[65]

Massachusetts courts expansively define "threat" as "the intentional exertion of pressure to make another fearful or apprehensive of injury or harm."[66] A threat to use lawful means to reach an intended result, however, is not actionable.[67] Intimidation is broadly defined as placing someone "in fear for the purpose of compelling or deterring conduct."[68] Coercion is expansively defined as "the application to another of such force, either physical or moral, as to constrain him to do against his will something he would not otherwise have done."[69]

In order to prove threats, intimidation, or coercion under the MCRA, evidence of an actual or potential physical confrontation, accompanied by a threat of harm is generally necessary.[70] An MCRA violation may also occur when evidence of an actual or physical confrontation between two people deprives a third person of his or her protected rights.[71] To violate the MCRA, however, the threatened harm or injury does not always need to involve a physical confrontation.[72] But a violation must include "some act by a defendant which, objectively viewed, would cause a person not to exercise a constitutional right or deprive that person of that right."[73] Similar to proving "threats" under the MCRA, "coercion" is not limited to actual or attempted physical force.[74] For example, moral force may raise a claim of coercion.[75] Additionally, economic coercion, standing alone, may violate the MCRA.[76] Based on its familiarity with the coercive economic, sometimes violent, tactics used during the struggle for civil rights in the South, Massachusetts courts have held that "economic pressure may be deployed in any number of commercial settings in the absence of actual or threatened physical force to coerce individuals to forgo the exercise of their secured rights."[77]

Indirect Violation of Secured Rights

In general, the MCRA is inapplicable to direct violations of an individual's civil rights, unless the direct violation, by itself, also involves threats, intimidation, or coercion. "[D]irect preemptive acts that do not seek to coerce a plaintiff to do or not do something," are distinguishable from cases involving threats, intimidation, or coercion in the denial of secured rights.[78] Liability under the MCRA may be established, however, when direct action by definition includes threats against or intimidation or coercion of a particular individual.[79] For example, excessive force by police officers was construed to constitute "threatening and intimidating physical acts," and therefore was covered by the MCRA.[80] The Massachusetts Supreme Judicial Court also stated that if a defendant has "some further purpose" in causing a deprivation of rights, conduct may contravene the MCRA.[81] Although not altogether clear, it also appears that in limited circumstances, a court may grant injunctive relief under the MCRA, where, for example, in engaging in a direct violation, a defendant acts out of malice or personal animosity.[82]

Responsibility for Natural Consequences of Conduct

Importantly, to obtain an MCRA injunction, the Massachusetts attorney general does not have to prove that a perpetrator acted with the specific intent to violate another person's secured rights. Rather, the MCRA "requires only the degree of intent 'that makes a [person] responsible for the natural consequences of his action.'"[83] The MCRA is satisfied if the natural consequence of the defendant's actions was to threaten, intimidate, or coerce the victim in the exercise of his or her rights.[84]

Although the MCRA does not require proof of specific intent, it does operate "almost entirely within the realm of intentional behavior."[85] Negligent conduct itself is insufficient to establish an MCRA violation.[86]

Applying a Reasonable Person Standard

The Massachusetts attorney general does not need to prove that a victim subjectively felt threatened, intimidated, or coerced by the defendant's conduct, because the state of mind of the victim is not controlling. Rather, Massachusetts courts apply an objective standard of whether a reasonable person would be threatened, intimidated, or coerced in the same circumstances to determine whether an action rises to an MCRA violation.[87]

An MCRA injunction case is "unlike a criminal case in which proof of the victim's state of mind may be indispensable in making the prosecution's case. We are not concerned here with the rights of a criminal defendant, but only with a civil action for an injunction" with no claim by the victims for an award of damages.[88] However, how an actual victim responds to an attempted or actual civil rights violation may serve as a guide to how a reasonable person would react in the same or similar circumstances.[89]

Holding Accountable Less Involved Hate Crime Participants

For purposes of issuing civil rights injunctions, an important enforcement feature of the MCRA is that a court may hold legally responsible less active hate crime contributors as participants in a joint venture or enterprise. On many occasions, the civil rights injunction is the only means to reach the conduct of certain participants where law enforcement determines it cannot successfully criminally prosecute participants less directly involved in the alleged hate crime.

Under the MCRA, even where a person does not directly violate a victim's rights, but shares the mental state of the other participants, "the act of each participant in the enterprise is chargeable vicariously against the rest."[90] An individual aiding or abetting a violation is also liable under the MCRA.[91] Furthermore, if the conduct is based on a common design or understanding, even a tacit one, the conduct of the active participant is deemed as an action engaged in by all the defendants.[92]

Factors in Seeking Judicial Relief

The Massachusetts Office of the Attorney General, through its Civil Rights Division, has taken into account various factors in determining whether to pursue an MCRA injunction case.[93] Generally, however, the decision whether to file a case is based on an assessment of the need for a preliminary injunction. Historically, the following factors, separately and in combination, have increased the likelihood the Civil Rights Division will seek to obtain a preliminary (or final) civil rights injunction order: (1) where the conduct against the victim occurred recently; (2) the civil rights violation is more serious than minor; (3) the conduct alleged reflects significant animus against the victim based on prejudice; (4) the offender has not shown any remorse for the conduct or its consequences; (5) the perpetrator has participated in prior hate crimes or previously committed civil rights violations against the victim or others; (6) a reasonable possibility exists that the victim and perpetrator will see or come in close proximity to each other (for example, because they live in the same neighborhood, are employed in the same workplace, attend the same school, shop in the same grocery store, walk the same streets, or travel to work or school by the same means of transportation); (7) there is a reasonable liklihood that the perpetrator will engage in additional civil rights violations against the victim or other persons who share similar legally protected characteristics to the victim; (8) the offender is already convicted of the hate crime, but is not incarcerated, or is imprisoned for only a brief period; (9) the perpetrator is a member of or associated with an organized hate group; (10) a court is likely to issue an injunction if it is sought; (11) the injunction is likely to have a deterrent effect on the defendant's future conduct; and (12) where the defendant is reasonably likely to violate the injunctive order, the increased penalties for its violation will improve the prospects for a more prolonged incarceration.

Additionally, when a criminal hate crime prosecution is pending for the same conduct, the following factors generally have increased the likelihood that the Civil Rights Division will seek to obtain a civil rights injunction order: (1) a long delay in the commencement of the criminal trial is anticipated; (2) the police, prosecutor, or victim believes that the pending criminal proceedings or the stay-away order issued pending resolution of the criminal charges will not adequately deter the offender from contacting, communicating with, or approaching near the victim or witnesses, or engaging in violations of civil rights against others before the criminal case's conclusion; (3) a conviction is unlikely; (4) more than a brief imprisonment after conviction is unlikely; and (5) the prosecutor does not articulate a reasonable concern that the civil proceedings will adversely affect the pending criminal prosecution, including the prosecutor's preparation for the criminal trial.

Tailoring Injunctions

Massachusetts courts are provided wide discretion in determining the appropriate scope of MCRA civil rights injunctive relief, including the terms and conditions governing the defendant's future conduct with the victim and others.

"The fact that [an] action [is] brought and an injunction [is] sought by the Attorney General, an elected official charged with the duty of protecting the public interest, lends support to the reasonableness of the judge's exercise of discretion," in circumscribing the future conduct of defendants.[94]

Generally, MCRA injunctions enhance the physical and emotional safety and well-being of victims by prohibiting the perpetrator or anyone acting in concert with the perpetrator from future attempts at interfering with or denying the secured rights of the victim through threats, intimidation, or coercion. If the conduct involves racially motivated threats and physical intimidation, for example, the order will commonly prohibit the perpetrator, or others acting with the perpetrator, from threatening, intimidating, or coercing, or causing or attempting to cause injury or damage to, the named victim and the person or property of any other person because of that person's race, color, or national origin, or the race, color, or national origin of any person with whom that person associates.

MCRA injunctions often prohibit perpetrators from approaching the victim, his or her residence, neighborhood, or place of employment or school (within 100 feet is the usual distance, but up to 500 feet has been granted in appropriate circumstances).[95] Injunctive provisions also protect witnesses, family members, friends, and associates of the victim. An injunction also commonly prohibits a perpetrator from communicating with the victim and his or her witnesses, except through defense counsel or through the attorney general's office. It may also require prior notification of the attorney general's office before the perpetrator's filing of any court action against the victim.[96]

The Record of Compliance

After a hate crime injunction issues, Civil Rights Division attorneys closely monitor compliance. In addition to periodic outreach to victims and police, division attorneys strongly encourage victims, police, and community members to notify the division if they believe a possible violation of an injunction has occurred.

The almost three decades of documented history of the attorney general's use of MCRA injunctions in Massachusetts demonstrates that civil hate crime injunctions in fact achieve their important deterrent and prevention goals. Almost all of the many hundreds of defendants have complied with their civil rights injunction orders, even though many of those orders remain in effect for many years. As a result, since the first MCRA injunction issued, the attorney general (or by agreement, a district attorney's office) has prosecuted only about 30 individuals for an alleged violation of a temporary, preliminary, or permanent civil rights injunctive order. Importantly, as discussed below, almost all of those prosecutions involved defendants who allegedly invaded and blockaded health clinics providing abortion services, rather than defendants allegedly involved in bias-motivated conduct.[97]

Offenders Who Violate Injunctions

When an MCRA violation occurs, however, the attorney general or a district attorney may prosecute for the breach of the injunction's provisions as a statutory violation or through criminal contempt proceeding.[98]

In order to prove a violation of a superior court's temporary, preliminary, or permanent civil rights injunctive order, the commonwealth must prove that the court had issued a civil rights injunction that provided the defendant clear and unequivocal prohibitions; that the order was in effect on the date of the alleged violation of the injunction; that the defendant knew of the order, either by in-hand service of the order (whether or not it is read) or by actual notice of the order; that the defendant clearly and intentionally disobeyed that order, and that the defendant was able to obey it.[99]

Unlike criminal hate crime prosecutions—where courts often sentence guilty defendants to probation, not prison—defendants are commonly incarcerated when they violate a court's MCRA injunction. For example, in 1982, the attorney general obtained one of its first MCRA civil rights injunctions. Eight white youths allegedly interfered, through racial threats, harassment, and assault, with the fair housing rights of two black families residing near a park in the Hyde Park section of Boston. The defendants consented to the court issuing a civil rights injunction following the Civil Rights Division's presentation of their case for a preliminary injunction. Part of the court order prohibited the defendants from harassing the victims

or congregating on the black victims' street or at or near the park where
their home was located. Three days after the injunction issued, one of the
defendants violated the injunction by standing in the park across the street
from one of the black family's houses and began yelling racial epithets at
one of the black families. He was promptly tried for an injunction violation,
found guilty, and sentenced to serve 60 days in a house of corrections.[100]
"Neighbors reported that thereafter the neighborhood was more peaceful
than it had been in years."[101]

Twenty of the 30 prosecutions for violation of an MCRA injunction involve defendants who allegedly blockaded and invaded abortion clinics in
violation of a preliminary or a permanent MCRA injunctive order. Some of
these individuals were not specifically named as parties in the court's order,
but were prosecuted for allegedly participating in violating the court order
with the named defendants. Eighteen of the 20 prosecutions were successful.[102] Sentences ranged from 60 days to 2.5 years.[103]

Police Collaboration

Police trained in hate crime enforcement work collaboratively with criminal prosecutors from district attorneys' offices and with assistant attorneys
general from the Civil Rights Division, to help determine the appropriateness for criminal charges and for seeking a civil hate crime injunction when
unlawful bias-motivated activity is reported. The responding officers who
initially arrive at the crime scene and the investigating officers who arrive
later to engage in a more comprehensive investigation of the incident both
play important, complementary roles.[104]

Upon arriving at the crime scene, responding officers first attempt to
restore order and take appropriate enforcement measures against the
perpetrator(s). The responding officers then attempt to identify the victims,
as well as any witnesses with knowledge of the crime, protect the evidence
at the crime scene, identify any injured person, and take steps to ensure
that medical assistance is provided. Attention is also given to address the
security of the victim. The responding officer is expected to conduct a preliminary investigation, including determining if any "bias indicators" are
present, clues that indicate the likelihood the crime was, at least in part, bias-
motivated. The responding officers must document such information in a
detailed police incident report. If any bias indicator is present, best practice
would dictate that the responding officer immediately contact a supervising
officer, who refers the case, where appropriate, for a hate crime investigation.
The police supervisor and the records department (as a second-level safeguard) are also expected to review all police incident reports and then refer
reports of all potential civil rights incidents (including those with "bias indicators") to the department's specialized civil rights unit, or the department's

specially trained civil rights officer, for investigation.[105] Police attention to the possibility that a civil rights violation occurred is essential for ensuring an appropriate law enforcement response and evaluation of the case. Investigating officers conduct comprehensive interviews with all victims and witnesses at the scene and canvass the neighborhood for additional witnesses. They marshal all evidence, including photographing, collecting, labeling, and submitting all physical evidence and all graffiti or markings present at the scene, consistent with department procedures.

Police work closely with the district attorney's office to determine appropriate criminal changes and whether the prosecutor has developed a legally adequate criminal hate crime case. As described in more detail below, at the same time, the investigating officer is working closely with an assistant attorney general from the Civil Rights Division of the Massachusetts attorney general's office, in investigating the incident to help determine the need and appropriateness for obtaining a civil hate crime injunction.

The investigating officer also maintains ongoing communication with the victim, ensuring that he and members of his family are safe and are receiving adequate assistance, while providing information as to the status of the investigation and the charges.

MCRA INJUNCTIONS OFFER MANY ADVANTAGES TO CRIMINAL PROSECUTIONS

In certain circumstances a civil hate crime injunction is a superior tool to criminal prosecutions in combating and deterring civil rights violators and criminal hate crime conduct.[106]

Lower Burden of Proof

In Massachusetts, even where law enforcement does not have a sufficient evidentiary basis to pursue a civil rights violation criminally, or where prosecutors are unable to establish the perpetrator's criminal hate crime violation "beyond a reasonable doubt," they may successfully proceed civilly to obtain a hate crimes injunction under a civil "preponderance of the evidence" standard.[107] In addition, unlike the criminal civil rights section of the MCRA,[108] where the prosecution must prove that the defendant acted with "force or threat of force," to obtain a civil rights injunction, the Massachusetts attorney general need only prove by a preponderance of the evidence that the defendant acted by "threats, intimidation, or coercion." In contrast to a civil injunctive case under the MCRA, where an objective standard is applied, in a criminal prosecution under the MCRA "proof of a victim's state of mind may be indispensable in making the prosecution's case."[109]

Flexibility of Orders

Injunctions offer the advantage of tailoring a remedy to an individual offender and the particular circumstances presented in the case. The MCRA provides Massachusetts courts, in effect, with the power to create a criminal law individualized to the perpetrator and the circumstances, including the nature and reasons for the prior conduct, the age, history, and motivation of the defendant, and the needs of the victim. Additionally, contrary to our criminal justice system, where, for due process purposes, members of the public are presumed to have notice of our criminal laws and the potential consequences for their violation, MCRA hate crime injunction orders provide defendants actual notice of the prohibited conduct that, if disregarded, will result in a criminal violation.

Finally, hate crime injunction orders may also include provisions that require participation in awareness, bias-reduction, or community service programs that encourage perpetrators to better understand the harm they have caused, recognize and modify the bigoted and hateful attitudes that motivated their unlawful behavior, and help develop the skills and strategies needed to succeed in their diverse schools, workplaces and communities.

Prompt Relief

Civil hate crime injunctive relief also has the added value of providing the victim and community with a prompt governmental response that provides immediate legal protections for the victim and those who reside in or visit the victim's community and share the victim's racial, ethnic, or other personal characteristic that motivated the bias-motivated violation. A criminal prosecution may take many months, and even at times years, while a court, where necessary, may issue a MCRA civil hate crime injunction within days or weeks after a hate crime incident occurs.

More Efficient Judicial Process

For purposes of obtaining a temporary restraining order or preliminary injunction, the attorney general's Civil Rights Division prepares the victim's and witnesses' affidavits. The division prepares and files court pleadings, including the complaint, affidavits, a proposed court order, and a memorandum in support of an injunction. If a juvenile is a defendant, a motion for appointment of a guardian ad litem, to represent the interest of the juvenile, is also prepared.[110]

Once the court pleadings are filed, a short order of notice is issued by the clerk of court, requiring the assistant attorney general assigned the case to provide notice to the defendant of the date of the preliminary injunction hearing, which usually occurs only days after the complaint is filed.

The attorney general has requested a temporary restraining order only in the few extraordinary cases that raise the most serious threats of ongoing violence. In those emergency circumstances, the court commonly will hear the request for a temporary order on the day the case is filed in an *ex-parte* hearing, where the attorney general requests an injunctive order without notice to or the presence of the defendant. This temporary order may remain in effect for a maximum of 10 days. A hearing on a motion for preliminary injunction, with notice to the defendant of the hearing, must follow as soon as possible, but not to exceed 10 days.[111]

If there is a parallel criminal case pending or contemplated, the Civil Rights Division will notify the district attorney's office that the attorney general's office is considering pursuing a hate crime injunction and will discuss whether pursuing an injunction may impede or negatively affect the criminal prosecution. On a very few occasions, the attorney general's office has delayed filing an injunctive action until completion of the trial on the criminal charges, where the district attorney has stated that the filing of the civil case could seriously compromise the prosecution.

Prior to the victim or witness reviewing or signing a finalized affidavit, the Civil Rights Division prepares and sends a draft affidavit to the assigned assistant district attorney for review. The draft affidavit is based on police reports and assistant attorney general interviews that occur with the same police officers assigned to the criminal investigation. The assistant district attorney reviews the draft affidavits to determine whether they are accurate and consistent with the information the district attorney's office received from the victim and witnesses. Since the attorney general and district attorney rely on the same police officers and police investigation for their cases, it is rare that evidentiary conflicts arise. Often, because of the specialized expertise of the Civil Rights Division's assistant attorneys general in hate crime matters, and their ability to focus on the case as an investigatory priority, the civil hate crime investigation assists the assistant district attorney in her preparation of the criminal case.

The court in general relies upon the victim, witness, and police affidavits in issuing temporary or preliminary relief. Perpetrators seldom file an opposing affidavit or an affidavit from a witness. Defendants also rarely request to testify at a court injunction hearing.[112] The assistant attorney general and defense counsel, and at times defendants on the relatively rare occasion they are unrepresented, then argue the appropriateness of the court issuing preliminary injunctive relief. At times defendants have challenged, generally without success, the evidence related to their identification or their bias-motivation, or their role or participation in the incident. On occasion they have argued, unsuccessfully, that an MCRA injunction is not warranted, claiming that the case involves an isolated incident that is not at all likely to repeat. On some occasions, defendants have challenged the attorney general's proposed injunction provisions, arguing that some restrictions are unfair, unnecessary, or overbroad. In some cases, the attorney general or the court has agreed to reasonable modifications of restrictions (e.g., geographic limitations, such as streets near the victim's residence on which the defendant is prohibited from walking or driving) that do not undermine the goal of protecting the victim and others.

On some occasions, a civil hate crime injunction defendant has sought discovery in the civil injunctive action, after a preliminary injunction has issued but while the criminal action is pending. The attorney general has successfully obtained protective orders for the stay of discovery pending the trial on the criminal charges. In filing motions to stay discovery, the attorney general's criminal bureau will typically represent the interests of the district attorney's office, while the Civil Rights Division represents the interests of the attorney general.

In these discovery motions, the Commonwealth of Massachusetts has successfully argued that the deposition of the victim will unjustly permit the defendant to circumvent the limits of pretrial discovery in the pending criminal action and thereby enable him to obtain discovery in a case in which he is otherwise not entitled; that the defendant will not be prejudiced if discovery is held in abeyance during the pendency of the criminal action, since the actual trial on a request for a final injunction order in general is not scheduled for a prolonged period, even years after the preliminary injunction issues; and that the protective order would have a chilling effect on the attorney general's statutory authority to seek civil rights injunctions.[113]

On most occasions, the superior court has been satisfied with the commonwealth's pleadings and issues injunctive relief at the conclusion of the preliminary injunction hearing. The defendant is ordered to remain in court until the formal injunctive order is prepared so the assistant attorney general may ensure that the police serve the injunction on the defendant in-hand, so the defendant may not later dispute receiving the order. In only a handful of cases, the commonwealth has failed in its effort to obtain requested temporary or preliminary injunctive relief. On a few occasions, the Civil Rights Division has been required to present witnesses at a preliminary injunction hearing, in addition to engaging in oral argument. This has arisen in cases, for example, of disputed identification of the defendant, or when the facts of who initiated the incident are hotly disputed.

On most occasions, once a preliminary injunction issues, defendants have agreed to consent to the entry of a time-limited final court injunctive orders. Defendants have consented, for example, to a final order remaining in effect for 3-, 5-, 7-, and 10-year periods. In the most serious cases, defendants have consented to injunction orders that will remain in effect permanently. The consent agreement obviates the need for a trial on the merits, and, most often, a finding or admission of liability by the defendant. Where a defendant does not enter a consent agreement after preliminary relief issues, investigations may continue, including the use of formal discovery. However, cases commonly remain largely dormant until a scheduled date for a pretrial conference approaches. At that point, an assistant attorney general attempts to negotiate a final judgment by consent. In a relatively small percentage of cases, defendants have refused settlement and have requested a final trial on the merits. None have succeeded in prevailing at this stage.[114]

Criminalizes Otherwise Lawful Conduct

In civil hate crime injunctive actions, courts criminalize conduct that is not otherwise criminal in nature. For example, an MCRA injunctive order may prohibit a defendant from entering a particular neighborhood or street where the prior violation occurred, subject to criminal sanction for violation. It may also criminalize future oral, written, or electronic communications with the victim or his or her family. If the defendant then enters that prohibited neighborhood or communicates with the victim, he is subject, if convicted, to a sentence of 2.5 years of incarceration.[115]

Broader Than Stay-Away Orders

In Massachusetts, a court may issue a stay-away order during the pendency of a criminal prosecution, which prohibits the defendant from communicating with or approaching the victim pending the criminal trial. Violation of a stay-away order, however, may only result in bail revocation and the court ordering the defendant into custody pending trial. On the other hand, a violation of the MCRA civil hate crime injunction constitutes an independent criminal violation, which prosecutors may separately charge and pursue. Another advantage of an injunction to a stay-away order is that the court may prohibit conduct not only in respect to the victim in that case, but also in respect to a whole potential class of similarly situated victims.

Increases Criminal Penalties

An additional benefit to obtaining an injunction is that an injunction may increase the defendant's exposure to more substantial criminal penalties for the same conduct. For example, in Massachusetts, a charge of simple assault and battery, a misdemeanor offense, would subject an offender to a maximum sentence of 2.5 years in a house of correction. If the defendant engages in the exact same conduct after a MCRA civil hate crime injunction issues, and if any bodily harm occurs, he is subject to a 10-year felony conviction, served in state prison, as well as subject to the general criminal law misdemeanor charge of assault and battery.[116]

Additionally, where a defendant commits a misdemeanor hate crime involving, for example, an assault and battery, without bodily injury, the defendant is subject to a maximum *one year* of incarceration for violating the state's criminal civil rights statute.[117] Where this same conduct is prohibited by a MCRA hate crime injunction, however, the defendant is subject to a maximum penalty of *2.5 years* in a house of corrections.[118]

Applies to Juveniles

Another substantial advantage of the use of a civil rights injunction is its applicability to juveniles. Juveniles are fully subject to the civil rights injunction procedures in the superior court, the state's highest trial-level court.[119] The formality of legal proceedings in the superior court underscores for juvenile offenders (and victims) that their case is serious and is taken seriously by law enforcement and the courts. Furthermore, if the attorney general (or a district attorney) pursues criminal contempt charges for a violation of a civil rights injunction, the superior court judge may, in her discretion, conduct the contempt proceedings against the juvenile in the superior court, rather than transferring the matter to the juvenile court.[120]

As the state's highest trial-level court, the formality of the session in superior court stands in sharp contrast to the typical juvenile court proceeding. The formality becomes even more pronounced in circumstances where, as often occurs, the offender receives a personal warning from the judge about the consequence of violating the court's own hate crimes injunctive order.

Increases Arrest Powers

MCRA injunctions provide law enforcement officers with the clear guidance they need to determine when they can arrest for a violation, particularly when the defendant violates communication or geographic restrictions (e.g., speaking to the victim or walking within 100 feet of the victim's residence), or where harassing or threatening behavior is involved. Furthermore, the police are provided special power to arrest without a warrant for violation of an injunctive order when there is probable cause to believe there is a violation of the injunction.[121] Otherwise, under Massachusetts common law, unless a misdemeanor offense breaches the peace and occurs in the presence of a police officer, he or she has no right to arrest without a warrant.[122]

CONCLUSION

Hate crimes remain a major public safety and community concern. They polarize communities and can lead to a cycle of retaliatory violence, threatening public safety and requiring the expenditure of substantial law enforcement resources. Civil hate crime injunctions are not only a valuable supplement to criminal prosecutions, but where criminal prosecutions fail, are inapplicable, or result in minor penalties, hate crime injunctions often provide law enforcement its most effective weapon in combating the hate-motivated conduct that tears at the social fabric of our schools, neighborhoods, and communities.

In addition to criminal hate crime laws, every state and national jurisdiction is strongly encouraged to provide its attorney general, or other leading law enforcement officials, with the authority to obtain civil hate crime injunctions. As described in some detail, states and other national jurisdictions may look to the Massachusetts civil rights injunction law, the MCRA, as a model law and practical civil enforcement scheme to deter bias-motivated crimes and related civil rights violations.

The experience of Massachusetts and other states that have applied similar civil hate crime enforcement laws demonstrates that hate crime injunctions are an indispensable enforcement and deterrent weapon. They help protect victims, decrease the level of fear in neighborhoods and schools where they occur, and assist communities in calming racial and ethnic tensions. Providing our law enforcement leaders with the authority to obtain hate crime injunctions, and employing them effectively, not only sends a powerful message reaffirming our intolerance for acts of hate-motivated terror and intimidation, but is also a practical necessity if we are to succeed in our fight for civil rights and against crimes of bias and bigotry.

NOTES

1. California: Cal. Civil Code 52.1(a); Florida: Fla. Stat. Ann. §§ 760.51; Maine: 5 M.R.S.A. § 4681; Massachusetts: M.G.L. c. 12, § 11H (West 2002); New Hampshire: N.H. Rev. Stat. Ann. §§ 354-B et seq.; New Jersey: N.J. Stat. Ann. § 10:6–2; Oregon: Or. Rev. Stat. Ann. § 30.200; Pennsylvania: 42 Pa. Cons. Stat. Ann. § 8309(b); Vermont: Vt. Stat. Ann. Tit. 13, § 1458 et seq.; and West Virginia: W.V.C.§ 5–11–20.

2. 1979 Mass. Acts 801 (approved November 16, 1979, effective February 1980). Mass. Gen. L. c. 12, § 11H, grants the Massachusetts attorney general civil rights enforcement authority. A second section of the MCRA, Mass. Gen. L. c. 12, § 11I, confers a private cause of action to persons whose rights have been interfered with in the manner described in § 11H, including the right to seek civil rights injunctions. A third section of the MCRA, M.G.L. c. 265, § 37, established the first Massachusetts criminal civil rights law (West 2002).

3. *Morgan v. Hennigan*, 379 F.Supp 410 (D. Mass. 1974); see *Batchelder v. Allied Stores Corp.*, 393 Mass. 819, 821, 473 N.E. 2d 1128, 1230 (1985); see also Marjorie Heins, Massachusetts Civil Rights Law, 76 Mass. L. Rev. 77, 81 (1991); Anthony P. Sager, *Rights Protected By The Massachusetts Civil Rights Act Against Interference on Account of Race or Color*, 17 Suffolk U. L. Rev. 53, 54–56 (1983).

4. Sager, 17 Suffolk U. L. Rev. at 55.

5. *Batchelder*, 393 Mass. at 821-823, 473 N.E. at 1129–30; Sager, 17 Suffolk U. L. Rev. at 45–56.

6.   See Mass. Gen. L. c. 12, § 11H (West 2002). The attorney general, however, may not seek monetary damages on behalf of the hate crime victim or the Commonwealth of Massachusetts. See Scott Harshbarger and Richard W. Cole, "The Attorney General's Sponsored Bill to Amend the Massachusetts Civil Rights Act," *Boston University Public Interest Law Journal*, vol. 3, no. 2 (Fall 1993). The author intends to highlight the reach and important law enforcement benefits of the application of the Massachusetts civil rights injunction law, because of his extensive familiarity with its use through 16 years of supervising the enforcement of Mass. Gen. L. c. 12, § 11H while in civil rights leadership positions in the Massachusetts Office of Attorney General, and because the MCRA is an example of a model law and practical approach that other states and countries should consider adopting in granting its attorney general or other key law enforcement officials with important civil enforcement powers to combat hate crimes and related civil rights violations.

7.   Where a violation results in "bodily injury," the defendant is subject to 10 years in state prison, rather than 2.5 years in a house of corrections for any other violation. See Mass. Gen, L. c. 12, §§ 11H and 11J (West 2002).

8.   Parts of California's civil rights legislation are known as the Ralph Civil Rights Act, and parts are known as the Tom Bane Civil Rights Act. Cal. Civil Code Section 52.1 was enacted as part of Assembly Bill 63 in 1987, and is part of the Bane Act. See *Stamps C. Superior Court Of Los Angeles County, B183741 (CA 2/27/06) (CA. 2006)*, at 6.

9.   *Stamps*, at 7. California, Florida, Maine, Massachusetts, and New Jersey's hate crime injunction laws provide that the attorney general (and in California, also the district and city attorneys) may bring an action where a person "interferes or attempts to interfere with" another person's secured rights under the U.S. and state constitutions and laws by "threats, intimidation or coercion." See California: Cal. Civil Code 52.1(a); Florida: Fla. Stat. Ann. §§ 760.51; 5 New Jersey: N.J. Stat. Ann. § 10:6–2. In addition to authorizing the state attorney general to bring hate crime injunction actions, California and Pennsylvania provide their district attorneys with this authority. California: Cal. Civil Code 52.1(a); Pennsylvania: 42 Pa. Cons. Stat. Ann. § 8309(b). Oregon's "civil injunction statute" authorizes any district attorney, upon reasonable belief, to bring a civil claim for such relief as may be necessary to restrain or prevent a violation of either of its criminal bias-motivated intimidation statutes. Oregon: ORS 30.200, Unlike the other nine states with civil hate crime injunction laws, however, the Oregon state attorney general has no such authority.

10.   Cal. Civil Code § 52(i) and Penal Code §422.9.

11.   N.H. Rev. Stat. Ann. §§ 354-B et seq. Under the New Hampshire law, "threatened physical force" and "threatened damage to or trespass on property, . . . is a communication, by physical conduct or by declaration, of an intent to inflict harm on a person or a person's property by some unlawful act with a purpose to terrorize or coerce."

12.   Maine, New Hampshire, and West Virginia use similar terms to define a violation: "actual or threatened physical force or violence" or "actual or threatened damage to or trespass on property." Maine: M.R.S.A. § 4681; New Hampshire: N.H. Rev. Stat. Ann. §§ 354-B B:1I, West Virginia: W.V.C. § 5–11–20.

13.   N.H. Rev. Stat. Ann. § 354-B:4:I.

14.   See 42 Pa. Cons. Stat. Ann. § 8309(b), referring to 18 Pa.C.S. § 2710; and 18 Pa.C.S. § 3307, respectively.

15.   See *Commonwealth v. Magliocco*, 883 A.2d. 479 (PA 2005) (a defendant's conviction for ethnic intimidation, 18 Pa.C.S. § 2710, could not be sustained in an instance where

the defendant had been charged with, but acquitted of, the predicate crime which is an element of the offense).

16.   Id.

17.   See 42 Pa. Cons. Stat. Ann. § 8309(d)

18.   Vt. Stat. Ann. Tit. 13, § 1458 et seq. ("Injunctions Against Hate Motivated Crimes").

19.   Vt. Stat. Ann. Tit. 13, § 1465.

20.   See, for example, *Bell v. Mazza*, 394 Mass. 176, 181–182, 474 N.E.2d 1111, 1114–1115 (1985); *Commonwealth v. Guilfoyle*, 402 Mass 130, 134, 521 N.E.2d 984, 986 (1988); Mass. Gen. L. c. 12, §§ 11H and 11I (West 2002).

21.   Mass. Gen. L. c. 12, § 11H, granting the Massachusetts attorney general civil rights enforcement authority, states in relevant part:

> Whenever any person or persons, whether or not acting under color of law, inter-
> fere by threats, intimidation or coercion, or attempt to interfere by threats, intimi-
> dation, or coercion, with the exercise or enjoyment by any other person or persons
> of rights secured by the constitution or laws of the United States, or of rights se-
> cured by the constitution or laws of the Commonwealth, the attorney general may
> bring a civil action for injunctive or other appropriate relief in order to protect the
> peaceable exercise or enjoyment of the right or rights secured.

22.   *Batchelder v. Allied Stores Corp.* 393 Mass 819, 822–23, 473 N.E.2d 1128, 1130–1131 (1985); *Ayasli v. Armstrong*, 56 Mass. App. Ct. 740, 749–750, 780 N.E.2d 926, 934 (Mass. App. Ct. 2002). The Massachusetts legislature, however, "did not intend to cre-ate [for private parties] a vast constitutional [and statutory] tort." *Bally v. Northeastern Univ.*, 403 Mass. 713, 718, 532 N.E.2d 49, 52 (1989); *Ayasli v. Armstrong*, 56 Mass. App. Ct. at 749–750, 780 N.E.2d at 934.

23.   *Batchelder*, 473 N.E.2d at1130; 393 Mass. at 822, 473 N.E.2d at 822; *Bell v. Mazza*, 394 Mass. at 181–182, 474 N.E.2d at 1114–1115.

24.   Mass. Gen. L. c. 12, §§ 11H and 11J (West 2002).

25.   *Commonwealth v. Mass. CRINC*, 392 Mass. 79, 88-89, 466 N.E. 792, 797–98 (1984).

26.   *Commonwealth v. Adams*, 416 Mass. 558, 566-567, 624 N.E.2d 102, 107 (1993).

27.   *Planned Parenthood League of Mass, Inc. v. Blake*, 417 Mass. 467, 479-480, 479 n.13, 631 N.E.2d 985, 992–993, cert. denied, 513 U.S. 868, 115 S.Ct. 188, 130 L.Ed.2d 122 (1994).

28.   Id., 417 Mass. at 479, 631 N.E.2d at 992.

29.   *Planned Parenthood League*, 417 Mass. at 479, 631 N.E.2d at 992.

30.   *Commonwealth v. Guilfoyle*, 402 Mass. at 135-136, 521 N.E.2d. at 987, *Common-wealth v. Mass. CRINC*, 392 Mass. at 88-89, 466 N.E. at 798.

31.   *Commonwealth v. Guilfoyle*, 402 Mass at 136, 521 N.E.2d at 987.

32.   *Commonwealth v. Adams*, 416 Mass. at 566, 624 N.E.2d at107; *Reproductive Rights Network v. President of the University of Massachusetts*, 45 Mass. App. Ct. 495, 500, 699 N.E.2d 829, 834 (Mass. App. Ct. 1998).

33.   *Commonwealth v. Mass. CRINC*, 392 Mass. at 88-89, 46 N.E.2d at798; *Common-wealth v. Guilfoyle*, 402 Mass. at 135, 521 N.E.2d. at 987.

34.   *Commonwealth v. Guilfoyle*, 402 Mass. at 135, 521 N.E.2d. at 987.

35.   Id.

36.   The Civil Rights Division was established by state statute, Mass. Gen. L. c 12, §
11A (West 2002).

37.   See, for example, *Commonwealth v. Guilfoyle*, 402 Mass. at 131–33, 521 N.E.2d. at
984–85.

38.   See Commonwealth of Massachusetts, Reports of the Attorney General, for the
Fiscal Year Ending June 30, 1992, to Fiscal Year Ending June 30, 2007, Civil Rights
Division.

39.   *Commonwealth v. Guilfoyle*, 402 Mass. at 131–33, 521 N.E.2d. at 984–985.

40.   See Commonwealth of Massachusetts, Report of the Attorney General, for the Fiscal Year Ending June 30, 1992, Civil Rights Division, at 155.

41.   See Commonwealth of Massachusetts, Report of the Attorney General, for the Fiscal Year Ending June 30, 1993, Civil Rights Division, at 126.

42.   Id. at 127.

43.   For example, the Massachusetts attorney general has obtained civil rights injunctions to protect a media news team, members of a church, a low-income housing
developer, an elected public official, gay demonstrators, a news reporter who with her
husband, a member of a local town board, had expressed views on race issues in a local
newspaper, women seeking abortion and counseling services at health clinics subject
to blockades and invasions, see *Planned Parenthood League*; and against police officers
for use of excessive force and for failing to report the use of excessive force, see *Commonwealth v. Adams*; Commonwealth of Massachusetts, Reports of the Attorney General
for the Fiscal Year Ending June 30, 1992, to the Fiscal Year Ending June 30, 2007, Civil
Rights Division. Similar to Massachusetts, by their language, California, Florida, Maine,
and New Jersey do not limit law enforcement's authority to obtain injunctions to bias-
motivated conduct. California: Cal. Civil Code 52.1(a); Florida: Fla. Stat. Ann. §§ 760.51;
Maine: 5 M.R.S.A. § 4681; New Jersey: N.J. Stat. Ann. § 10:6–2. Unlike Massachusetts,
the language in New Hampshire, Pennsylvania, Vermont, and West Virginia's hate crime
injunction laws limit the right of action to bias-motivated conduct. See New Hampshire:
N.H. Rev. Stat. Ann. §§ 354-B: 1; § 30.200; Vermont: Vt. Stat. Ann. Tit. 13, § 1458 e, Part
I(6); West Virginia: W.V.C. § 5–11–20 (a)(1) and (b).

44.   Under the companion state civil rights statute granting private parties the right
to seek civil rights injunctions, Mass. Gen. L. c. 12, § 11I, however, Massachusetts courts
have applied the MCRA to violations of rights unrelated to bias-motivated conduct or
fundamental constitutionally protected rights. See, for example, *Bell v. Mazza* (where defendant threatened to "do 'anything,'" "at any cost," to prevent plaintiffs' construction of
a tennis court on their property).

45.   Mass. Gen. L. c. 12, §§ 11H and 11I (West 2002).

46.   *Reproductive Rights Network*, 45 Mass. App. Ct. at 507–09, 699 N.E.2d at 838–
839 (secured right under First Amendment and Article 16 of the State Constitution).

47.   *Langton v. Secretary of Public Safety*, 37 Mass. App. Ct. 15, 19–20, 636 N.E.2d 299,
302 (Mass App. Ct. 1994) (secured by First and Fourteenth Amendments to the U.S. constitution and Part 1, Article 11 of the state constitution and state law); *Murphy v. Cruz*, 52
Mass. App. Ct. 314, 319, 753 N.E.2d 150, 154 (Mass. App. Ct. 2001) (retaliation against
prisoner for exercising rights secured under First Amendment to petition the courts).

48.   *Commonwealth v. Adams, 416 Mass. at 562–563, 624 N.E.2d at 104–105* (action
brought by Attorney General under Mass. Gen. L. c. 12, § 11H; right secured under federal
and state constitution and laws).

49.   *Planned Parenthood League*, 417 Mass. at 475, 631 N.E.2d at 990 (action brought by the Attorney General under Mass. Gen. L. c. 12, § 11H; right secured under federal and state constitution).

50.   *Batchelder*, 388 Mass. at 88–89, 445 N.E.2d at 593 (right secured under Article 9 of the state constitution).

51.   *O'Connell v. Chasdi*, 400 Mass. 686, 692–693, 511 N.E.2d 349, 353 (1987) (in violation of Article I of the Massachusetts Declaration of Rights, under Equal Rights Amendment).

52.   *Commonwealth v. Guilfoyle*, 402 Mass. at 131–132, 521 N.E.2d at 685 (action brought by attorney general under Mass. Gen. L. c. 12, § 11H) (right to walk public streets and use public parks free of discrimination secured by Mass. Gen. L. c. 272, §§ 92A and 98) (West 2000).

53.   *Redgrave v. Boston Symphony Orchestra*, 399 Mass. 93, 99–100, 502 N.E.2d 1375 (1987), answer to certified questions, 855 F.2d 888 (1st Cir. 1988), cert. denied, 498 U.S. 1043, 109 S.Ct.869, 102 LEd.2d 993 (right secured by state law).

54.   *Tortora v. Inspectors of Bldgs. of Tewksbury*, 41 Mass. App. Ct. 120, 122–124, 668 N.E.2d 876, 877–878 (Mass. App. Ct. 1996) (right against threats of retributive arrests and official action for lawful conduct—to pursue legal avenues to enlarge their property—secured by federal and state constitution); *Bell V. Mazza* (right to build a tennis court on their property secured by Articles 1, 2, and 10 of the Massachusetts Declaration of Rights); *Haufler v. Zotos*, 446 Mass. 489, 507–508, 845 N.E.2d 322, 337–338 (2006) (right secured under state law).

55.   *Sarvis v. Boston Safe Deposit and Trust Co.*, 47 Mass. App. Ct. 86, 711 N.E.2d 911 (Mass. App. Ct. 1999) (right against being removed from property except through a summary process action in court secured by state statute).

56.   *Brunelle v. Lynn Public Schools*, 433 Mass. 179, 182, 740 N.E.2d 625, 628 (2001) (right secured by state statute).

57.   See generally, Sager, *Rights Protected By The Massachusetts Civil Rights Act Against Interference on Account of Race or Color*, 17 Suffolk U. L. Rev. 53 (1983).

58.   Mass. Gen. L. c. 151B, § 4 (West 2004); Mass. Gen. L. c. 93 §§ 102 & 103 (West 2006); Title VIII of Civil Rights Act of 1968, 42 U.S.C. Section 3601–3631 (West 2003).

59.   Id.

60.   See Mass. Gen. L. c. 272, §§ 92A and 98 (West 2000).

61.   See Mass. Gen. L. c. 76, § 5 (West Supp. 2008) (discrimination in public schools); Mass. Gen. L. c. 151C, § 2 (West 2004) (discrimination in educational institutions, including colleges and universities); Title VI of the Civil Rights Act of 1964, 42 U.S.C. § 2000d (race, color, national origin discrimination) (West 2003); Title IX of the Education Amendments of 1972, 20 U.S.C § 1681 et seq. (sex or gender discrimination) (West 2000); Section 504 of the Rehabilitation Act of 1973, 29 U.S.C. § 794 (disability discrimination) (West 1999); and Title II of the Americans with Disabilities Act of 1990 (ADA), 42 U.S.C. § 12132 (disability discrimination) (West 2005).

62.   See Mass. Gen L. c. 151B, § 4 (West 2004); Mass. Gen L. c. 93, §§ 102 and 103 (West 2006); 42 U.S.C. § 1981 (West 2003); Title VII of the Civil Rights Act of 1964, 42 U.S.C. 2000e-2000e-17 (West 2003).

63.   *Planned Parenthood League*, 417 Mass. at 474, 631 N.E.2d at 990.

64.   *Reproductive Rights Network*, 45 Mass. App. Ct. at 506, 699 N.E.2d at 837.

65.   *Haufler*, 446 Mass. at 504–505, 845 N.E.2d at 335–336.

66.   *Planned Parenthood League*, 417 Mass. at 474, 631 N.E.2d at 990 (internal citations omitted). By citing favorably to definitions used in other Massachusetts court decisions, the Massachusetts Supreme Judicial Court incorporated into its "threats" definition "acts or language by which another is placed in fear of injury or damage," and "reasonable apprehension on the part of the recipient of a criminal threat"; see also *Haufler*, 446 Mass. 489, 505, 845 N.E.2d at 335.

67.   *Buster v. George W. Moore, Inc.* 438 Mass. 635, 648, 783 N.E.2d 399, 411, citing *Sena v. Commonwealth*, 417 Mass. 250, 263, 629 N.E.2d. 986 (1994).

68.   *Planned Parenthood League*, 417 Mass. at 474, 631 N.E.2d at 990 (internal citations omitted); *Buster*, 438 Mass. at 646–648, 783 N.E.2d at 410–411; *Kennie v. Natural Resource Dept. of Dennis*, 69 Mass. App. Ct. 158, 163–64, 866 N.E.2d 983, 988 (Mass. App. Ct. 2007); *Haufler*, 446 Mass. at 505, 845 N.E.2d at 335.

69.   In *Planned Parenthood* League, 417 Mass. at 474, 631 N.E.2d at 990 (internal citations omitted), the Supreme Judicial Court also incorporated into its definition of "coercion" the "creation of fear to compel conduct," and "the active domination of another's will." See also *Haufler*, 446 Mass. at 505, 845 N.E.2d at 335–336.

70.   *Planned Parenthood League*, 417 Mass. at 473–474, 473, n.8, 631 N.E.2d at 989, 989–990 n.8. See also *Willitts v. Roman Catholic Archbishop of Boston*, 411 Mass. 202, 210, 581 N.E.2d 475 (1991); *Layne v. Supt. Mass. Correctional Inst. Cedar Junction*, 406 Mass. 156, 158, 546 N.E.2d 166, 168 (1989); *Bally v. Northeastern Univ.*, 403 Mass. 713, 719–720, 532 N.E 2d 49, 53 (1989).

71.   *Sarvis v. Boston Safe Deposit and Trust*, 47 Mass. App. Ct. 86, 92, 711 N.E.2d 911, 918 (Mass. App. Ct. 1999); see also *Redgrave*, 399 Mass. at 100–101, 502 N.E.2d at 1379.

72.   *Buster*, 438 Mass. at 646–648, 783 2d at 410–411; *Haufler*, 446 Mass. at 505, 845 N.E.2d at 336.

73.   *Doe v. Senechal*, 66 Mass. App. Ct. 68, 79, 845 N.E.2d 418, 428 (Mass. App. Ct. 2006), review denied, 447 Mass 1103, 846 N.E.2d 1212.

74.   *Haufler*, 446 Mass. at 505, 845 N.E.2d at 336; *Buster*, 438 Mass. at 647–648, 783 N.E.2d at 411 (comparing Mass. Gen. L. c. 12, §§ 11H and 11I, "civil violations to use threats, intimidation or coercion to interfere with secured rights with Mass. Gen. L. c. 265, § 37 criminal violation to use 'force or threat of force' to interfere with secured rights") (fn10); see also *Kennie*, 69 Mass. App. Ct. at 162, 866 N.E.2d at 164–165.

75.   *Buster*, 438 Mass. at 646–648, 783 N.E.2d at 410–411.

76.   *Buster*, 438 Mass. at 646–648, 783 N.E.2d at 410–411; see also *Reproductive Rights Network*, 45 Mass. App. Ct. at 507–508.

77.   *Buster*, 438 Mass. at 647, 783 N.E.2d at 411.

78.   See *Longval v. Comm'r of Correction*, 404 Mass. 325, 333, 535 N.E.2d 588, 593 (1989) (no coercion involved when correctional officers, authorized to use force, directly employed force to compel conduct); *Pheasant Ridge Assocs. Ltd. Partnership v. Burlington*, 399 Mass. 771, 781, 506 N.E.2d 1152, 1158–1159 (1987) (even if unlawful, land taking by board empowered to take land involved direct denial of rights, and therefore lacks the necessary quality of coercion); *Layne*, 406 Mass. at 158, 546 N.E.2d at 168 (direct action of moving prison library to basement which made it inaccessible to inmates with disabilities not coercive under MCRA).

79.   *Planned Parenthood League*, 417 Mass. at 473, 631 N.E.2d at 989–990.

80.   *Commonwealth v. Adams*, 416 Mass. at 565, 624 N.E. 2d at 106.

81.   *Longval*, 404 Mass. at 333, 535 N.E.2d at 593.

82. See *Commonwealth v. Adams*, 416 Mass. at 569 (Liacos, C.J., concurring in part and dissenting in part) (MCRA relief warranted where police participated in or allowed the direct violation of civil rights "out of anger and personal animosity").

83. *Redgrave*, 399 Mass. at 99–100, citing *Monroe v. Pape, 365 U.S. 167, 187 (1961)*.

84. Id.; *Batchelder*, 393 Mass. at 823, 473 N.E. 2d at 1131.

85. *Breault v. Chairman of the Bd. of Fire Comm'rs of Springfield*, 401 Mass. 26, 36, 513 N.E.2d 1277 (1987).

86. *Planned Parenthood*, 417 Mass. at 48, 631 N.E.2d at 993–994; *Deas v. Dempsey*, 403 Mass. 468, 471, 530 N.E.2d 1239, 1241 (1988).

87. *Kennie*, 69 Mass. App. Ct. at 162, 866 N.E.2d at 987, *Haufler*, 446 Mass. at 505, 845 N.E.2d at 335, *Planned Parenthood*, 417 Mass. at 474–475, 631 N.E.2d at 990.

88. *Planned Parenthood*, 417 Mass. at 476–477, 631 N.E.2d at 991.

89. *Planned Parenthood League*, 417 Mass. at 474, 476–77, 631 N.E.2d at 991.

90. *Commonwealth v. Adams*, 416 Mass. at 565, 624 N.E.2d at 106; *Bell v. Mazza*, 394 Mass. at 184, 474 N.E. 2d at 1116.

91. *Planned Parenthood League*, 417 Mass. at 480–481, 631 N.E.2d at 993–994.

92. *Bell v. Mazza*, 394 Mass. at 184, 474 N.E. 2d at 1116.

93. Generally, the Massachusetts Attorney General's decision to file an MCRA injunction case is based on the evaluation of the need for a preliminary injunction. For a list of relevant factors, see also *The United States Department of Justice's Hate Crime Training: Core Curriculum for Patrol Officers, Detectives & Command Officers*, Session D, section C., titled, "Factors Law Enforcement Professionals Should Consider in Determining Whether to Pursue Injunctive Relief," at pages 122–125, drafted by this author, Richard W. Cole. The training module for multilevel state and local law enforcement professionals may be obtained by contacting the Bureau of Justice Clearinghouse, Office of Justice Programs, in Rockville, Maryland.

94. *Commonwealth v. Adams*, 416 Mass. at 566–567, 624 N.E.2d at 107.

95. See, for example, *Commonwealth v. Guilfoyle*, 402 Mass. at 135, 521 N.E.2d at 987 (held that 100 yards was highly reasonable under the circumstances).

96. In *Commonwealth v. Guilfoyle*, 402 Mass. at 133 n.4, 521 N.E.2d. at 985–986 n.4, the court sanctioned the provisions that are commonly sought for injunctive relief by the Massachusetts Attorney General.

IT IS HEREBY ORDERED AND ADJUDGED THAT:

A. Defendant Michael Guilfoyle and all persons in concert or participation with him shall be permanently enjoined from directly or indirectly:

1. assaulting, threatening, intimidating or harassing or attempting to assault, threaten, intimidate or harass, or causing or attempting to cause injury or damage to the person or property of Jesse Coleman, Mary Deshaies, Kristyn Atwood, Emily Harr, members of their families or persons known to the defendants to be students of the Mather School, Dorchester, Massachusetts.

2. assaulting, threatening, intimidating or harassing or attempting to assault, threaten, intimidate or harass, or causing or attempting to cause injury or damage to the person or property of any person because of that person's race, color or national origin or the race, color or national origin of any person with them.

3. assaulting, threatening, intimidating or harassing, or attempting to cause injury or damage to the person or property of any person because he or she did

or might complain or testify about acts prohibited by Massachusetts or Federal Law or did or might cooperate in any investigation concerning such acts.

4. preventing Jessie Coleman, Mary Deshaies, Kristyn Atwood, or Emily Harr, members of their families, or any other person, from enjoying full access to schools, homes, streets, beaches, and other places of public accommodation in Dorchester, because of that person's race, color, or national origin, or the race, color, or national origin of any person with them.

And further, defendant Michael Guilfoyle shall be enjoined from

1. being present on or entering the grounds and property of the Mather School, Dorchester, Massachusetts during the hours of 6:00 a.m. to 6:00 p.m. on all days when school is in session;
2. knowingly approaching within one hundred (100) yards of Jesse Coleman, Mary Deshaies, Kristyn Atwood, or Emily Harr;
3. speaking to, telephoning, writing to or otherwise communicating with Jesse Coleman, Mary Deshaies, Kristyn Atwood, or Emily Harr or members of their families or any student of the Mather School, Dorchester, Massachusetts; except through defendant's counsel or by arrangement with the Civil Rights Division of the Department of the Attorney General;

Pursuant to G.L. c. 12, §11J, VIOLATION OF THIS ORDER IS A CRIMINAL OFFENSE.

97. See Commonwealth of Massachusetts, Reports of the Attorney General, for the Fiscal Year Ending June 30, 1981, to Fiscal Year Ending June 30, 2007, Civil Rights Division.

98. See G.L. c. 12 § 11J (West 2002); see also *Commonwealth v. Brogan*, 415 Mass. 169, 612 N.E.2d 656 (1993); *Commonwealth v. Guilfoyle*, 521 N.E.2d at 987, 402 Mass. at 134–135.

99. See *Commonwealth v. Brogan*, 415 Mass. 169, 171, 612 N.E.2d 656, 657 (1993), citing *Furtado v. Furtado*, 380 Mass. 137, 145, 402 N.E 2d 1024 (1980).

100. See Commonwealth of Massachusetts, Report of the Attorney General for the Fiscal Year Ending June 30, 1983, Civil Rights Division, referring to *Commonwealth v. Gilligan, et. al.*, at 36.

101. Id.

102. See Commonwealth of Massachusetts, Report of the Attorney General for the Fiscal Year Ending June 30, 1994, Civil Rights Division, at 117. Four of the 18 defendants unsuccessfully appealed the court holding them in criminal contempt. See *Commonwealth v. Brogan*, 415 Mass. 169, 612 N.E.2d 656 (1993); *Commonwealth v. Cotter*, 415 Mass. 183, 612 N.E.2d 1145 (1993); *Commonwealth v. Filos*, 420 Mass. 348, 649 N.E.2d 1085 (1995); *Commonwealth v. Blake*, 39 Mass. App. Ct. 906, 654 N.E.2d 64 (Mass. App. Ct. 1995); see also Commonwealth of Massachusetts, Reports of the Attorney General for the Fiscal Year Ending June 30, 1982, to the Fiscal Year Ending June 30, 2007, Civil Rights Division.

103. See, for example, *Commonwealth v. Cotter*, 415 Mass. at 186, 612 N.E.2d at 1146 (sentenced to 2.5 years in a house of corrections, with one year to serve, the balance suspended for 3 years).

104. See "The United States Department of Justice's Hate Crime Training: Core Curriculum for Patrol Officers, Detectives & Command Officers," Session E and F, for a sum-

mary of the steps responding and investigating officers should take in a potential hate crime.

105.   Some larger departments maintain a specialized civil rights unit to investigate all cases involving civil rights or bias indicators. In Boston, for example, a specialized civil right investigative unit exists called the Community Disorders Unit (CDU), which has been recognized as a national model. The officers of the CDU are specially trained to identify bias indicators, to locate civil rights violators, and to evaluate incidents to determine if a victim's civil rights have been violated. In many departments that do not maintain a specialized civil rights investigation unit, the chief designates an officer, trained in hate crime investigations and enforcement, to serve as the department's "civil rights officer" to supervise or directly participate in investigating all civil rights incidents. The civil rights officer also trains and acts as a resource for other officers in the department and serves as a bridge to community groups, to individual victims, and to the district attorney and attorney general's office.

106.   See itemized list of advantages of civil rights injunctions, drafted by Richard W. Cole in the "United States Department of Justice's Hate Crime Training: Core Curriculum for Patrol Officers, Detectives & Command Officers," Section D, page 122.

107.   *Commonwealth v. Guilfoyle*, 402 Mass. at 135–136, 521 N.E.2d. at 987. New Hampshire, however, requires its state attorney general to obtain a civil hate crimes injunction by proving the violation by "clear and convincing evidence"; N.H. Rev. Stat. Ann. § 354-B:2 IV.

108.   Mass. Gen. L. c 265, § 37 (West 2000).

109.   *Planned Parenthood League*, 417 Mass. at 476–477, 631 N.E.2d at 991.

110.   See Rule 17b, Massachusetts Rules of Civil Procedure (West 2007). See also *Commonwealth v. Guilfoyle*, 402 Mass. at 131, 521 N.E.2d at 985, where the court took note that the superior court had properly appointed a parent as guardian ad litem for a minor defendant, in accordance with Rule 17(b) of the Massachusetts Rules of Civil Procedure.

111.   See Rule 65(a), Massachusetts Rules of Civil Procedure (West 2008).

112.   The affidavits a defendant files and the live testimony he provides in the civil injunction case are available for prosecutors to use in their criminal case. In New Hampshire, testimony in a civil rights injunction action is not admissible in criminal proceedings related to the same event. N.H. Rev. Stat. Ann. § 354-B:2(III).

113.   See Rule 26(a)(b), Massachusetts Rules of Civil Procedure (West 2008); *Commonwealth v. Balliro*, 349 Mass. 505, 209 N.E.2d 308 (1965); *Commonwealth v. St. Pierre*, 377 Mass. 650, 387 N.E.2d 1135 (1979).

114.   See, for example, *Planned Parenthood League; Commonwealth v. Adams.*

115.   See M.G.L. c. 12, §§ 11H and 11J (West 2002).

116.   Id.

117.   M.G.L. Chapter 265, § 37 (West 2002).

118.   Through Mass Gen. L. c. 12, § 11J, or through criminal contempt.

119.   *Commonwealth v. Guilfoyle*, 402 Mass. at 135, 521 N.E.2d. at 987; see also *Doe v. Commonwealth*, 396 Mass. 421, 423, 486 N.E. 2d 698, 700 (1985). The court, however, in its discretion, but within constitutional limits, may decide "to impound papers in the case, to protect the juvenile's identity and to close the proceeding to the public." Vermont, in enacting its hate crime injunction statute, was particularly concerned with the potential effects of the hate crime legislation on juveniles, including "inappropriate or counterproductive publicity and stigmatization" and the effect of "injunctions on the illegal behavior or those similarly situated to the defendant who are subject to the injunctions." See Vt. Stat. Ann. Tit. 13, §§ 1460.

120.   *Doe v. Commonwealth*, 396 Mass. at 423, 486 N.E. 2d at 700; *Commonwealth v. Guil-foyle*, 402 Mass. at 134–135, 521 N.E.2d at 986–987.

121.   Mass. Gen. L. c 12, § 11J (West 2002). Similarly, under Vermont's hate crime injunction law, a law enforcement officer is authorized to arrest without a warrant a person whom the officer has probable cause to believe has violated a hate-motivated crime injunction issued under this statute.

122.   See *Commonwealth v. Howe*, 405 Mass. 332, 334, 540 N.E.2d 677 (1989).

CHAPTER 7

HATE CRIMES AND THE WAR
ON TERROR

Cynthia Lee

On September 11, 2001, 19 Arab Muslims hijacked four commercial airplanes in the United States. They flew two of these planes into the World Trade Center in New York City, killing an estimated 2,759 people.[1] They flew a third plane into the Pentagon in Northern Virginia, just minutes from Washington, D.C., killing another 125.[2] The fourth plane never made it to its intended target, presumably the White House in Washington, D.C., crashing instead into a remote field in Pennsylvania, killing all 44 on board.[3]

In the days, weeks, and months immediately following the September 11 attacks, Arab Americans, South Asian Americans, Muslim Americans, and Sikh Americans were the targets of widespread hate violence.[4] Many of the perpetrators of these acts of hate violence claimed they were acting patriotically by retaliating against those responsible for September 11.

This chapter situates the private acts of hate violence committed against Arab Americans, Muslim Americans, Sikh Americans, and South Asian Americans in the aftermath of September 11 into the broader context of the war on terror. Despite public pronouncements condemning these private acts of hate violence, the government engaged in its own acts of psychological and physical violence against Arabs, Muslims, Sikhs and South Asians, all in the name of the war on terror.[5] Like Muneer Ahmad, Leti Volpp, and others, I argue that both private and public acts of violence against individuals perceived to

I thank Dean Fred Lawrence for inviting me to write this chapter. A special thanks to Deepa Iyer and Anil Kalhan for directing me to helpful community resources. I also thank Hans Christian-Latta for excellent research assistance and Jason Hawkins, Lesliediana Jones, and Herb Somers for outstanding library assistance.

be Arab or Muslim can be understood as two sides of the same coin—a coin made possible by the social construction of the Arab-as-Terrorist stereotype.[6] Obviously, this stereotype affects Arabs, Muslims, and those individuals perceived to be Arab or Muslim. In addition, the Arab-as-Terrorist stereotype affects us all by encouraging lawmakers to give police expanded authority that encroaches on the civil liberties of all citizens.

After providing some general background information on hate crimes, I discuss some of the hate crimes committed in the aftermath of September 11. I examine two common stereotypes about Arabs and Muslims that likely contributed to the post–September 11 backlash against Arabs and Muslims and those perceived to be Arab or Muslim: the Arab-as-Terrorist stereotype and the Arab-as-Foreigner stereotype. I suggest that government action in the war on terror was influenced by and reinforced these stereotypes.

HATE CRIMES IN THE AFTERMATH
OF SEPTEMBER 11

A hate crime is a crime against an individual on account of his race, religion, national origin, ethnicity, or some other protected characteristic.[7] Supporters of hate crime legislation argue that hate crimes merit enhanced punishment because of the greater harm they cause. For example, Frederick Lawrence notes that the harm caused by hate crimes is greater than the harm caused by other crimes because of "the nature of the injury sustained by the immediate victim of a bias crime; the palpable harm inflicted on the broader target community of the crime; and the harm to society at large."[8] Andrew Taslitz argues that "hate crimes contribute to a racist culture that creates subordinate status for marginalized groups and raises the risk of physical harms, such as further assault."[9]

Hate crime statutes tend to follow one of two models: (1) the *discriminatory selection* model and (2) the *racial animus* model.[10] Under the discriminatory selection model, a defendant's punishment is enhanced if he chose his victim because of the victim's membership in a protected group.[11] The prosecutor need not show that defendant acted because of any animus or hostility toward the victim because of his race, religion, ethnicity, gender, or other protected status.

Lu-in Wang gives examples of two defendants who could be punished under the discriminatory selection model. First, "[o]ne such perpetrator would be the purse snatcher who preys exclusively on women, not because he feels hostility toward women as a group, but because their general practice of carrying handbags or their typically small stature makes them, for the most part, easier targets than men."[12] Second, "a juvenile delinquent who chooses to rob grocery stores owned by recent immigrants from Asia because she presumes that those merchants have lots of cash on hand" would be punishable under the discriminatory selection model even if she bore no hostility toward Asians as a group.[13]

Under the racial animus model, the defendant must choose his victim because of the victim's membership in a protected group *and* "hatred or hostility toward the target group."[14] The individuals described above (the purse snatcher who targets women and the juvenile delinquent who targets recent immigrants from Asia) would not be subject to enhanced punishment under the racial animus model because they were not acting out of hostility toward the victim's group.

Wang notes that the cases that tend to be prosecuted are those that conform to the racial animus model.[15] This is problematic because the racial animus model perpetuates an overly simplistic view of the bias criminal as an irrational deviant unlike most of us.[16] The racial animus model makes it easy for us to distance ourselves from the perpetrators of hate crimes even though we often share many of the same underlying biases.

One of the first laws exclusively criminalizing bias-motivated conduct in the United States is found in Section 245 of volume 18 of the U.S. Code, enacted in the 1960s.[17] This statute makes it a crime to try to stop another person on the basis of race, color, national origin, or religion from engaging in any one of six federally protected activities: (1) enrolling in or attending a public school; (2) participating in a service or facility provided by a state; (3) engaging in employment; (4) serving as a juror; (5) traveling or using any common carrier (motor, rail, water, or air) in interstate commerce; and (6) enjoying the services of any hotel or motel or any restaurant, cafeteria, lunch counter, gas station, motion picture house, theater, concert hall, sports arena, stadium, or any other establishment that serves the public.[18]

Because Section 245 is limited to attempts to interfere with the exercise of a civil right,[19] many states began enacting hate crime laws of their own in the 1980s and 1990s.[20] Today, 45 of the 50 states and the District of Columbia have hate crime laws on the books.[21] All of these statutes criminalize or enhance punishment for conduct motivated by bias on the basis of race, ethnicity, and religion.[22] At least 26 states include crimes motivated by sexual orientation bias.[23] At least 24 states include crimes motivated by bias on the basis of gender.[24]

In 1990, Congress passed the Hate Crimes Statistics Act, which requires the United States Department of Justice to collect data on hate crimes from law enforcement agencies.[25] Specific data about hate crimes against Arabs and Muslims and those perceived to be Arab or Muslim, however, is not collected.[26] Because the data collected by the Department of Justice under this statute inadequately captures information regarding hate violence directed against Arabs and Muslims and those perceived to be Arab or Muslim, it is necessary to look to other sources for such information. A few community-based organizations filled this void by specifically collecting information about acts of hate violence in the wake of September 11.

For example, South Asian American Leaders of Tomorrow (SAALT) found that in just the first week following the September 11 attacks, 645 bias incidents directed at individuals perceived to be of Middle Eastern descent, including shootings, verbal harassment in the streets, telephone threats to individuals in their homes, property damage and violence at places of worship, and racial jokes made in the workplace, were reported by newspapers and other media.[27] The Council on American-Islamic Relations (CAIR) received reports of 1,717 anti-Muslim and anti-Arab bias incidents, including violence, threats, hate messages and harassment, airport profiling, and workplace and school discrimination, after September 11, 2001.[28] While some of the incidents included in these numbers are bias incidents, not hate crimes,[29] these reports nonetheless are consistent with information collected by the FBI showing a 17-fold increase in anti-Muslim crimes nationwide in 2001.[30]

Just after September 11, numerous Arabs, Muslims, and individuals perceived to be Arab or Muslim were assaulted, and some killed,[31] by individuals who believed they were responsible for or connected to the attacks on the World Trade Center and Pentagon.[32] The first backlash killing occurred four days after September 11.[33] Balbir Singh Sodhi was shot to death on September 15 as he was planting flowers outside his Chevron gas station.[34] The man who shot Sodhi, Frank Roque, had told an employee of an Applebee's restaurant that he was "going to go out and shoot some towel heads."[35] Roque mistakenly thought Sodhi was Arab because Sodhi, an immigrant from India, had a beard and wore a turban as part of his Sikh faith.[36] After shooting Sodhi, Roque drove to a Mobil gas station a few miles away and shot at a Lebanese-American clerk.[37] He then drove to a home he once owned and shot and almost hit an Afghani man who was coming out the front door.[38] When he was arrested two hours later, Roque shouted, "I stand for America all the way."[39]

The next two killings were committed by a man named Mark Stroman. On September 15, 2001, Stroman shot and killed Waqar Hassan, an immigrant from Pakistan, at Hassan's grocery store in Dallas, Texas.[40] On October 4, 2001, Stroman shot and killed Vasudev Patel, an immigrant from India and a naturalized U.S. citizen, while Patel was working at his Shell station convenience store.[41] A store video camera recorded the killing, helping police to identify Stroman as the killer.[42] Stroman later told a Dallas television station that he shot Hassan and Patel because, "We're at war. I did what I had to do. I did it to retaliate against those who retaliated against us."[43]

Beyond these killings, there were more than a thousand other anti-Muslim or anti-Arab acts of hate that took the form of physical assaults, verbal harassment and intimidation, arson, attacks on mosques, vandalism, and other property damage.[44] Many individuals reported being intimidated on the road by drivers and pedestrians who pointed fingers at them as if shooting them.[45] Businesses were hit with gasoline bombs, and homes and places of worships were vandalized.[46] In approximately one in every five cases, the victim suffered bodily injury from physical assault.[47] In each of these acts of hate violence, the perpetrators chose their victims because they believed them to be Arab or Muslim. Their acts of violence were intended as payback for the death and destruction brought about by terrorists on September 11. Payback, however, makes sense only if the targets of the post–September 11 hate violence were in fact linked to the September 11 terrorists. No evidence has come to light indicating that any of the backlash victims had anything to do with the September 11 attacks. The September 11 terrorists were Arab Muslim men with links to Al Qaeda. Many of the victims of post–September 11 hate violence were neither Arab nor Muslim, yet these men were selected because their perpetrators thought they were Arab or Muslim and in some way responsible for September 11. How could so many individuals leap to such an erroneous conclusion? The answer lies in the construction of the Arab-as-Terrorist stereotype.

STEREOTYPES ABOUT ARABS AND MUSLIMS

Many Americans do not know the difference between Arabs[48] and Muslims and think that all Arabs are Muslim and all Muslims are Arab. Not all Arabs, however, are Muslim and not all Muslims are Arab. Muslims are people who believe in or adhere to the religion of Islam.[49] Though the vast majority of Arabs are Muslim,[50] approximately 15 million Arab Christians reside in Arab-speaking countries today.[51] The majority of Arabs living in the United States today are Christian, not Muslim.[52] A 2001 Zogby survey found that 42 percent of Arab Americans are Catholic, 23 percent are Orthodox, 12 percent are Protestant, and only 23 percent are Muslim.[53] In other words, approximately 77 percent of the Arabs in America are not Muslim.

As noted above, not all Muslims are Arab. Islam has nearly 1.5 billion adherents of many ethnic, national, and racial backgrounds throughout the world.[54] Only 12 percent of Muslims worldwide are Arab.[55] In the United States, Arab Americans represent only a small percentage of the total Muslim population. According to one survey, 42 percent of Muslims in the United States are African American, 24.4 percent are South Asian, and only 12.4 percent are Arab.[56]

One reason why Arabs and Muslims may often be confused is that over 90 percent of all Arabs are Muslim.[57] In addition, there is considerable overlap between Arab and Muslim cultures.[58] According to Sylvia Nassar-McMillan:

> Islam is believed to have begun sometime between the 7th and 10th centuries A.D., when the Prophet Mohammed became known to the people inhabiting the Arabian Peninsula. He claimed to be the messenger of God, delivering the word of God as communicated to him by the Archangel Gabriel. Unifying within their new common faith, the people formed a nation, henceforth known as the Arab Nation.[59]

The Arab-as-Terrorist Stereotype

The conflation of Arabs and Muslims has contributed to the construction of the Arab (or Muslim)-as-Terrorist stereotype.[60] The Arab-as-Terrorist stereotype, however, is not a new stereotype. Even before September 11, Arabs and Muslims were stereotyped as terrorists.[61] As Karen Engle notes, in America, Arabs are presumed to be Muslim, and Muslims are "suspected of having greater fealty to their religion—one that is often equated with terrorism—than to the United States."[62] Engle points out that "the terrorism-Islam conflation has become so ingrained in the American mind set that initial media reports after the 1995 bombing of the federal building in Oklahoma simply assumed that the culprits were from the Middle East."[63] As we now know, an American named Timothy McVeigh was responsible for that act of terrorism.[64] Nonetheless, the government received more than 200 reports of harassment, threats, and assaults against Arab-Americans and Muslim-Americans following this incident.[65]

In 1980, Dr. Jack Shaheen, professor emeritus at Southern Illinois University, began research on motion pictures with Arab portraits and themes.[66] By the completion of his project, Shaheen had found more than 900 feature films released between 1896 and 2001 that contained Arab storylines, settings, and character casts.[67] Not surprisingly, Arabs were portrayed as bad guys in the vast majority of these feature films.[68] Only a handful of films depicted Arabs as heroes or ordinary people.[69]

One example of this anti-Arab view can be found in *Rules of Engagement* (2000), a film starring Samuel Jackson and Tommy Lee Jones, which Shaheen describes as "promot[ing] a dangerously generalized portrayal of Arabs as rabidly anti-American."[70] During the film, U.S. Marines open fire on 83 Yemeni men, women, and children.[71] Initially, the audience is led to sympathize with the Yemeni victims. The camera follows a young girl with only one leg who was disabled in the gunfire, then shows other men, women, and children suffering from gunshot wounds at a nearby hospital. As the story unfolds, however, the audience learns that the disabled girl and other apparently innocent victims were not so innocent after all. We find out that the men, women, and children in the crowd had weapons and began firing on the Marines, who shot back in self-defense.[72] In the end, the U.S. Marines are vindicated. The attack on the Yemeni civilians is portrayed as a justified act.

Another example Shaheen uses is *True Lies* (1994), a film in which Arnold Schwarzenegger plays a secret agent whose mission is to track down nuclear warheads stolen from Kazakhstan. Schwarzenegger finds out that a radical Islamic terrorist group named Crimson Jihad is trying to smuggle the nuclear warheads into the United States. The story follows Schwarzenegger's battles with Salim Abu Aziz, the leader of the terrorist group.

In the meantime, Schwarzenegger's wife, played by Jamie Lee Curtis, is unaware that her husband is a spy and believes he is a boring computer salesman. Curtis craves adventure, which she thinks her husband can't give her. Schwarzenegger finds out that his wife is on the verge of having an affair with a man pretending to be a spy. Schwarzenegger decides to engage his wife in a fake spy operation and gets her to perform a striptease in front of him while he hides his face in the shadows. Eventually, Curtis finds out that her husband is a true spy and they live happily ever after.

When *True Lies* was released, it garnered mostly positive reviews. The movie earned $146 million in the United States and more than $200 million abroad, making it the third best grossing movie in 1994.[73] Jamie Lee Curtis received a Golden Globe for best actress in a musical/comedy.[74] For most people who saw this film when it first came out, Jamie Lee Curtis's striptease scene was probably the most memorable part of the movie, *not* that the movie portrayed Arabs as crazed terrorists intent on harming Americans. This portrayal may not have been particularly striking because it fit within our expectations of what Arab people are like.

While the image of the Arab-as-Terrorist is not a new stereotype, it has become increasingly entrenched in the public imagination since September 11 because of the increased frequency of news coverage of actual Islamic terrorism. Burned into our memories is the real-life image of hooded masked men holding American journalist Daniel Pearl hostage and declaring his beheading to the world.[75] Anyone who watches the news has seen video footage of jihadist training camps depicting men in black face masks with assault-style machine guns engaging in rigorous boot camp exercises as if preparing for hand-to-hand combat. Increasingly we hear of Arab men, and sometimes Arab women,[76] strapping bombs to themselves and acting as suicide bombers.

The effect of these fictional and real-life images of Arabs as terrorists came to a head with the attacks on the World Trade Center and Pentagon. Despite widespread contemporary condemnation of the internment of Americans of Japanese descent during World War II,[77] a Gallup Poll taken after September 11 found that one in every three Americans supported internment for

Americans of Arab descent.[78] And even though racial profiling of African Americans and Latinos was widely condemned just prior to September 11,[79] a CNN/USA Today/Gallup Poll taken shortly after September 11 found that a majority of Americans supported the racial profiling of persons of Middle Eastern descent.[80] The same poll found that 49 percent of the adults surveyed thought all Arab-Americans should have to carry special identification cards.[81] As Sharon Davies notes, the post–September 11 racial profiling of individuals of Middle Eastern descent was euphemistically called "ethnic profiling" and "was met with shrugs of resignation rather than shouts of protest, signaling a sea change in the nation's thinking about profiling practices from its new, post 9/11 perspective."[82]

There is such anti-Muslim sentiment in America today that during the 2008 presidential campaign, opponents of presidential candidate Barack Obama attempted to spread false rumors over the Internet alleging that Obama is Muslim and a "Muslim plant" in a conspiracy against America.[83] In a poll of American citizens conducted by the Pew Research Center for the People and the Press in August 2007, 45 percent of respondents said they would be less likely to vote for a candidate who is Muslim than any other candidate, compared with 25 percent who said the same about a Mormon candidate and 16 percent who said the same for a candidate who is an evangelical Christian.[84] In the month before the election, the chairman of the Virginia Republican Party compared Barack Obama to Osama bin Laden, telling volunteers working for GOP nominee John McCain that Obama and bin Laden "both have friends that bombed the Pentagon."[85] During several campaign stops, GOP vice presidential nominee Sarah Palin accused Obama of "palling around with terrorists."[86] Even though Barack Obama is neither Muslim nor Arab, speakers at McCain-Palin rallies referred to Obama as "Barack Hussein Obama," in an attempt to further associate Obama with the Arab-as-Terrorist stereotype.[87]

The Arab (or Muslim)-as-Terrorist stereotype victimizes more than just Arabs and Muslims. Anyone who "appears" to be Arab or Muslim is suspect. I put the word "appears" in quotes because Muslim people (adherents of Islam) are of all different colors, races, and ethnicities, and one cannot tell simply by a person's appearance whether he or she is Muslim.[88] Moreover, it is difficult to tell from appearance alone whether an individual is Arab. South Asians—individuals from India, Pakistan, Bangladesh, Sri Lanka, Nepal, and Bhutan—are often misidentified as Arab because of their dark skin and dark hair.[89] Sikhs—adherents of the Sikh religion—are also often misidentified as Arab or Muslim because of their long beards and turbans, which may remind people of Osama bin Laden, often seen in news footage wearing a long beard and turban.[90] It is telling that the first three individuals killed as part of the backlash against the September 11 terrorist attacks—Waqar Hasan, Balbir Singh Sodhi, and Vasudev Patel—were of South Asian descent.[91] According to one report, 96 percent of the victims of backlash violence in the three months following September 11 were of South Asian descent.[92]

Besides broadening the pool of potential victims, the Arab-as-Terrorist stereotype has also broadened the pool of possible perpetrators of bias-motivated conduct, though not necessarily conduct that would be punishable as a hate crime. Trigger-happy individuals filled with hatred are not the only ones who have been influenced by the Arab-as-Terrorist stereotype. On May 22, 2006, one nervous American Airlines passenger grabbed a fellow passenger sitting directly in front of him as that passenger was settling down with a book and a ginger ale less than an hour into the flight.[93] Thinking he was apprehending a would-be Islamic terrorist, Michael Wilk grabbed the passenger from behind and held him in a headlock.[94] He then went into the passenger's pocket and removed his passport and iPod.[95]

It turns out the suspicious-looking passenger wasn't an Islamic terrorist but rather a British interior designer with Jewish roots named Seth Stein.[96] Mr. Stein was later told by airline personnel that he was targeted by Wilk because he was using an iPod, had used the lavatory when he got on the plane, and had tan skin that made him appear Arab.[97] Even worse, one or two passengers went up to Wilk (the passenger who assaulted Stein) afterwards and thanked him for his action.[98] American Airlines apologized to Stein and offered him $2,000, but later withdrew their offer fearing that it would be seen as an admission of liability.[99] In other incidents, commercial airline personnel have barred passengers who were or looked like they were from the Middle East from getting on flights.[100]

Another example occurred on September 13, 2002, when a woman eating breakfast at a Shoney's restaurant in a small town in north Georgia saw three men who appeared to be of Middle Eastern descent and thought she overheard them plotting another September 11-like attack.[101] Eunice Stone claimed she heard the men say, "Well, if they're mourning 9/11, what are they going to do about 9/13?"[102] They then laughed and talked about "bringing it down."[103] Stone took down the license plate numbers from the cars the men were driving and called police.[104]

About 1:00 A.M. the next day, the three men were pulled over by police on a section of Florida's Interstate 75 known as Alligator Alley.[105] They were handcuffed, interrogated, and held in separate police cars all night.[106] Seventeen hours after they were pulled over, they were finally released.[107]

It turns out the three men were medical students heading to a nine-week course in Miami. They were also U.S. citizens of Middle Eastern descent.[108] One was born in Detroit, Michigan, to Pakistani immigrant parents.[109] The other two men were naturalized U.S. citizens from Jordan living in Chicago.[110] All three men denied joking or talking about September 11 or another terrorist attack. Stone had also told police that the men she overheard were speaking in Arabic, but only one of the three men knew Arabic, so it would have been impossible for the three of them to carry on a conversation in Arabic.[111]

In response to negative publicity about the incident, Stone stated, "First off, I would like to say that I didn't do any of this for any kind of publicity. I did it as an American." Law enforcement authorities and citizens alike praised Eunice Stone for reporting her suspicions to police. Former Senator Bob Graham of Florida, who was serving as the Chair of the Senate Select Committee on Intelligence at the time,[112] told news media, "I especially commend the actions of the private citizen in Calhoun, Georgia, who reported this suspicious activity to the proper authorities. This is exactly the kind of citizen involvement that this war on terrorism is going to require as we seek to protect our homeland."[113] Tim Moore, a Florida state official, also commended Stone. "Just think if we could get every American to do that, then every town would be safe."[114]

The Arab-as-Foreigner Stereotype

The "race-ing" of Arab-Americans, Muslim Americans, and those perceived to be Arab or Muslim is multifaceted.[115] The Arab-looking person is not just raced as a terrorist; he is also raced as foreign.[116] As Leti Volpp notes, many of those who were the targets of post–September 11 hate violence were formally citizens of the United States, either through birth or naturalization.[117] Nonetheless, they were not considered citizens as a matter of identity.[118] Just as Japanese Americans during World War II were considered first and foremost Japanese, rather than Americans of Japanese descent (even though many had never even been to Japan), Arab Americans today are considered first and foremost Arabs, rather than Americans of Arab descent.

Recognizing that the "Arab (or Muslim)-looking" person is raced not only as a terrorist, but also as a foreigner, helps us understand why the Bush administration has increased funding in two main areas: counter-terrorism and immigration enforcement. In October 2007, the *Washington Post* reported that under the Bush administration, the Department of Justice retreated from vigorous prosecutions of mobsters, white-collar criminals, environmental crimes, and traditional civil rights infractions and instead focused on immigration and terrorism related investigations.[119] Apparently, the Bush administration believes that in order to prevent the next terrorist attack, we must be vigilant about ferreting out illegal immigrants.

The public seems to feel the same way. Since September 11, anti–illegal-immigration fervor has become more pronounced. For example, under mounting pressure from constituents opposed to illegal immigration, in October 2006, Congress passed legislation authorizing the construction of 700 miles of fencing along the U.S. and Mexican border.[120] Also in 2006, anti–illegal-immigration forces launched a "Send-A-Brick" campaign, encouraging its supporters to send bricks to members of Congress, asking them to stop the flood of illegal immigration.[121] In 2007, President George W. Bush's attempts to enact immigration reform legislation met with fierce opposition from his Republican base because of provisions that would have allowed undocumented immigrants to become lawful permanent residents if they fulfilled certain requirements.[122] Since July 2006, more than a hundred municipalities have passed legislation designed to penalize businesses that hire and landlords who rent to undocumented immigrants.[123] Some counties have deputized their police officers to act as immigration officers.[124] In September 2007, Virginia government officials announced they were considering a proposal—the first of its kind in the nation—to build a prison just for illegal immigrants accused of crimes.[125] Eventually, the Virginia Crime Commission's Immigration Task Force rejected the proposal.[126]

THE WAR ON TERROR

In the days, weeks, and months after September 11, 2001, the Bush administration took conscientious steps to assure the public that its fight was against terrorism, *not* against all Arabs and Muslims. On September 17, 2001, President George W. Bush visited the Islamic Center of Washington, D.C., where he stated, "The face of terror is not the true faith of Islam. That's not what Islam is all about. Islam is peace. These terrorists don't represent peace. They represent evil and war."[127] On September 19, 2001, President Bush told President Megawati of Indonesia, the country with the world's largest Muslim population,[128] "I've made it clear, Madam President, that the war against terrorism is not a war against Muslims, nor is it a war against Arabs. It's a war against evil people who conduct crimes against innocent people."[129] Again on September 27, 2001, President Bush told airline employees at O'Hare International Airport in Chicago, Illinois, "Americans understand we fight not a religion; ours is not a campaign against the Muslim faith. Ours is a campaign against evil."[130]

President Bush also explicitly condemned the acts of bigotry and hatred committed by private individuals against Arabs, Muslims, and those perceived to be Arab or Muslim. In a speech in San Jose, California on April 30, 2002, President Bush declared:

> America rejects bigotry. We reject every act of hatred against people of Arab background or Muslim faith. America values and welcomes peaceful people of all faiths—Christian, Jewish, Muslim, Sikh, Hindu and many others. Every faith is practiced and protected here, because we are one country. Every immigrant can be fully and equally American because we're one country. Race and color should not divide us, because America is one country.[131]

Despite these public pronouncements, post–September 11 government action in the war on terror has helped foster the belief that all Muslims and Arabs are to be viewed with suspicion. Three government actions in particular deserve mention.[132]

Post–September 11 Detentions

First, in the weeks immediately following the September 11 attacks, the government began secretly arresting and detaining Arab, Muslim, and South Asian men.[133] Within the first two months after the attacks, the government had detained at least 1,200 men.[134]

The September 11 detainees were not immediately informed of the charges against them.[135] Some were discouraged from obtaining counsel and others were denied access to counsel.[136] Family members were kept in the dark as to their loved ones' whereabouts.[137] Most of the detainees were held for minor immigration violations and had no connection to terrorism.[138] Nonetheless, they were treated like violent criminals and verbally and/or physically abused by corrections officials.[139] Some detainees complained of being called "Bin Laden, Jr." and of being told, "You're going to die here," and "You're never going to get out of here."[140] Others reported painfully tight handcuffs and being repeatedly slammed against the wall.[141] One detainee said that a corrections officer bent his finger back until it touched his wrist.[142] Another detainee said officers repeatedly twisted his arm, which was in a cast, and a finger that was healing from a recent operation.[143]

Although the Bureau of Prisons directed the wardens of correctional facilities where the September 11 detainees were being held to preserve videotapes of the detainees in their cells and detainee movement outside the cells, correctional staff destroyed hundreds of tapes, allegedly to free up storage space.[144] Consequently, videotapes that could have helped prove or disprove allegations of abuse raised by September 11 detainees were not available to the Office of Inspector General for the Department of Justice when it conducted an investigation into the treatment of aliens held on immigration charges in connection with the investigation into the September 11 attacks.[145]

"Voluntary" Interview Program

Second, in November 2001, the Department of Justice began efforts to "interview" approximately five thousand men between the ages of 18 and 33 from Middle Eastern or Muslim nations who had arrived in the United States within the previous two years on a temporary student, tourist, or business visa; these men were lawful residents of the United States.[146] Four months later, the government announced it would seek to interview an additional 3,000 men from countries with an Al Qaeda presence.[147] According to then Attorney General John Ashcroft, these men were selected *not* because of their ethnicity or religious affiliation, but because they "fit the criteria of persons who might have knowledge of foreign-based terrorists."[148] To carry out this program, the Justice Department sent out letters inviting these men to come for supposedly voluntary interviews.[149]

Arab American groups protested that the government was engaging in racial profiling.[150] Ashcroft, however, responded that "[t]hese individuals were not selected in order to single out a particular ethnic or religious group, which suggests that one ethnic or religious group is more prone to terrorism than another. I emphatically reject that proposition."[151] A few weeks later, however, an internal memo from the INS was leaked to the press, suggesting that the interviews were being used to identify immigration violations and persons connected with the September 11 attacks.[152]

Professor Tracey Maclin notes that while reasonable minds might differ with the Attorney General's assertion that the individuals were not racially or ethnically profiled, there was no debate concerning one key point: "[t]here was no evidence revealed to the public that the men targeted for interrogations had any connection with terrorism or the events of September 11."[153] Maclin concludes, "[T]he government's investigative procedure following September 11 amounted to an ethnic-based fishing expedition."[154]

Nonetheless, several prominent legal academics have defended the government's so-called voluntary interview program. Samuel Gross and Debra Livingston, for example, argue that even if the voluntary interview program constituted ethnic profiling, as long as government agents treated the young man of Middle Eastern descent who were asked to come in for interviews with respect, then the program is not objectionable.[155]

Sherry Colb uses the voluntary interview program to examine whether the post–September 11 ethnic profiling of Middle Eastern men is different from the racial profiling of black and brown drivers and concludes that ethnic profiling of men of Middle Eastern descent, what she calls nationality-profiling for terrorists, is distinguishable from Driving While Black (a.k.a. DWB) profiling for drug couriers.[156] Colb asserts, "By contrast to *the extremely high probability that an aspiring terrorist will turn out to be Arab and/or Muslim*, the DWB profiling that has for years drawn large-scale condemnation does not carry a similar likelihood of success."[157] She continues, "[T]he likelihood that a minority driver has drugs in his car, just because he is engaged in one of the minor traffic violations of which almost everyone on the highways guilty, is quite small."[158] Colb concludes, "under limited circumstances, profiling on the basis of nationality may be constitutionally permissible and even appropriate."[159]

The problem with Colb's argument is that she is not comparing apples to apples. If we are asking about the likelihood that a suspect of a particular race or ethnicity will be a terrorist, the question we should be asking is,

"What is the likelihood that any given Arab American or Muslim American is a terrorist?" *not* "What is the likelihood that a suspected terrorist will turn out to be Arab or Muslim?" Just as a large percentage of African Americans and Latinos have nothing to do with illegal drugs, a large percentage of Arab Americans and Muslim Americans have nothing to do with terrorism. Therefore the likelihood that any given Arab American or Muslim American is a terrorist is probably quite small.[160]

Special Registration Program (NSEERS)

Third, in September 2002, the government implemented a Special Registration program also known as NSEERS (National Security Entry-Exit Registration System), requiring immigrant men from 26 mostly Muslim countries[161] to register with the government their name, address, telephone number, place of birth, date of arrival in the United States, height, weight, hair and eye color, financial information, and the addresses, birth dates, and phone numbers of parents and any foreign friends.[162] Under NSEERS, citizens and nationals of certain countries designated by the Attorney General had to report to the Immigration and Naturalization Service (INS) upon arrival, within 30 days after arrival, every 12 months after arrival, upon changing address, employment, or school, and when departing from the United States.[163] Individuals from designated countries already present in the United States had to submit to a call-in registration program and present themselves in person to the INS by a deadline specified in the Federal Register.[164] They also had to provide photographs and fingerprints.[165] Failure to comply with any of the special registration rules, including failing to report an address change within 10 days, could lead to criminal charges, removal from the United States, and future inadmissibility.[166] Additionally, if an individual failed to comply with these rules, his or her name would be entered into the FBI's national crime database that is available to state and local police.[167]

Initially, hundreds of noncitizens, including many who were lawfully in the United States pursuing applications for permanent residency, dutifully reported for special registration and found themselves arrested and detained by the INS, such that "a climate of fear and feeling of betrayal was created among immigrant communities targeted for special registration."[168] Many in the affected communities complained that these arrests unfairly penalized individuals simply attempting to comply with the law.[169] Fearing arrest and imprisonment, many noncitizens from the designated countries left homes and well-established businesses and fled to Canada rather than report, even though they were lawfully in the United States.[170] Aziz Huq, Deputy Director of the Justice Program at the Brennan Center at New York University School of Law, notes that by the program's conclusion on December 1, 2003, 83,519 men had come forward voluntarily.[171] Of these voluntary registrants, 13,799 had been placed in deportation proceedings.[172] According to James Zogby of the Arab American Institute, "In the end, there was no evidence that any terrorists were apprehended as a result of the effort."[173]

Broader Implications

The Arab-as-Terrorist stereotype has even broader implications beyond the private acts of hate violence and government action discussed above. The specter of the Arab-as-Terrorist conjures up images of sleeper cells waiting to launch another attack on American soil and encourages citizens and legal decision makers alike to embrace expansive law-enforcement measures that curtail the civil liberties of us all. For example, shortly after September 11, Congress hastily passed the USA PATRIOT Act, giving police the authority to engage in secret searches under a provision known as the "sneak and peek" warrant provision.[174] Under this provision, police can delay giving notice of a search warrant until after executing the search.[175] This provision is not limited to searches of the homes of suspected terrorists. It can be applied to the search of any person's home as long as the court "finds reasonable cause to believe that providing immediate notification of the execution of the warrant may have an adverse result."[176]

The Patriot Act also expanded the application of the Foreign Intelligence Surveillance Act (FISA) from situations in which foreign intelligence gathering is the sole or primary purpose of the investigation to situations in which foreign intelligence gathering is a "significant" purpose of the investigation.[177] FISA allows the electronic eavesdropping (wiretapping) of citizens and noncitizens in the United States upon a showing of probable cause that the target is a foreign power or an agent of a foreign power.[178] This is a significant departure from the probable cause showing required under the Fourth Amendment. Probable cause to search means there must be reasonable grounds to believe evidence of a crime will be found in the place to be searched. Probable cause to arrest means there must be reasonable grounds to believe a crime has been committed and that the person being arrested committed it. FISA, in contrast, only requires reasonable grounds to believe the target is a foreign power or an agent of a foreign power. Previously, FISA was understood to cover foreign intelligence investigations, not ordinary domestic law enforcement investigations. As amended, FISA can now be used to collect evidence against a U.S. citizen for use in a domestic criminal case as long as a "significant" purpose of the investigation is foreign intelligence.[179]

The fear of another terrorist attack has already fueled other proposals to enhance police power. For example, Harvard law professor Bill Stuntz suggests that September 11 justifies (1) increased police power to seize, search, and question groups of individuals without the usual showing of individualized suspicion, (2) secret searches whenever the police want to engage in them, and (3) doing away with the *Miranda* rule.[180]

Acknowledging that young men of Middle Eastern descent have found themselves increasingly the target of suspicion in a post–September 11 world, Stuntz concludes that such ethnic profiling is an inevitable fact of life.[181] Given that the system cannot eliminate the race-based selection of suspects, Stuntz argues it should attempt to reduce the injury those suspects feel once they are selected by law enforcement personnel.[182] Stuntz's solution to the problem of post–September 11 racial profiling is: (1) to provide incentives for police to engage in group, rather than individual, seizures, and (2) to encourage police to treat all suspects more politely.[183]

Stuntz also argues that in light of September 11, police should be allowed to engage in secret searches "whenever the police want to engage in [them], but [would] forbid public disclosure of anything uncovered save in a criminal trial."[184] He would also limit the types of crimes the government could prove using evidence gathered in a secret search.[185]

Finally, Stuntz suggests that the *Miranda* rule is untenable in a post–September 11 world because a terrorist is more likely than the average suspect to invoke his *Miranda* rights.[186] He therefore proposes doing away with the *Miranda* rule, which requires police to cease questioning of a suspect in custody as soon as that person invokes his right to remain silent or his right to counsel. Stuntz would allow police to continue interrogating anyone in custody even if they expressed a desire not to talk or asked to see an attorney.[187] To decrease the possibility of coercion, Stuntz would require all interrogations to be video- and audiotaped.[188] As recent events have made clear, however, incriminating videotapes have a habit of getting erased or destroyed, and thus are unlikely to provide much deterrent effect.[189]

It is unclear whether Stuntz's proposals have caught the attention of any legislators who may put his proposals into action. Nevertheless, the point is that before September 11, proposals to allow the police to engage in group seizures without individualized suspicion as a means of dealing with the problem of racial profiling, allowing police to engage in secret searches whenever they want to (not just when a judge preauthorizes such a search), and allowing police to interrogate suspects who have asked to speak to a lawyer, would have been unthinkable. September 11 and the specter of the Arab-as-Terrorist have made proposals such as Stuntz's seem more mainstream than they might have appeared before September 11.

CONCLUSION

Much work needs to be done to mitigate the damage caused by private and public actors responding to September 11 and the fear of the Arab-as-Terrorist. As Frederick Lawrence has noted, "America, on the whole, has been a staunch defender of the right to be the same or different, although it has fallen short in many of its practices. The question before us is whether progress toward tolerance will continue, or whether, as in many regions of the world, a fatal retrogression will set in."[190] One step in the right direction is recognizing that Arabs and Muslims are not one and the same and that not all Arabs and Muslims are terrorists. Acknowledging the humanity of Arabs and Muslims is a small first step we can take towards combating the Arab (or Muslim)-as-Terrorist stereotype and the hate violence that can result from this stereotype. Beyond this, we must also recognize that the fear engendered by promotion of the Arab-as-Terrorist stereotype can have the deleterious effect of encouraging lawmakers to pass legislation that is aimed at making it easier to detain, question, and search suspected terrorists, but which at the same time can undermine the civil liberties of us all.

NOTES

1. "9/11 Attacks," *New York Times*, Times Topics. http://topics.ny times.com/top/reference/timestopics/subjects/s/sept_11_2001/attacks/index.html (accessed December 21, 2007).

2. Id.

3. Id. The 9/11 Commission determined through testimony, tapes of passengers' phone calls, and flight data recorders recovered from the crash that crew and passengers on United Airlines flight 93 attempted to overpower the terrorists, which led the terrorists to crash the plane in Pennsylvania (*The 9/11 Commission Report: Final Report of the National Commission on Terrorist Attacks on the United States*, Authorized Edition [New York: Norton, 2004]).

4. South Asian American Leaders of Tomorrow (SAALT), *American Backlash: Terrorists Bring War Home in More Ways Than One* (Washington, DC: SAALT 2001), http://www.saalt.org/attachments/1/American%20Backlash%20report.pdf (accessed October 1, 2008); June Han, *"We Are Americans Too": A Comparative Study of the Effects of 9/11 on South Asian Communities* (Cambridge, MA: Discrimination and National Security Initiative, 2006), http://www.geocities.com/dnsinitiative/911_Report.pdf (accessed October 1, 2008).

5. Muneer I. Ahmad, "A Rage Shared by Law: Post-September 11 Racial Violence as Crimes of Passion," 92 *California Law Review* 1259 (2004) (arguing that "we might view physical hate violence as the end product of racial profiling's flawed logic, just as racial profiling may be viewed as a form of violence—whether psychic or physical—flowing from bias").

6. I am not the first person to make this argument. In "A Rage Shared by Law: Post-September 11 Racial Violence as Crimes of Passion," 92 *California Law Review* 1259 (2004), Professor Muneer Ahmad argues that physical violence against Arabs, Muslims, and South Asians by private individuals and racial profiling of the same communities by government entities "are best understood as different facets of the same social, political, and cultural phenomena." Id. at 1277; see also Leti Volpp, "The Citizen and the Terrorist," 49 UCLA *Law Review* 1575 (2002) (arguing that "we can conceptualize the actions of the U.S. populace, in the form of hate violence attacks, as bearing a relationship to the explicit racial profiling by the government").

7.   A common definition of "hate crime" is "[a] crime motivated by the victim's race, color, ethnicity, religion, or national origin," *Black's Law Dictionary*, 8th ed. (Eagan, MN: Thomson West, 2004), 399. For an excellent resource on hate crimes law, see Lu-in Wang, *Hate Crimes Law* (Deerfield, IL: Clark Boardman Callaghan, 2001).

8.   Frederick M. Lawrence, *Punishing Hate: Bias Crimes Under American Law* (Cambridge, MA: 1999), 4.

9.   Andrew E. Taslitz, Condemning the Racist Personality: Why the Critics of Hate Crimes Legislation are Wrong, 40 *Boston College Law Review* 739, 742 (1999).

10.   Lu-in Wang, "The Complexities of 'Hate,'" 60 *Ohio State Law Journal* 799, 809 (1999).

11.   Id. at 810.

12.   Id. at 811.

13.   Id.

14.   Id. at 812.

15.   Id. at 815.

16.   Id. Wang argues that the racial animus model makes three erroneous assumptions: (1) that the perpetrator's bias is personal and based on his own negative attitudes toward the targeted social group, (2) that the perpetrator's bias is deviant and irrational, and (3) that the perpetrator commits his crime for no other reason than to inflict harm on a member of the target group. Id. at 816. Wang challenges these assumptions by examining two classic forms of hate crime: racial violence against blacks during the country's lynching era and antigay violence today. She shows that lynchings during the late 1800s and early 1900s were often motivated by economic considerations and that gay bashings today are often motivated by social considerations. Id. at 833–883. Thus, the prototypical hate criminal's bias is not deviant. Rather, it is shared widely by members of his social group. Id.

17.   18 U.S.C § 245 (1994).

18.   Id.

19.   Some say the "federally protected activities" requirement in Section 245 makes current federal hate crime legislation useless. See Jason A. Abel, "Americans Under Attack: The Need for Federal Hate Crime Legislation in Light of Post-September 11 Attacks on Arab Americans and Muslims," 12 *Asian Law Journal* 41, 45 (2005).

20.   Amardeep Singh, ""We Are Not the Enemy": Hate Crimes Against Arabs, Muslims, and Those Perceived to Be Arab or Muslim after September 11," *Human Rights Watch* 6 (November 2002), http://www.hrw.org/re ports/2002/usahate/usa1102.pdf (accessed October 1, 2008).

21.   Id. The states that do not have any hate crimes legislation are Arkansas, Indiana, New Mexico, South Carolina, and Wyoming. Id. at 6 (citing Anti-Defamation League, State Hate Crime Statutory Provisions). http://www.adl.org/99hatecrime/intro.html (follow "State Hate Crime Laws" hyperlink) (accessed January 4, 2008).

22.   Id.

23.   Id.

24.   Id.

25.   Hate Crimes Statistics Act, Public Law No. 101–275, 104 Stat. 140 (1990) (codified as amended at 28 U.S.C. § 534 (2007)).

26.   The types of hate crimes that are supposed to be reported to the FBI's Uniform Crime Reporting Program include crimes motivated by bias based on "race, religion, disability, sexual orientation, or ethnicity." U.S. Department of Justice Federal Bureau of Investigation, Criminal Justice Information Services Division, *Hate Crime Data Collection*

Guidelines 2 (October 1999), http://www.fbi.gov/ucr/hatecrime.pdf (accessed October 5, 2008). The term *ethnicity* in the statute, however, refers only to whether or not a person is Hispanic. Id. In recognition of the fact that there are other ethnicities, the term *ethnicity/national origin* was later adopted to denote "a group of persons of the same of race or national origin who share common or similar traits, languages, customs, and traditions, *e.g.*, *Arabs*, Hispanics." Id. at 2 (emphasis added). This category—ethnicity/national origin—is meant as an umbrella term encompassing "Anti-Hispanic" bias on the one hand and "Anti-*Other* Ethnicity/National Origin" bias, on the other. Id. at 4 (emphasis added). Under this scheme, anti-Muslim bias would fall under the category of religious bias and anti-Arab bias would fall under the category of other ethnicity/national origin bias, but neither is tracked separately.

27.   SAALT, *American Backlash*, supra note 4 at 3.

28.   Council on Arab-Islamic Relations (CAIR), *Stereotypes and Civil Liberties: The Status of Muslim Civil Rights in the United States: 2002* (Washington, DC: CAIR, 2002), 9.

29.   "Hate crimes" are by definition criminal in nature, whereas "bias incidents" are noncriminal bias-motivated actions. See, for example, Alix Pianin, "What's the Difference Between a Bias Incident and a Hate Crime?" *Columbia Spectator: Online Edition*, October 17, 2007, http://www.columbiaspectator.com/?q = node/27520; see also Justin Wieland, Note, "Peer-on-Peer Hate Crime and Hate-Motivated Incidents Involving Children in California's Public Schools: Contemporary Issues in Prevalence, Response and Prevention," 11 *U.C. Davis Journal of Juvenile Law and Policy* 235, 237–38 (2007).

30.   Singh, "We Are Not the Enemy," supra note 20, at 3.

31.   There is widespread disagreement over how many post-9/11 killings of Arabs, South Asians, Sikhs, and/or Muslims, should be counted as hate crimes. The Justice Department's Civil Rights Division listed nine killings across the country as "possible hate crimes" committed in response to 9/11. The Council on American-Islamic Relations counted eight deaths as part of the backlash. The American-Arab Anti-Discrimination Committee thought six killings constituted hate crimes. Alan Cooperman, "September 11 Backlash Murders and the State of 'Hate': Between Families and Police, a Gulf on Victim Count," *Washington Post*, January 20, 2002, at A3. According to Human Rights Watch, at least three and perhaps as many as seven individuals were killed as a result of September 11 backlash. Singh, "We Are Not the Enemy," supra note 20, at 18.

32.   Singh, "We Are Not the Enemy," supra note 20, at 18–21 (summarizing post-September 11 anti-Arab and anti-Muslim murders and assaults).

33.   Julian Borger, "September 11 Revenge Killer To Die for Shooting Sikh," *Guardian*, October 11, 2003, at 17 ("The murder of Balbir Singh Sodhi, an immigrant from India and the owner of a petrol station, was the first and one of the worst of the reprisal attacks across the US after September 11, 2001").

34.   Robert E. Pierre, "Victims of Hate, Now Feeling Forgotten; Family of Man Killed after 9/11 Finds Little Charity, But Much Hardship," *Washington Post*, September 14, 2002, at A1.

35.   Jim Walsh, "'World Is Watching' Trial in Post-9/11 Sikh Killing," *Arizona Republic*, September 3, 2003, at 1A.

36.   Michael Kiefer and Jim Walsh, "9/11-Tied Slayer Won't Be Executed," *Arizona Republic*, August 15, 2006, at 1.

37.   Mike Anton, "After the Attack; The Psychic Toll; Collateral Damage In War on Terrorism," *Los Angeles Times*, September 22, 2001, at A26.

38.   Id.

39.   Id. Roque's attorneys argued that he should be found not guilty by reason of insanity. A jury rejected Roque's insanity defense and found him guilty of first-degree murder, attempted first-degree murder, reckless endangerment, and three counts of drive-by shooting. Roque was then sentenced to death. The Arizona Supreme Court later commuted Roque's death sentence to life in prison without the possibility of parole on the ground that his mental illness and low IQ were mitigating factors. Kiefer and Walsh, "9/11-Tied Slayer Won't Be Executed," supra note 36.

40.   Charles Stile, "FBI Probes Slaying of Former New Jersey Shopkeeper," *Record*, September 19, 2001, at A22.

41.   Katherine Morales, "Murdered Man's Wife Keeps Alive His Dream," *Dallas Morning News*, October 6, 2003, at 5B; Frank Trujo, "Slain Man's Family in Limbo," *Dallas Morning News*, February 13, 2003, at 28A.

42.   Singh, "We Are Not the Enemy," supra note 20, at 18.

43.   Diane C. Walsh, "Permit Extensions Allow Hate Victim's Kin to Stay," *Star Ledger*, April 16, 2003, at 27.

44.   Ahmad, *A Rage Shared by Law*, supra note 5, at 1266; *see also* CAIR, *Stereotypes and Civil Liberties*, supra note 28, at 9; Singh, "We Are Not the Enemy," supra note 21, at 18–24.

45.   National Asian Pacific American Legal Consortium (NAPALC), *Backlash: When America Turned on Its Own* (Washington, DC: National Asian Pacific American Legal Consortium, 2002), 6.

46.   Id.

47.   Id. at 7.

48.   There is no single definition of the word *Arab.* A common definition focuses on linguistics and/or country of origin and defines Arabs as Arabic-speaking people from one of a number of countries (*New Encyclopaedia Britannica*, vol. 1, 504 [1995]). The League of Arab States includes the following 22 countries: Algeria, Bahrain, Comoros, Djibouti, Egypt, Iraq, Jordan, Kuwait, Lebanon, Libya, Mauritania, Morocco, Oman, Palestine, Qatar, Saudi Arabia, Somalia, Sudan, Syria, Tunisia, United Arab Emirates, and Yemen. Sylvia C. Nassar-McMillan, "Counseling Arab-Americans: Counselors' Call for Advocacy and Social Justice," *Counseling & Human Development* 35 (2003): 1, 3. However, even in scholarly circles of Arab-Americans, "there is debate over which of these countries should be included as countries of origin for Arab Americans." Id.

49.   Muslims are people who are adherents of or believers in Islam. *Webster's Third New International Dictionary of the English Language (Unabridged)* (Springfield, MA: Merriam-Webster, 2002), 1491.

50.   Mohammed T. Mehdi, "Arabs and Muslims in American Society," in *The Politics of Minority Coalitions: Race, Ethnicity, and Shared Uncertainties* 249, 249 (Wilbur C. Rich ed., Westport, CT: Praeger, 1996) (noting that 94 percent of Arabs are Muslim); see also Margaret K. Nydell, *Understanding Arabs: A Guide for Modern Times* (2006), 83 (noting that "today over 90 percent of all Arabs are Muslims").

51.   Jack G. Shaheen, *Reel Bad Arabs: How Hollywood Vilifies a People* (Fowlerville, MI: Olive Branch Press, 2001), 5. See also Douglas Stewart, *What You Should Know about Arabs and Arab-Americans*, http://www.detroit chamber.com/detroiter/articles.asp?cid=103&detcid=182 (accessed January 4, 2008) (noting that 90 percent of all Arabs are Muslim).

52.   Shaheen, *Reel Bad Arabs*, supra note 51, at 5.

53.   Nassar-McMillan, "Counseling Arab-Americans," supra note 47, at 4 (noting that "the major religious affiliations of Arab-Americans are as follows: Catholic [42%], Orthodox [23%], Muslim [23%], and Protestant [12%]").

54.   Mehdi, *Arabs and Muslims in American Society*, supra note 49, at 249. According to Mohammed T. Mehdi, Arabs number approximately 200 million, so even if all Arabs were Muslim, they would still represent only a small percentage of the overall Muslim population in the world. Id.

55.   Rachel Saloom, "I Know You Are, But What Am I?: Arab-American Experiences Through the Critical Race Theory Lens," 27 *Hamline Journal of Public Law and Policy* (2005): 55, 57, citing Stewart, *What You Should Know About Arabs and Arab-Americans*, supra note 51 (noting that only 12 percent of Muslims are Arabs).

56.   Ilhan Kaya, "Muslim American Identities and Diversity," 106 *Journal of Geography* 29, 30 (2007), citing K. I. Leonard, *Muslims in the United States: The State of Research* (2003); Saloom, "I Know You Are, But What Am I?: Arab-American Experiences Through the Critical Race Theory Lens," supra note 55, at 58, citing Joyce Howard Price, "1.2 Million Arabs in U.S., Census States," *Washington Times*, December 3, 2003, http://www.wash times.com/news/2003/dec/03/20031203-113839-9531r/ (accessed October 6, 2008).

57.   Mehdi, "Arabs and Muslims in American Society," supra note 50, at 249.

58.   Nassar-McMillan, "Counseling Arab-Americans," supra note 48, at 4.

59.   Id.

60.   Ahmad, "A Rage Shared by Law," supra note 5, at 1278 (discussing the construction of a new racial construct called the "Muslim-looking" person); Natsu Taylor Saito, "Symbolism Under Siege: Japanese American Redress and the 'Racing' of Arab Americans as 'Terrorists,'" 8 *Asian Law Journal* 1, 11–15 (2001) (discussing the "racing" of Arab-Americans as terrorists).

61.   Karen Engle, "Constructing Good Aliens and Good Citizens: Legitimizing the War on Terror(ism)," 75 *University of Colorado Law Review* 59, 75 (2004).

62.   Id.

63.   Id.

64.   See Lois Romano, "McVeigh Halts Appeals; U.S. Court Rejects Delay; Bomber to Die Monday," *Washington Post*, June 8, 2001, at A1; Jo Thomas, "The Oklahoma City Bombing: The Verdict; McVeigh Jury Decides on Sentence of Death in Oklahoma Bombing," *New York Times*, June 14, 1997, at 1.

65.   Abel, "Americans Under Attack," supra note 19, at 48.

66.   Shaheen, *Reel Bad Arabs*, supra note 51, at 12.

67.   Id.

68.   Id. at 13.

69.   Id. at 10, 13.

70.   Id. at 15.

71.   Id.

72.   *Reel Bad Arabs* (Media Education Foundation, 2006).

73.   Andrew Hindes, "T2 Ushered in $ 100 mil Era," *Variety*, April 29, 1996—May 5, 1996, at 153; Anne Thompson, "They Dubbed to Conquer," *Entertainment Weekly*, October 27, 1995, at 54.

74.   Hollywood Foreign Press Association database of Golden Globe awards, http://www.goldenglobes.org/browse/member/29158 (accessed January 13, 2008).

75.   Felicity Barringer and Douglas Jehl, "U.S. Says Video Shows Captors Killed Reporter," *New York Times*, February 22, 2002, at A1.

76.   Amit R. Paley, "Female Suicide Bomber Attacks in Diyala," *Washington Post*, January 17, 2008, at A16.

77.   See, for example, Samuel R. Gross and Debra Livingston, "Racial Profiling Under Attack," 102 *Columbia Law Review* 1413, 1424 (2002) (noting that "[p]erhaps

the worst instance of ethnic profiling in American history began on February 19, 1942, when President Franklin Delano Roosevelt signed Executive Order 9066, giving the Secretary of War the power to order over 110,000 Japanese-Americans on the West Coast to be 'resettle[d]' in 'relocation centers' for the duration of the war"); see also Saito, "Symbolism Under Siege," supra note 60, at 6–8 (discussing the narrative of the internment as having "the markings of a feel-good story: a terrible thing happened, but the nation recognized its wrong and stepped forward to provide some redress").

78. Volpp, "The Citizen and the Terrorist," supra note 6, at 1591, citing *Gallup Poll Analysis: The Impact of the Attacks on America*, http://www.gal lup.com/poll/releases/pr010914c.asp (showing that one in three Americans polled shortly after 9/11 favored internment for people of Arab descent).

79. A December 1999 Gallup Poll found that 81 percent of the public disapproved of racial profiling. Florangela Davila, "ACLU Ads to Spotlight 'Racial Profiling' Issue," *Seattle Times*, April 20, 2000, at B5.

80. Sharon L. Davies, "Profiling Terror," 1 *Ohio State Journal of Criminal Law* 45, 46 n. 6 (2003).

81. Id.; see also David Van Biema, "As American As . . . ," *Time*, October 1, 2001, at 72.

82. Davies, "Profiling Terror," supra note 80, at 48.

83. Perry Bacon, Jr., "Foes Use Obama's Muslim Ties to Fuel Rumors about Him," *Washington Post*, November 29, 2007, at A1. Senator Obama, a member of the congregation of the United Church of Christ in Chicago, has openly acknowledged that his paternal grandfather, a Kenyan farmer, was Muslim and that he (Senator Obama) spent part of his childhood living in Indonesia, a predominantly Muslim country. Id.

84. Id.

85. Tim Craig, "GOP Head Compares Obama to Bin Laden," *Washington Post*, October 13, 2008, at B1 (noting that the chairman of the Virginia Republican Party made this comparison because of Obama's "past association with Bill Ayers, who has confessed to domestic bombings as a member of the Vietnam War-era Weather Underground.").

86. Kate Phillips, "Palin: Obama is 'Palling Around with Terrorists,'" *The New York Times Politics Blog*, available at http://thecaucus.blogs.nytimes.com/2008/10/04/palin-obama-is-palling-around-with-terrorists/ (accessed October 15, 2008) (noting that in remarks at a Colorado airport hangar, Palin told supporters that Obama "is someone who sees America it seems as being so imperfect that he's palling around with terrorists who would target their own country"). *See also* The Associated Press, "Palin Defends Terrorist Comment Against Obama," MSNBC.com, available at http://www.msnbc.msn.com/id/27022487/ (accessed October 15, 2008) (noting that while Bill Ayers, a founder of the Weather Underground group during the Vietnam War era, and Barack Obama both served on the same Chicago charity, "the charge that they 'pal around' is a stretch of any reading of the public record" and that Obama was only 8 years old at the time the Weather Underground claimed credit for numerous bombings).

87. Khaled Hosseini, "McCain and Palin are Playing with Fire," *Washington Post*, October 12, 2008, at B5 (editorial by the author of *The Kite Runner* and *A Thousand Splendid Suns*).

88. It does not make sense to say that someone appears to be Muslim because being Muslim is a religious identity, not a racial identity. See infra note 49.

89. Han, "We Are Americans Too," supra note 4, at 1 n. 1.

90. Id. at 2 ("Turban-wearing Sikhs have been targeted for hate crimes and profiling incidents since 9/11 because they are often misidentified as Arabs and Muslims.").

See also *Backlash*, supra note 45, at 3 (noting that during coverage of the 9/11 attacks, the media repeatedly showed pictures of Osama Bin Laden with a long beard and turban, which may have led "certain segments of the public [to] identify the turbans and beards worn by Sikh American men with Bin Laden, even though the style of the turbans are not the same.").

91.   Singh, "'We Are Not the Enemy,'" supra note 20, at 18.

92.   *Backlash*, supra note 45, at 7 (noting that "[n]early all (96%) of the 243 [post–September 11 backlash] incidents documented by NAPALC and its Affiliates involved victims of South Asian descent, namely immigrants from India or Pakistan"). NAPALC (National Asian Pacific Asian Pacific American Legal Consortium) also found that in contrast to past practice, the victims and perpetrators of post–September 11 hate violence included women, senior citizens, and even children. Id. at 2.

93.   Sophie Goodchild, "Humiliation at 33,000 Feet," *Independent on Sunday* (London), October 1, 2006, at 3.

94.   Id.

95.   Id.

96.   Id.

97.   Id.

98.   Id.

99.   Id.

100.   Davies, "Profiling Terror," supra note 80, at 47 n. 7.

101.   David Ballingrud et al., "Terror Alert Shuts Florida Road; Three Questioned," *St. Petersburg Times Online*, September 14, 2002, available at http://www.sptimes.com/2002/09/14/news_pf/State/Terror_alert_shuts_Fl.shtml (accessed October 6, 2008).

102.   Id.

103.   Id.

104.   Id.

105.   Id.

106.   Kelli Arena et al., *Man in Terror Scare Says Woman Is Lying*, CNN.com, September 13, 2002, available at http://archives.cnn.com/2002/US/09/13/alligator.alley/index.html (accessed October 7, 2008).

107.   Id.

108.   Id.

109.   Id. Ballingrud, "Terror Alert Shuts Florida Road," supra note 101.

110.   Arena et al., *Man in Terror Scare Says Woman is Lying*, supra note 106.

111.   *Larry King Live* (CNN television broadcast September 16, 2002) (interview with three men detained by police after a woman thought she overheard them plotting another terrorist attack).

112.   *Biographical Directory of the United States Congress, 1774—Present*, available at http://bioguid.congress.gov/scripts/biodisplay.pl?index=G000352/ (noting that Graham chaired the Senate Committee on Intelligence during the 107th Congress, January 3–20, 2001, and June 6, 2001—January 3, 2003).

113.   Ballingrud, "Terror Alert Shuts Florida Road," supra note 101.

114.   Id.

115.   Natsu Saito notes that "Arab-Americans and Muslims have been 'raced' as 'terrorists': foreign, disloyal, and imminently threatening." Saito, "Symbolism under Siege," supra note 60, at 12.

116.   Id. Other groups, such as Asian Americans and Latinos, have been raced as foreigners. See Cynthia Kwei Yung Lee, "Race and Self-Defense: Toward a Normative Conception of Reasonableness," 81 *Minnesota Law Review* 367, 428–438, 441–442 (1996).

117.   Volpp, "the Citizen and the Terrorist," supra note 6, at 1592.

118.   Id.

119.   Dan Eggen and John Solomon, "Justice Department's Focus Has Shifted: Terror, Immigration Are Current Priorities," *Washington Post*, October 17, 2007, at A1. See also "DOJ White Collar Prosecutions Drop As Terrorism Cases Rise, Study Says," 78 U*nited States Law Week* 2232, 2232 (2007) (noting that a survey of federal prosecutions during the Bush administration conducted by the Transactional Records Access Clearinghouse [TRAC] at Syracuse University found that Justice Department prosecutions for white-collar crime and official corruption cases dropped significantly while terrorism-related and immigration prosecutions showed substantial increases since fiscal year 2000).

120.   Michael A. Fletcher and Jonathan Weisman, "Bush Signs Bill Authorizing 700-Mile Fence for Border," *Washington Post*, October 27, 2006, at A4.

121.   Carl Hulse, "A Build-a-Protest Approach to Immigration," *New York Times*, May 31, 2006, at A15.

122.   See Michael Abramowitz, "Immigrant Legislation Splits GOP; Right Lashes Out at Bush and Senate over Compromise," *Washington Post*, May 19, 2007, at A1.

123.   Stephen Deere, "City Tries to Sidestep Lawsuits," *St. Louis Post-Dispatch*, September 27, 2006, at D1 (noting new St. Louis ordinance penalizing businesses and landlords that hire and rent to illegal immigrants); Jennifer Edwards, "Butler County Pushes Pledge," *Cincinnati Enquirer*, February 7, 2006, at 1C (noting that Butler County, Ohio, is considering a plan that would require business owners to sign pledges not to hire illegal immigrants as a condition necessary to receive and keep a license to do business); Jim Lockwood and Maura McDermott, "Law Targeting Illegals Takes Shape in Newton," *Star-Ledger*, September 1, 2006, at 1 (noting that officials in Newton, New Jersey, are considering legislation that would deny business permits and city contracts for five years to any business owner who hires an illegal immigrant and impose fines on landlords who rent to illegal immigrants ranging from $1,000 for a first offense to $10,000 for three or more offenses); Emilie Lounsberry, "Illegal Immigrant Laws Spur Two Suits," *Philadelphia Inquirer*, August 16, 2006, at A1 (noting that Riverside, California, bans hiring or renting to illegal immigrants, with employers and landlords facing a fine of $1,000 for each violation and the denial of business permits and municipal contracts and grants); Laura Parker, "Court Tests Await Cities' Laws on Immigrants," *USA Today*, October 9, 2006, at 3A (noting that under Hazelton, Pennsylvania's new ordinance, business owners and landlords are penalized if they employ or rent to illegal immigrants by having their licenses to do business revoked); Amy Worden and Mario F. Cattabiani, "Court Voids Hazelton Law," *Philadelphia Inquirer*, July 27, 2007, at A1 (noting that more than 100 municipalities have passed legislation modeled after an ordinance enacted in Hazelton, Pennsylvania, penalizing businesses that hire and landlords that rent to illegal immigrants). In July 2007, the Hazelton ordinance was struck down by a federal district court judge. Amy Worden and Mario F. Cattabiani, "Court Voids Hazelton Law," *Philadelphia Inquirer*, July 27, 2007, at A1.

124.   Dan Genz, "Crackdown on Illegal Immigration Hitting Its Stride," *Examiner* (*V*irginia ed.), December 28, 2007, at 4 (noting that police officers in Prince William County, Virginia, will soon start checking whether people pulled over for a traffic offense or stopped for a minor misdemeanor are legally in the United States); Nick Miroff, "Questions Remain on Illegal Immigrants," *Washington Post*, July 12, 2007, at B1 (noting that the Board of County Supervisors in Prince William County, Virginia, unanimously approved a resolution that authorizes police officers to inquire about the residency status of a person if they have probable cause to believe that person is not

legally in the United States); Jean O. Pasco, "City's Border Policy Sparks Outcry," *Los Angeles Times*, January 4, 2006, at B1 (noting that Costa Mesa in Orange County, California, was the first county to authorize its police department to enforce the nation's immigration laws).

125. Tim Craig, "Virginia Considers Detention Center for Immigrants," *Washington Post*, September 26, 2007, at A1.

126. Nick Miroff and Kristen Mack, "As Hundreds Testify, Prince William's Vote on Immigrant Plan Goes Late," *Washington Post*, October 17, 2007, at A1.

127. WhiteHouse.gov, *Backgrounder: The President's Quotes on Islam: In the President's Words: Respecting Islam*, http://www.whitehouse.gov/infocus/ra madan/islam.html (accessed January 4, 2008).

128. See *CIA World Factbook*, https://www.cia.gov/library/publications/the-world factbook/geos/id.html#People (accessed February 1, 2008).

129. Id.

130. Id.

131. Id.

132. For a more in-depth critique of government actions in the war on terror and how these actions have contributed to the Arab or Muslim-looking person-as-Terrorist stereotype, see Ahmad, "A Rage Shared by Law," supra note 5.

133. Ahmad, "A Rage Shared by Law," supra note 5, at 1270; Susan M. Akram and Kevin R. Johnson, "Race, Civil Rights, and Immigration Law after September 11, 2001: The Targeting of Arabs and Muslims," 58 *New York University Annual Survey of American Law* 295, 331 (2002); David Cole, "Enemy Aliens," 54 *Stanford Law Review* 953, 960 (2002); Office of the Inspector General for the Department of Justice, *The September 11 Detainees: A Review of the Treatment of Aliens Held on Immigration Charges in Connection with the Investigation of the September 11 Attacks* (2003), http://www.usdoj.gov/oig/special/0306/full.pdf [hereinafter *OIG Report*] (confirming that within two months of the September 11 attacks, law enforcement authorities had detained, at least for questioning, more than 1,200 citizens and aliens nationwide). According to David Cole, every aspect of the proceedings was closed to the public press and even family members. David Cole, "In Aid of Removal: Due Process Limits on Immigrant Detention," 51 *Emory Law Journal* 1003, 1005 (2002). Susan Akram and Maritz Karmely explain the various ways in which these detentions were conducted in secret. Susan M. Akram & Maritza Karmely, "Immigration and Constitutional Consequences of Post-9/11 Policies Involving Arabs and Muslims in the United States: Is Alienage a Distinction Without a Difference?," 38 *U.C. Davis Law Review* 609, 625–26 (2005).

134. *OIG Report*, supra note 133, at 1. The Department of Justice stopped reporting the number of individuals detained once the number reached approximately 1,200 because "the statistics became too confusing." Id.

135. Id. at 2 (noting that detainees and their attorneys "alleged that the detainees were not informed of the charges against them for extended periods of time; were not permitted contact with attorneys, their families, and embassy officials; remained in detention even though they had no involvement in terrorism; or were physically abused, verbally abused, and mistreated in other ways while detained").

136. John W. Whitehead and Steven H. Aden, "Forfeiting 'Enduring Freedom' for 'Homeland Security': A Constitutional Analysis of the USA PATRIOT Act and the Justice Department's Anti-Terrorism Initiatives," 51 *American University Law Review* 1081, 1117 (2002).

137. *OIG Report*, supra note 133, at 2.

138.   Id. at 27 (noting that while some of the arrests resulted in criminal charges, "the vast majority of September 11 detainees were charged with civil violations of federal immigration law"); see Ahmad, "A Rage Shared by Law," supra note 5, at 1271.

139.   *OIG Report*, supra note 133, at 142–132.

140.   Id. at 143.

141.   Id. at 143, 145.

142.   Id. at 144.

143.   Id.

144.   Id. at 150.

145.   Id.

146.   Tracey Maclin, "'Voluntary' Interviews and Airport Searches of Middle Eastern Men: The Fourth Amendment in a Time of Terror," 73 *Mississippi Law Journal* 471, 479 (2003), citing Florangela Davis and Mike Carter, "Immigrants Urged to Exercise Rights," *Seattle Times*, November 21, 2001, at B1; see Samuel R. Gross and Debra Livingston, "Racial Profiling Under Attack," 102 *Columbia Law Review* 1413, 1417 (2002).

147.   Gross and Livingston, "Racial Profiling Under Attack," supra note 146, at 1417.

148.   Maclin, "'Voluntary' Interviews and Airport Searches of Middle Eastern Men," supra note 146, at 480, citing *Memorandum from the Attorney General to All United States Attorneys and all Members of the Anti-Terrorism Task Forces* (November 9, 2001), http://www.usdoj.gov/ag/readingroom/terror ism1.htm (accessed October 6, 2008).

149.   Id. at 481.

150.   Id.

151.   Id. at 480, citing *Memorandum from the Attorney General to All United States Attorneys and All Members of the Anti-Terrorism Task Forces* (November 9, 2001), http://www.usdoj.gov/ag/readingroom/terrorism1.htm (accessed October 6, 2008).

152.   Id. at 482–483.

153.   Id. at 486.

154.   Id. at 493.

155.   Gross and Livingston, "Racial Profiling Under Attack," supra note 146, at 1436–1437.

156.   Sherry F. Colb, "Profiling with Apologies," 1 *Ohio State Journal of Criminal Law* 611, 613 (2004).

157.   Id. at 616 (emphasis added).

158.   Id.

159.   Id. at 624.

160.   In Colb's defense, she does not suggest that pulling over Arabs and Muslims driving on the highway is a sensible way to catch terrorists. Rather, she suggests that if someone in the Arab or Muslim community is likely to have been involved in a terrorist attack, then interviewing a large proportion of the Arab-Muslim community in a respectful manner and compensating the individuals interviewed is likely to bring authorities into contact with someone who has something useful to share with authorities. Communication with Sherry Colb on January 23, 2008 (copy on file with author).

161.   Besides North Korea, all of the countries designated for special registration are predominantly Arab or Muslim. Dan Kesselbrenner and Lory D. Rosenberg, *Immigration Law and Crimes* 8–10 (New York: Clark Boardman, 1985). Armenia, a non-Muslim non-Arab country, was designated for a short time, "then removed after a public outcry by the politically-influential US Armenian American community." Id. at 8–10—8–11.

162.   Ahmad, "A Rage Shared by Law," supra note 5, at 1274 n. 55; see also Victor Romero, "Race, Immigration, and the Department of Homeland Security," 19 *St. John's Journal of Legal Commentary* 51, 55–59 (2004) (discussing the NSEERS program).

163.   Kesselbrenner and Rosenberg, *Immigration Law and Crimes*, supra note 159, at 8–8.

164.   Id. at 8–8 to 8–9.

165.   Id. at 8–9.

166.   Id. at 8–12.

167.   Id.

168.   Id. at 8–11.

169.   Id.

170.   Id.

171.   Aziz Z. Huq and Christopher Muller, "The War on Crime as Precursor to the War on Terror," *International Journal of Law, Crime and Justice* [forthcoming 2008]), at 10.

172.   Id.

173.   Id., citing James Zogby, "Injustice toward Immigrants," *Baltimore Sun*, January 13, 2006.

174.   *Uniting and Strengthening America by Providing Appropriate Tools Required to Intercept and Obstruct Terrorism (USA PATRIOT) Act of 2001*, Public Law 107–56, § 213, 115 Stat. 272, 285–86 (2001) (hereinafter *USA Patriot Act*).

175.   Id.

176.   Id.

177.   Id. § 218; see also Whitehead and Aden, "Forfeiting 'Enduring Freedom' for 'Homeland Security,'" supra note 134, at 1103 (noting that this change in language "greatly expands the power of federal authorities to apply the relatively loose FISA standards to investigations of both U.S. citizens and residents that only tangentially touch on national security").

178.   *USA Patriot Act* § 218.

179.   Id.; see also Akram and Karmely, "Immigration and Constitutional Consequences of Post-9/11 Policies Involving Arabs and Muslims in the United States," supra note 131, at 639 (noting that § 218 enables law enforcement agencies conducting a criminal investigation to "subvert Fourth Amendment requirements simply by claiming that foreign intelligence-gathering is 'a significant purpose' of their investigation").

180.   William J. Stuntz, "Local Policing after the Terror," 111 *Yale Law Journal* 2137 (2002).

181.   Id. at 2179.

182.   Id.

183.   Id. at 2179–80. Stuntz would not allow law enforcement to use race, sex, alienage or occupation as a basis for a group search. Id. at 2163. He would only allow police to search "classes of people defined by place and time—everyone who happens to be driving past a particular point on a particular road at a particular time, everyone who occupies a given building or public space at a given time, and so forth." Id.

184.   Id. at 2183–84.

185.   Id. at 2137.

186.   Id. at 2189.

187.   Id.

188.   Id.

189.   Dan Eggen and Joby Warrick, "CIA Destroyed Videos Showing Interrogations; Harsh Techniques Seen in 2002 Tapes," *Washington Post*, December 7, 2007, at A1; Joby Warrick and Walter Pincus, "Station Chief Made Appeal to Destroy CIA Tapes," *Washington Post*, January 16, 2008, at A1.

190.   Frederick Lawrence, "The Punishment of Hate: Toward a Normative Theory of Bias-Motivated Crimes," 93 *Michigan Law Review* 320 (1994).

CHAPTER 8

SCHOOL–BASED ANTIHATE INITIATIVES

Lindsay J. Friedman, Esther Hurh, Nicole Manganelli, and Stephen Wessler

I felt emotionally and physically weak. I was out of synch. I couldn't think anymore, my grades and self-esteem dropped. My life became a disaster. I was contemplating taking my own life or maybe that of other kids.

—11th grader, Vermont

This quote offers a troubling and frightening picture of the impact of verbal and physical bullying and harassment on one young student in our nation's schools. As is the case with many school-based hate incidents and crimes, this student's experiences began first with a daily torrent of words, sneers, and jokes, eventually culminating in physical assault. Hate incidents and crimes are intended to intimidate and harass, and generate humiliation, fear, and anxiety not only in the target but also in the target's community. When such an incident occurs at school, the entire school community is negatively impacted: learning is disrupted, instruction is occupied with classroom management, and school safety and sense of community is threatened.

School-based antihate initiatives are important in large measure because youth are reported to commit a significant portion of hate crimes, most of which occur in school or in their neighborhoods. Data based on reports of hate crimes sent to the Federal Bureau of Investigation (FBI) by local and state police departments show that 33 percent of all hate crimes are committed by offenders who are less than age 18. Further, youth commit 31 percent of all violent hate crimes and 46 percent of all property hate crimes. An additional 29 percent of offenders are between ages 18 and 24. A total of 62 percent of hate crimes are committed by young adults and teens under 24 years of age (Strom, 2001). Data compiled by the Federal Bureau of Investigation (FBI) in 2006 based on reports from reporting agencies establishes that 12.2 percent of hate crimes occur in school (2007).

The reasons why youth commit such a high percentage of hate crimes vary. It may be because many of today's teens have greater contact with people of diverse backgrounds, giving rise to hateful expressions of stereotypical thinking and prejudicial attitudes, or it may be that young people who are confused or angry about their personal life circumstances may be more prone to turn to violence towards others. Regardless of the reasons, the growing diversity of the youth population requires school leaders and educators to think about how the school setting will manage this diversity. Today, more than 40 percent of the children in public schools are from what have traditionally been called minority groups (Planty et al., 2007). It is projected that this figure will rise to almost 50 percent within the next two decades. While this shift represents tremendous opportunities for cross-cultural learning and understanding, the daily interaction in school between students who are different from one another can bring forth anxieties and prejudices, which can escalate to hate incidents and hate crimes.

A comprehensive review of responses to hate crimes cannot be complete without an examination of the education response, specifically efforts within public, private, and parochial middle and high school settings, to address the problem. School-based efforts, however, should not be limited to merely an understanding of and compliance with the legal steps school administrators and educators must take if a hate crime or incident occurs, but should also include comprehensive and preventative efforts that build mutual respect and safe, inclusive learning environments for all students. Diligent and consistent responses by public officials and law enforcement authorities can play an essential role in deterring and preventing hate crimes. Nonetheless, to eliminate stereotyping and biases that fuel hateful words and potentially violent acts requires an education intervention.

The educational response to hate crime prevention must dig deep to examine where the seeds of hatred and bias take root and to take measures to interrupt this growth at its base. Rarely are school-based hate crimes or bias incidents isolated moments that appear without precedent. Hate crimes and bias-based violence are often the end result of a long socialization process that permits small acts of intolerance to escalate into larger, more pronounced forms of discrimination. This progression can be understood by imagining a pyramid with different levels (see Figure 8.1), starting at the base with stereotyping and acts of bias (e.g., jokes and slurs, insensitive comments), and escalating into prejudice and bigotry (e.g., name-calling, epithets), to discrimination and scapegoating, leading potentially to vandalism and violence. If people or institutions treat behaviors on the lower levels as benign or acceptable, it can result in the behaviors at the next

Figure 8.1 Pyramid of Hate

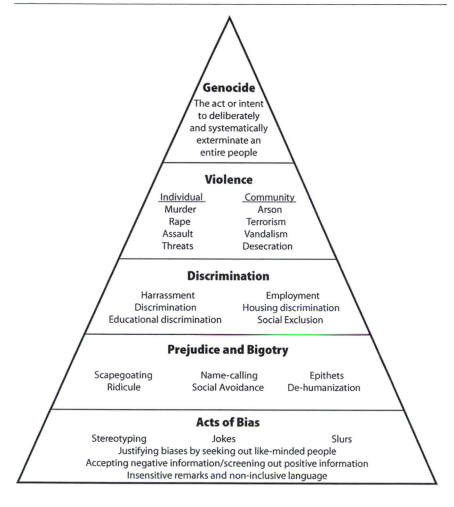

Genocide
The act or intent
to deliberately
and systematically
exterminate an
entire people

Violence

Individual	Community
Murder	Arson
Rape	Terrorism
Assault	Vandalism
Threats	Desecration

Discrimination

Harrassment   Employment
Discrimination   Housing discrimination
Educational discrimination   Social Exclusion

Prejudice and Bigotry

Scapegoating   Name-calling   Epithets
Ridicule   Social Avoidance   De-humanization

Acts of Bias

Stereotyping   Jokes   Slurs
Justifying biases by seeking out like-minded people
Accepting negative information/screening out positive information
Insensitive remarks and non-inclusive language

level becoming more tolerated, if not acceptable. In order to curb this tide, it's important for teachers, school administrators, parents—and students themselves—to work diligently to interrupt the escalation, especially starting at the lower levels.

This chapter begins by reviewing the current state of bias and harassment in schools: What is the day-to-day experience of youth as they navigate the hallways and classrooms of the average school? What is the impact of bias and hate on students who are the targets as well as on the larger school population? The following two sections of the chapter will provide a review of effective models of intervention and training for students as well as educators and administrators, outlining specific approaches and methods that can

be employed to effectively respond to hate and bias and create an environment built on mutual respect, understanding, and achievement for all members of the school community.

BIAS AND HARASSMENT IN SCHOOLS

> I have been verbally attacked and ridiculed many times in my life but no
> words can begin to describe how it feels to see one of your peers trying
> to imitate your limping or the way you walk right in front of you. And
> no words can describe what it feels like to hear laughter accompanied
> with degrading remarks behind you, as you walk away, trying to es-
> cape.
>
> —*12th grader, Connecticut*

From the moment of birth, each of us begins a long and complex journey
of identity development and socialization. From the earliest years, we are
socialized on a personal level by parents and caregivers, educators, relatives,
and others whom we trust, each of whom shape and define our norms and
values. This cycle of socialization becomes more complex as conscious and
unconscious messages from our culture, house of worship, education institutions, media, and institutions inform the lens through which we see the world
and our and others' place in it (Adams, Bell, & Griffin, 1997). Thus while no
one is born prejudiced or full of animus towards others based on the color of
their skin or the language that they speak, for example, it is in these critical
years that the seeds of intolerance and bias can be planted. Research in fact
indicates that by preschool, some children have already acquired stereotypes
or negative attitudes toward those they perceive as "others" (Derman-Sparks
as cited in Anti-Defamation League, 2000). In an attempt to minimize the
development of prejudice, well-meaning adults often teach children to ignore
differences and value and focus only on similarities, inadvertently reinforc-
ing the notion that being different from one another is a negative aspect of
one's character, personality, or identity. Further, a lack of intervention when
stereotypes are expressed or acted upon, or a reinforcement of prejudicial
thinking and stereotypical attitudes by parents, family members, and others
who influence the psychosocial development of young children can further
contribute to cross-cultural misunderstanding, mistrust, and the expression
of biased attitudes and behaviors.

In the preteen and teen years, young people are developing and questioning not only their own identity and their place in the world. As anyone who
works with preadolescents and adolescents knows, a sense of belonging is
critical. For some, this belonging is only achieved through a lens of "us" and
"them" or "other" in order to strengthen one's sense of place within the powerful social structure of the school setting. The "other" may be classified as a
student or students who are interpersonally awkward, have unusual hobbies

or interests, or have little or no social group network. In addition, however, the "other" can be and often is defined by someone's social group identity such as his or her race, immigration status, religion, gender, and sexual orientation. While these divisions may organize and simplify our surroundings to help shape interactions, such divisions with the overlay of negative, overgeneralized, or incorrect attitudes and information have a highly detrimental effect on intergroup interactions. Such manifestations of prejudicial thinking on behavior can be found in the following statistics:

- More than a third of all students ages 12–18 report having observed hate-related graffiti and one in nine students have had hate-related words used against them (Dinkes, Cataldi, Kena, & Baum, 2006).
- 90 percent of students hear gay epithets in school on a regular basis (Kosciw & Diaz, 2006).
- In a study of bullying, teasing, and sexual harassment in school, 83 percent of girls and 79 percent of boys report having ever experienced harassment at school, with over one in four students experiencing it "often." Seventy-six percent of students have experienced nonphysical harassment while 58 percent have experienced physical harassment, with one-third of all students reporting that they experience physical harassment "often or occasionally." Eighteen percent of students fear being hurt by someone in their school life "some" or "most" of the time, and less than half (46 percent) are "never" afraid in school (American Association of University Women Educational Foundation, 2001).

Further, with increases in technological capabilities and the increased access of this equipment to teens, there are increasing reports that some youth are misusing Internet and cell phone technology to harass and bully others, and even to incite violence against them. The organization entitled Fight Crime: Invest in Kids reported that approximately 13 million children aged 6 to 17 have been the targets of cyberbullying (2006a, 2006b). For some of these youth, online cruelty may be a precursor to more destructive behavior, including involvement in hate groups and bias-related violence.

School administrators and classroom teachers, who are at the center of the education experience of children, do not always feel well prepared to work with their students on issues related to prejudice and stereotyping or feel equipped to respond to the incidents of bias that may emerge within the classroom and hallways. This lack of preparedness or response may result from unclear or ill-defined school policies and expectations regarding name-calling, bullying, harassment, or vandalism, from a lack of confidence in the best methods to raise these topics or confront incidents, or even in some cases from the adult's own personal biases or beliefs.

Despite a demographic disparity between an 85 percent white teaching force (National Center for Education Information, 2005) and an increasingly diverse student population, educators must possess the knowledge and skills to effectively teach and reach all students, regardless if their students' culture, language, learning style, and experiences are ones with which they may not be familiar. However, according to a 2000 survey by the U.S. Department of Education, only one in three public school teachers said that they felt well prepared to address the needs of students from diverse cultural backgrounds or with limited English proficiency (Parsad, Lewis, & Farris, 2001). Perhaps not surprising, research also indicates a significant disparity between the educational experiences of students of color versus those of most of their white peers. A recent school climate survey shows that students of color feel less respected by their teachers and are less likely to believe that teachers treat everyone fairly or care about their academic success (Perkins, 2007).

How do these various factors play out in schools? A 2003 survey conducted by Widmeyer Communications for the Health, Resources, and Services Administration (HRSA) of the U.S. Department of Health and Human Services underscores the "omnipresent fear of physical violence and name-calling" that students age 9–13 feel. The report describes the prevailing view among students that teachers and administrators "don't get it" when it comes to verbal and emotional bullying, instead simply focusing on physical bullying. Students who participated in the HRSA survey report that it is not worth the effort to tell an adult about bullying because bullies are rarely punished severely enough to deter them from future bullying. Students in the study describe "unsympathetic and apathetic teachers and principals" as "difficult to motivate to take action," who dole out "weak and ineffective penalties and punishments for bullies that allows bullying to flourish." For those who become the targets of these expressions of bias and animus and who feel unsupported by school adults, the school experience is one of isolation, harassment, and even violence.

THE IMPACT OF BIAS AND HATE

One of my fantasies is going to heaven because I believe that I when I get there I won't have to worry about all this harassment. . . . I just won't have pain, and no one will be going through pain. I look forward to it because it will be like the better place than this world.

—*Middle school student, Illinois*

Bias-motivated harassment and violence in schools has an immensely destructive impact on targeted students, on bystanders, and on school climate itself. Schools in which harassment and violence are widespread become places where many students suffer deep emotional pain, have trouble focusing on academic work, and lose the opportunity to experience their school years with joy and hope.

Social and Emotional Harm

The middle-school student who made the opening statement to this chapter section was asked to imagine a place where there was no harassment. The old adage that "sticks and stones can break your bones but words can never hurt you" simply does not apply to this and countless other students. For many students the damage of a punch or a kick is short- lived. However, the social impact and emotional pain and damage of verbal harassment, slurs, and put-downs can last for years and, for some, a lifetime. Some students, like the one quoted above, cannot even imagine a school in which they will be respected. Rather, these students both expect and experience school as a place where humiliation and degradation are daily phenomena. The social and emotional impact of bias and harassment on targeted students—in the form of fear, anger, withdrawal, and loss of spirit and hope—is both deeply destructive and deeply disturbing.

Fear

Verbal harassment directed at students who are perceived to be different from the norm, whether because of race, religion, gender, sexual orientation, gender identity, ability, or other reasons, often creates fear. This fear can range from mild anxiety to overwhelming terror. As one student reports, "I have a friend who has been picked on so much that every time he goes to school he is scared because he thinks someone is going to hurt him. Every day when he comes to school, a group of friends have to walk him to class or wherever he goes so he will feel safe."

Bias-motivated harassment leads to fear primarily for two reasons. First, students who are regularly subject to verbal abuse and degradation expect that the harassment will continue. This expectation and anticipation can create fear of what will happen after the next class, at lunch, in gym, and on the bus ride home. Sadly, students do not escape this anticipatory fear when they get home because they know that the harassment may continue at home through text messages or e-mails and that early the next morning the barrage of hateful words will begin again the moment they step on the bus. In fact, a 2006 Illinois study about cyberbullying reported that 70 percent of the harmful messages that teens receive come while they are at home (Fight Crime: Invest in Kids, 2006b).

Second, students who are subject to racial, religious, gender, and antigay harassment know that the words may escalate to stronger words, to threats, and finally to violence. The fear of being humiliated daily is ratcheted up significantly for those students who worry that they may be targeted with serious violence. For those students who have experienced violence the fear can become immense. Consider for example a report several years ago of a gay high school student who was walking home from school on a fall afternoon when he was chased down, taunted with homophobic slurs, and ultimately beaten. The attack was preceded by weeks of taunting and verbal harassment. After the attack, when approached by a hate crime prosecutor to check on the boy's state, his mother reported that their son continued to be so traumatized by the event and fearful that his classmates would return to "kill him in his sleep" that he had taken to climbing out of his second story bedroom window to sleep (or attempt to sleep) on a flat part of the roof.

Anger

In addition to fear and anxiety caused by bias-motivated harassment, students may also, and do often, become angry. In many instances anger can turn the target of harassment into the perpetrator of degrading language or even violence. And ironically, often it is this angry and violent response by the victim of harassment that receives the greater disciplinary response from the school or even the juvenile criminal justice system. One high school student described her anger caused by a school climate rife with degrading language.

> Every day I feel like I'm getting closer to going insanely psycho. This is mostly because of how racist, prejudice, and homophobic my school is. I get so mad when I hear people say words like "nigger, gay, fag" and "retard" or when people come up to me and say, "Can I pet your hair?" I'm just hoping that I don't snap one day and do something I'll regret forever.

Examples of the target of harassment and bullying becoming the perpetrator of extreme school violence have been often reported and documented in several recent cases. In less severe forms, the contagious effect of prejudice and bias is also common. In a 2007 study of 177 grade seven middle school students, 85.5 percent of those who reported bullying others said that they had also been targets of bullying (Li, 2007).

Withdrawal

Students who experience daily or even intermittent harassment or bullying may often withdraw from others in the school, home, and community environments. These students may isolate themselves in an attempt to avoid degrading language and conduct or they may do so out of fear of further rejection by others. Both types of isolation can cause loneliness and depression and lead to even greater negative outcomes.

At a recent focus group about racial harassment with students of color at a high school, a Latino student refused to make eye contact and consistently denied that he had been subject to any racial bias. However, when asked if he could describe one incident he had seen or heard at school involving harassment directed at students of color, he revealed that he had become "sick and tired" of the constant racial slurs and stereotypes directed at him. He added that he had "dealt" with the harassment, and it no longer bothered him. When asked how he had dealt with it, he responded that he "had stopped playing football, had no friends," did not participate in any extracurricular activities and left school as soon as the last bell rang to avoid any conversations with students. He avoided any contact with students in an attempt to avoid bias and harassment.

The withdrawal and loss of spirit experienced by this and many students is, in some sense, both the most difficult form of impact to measure, as well as the most disturbing. It is difficult to know how many students "disappear" in school: withdrawing from social activities and classroom participation, giving up on interests they once pursued and melting into the background of busy school environments. These students often become the silent casualties of bias and harassment, as they minimize or end completely their contributions to their school and community.

Self–Destructive Conduct

Some students who experience fear, anger, withdrawal, and other social and emotional impacts of bias and harassment sometimes turn to selfdestructive conduct. The range of harmful conduct is broad: drug and alcohol abuse, cutting or other forms of self-injury, eating disorders, sexual promiscuity, attempted suicide, and suicide. Many high school students know classmates who engage in one or more of these harmful activities. In a 2002 study of Canadian high school students, 13.9 percent of urban and suburban students reported that they had performed acts of self-injury (Ross & Heath, 2002). A survey of 633 9th- to 12th-grade students in the southern and Midwestern United States found that 28 percent of the students studied had engaged in "moderate to severe forms" of self-injury (Lloyd-Richardson, Perrine, Dierker, & Kelley, 2007). In another survey, children who are bullied are five times more likely to be depressed than their peers; bullied boys are four times more likely to be suicidal, and bullied girls are eight times more likely to be suicidal (Fox, Elliott, Kerlikowske, Newman, & Christeson, 2003).

Impact on Academic Performance and Attendance

Students who spend their hours at school reacting to the most recent incident of humiliation and worrying about the next are likely to have difficulty focusing on academics. In a 2003 study of over 800 gay, lesbian, bisexual, and transgender youth, the Gay Lesbian Straight Education Network (GLSEN)

found that lesbian, gay, bisexual, and transgender youth who report significant verbal harassment are twice as likely to report they do not intend to go
to college and their GPAs are significantly lower than their peers (Kosciw,
2003).

For similar reasons, some students who are targeted with harassment
begin staying away from school and in some instances drop out completely.
As many as 160,000 students may stay home from school on any given day
because they are afraid of being bullied (Coy, 2001). In 2006, the U.S. National
Center for Education Statistics reported that 6 percent of the 12–18-year-old
students they surveyed in 2005 had skipped school or extracurricular activities, or avoided specific places in school because they were fearful (Dinkes,
Cataldi, Kena, & Baum, 2006).

Impact on Bystanders

Bias-motivated harassment impacts not only those students who are directly involved in particular incidents, but also those student bystanders
who witness the harassment. The importance of the bystander role has been
documented in numerous studies, including a 1970 research project by two
psychologists who attempted to determine how likely participants were to
intervene in an emergency situation if they were the sole bystander versus
being in a group of bystanders (Latane & Darley, 1970). The researchers
found that individuals would assist someone in need 75 percent of the time if
they were alone, and only 53 percent of the time if they were in a group.

A similar dynamic takes place among students. Oliver, Hoover, & Hazler
(1994) found that many students believed that "teasing is playful" and most
(61 percent) felt that bullying can "toughen" a weak student. In another study
in Washington state, more than half of the adolescents surveyed (57 percent)
would not take action if they witnessed another student being bullied or
teased (Smyser & Reis, 2002). While between 36 percent (6th graders) to
46 percent (12th graders) of these students said that they would "tell that
kid to stop," between one-third and one-fourth of 8th, 10th, and 12th graders
said they would "walk away" or "mind their own business." A full 20 percent
indicated that they would "stay and watch" (Smyser & Reis, 2002).

Reason for students remaining in the bystander role varies. Some of these
students pick up the message that denigrating others is "no big deal." Because of the pressure to fit in, other students would rather not call attention to themselves by standing up for a student who is harassed. Those who
share the same characteristic of the targeted student (e.g., are gay, black,
or Muslim) recognize that the harassers could just as easily focus their discrimination on them, and therefore are highly motivated not to act. In this
case, these bystanders may be impacted by bias and harassment with similar
intensity. Finally, students who do not share the same characteristic of those

targeted may also be impacted emotionally if they belong to groups that are frequently harassed. These students also know that the harassers may turn on them.

Instead of being allies to the targets, some students choose to become harassers themselves. Some have come to believe that this conduct is acceptable. Others, feeling the same peer pressure of fitting in like some bystanders, permit themselves to participate in the harassment, when they would otherwise not do so as individuals.

Whether many students just remain silent or become active participants in harassment, they may leave high school with the belief that degrading others for their race, disability, gender, or other characteristic is an acceptable form of behavior. This can lead to a continuation of bias and harassment in their adult lives. However, the good and hopeful news is that an increasing number of students, many of whom have participated in antibias programs, have gained the confidence and courage to intervene. Model programs for students and their positive impact will be discussed in the next section.

MODELS OF PROGRAMMING WITH STUDENTS

(As a Peer Trainer) the students really listened to what we were discussing. A lot of new areas were introduced and I know some of (my peers) were hesitant but did open up to us. That's a great thing in itself because they acknowledge there are biases and issues out there that we have to deal with.

—*10th grader, Arizona*

As identified earlier in this chapter, bias-motivated harassment and violence are serious problems in schools across the United States, negatively impacting both the targets of bias and passive bystanders. In addition, young people who are the perpetrators of bias-motivated harassment also experience the negative and lasting impacts of their own behavior, and are often targets as well as perpetrators of harassment. Civil rights and antibias organizations, however, are working with students, to provide them with the knowledge, empathy development opportunities, and skills needed to confront stereotypical attitudes and behaviors and the pervasiveness of harassment among young people.

As discussed above, peer pressure plays a critical role in the occurrence of bias-motivated harassment and violence, particularly the pressure to not intervene. Further, school-based incidents of prejudice tend to occur during times when teachers or other adults are not present, in the hallways and cafeterias of schools, on the school grounds before and after school, and on community streets and neighborhoods. As indicated earlier, students who are targets of prejudice rarely report the incident to an adult; but if they talked to anyone, it would be a peer. Research has shown that comprehensive peer education/leadership programs can have a measurable positive impact on school climate and peer relationships (Stevens, Van Oost, & de Bourdeauhuil, 2000). For these reasons, many successful antibias and harassment prevention programs focus on harnessing the power of peer influence and guiding students toward positive peer interventions.

Peer programs provide students who are viewed as leaders by other students with the opportunity to understand the impact of bias and harassment on others, and the knowledge, skills, and confidence to speak up in the hallways, classrooms, and locker rooms of their schools. These students have the potential to change the school culture from one that allows students to engage in or remain silent in the presence of harassment, to a school that values standing up for someone else.

Peer Leader Programs

Peer leader programs offer one option for working with students to prevent bias and harassment in school. The programmatic outline to follow describes a highly effective model used by the Center for the Prevention of Hate Violence (CPHV).

The CPHV Peer Leader program is a day-long leadership workshop designed to help students identify the extent and the damaging impact of bias and harassment in their school, and to provide them with the skills and confidence to intervene whenever they witness bias and harassment in the hallways, classrooms, and other areas in their school. The program includes highly interactive activities that define bias and harassment, build empathy for the targets of harassment, identify specific issues of bias and harassment that exist in the students' school environment, and assist students in practicing interpersonal intervention through role-playing activities. The mix of intense, content-based material about bias and team-building activities helps to create like-minded and committed peer leaders, increasing the likelihood that these students will assist each other when future situations call for intervention. Programs are often held off school grounds to send the message that the program is a special and significant event.

Students selected in the CPHV program are identified based on two main factors. First, a successful peer leader group will include students who represent different racial, ethnic, religious, or cultural groups at the school, as well as students of different sexual orientations, economic backgrounds, levels of academic achievement, and levels of involvement in school-related activities. Second, their level of social influence within their peer groups is considered, and how they can impact their peers, and where their impact will be greatest. When choosing student participants, leadership should be defined broadly. Some students may be more traditional leaders, excelling in the arts or academics, and thriving within the school community. Other students may be effective social leaders, whose opinions and attitudes act as a social barometer for their peers. It is also important to include in peer leader trainings both students who have demonstrated their ability to negatively influence their peers (by either encouraging or participating in name-calling or harassing behaviors) as well as those students who are more positive role models for their peers. Often students who are viewed by their peers as more negative leaders can have a significant positive impact on their peers after being given the opportunity to understand and internalize the impact of degrading language and harassment. Such leaders have been found to flourish when given the opportunity to participate in making their school a safer, more respectful place.

Using these two criteria for selecting student leaders provides the opportunity for the peer leader training program to create a ripple effect throughout the school community. In some cases, this influence may mean that student leaders model respectful behavior and intervene in situations of bias. In other cases, through modeling and actively encouraging, these peer leaders can influence their friends and peers to stand up and speak out when they see bias and harassment at school.

The follow-up meetings with students after a peer leader training program are a key part of ensuring the lasting impact of the program. Beginning about two weeks after the CPHV program, peer leaders are gathered for a short follow-up meeting to measure their progress and to receive encouragement and appreciation for their efforts. Follow-up meetings continue to build students' skills in confronting and intervening in the face of bias and provide a forum for students to discuss difficult situations they've encountered. These meetings help remind students that they are important contributors to the prevention of bias and harassment at their school and that they are part of a community of students who are trying to create positive change.

A variation on this peer leader program is to establish teams of student leaders who meet regularly during the school year to develop projects to improve school climate.

Peer Training Program

Another model of developing peer leadership to combat hate in schools is the Peer Training Program approach, which prepares selected peer leaders to lead antibias and antihate workshops with their peers. The Anti-Defamation League's A WORLD OF DIFFERENCE® Institute Peer Training Program model assists schools in establishing a peer-focused, peer-led program and process to mobilize and involve students in school-wide efforts to combat bigotry. The Peer Training Program uses a unique combination of instructional and peer influence strategies to combat name-calling, bullying, and harassment, and create safe and inclusive school communities.

This model was created following the riots in Crown Heights, Brooklyn, in 1991 when the staff of A WORLD OF DIFFERENCE® Institute began working with a group of students from Clara Barton High School in Crown Heights. The motivation of this group of young people to take action against prejudice resulted in the creation of ADL's Peer Training Program. The Peer Training Program is based on the following research premises: (1) Peer Trainers need certain basic skills and competencies to be effective; (2) this skill development occurs best when Peer Trainers are first exposed to a body of knowledge and then share opportunities to integrate that knowledge into their lives; and (3) Peer Trainers need to be supported on an ongoing basis at the school level by administrators and educators (Ender & Newton, 2000; Gottfredson, Gottfredson, & Czeh, 2000).

The multiyear program begins with antibias training for peer trainers and program coordinators. Facilitated by ADL training specialists, the initial three-day training is interactive and experiential, and designed to address the specific issues faced by peer trainers in their schools and communities. Following this initial training, peer trainers meet weekly with an ADL-trained School-Based Coordinator (e.g., teacher). These regular meetings help students further their understanding of social justice and equity as they related to their school setting; to continue to develop their leadership and facilitation skills; and to empower them to be a part of making justice and equity realities in the world.

In 2005–2006, Yale University conducted a national evaluation of the Peer Training Program, and on the basis of data gathered from over 500 students in 10 schools, located in urban, suburban, and rural settings across the United States, Yale researchers determined that the Peer Training Program "can have an important effect on reducing bias in schools" (Paluck & Green, 2006, p. 6). Yale evaluators concluded that the program's approach—combining instructional and peer influence strategies—had a positive impact on students' knowledge and awareness about issues of prejudice and discrimination in their environments, as well as their response to incidents of bias they witness.

Training of Trainers Programs

A variation on the Peer Training Program model is to train adult members of a school community to lead peer programs to ensure the sustainability of bias and harassment prevention efforts within a particular school or district. Training of Trainers Programs (TOT) are intensive trainings that provide a select group of teachers, counselors, administrators, school resource officers, or other school personnel with the curriculum and skills to implement and lead peer leadership workshops and antiharassment team programs in their schools. TOT programs include antibias professional development for participants to consider their own behaviors and beliefs related to bias, prejudice, and harassment. Following the TOT, trainers provide several workshops during each school year, and receive updated materials and support from the providing organization to strengthen their implementation and sustainability efforts.

The benefit of hosting a TOT in the school community goes beyond the ability to implement peer leadership workshops. Not only do these trainers provide an ongoing message of the importance of bias and harassment prevention work, but they often possess a high level of investment in the program as they see it work in their own community. This sends a powerful and positive message to students, faculty, staff, and community members that these issues are of great importance to the school community.

Conflict Resolution Dialogues

Conflict resolution dialogue programs in high schools are used for students to discuss controversial and often highly charged issues of bias, harassment, and stereotyping with a trained adult facilitator. Dialogue groups are often used in schools experiencing heightened tensions or violence relating to race, ethnicity, or religion. The goal of the dialogue programs is to encourage respectful communication and develop relationships among groups of students who may not otherwise reach across social and cultural barriers, thereby increasing the likelihood of dispelling stereotypes about each other while decreasing the likelihood of intergroup conflict and harassment. Unlike more instructional peer leader training programs, dialogue programs use structured, focused conversations to allow students to share their personal experiences with bias and stereotypes.

Typically, the model employed by CPHV consists of 20 students who meet weekly for 90 minutes, over four to six weeks. Participating students include those who are in conflict with each other as well as students who are viewed as peacemakers. Peacemakers are not directly involved in conflict, but are passionate about their school being a safe and respectful place, and are often able to help build bridges between the polarized students during each session. The role of the adult facilitator includes asking students to listen to the different perspectives and to develop strategies for reducing bias, harassment, and violence.

In the initial sessions, some students express anger or frustration directed at the students they have been in conflict with. Over the course of the dialogue sessions, however, many students develop strong personal bonds with classmates whom they previously viewed with hostility and fear. In addition, many students leave the group with intense (and even passionate) commitments to eliminating racism and other forms of bias.

It is important that this type of dialogue program should include a number of elements designed to ensure the physical and emotional safety of the students involved. The adult facilitator should work with the students in the first session to develop clear ground rules for behavior for all meetings. The facilitator should also structure each session so that students are able to express and process intense emotion during the session, and leave each meeting not necessarily with a solution to the conflict, but with a sense of hope.

The success of the program is reflected in this comment from a participating white student: "When (racial) issues surfaced, it really brought high emotions in the first meeting. I got in a little squabble with a black student and it was just really heated and we didn't understand each other. We were yelling back and forth but we weren't really *listening* to each other and that is pretty much what this project has opened up, a group of students having a chance to talk to one another. We never would have talked or spoken a word to each other if we hadn't been in this dialogue." Dialogues can be an effective tool for addressing specific issues of conflict as well as general underlying tensions in a school, and for creating positive, lasting relationships among students from different social groups.

The Power of One

A conversation with an 11th-grade high school female student illustrates both the depths of the problem of harassment and the heights to which each single student can rise in creating solutions. She attended a peer leader antibias program during the fall. Shortly afterwards she was leaving school at the end of the day, threading her way through the halls with hundreds of other students, when she saw a 9th grade student sitting on the floor with her back up against a locker. The 9th grade student, who looked "miserable," was staring vacantly across the hallway. The older student did not know the younger student's name but sat down beside her and asked her if she was doing okay. With nothing more said, the 9th grader let loose a cascade of tears and an account of the constant harassment directed at her because of her body size, her race, and the perception of others that she was sexually promiscuous.

As she spoke she gestured with her hands, causing the sleeves of her shirt to ride up her arms. The 11th grader saw several long red cut marks on her arms and then asked why she was cutting herself. The 9th grader responded that the only time during her life when she did not feel the intense emotional pain of harassment was when she could focus on the physical pain of cutting herself. She added that for a while she had stopped cutting herself because she had put a rubber band around her sleeve to remind her not to cut. But she was nervous and picked at the rubber band until it broke. The older student then pulled off her wrist a thick rubber band and said to the younger student that she gave the band to her so that she would know that she cared about her and that the younger student would never have to cut herself again because this band will not break. As a postscript, eight months later, the younger student was still wearing the band and had not cut herself in that time.

MODEL OF PROGRAMMING AND INTERVENTION WITH SCHOOL ADULTS

> I entered the classroom with a personal belief that I was not prejudiced or biased in any way, shape or form. I have come to see the true meaning of these terms and the subconscious ways in which I commit these errors in relationships with my students. I see the impact I have.
> —*Teacher, California*

Addressing the escalation of bias-motivated violence among youth is not the work of students alone. School adults play a critical role in creating and sustaining safe and inclusive schools so that students can experience and learn how to live in a diverse and democratic environment. In this section, we will discuss how school adults create such an environment through participating in antibias professional development workshops, embracing a more transformative and social justice-minded curriculum, and developing and sustaining school policies, procedures, and practices of nondiscriminatory behavior.

Antibias Diversity Training Programs

Talking about prejudice and discrimination, related to race, gender, sexual orientation, and the like, can be an exercise in anxiety for many people, to the point where many practice "active avoidance" (Lawrence and Tatum, 1997) or "color muteness" (Pollock, 2001) in order to avoid talking about these topics. Silence, however, doesn't rid discrimination but makes it invisible and allows it to continue to escalate undetected until it results in very public acts of hate incidents and hate crimes. In order to both reduce the anxiety associated with such conversations and raise educators' awareness of the various manifestations of prejudice and discrimination, antibias professional development workshops can provide a safe environment to acquire the knowledge, attitude, and skills to work towards eradicating discrimination and intolerance in themselves, in their students, and in the school at large.

Because there are several approaches to addressing diversity (see Sleeter & Grant, 2006, for explanation of typographies), for the purposes of the chapter, the A WORLD OF DIFFERENCE® Institute's antibias professional development workshop model will be used to describe one approach. Based on the institute model, effective workshops encourage participants to understand the various dimensions of identity and how identity impacts thinking and behavior; to examine how prejudice and discrimination are acquired and manifest in intergroup and teacher-student relationships, curriculum, policies, and practices; to develop and put into practice skills to confront bias and discrimination; and to cultivate the capacity to create and sustain environments that are fair, equitable, and respectful.

To work toward these goals, workshops utilize both instructional and experiential methods. Instructional methods deliver information in a straightforward manner to fill in knowledge gaps that participants have identified, such as presenting the state of name-calling, bullying, and hate crimes and providing a skill building to address these issues in school. Experiential methods take on a more personalized and cooperative approach, mostly asking participants to answer the question, "How does this information relate to and affect me as an educator?" Participants use themselves as a point of reference to understand bias and discrimination, building on the premise that everyone has been affected by discrimination and bias, regardless of their background. For example, in one activity participants are asked to reflect on and discuss both their multiple and cross-cutting social group membership (e.g., white, female, middle class) and how their different group membership places them in advantageous or disadvantageous situations in the context of the larger society. In another activity, participants are asked to consider the roles in a bias-related incident—target, perpetrator, bystander, and confronter/ally—and provide examples of when they played these roles, to recognize both the universality of these roles and the importance of being a confronter/ally.

In addition to providing the knowledge and skills and capacity to develop empathy, effective antibias professional development workshops utilize group work techniques that help break down barriers and build trust. Based on adult learning principles (see Sheal, 1989) and intergroup relations research (see Stephan & Stephan, 2004), group structures such as pairs, and small and large groups, encourage participants to fully engage in the learning process rather than passively taking in information without relating it back to the self and others. Such structures increase self-disclosure to reveal a more complex view of people and the many groups they represent. Another participatory structure is the creation of diverse, superordinate groups (groups with which members of all the other groups in a situation identify) to create both a common in-group identity focused on goals outside of social identity groups (e.g., participants working together on a project) and a situation of interdependence in order to achieve these goals. This in-group identity is based on research that has found that when membership of superordinate groups is salient, stereotypes and other biases associated with individuals from different groups become less important to the situation and task at hand (Stephan & Stephan, 2004). Furthermore, it provides an opportunity for those in-groups to learn about others who share some aspect of their identity, even though they may differ in other areas (Banks et al., 2001). Following, members of this group can work together toward a common goal in challenging discrimination, whether it's speaking in unison against bias-motivated bullying and harassment or examining school policies for structural discrimination.

As a result of these professional development workshops, educators become more sensitized to how prejudice and discrimination are manifested in the school community, and particularly how they impact students. By better understanding the issues faced by different social groups and possessing empathy for those who are targets of bias and discrimination, educators are more willing to intervene, knowing the negative academic, social, psychological, and emotional consequences that could follow if left unaddressed.

Curriculum: Knowledge Construction and Teaching

A major responsibility of educators is their teaching. What and how they teach impacts how students view the world and how they regard one another in the context of society. Curriculum content and its transmission should be examined for its support of or detraction from a more inclusive and safe school environment.

While there have been improvements in the past decade, more often than not, the typical curriculum in U.S. schools takes on a monocultural approach, highlighting the mainstream (e.g., male, Christian, middle-class, white) group's representation, perspectives, experiences, and interpretations while minimizing or distorting other groups' representation, perspectives, experiences, and interpretations (Banks, 1994; Takaki, 1993). Using gender as an example, Zittleman and Sadker (2002), recognizing that teachers educate their students based on their teacher education training, found that teacher textbooks are complicit in perpetuating sexist curriculum. Among 23 teacher education textbooks published from 1998 to 2001 they found that the average text coverage to the issues of sexism and gender is 3.3 percent, up from 1 percent 20 years ago. Furthermore, while introductory/foundation texts offer the most gender coverage at 7.3 percent, the content is segregated into one section or chapter. Zittleman and Sadker (2002) conclude, "Every day (teachers) will confront bias in classroom interactions, harassment in the hallways, stereotypes in the curriculum, imbalance in school staffing and a whole host of educational and political challenges. Current (teacher education) textbooks are unlikely to prepare teachers to respond to these challenges" (p. 178). Women and their issues in both children's books and teaching texts have been omitted, minimized, and relegated to a "special section," sending a message to both teachers and their male and female students that girls and women are not important, and, by extension, taking the risk of ignoring or minimizing problems of sexual harassment in schools.

Several methods have been used to counter a monocultural curriculum. However, some of these efforts may inadvertently only serve to reinforce stereotypes or escalate anxiety or even intergroup tensions and hostilities. One common well-intentioned practice is hosting "diversity days" or "international days" where food, fashion, and festivals from different cultural groups are exhibited. These special events provide students a time to celebrate their and others' cultures. However, if done in isolation from the school's daily culture and norms, these events can unintentionally serve to reinforce certain groups' peripheral place in the school's culture, exoticize these cultures as different from the norm, and, especially if done superficially, reinforce stereotypes about cultures (e.g., Mexicans only eats tacos or Native Americans only live in teepees). More importantly, without a critical analysis of the discrimination that these cultures face, these events deny students and their families a fuller, more complex understanding of these cultures' experiences.

Another example of a well-intentioned but potentially harmful approach is to create simulation activities that ask students to "walk in someone else's shoes" to experience the full effect of discrimination. While some educators are able to employ this technique skillfully, paying great attention to setting the stage, managing the process, and attending to students' emotional and social needs under stressful circumstances, many do not prepare carefully, resulting in sloppy execution and a compromised sense of safety. Such misguided efforts include enforcing "For White Only" and "For Colored Only" signs at water fountains to teach white and black students about racism; calling black students the "n" word to teach them how name-calling is hurtful; asking students to pretend to be Jews in a concentration camp under the Nazi regime to teach them about the Holocaust.

In order to more fully understand the ways in which the classroom curriculum can assist in combating racism and discrimination and diminish intergroup bias, Banks (1994) identified four approaches to multicultural curriculum: contribution approach, additive approach, transformative approach, and social action approach. At the most basic level, the contribution approach focuses on holidays, heroes, and discrete cultural elements that are not integrated in the common curriculum, exemplified by the diversity days as described above. Following, the additive approach provides cultural content, concepts, and themes in the curriculum, but in symbolic ways. The curriculum, in this case, does not change the basic framework or dominant perspective, and can create a multitiered curriculum, with these additions relegated as separate and disjointed, as seen in the above discussion about gender treatment in teacher textbooks. Both approaches do not question the existing structure and prevailing content in the curriculum, and do not actively address issues of bias and discrimination on a personal, historical, or institutional level.

The transformation approach questions the framework and perspective of curriculum, and enables students to learn concepts, ideas, perspectives, and events from diverse groups. Here, critical and analytical thinking skills are valued, and are used to counter ignorance, challenge prejudice, and offer a legitimate space for other groups' voices. While providing additional voices from diverse groups is important, it is also important to provide multiple perspectives within these diverse groups to undercut the tendency to either lump all members in the group together, or else create exceptions to the rule, which does little to dispel stereotypes (Stephan & Stephan, 2004).

Care and consideration should also be taken when addressing topics that highlight oppression of groups that are represented in the classroom. For example, when teaching U.S. slavery, feelings of discomfort and embarrassment may arise, not only from teachers but also from African American students. In addition, if taught from the perspective of white Northern abolitionists, it can potentially communicate to other students that African American slaves were helpless and passive. Lawrence and Tatum (1997) recount how one teacher was able to discuss the topic of slavery while upholding the dignity of his African American students: "I have chosen to focus more on the resistance shown by the slaves, rather than the oppression directed against them. This resistance, both spiritual and physical, seemed to be a more positive side of the institution of slavery. I have come to realize that the African-American students do not want to be saturated with details of cruelty to the slaves" (172). Informed by participating in an antibias professional development workshop, this teacher was able to couple his empathy and understanding of the African American community with his knowledge about African American history to discuss slavery in a way that put African Americans in a more positive light.

The last approach is social action, which extends the transformative approach by carving space for students to pursue projects and activities that address discrimination. Particularly for students from oppressed groups, this aspect is essential to building their resiliency. Awareness of racism, sexism, and classism, for example, does not automatically result in healthy student development. Without a model to move from awareness to social action, feelings of hopelessness, cynicism, alienation, and lower achievement aspirations can result among students in oppressed groups (Pastor, McCormick, & Fine, 1997). Projects that challenge discrimination serve as opportunities for students to take ownership and responsibility for making positive change. For example, after students at a Massachusetts urban high school with limited resources learned about the structural and systemic nature of school inequities, they were able to understand the complex nature of the achievement gap in their school. Because the course took a social action approach, they channeled their disappointment, anger, and frustration into producing a video documentary comparing the educational resources and opportunities between urban schools and suburban and magnet schools. They presented their findings and recommendations to various decision makers in the school community to dispel the racial myth that low levels of intelligence and motivations of African American and Latino students were to blame. Reflecting on the project, one of the student researchers said, "It makes me think more about making the change and speaking out about what you don't have and what you should have. . . . I think that that's very important to me and very important to other people who are coming to other public schools to know that they have a voice and that voice is valid. And if they speak out and they appreciate their voice, then they can make change." The project not only achieved knowledge and critical thinking standards; it also allowed students to practice democracy on a more meaningful and fulfilling level.

Policies, Procedures, and Practices: Larger School Environment

Empathetic and knowledgeable educators and a more transformative and action-oriented approach to curriculum can allow students to experience positive intergroup relations, and a richer and more informed curriculum. However, these factors are not enough for students to feel safe, valued, and included in the school community. School is an institution with policies, procedures, and practices that "embody a school's beliefs, attitudes and expectations of its students" (Nieto, cited in Banks et al., 2001). As such, schools must participate in a four-part process to ensure an inclusive and safe environment—to create policies and procedures that respect all students and condemn discrimination and inequity; to develop and communicate procedures that reflect the norms and expectations to school adults, students, and other school members-at-large; to consistently enforce these policies through equitable practices; and to periodically review the effectiveness of the policies, procedures, and practices.

Schoolwide policies can set the tone for how students interact with each other. While some believe that people must be persuaded to engage in certain types of behavior, research has continually shown that even when mandated, behavioral change can result in attitudinal change. Youth and adults alike will conform to the expectations stated when they are given, and when norms promoting positive intergroup relations and nondiscriminatory behavior are presented, behavior aligned to the norms can result in people respecting one another (Pettigrew, 2004). Nondiscriminatory policies about name-calling, bullying, and harassment (which highlight protected groups such as gay students), and codes of conduct detailing basic human rights can establish up front how seriously schools take their goal to practice democracy and respect for diversity. The most effective policy development comes when all members of the school community are included and given equal voice and voting power, particularly students and, by extension, their parents and caregivers.

To put these nondiscriminatory policies into practice, developing clear procedures and communicating them to adult educators and students are essential. Using staff meetings or professional development days for school adults; homeroom, advisory periods, or other formal gatherings for students; and PTA meetings, newsletters, or open houses for parents and caretakers, administrators can provide staff, students, and family members with a clear understanding of these policies and procedures as well as its consequences. Rather than simply reporting what these policies and procedures are, administrators should provide opportunities for people to ask questions so they fully understand how these policies will be enforced. Particularly for school adults, engaging them in role playing, case studies, or other methods of application can help them better anticipate how to respond to name-calling, bullying, and harassment, and learn effective approaches from others.

Following the development and communication of policies and procedures is the practice of their application and enforcement. While it is difficult for school adults to address every single instance of name-calling, bullying, and harassment in the hallway, letting such situations slip by communicates an insincere and untrustworthy message. When discrimination is not addressed seriously or consistently (especially among different social identity groups), students will indirectly learn about the unequal treatment of different groups, which will affect how they perceive themselves and others in the group, and will contribute to a growing chasm among groups. To see an educator reprimand a student for using the phrase *Jew down* but not respond to another student's use of the word *retarded* in a demeaning way teaches students that the disability community is less deserving of the same protection as the Jewish community. It is important, therefore, to carefully monitor how policies are being interpreted and practiced.

Lastly, those involved in the policy development should periodically review, revise, and update policies and procedures, as well as assessing the effectiveness of the practice on the ground. For example, with a growing concern of cyberbullying, policies and procedures should include online cruelty as a form of bullying, and identify technology-oriented ways to address it, such as a log-in warning about the limited nature of student privacy when using school computers. Another example is the recent inclusion of transgender students as a protected group by many schools, and, in response, the establishment of gender-neutral bathrooms for their use and safety. Any changes to policies and procedures should be communicated and their enforcement monitored for consistency and fairness.

CONCLUSION

Bias and harassment are widespread in schools throughout the United States. The impact of this conduct is deeply destructive to the emotional and physical well-being of students, to their chances for succeeding academically, and to the likelihood that they will leave high school with the knowledge and skills necessary for navigating successfully in an increasingly diverse nation.

When practicing effective, inclusive antibias ideals, schools can be exemplary models of democracy and justice and can serve as apprenticeships (Banks et al., 2001) of these values, an important fundamental learning experience for students. Concepts of fairness, respect, and dignity become realities and the practice of discrimination and violence based on group membership is discouraged and recognized as antithetical to the fundamental ideals of larger communities.

Creating schools in which every student feels safe and respected is not an easy task. However, antibias organizations know that it is possible to significantly decrease bias and harassment in schools while at the same time significantly increase the confidence and skills of students to speak up and stand up for others. This change only can occur when administrators, faculty, staff, and, most importantly, students join in with commitment and courage to become part of a comprehensive and multiyear antibias and harassment effort.

REFERENCES

Adams, M., Bell, L. A., & Griffin, P. (Eds.). (1997). *Teaching for diversity and social justice: A sourcebook.* New York: Routledge.

American Association of University Women Educational Foundation. (2001). *Hostile hallways: Bullying, teasing, and sexual harassment in school.* Retrieved October 18, 2007, from http://www.aauw.org/member_center/publications/HostileHallways/ hostilehallways.pdf

Anti-Defamation League. (2000). *A WORLD OF DIFFERENCE® Institute anti-bias study guide elementary/intermediate level.* New York: Anti-Defamation League.

Banks, J. A. (1994). *An introduction to multicultural education.* Boston: Allyn and Bacon.

Banks, J. A., Cookson, P., Gay, G., Hawley, W. D., Irvine, J. J., Nieto, S., et al. (2001). *Diversity within unity: Essential principles for teacher and learning in a multicultural society.* Seattle: University of Washington at Seattle Center for Multicultural Education.

Coy, D. R. (2001). *Bullying.* Washington, DC: Education Resources Information Center.AQ

Dinkes, R., Cataldi, E. F., Kena, G., & Baum, K. (2006). *Indicators of school crime and safety: 2006.* Washington, DC: U.S. Departments of Education and Justice. Retrieved October 18, 2007, from http://nces.ed.gov/programs/crimeindicators/ index.asp

Ender, S. C., & Newton, F. B. (2000). *Students helping students.* San Francisco: Jossey-Bass.

Federal Bureau of Investigation. (2007). *Hate crime statistics, 2006.* Washington, DC: U.S. Department of Justice.

Fight Crime: Invest in Kids. (2006a). *Cyber bully: Pre-teen.* Princeton, NJ: Opinion Re-search Corporation. Retrieved November 21, 2007, from http://fightcrime.org/cyberbullying/cyberbullyingpreteen.pdf

Fight Crime: Invest in Kids. (2006b). *Cyber bully: Teen.* Princeton, NJ: Opinion Re-search Corporation. Retrieved November 21, 2007, from http://fightcrime.org/cyberbullying/cyberbullyingteen.pdf

Fox, J. A., Elliott, D. S., Kerlikowske, R. G., Newman, S. A., & Christeson, W. (2003). *Bullying prevention* is *crime prevention.* Washington, DC: Fight Crime: Invest in Kids. Retrieved December 3, 2007, from http://www.fightcrime.org/reports/BullyingReport.pdf

Gottfredson, G. D., Gottfredson, D. C., & Czeh, E. R. (2000). *National study of delin-quency prevention in schools.* Ellicott City, MD: Gottfredson Associates.

Kosciw, J. G. (2003). *The 2003 national school climate survey: The school-related experi-ences of our nation's lesbian, gay, bisexual and transgender youth.* New York: GLSEN.

Kosciw, J. G., & Diaz, E. M. (2006). *The 2005 national school climate survey: The experi-ences of lesbian, gay, bisexual and transgender youth in our nation's schools.* New York: GLSEN.

Latane, B., & Darley, J. (1970). *The unresponsive bystander: Why doesn't he help?* New York: Appleton-Century-Crofts.

Lawrence, S. M., & Tatum, B. D. (1997). Teachers in transition: The impact of an-tiracist professional development on classroom practices. *Teachers College Record, 99*(1), 162–178.

Li, Q. (2007). New bottles but old wine: A research of cyberbullying in schools. *Computers in Human Behavior, 23,* 1777–1791.

Lloyd-Richardson, E., Perrine, N., Dierker, L., & Kelley, M. L. (2007). Characteristic and functions on non-suicidal self-injury in a community sample of adolescents. *Psychological Medicine, 37*(8), 1183–1192.

National Center for Education Information. (2005). *Profile of teachers in the U.S. 2005.* Washington, DC: Author.

Oliver, R., Hoover, J. H., & Hazler, R. (1994). The perceived roles of bullying in small-town Midwestern schools. *Journal of Counseling and Development, 72*(4), 416–423.

Paluck, E. L., & Green, D. P. (2006). *Anti-bias education and peer influence as two strat-egies to reduce prejudice: An impact evaluation of the Anti-Defamation League Peer Training Program.* New Haven: Yale University.

Parsad, B., Lewis, L., & Farris, E. (2001). *Teacher preparation and professional develop-ment: 2000.* Washington, DC: National Center for Education Statistics. Retrieved October 18, 2007, from http://nces.ed.gov/surveys/frss/publications/2001088/index.asp?sectionID=1

Pastor, J., McCormick, J., & Fine, M. (1997). Makin' homes: An urban girl thing. In B.J.R. Leadbeater & N. Way (Eds.), *Urban girls: Resisting stereotypes, creating ideas* (pp. 15–34). New York: NYU Press.

Perkins, P. K. (2007). *Where we learn: The cube survey of urban school climate.* Alexan-dria, VA: National School Boards Association. Retrieved October 18, 2007, from http://www.nsba.org/site/docs/38100/38081.pdf

Pettigrew, T. (2004). Intergroup contact: Theory, research, and new perspectives. In J. Banks, & C.A.M. Banks (Eds.), *Handbook of research on multicultural education* (2nd ed., pp. 770–780). San Francisco: Wiley.

Planty, M., Provasnik, S., Hussar, W., National Center for Education Statistics, Kena, G., Hampden-Thompson, G., et al. (2007). *The condition of education 2007.* Washington, DC: U.S. Department of Education, National Center for Education Statistics.

Pollock, M. (2001). How the question we ask most about race in education is the very question we most suppress. *Educational Researcher, 30*(9), 2–12.

Ross, S., & Heath, N. (2002). A study of the frequency of self-mutilation in a community sample of adolescents. *Journal of Youth & Adolescence, 31,* 67–77.

Sheal, P. (1989). *How to develop and present staff training courses.* New York: Nichols Publishing.

Sleeter, C., & Grant, C. (2006). *Making choices for multicultural education: Five approaches to race, class and gender.* Hoboken, NJ: Wiley.

Smyser, M., & Reis, E. (2002). Bullying and bias-based harassment in King County Middle Schools. *Public Health Data Watch, 5*(2), 1–15.

Stephan, W. G., & Stephan, C. W. (2004). Intergroup relations in multicultural education programs. In J. Banks, & C.A.M. Banks (Eds.), *Handbook of research on multicultural education* (2nd ed., pp. 781–798). San Francisco: Wiley.

Stevens, V., Van Oost, P., & de Bourdeauhuil, I. (2000). The effects of an anti-bullying intervention on peers' attitudes and behavior. *Journal of Adolescence, 22*(4), 21–34.

Strom, K. J. (2001). *Hate crimes reported in NIBRS, 1997–99.* Rockville, MD: U.S. Department of Justice.

Takaki, R. (1993). *A different mirror: A history of multicultural America.* Boston: Little, Brown.

Zittleman, K., & Sadker, D. (2002). Gender bias in teacher education texts: New (and old) lessons. *American Association of Colleges for Teacher Education, 53*(2), 168–180.

CHAPTER 9

VICTIM SERVICES AND COUNSELING FOR VICTIMS AND COMMUNITIES THAT EXPERIENCE HATE CRIME

Kellina Craig-Henderson

There are many ways to respond to hate crime victimization.[1] Indeed, as all of the papers in this volume attest, the problems created by hate crimes are very real and extend well beyond the actual incident. What is most salient, however, is the impact of the incident on the actual victim or survivor. This chapter identifies the services that are available and most likely to assist victims in the wake of hate crime. Consequently, particular attention is paid to the postvictimization experience of the victim. In some of the more heinous hate crimes involving extreme violence, it may be appropriate to refer to the victim as a survivor. Doing so underscores the severity of the crime. Although I will generally refer to the *victim* throughout this discussion, the term *survivor* will be used occasionally.

What are some of the ameliorative recommendations for victims of hate crime? Following the incident, are there specific services to which victims can avail themselves? Are hate crime victims unique among those whom mental health service professionals encounter? What are the best practices for victim service providers (e.g., police, social workers, attorneys)? This chapter seeks to address each of these questions while considering the distinctive characteristics among the different types of hate crime victims.

By examining the unique characteristics of bias crime victims relative to victims of nonbias crime, this chapter can provide useful recommendations for mental health professionals and other service providers who interact with victims following a hate crime incident. Given that the

Any opinion, findings, and conclusions or recommendations expressed in this material are those of the author and do not necessarily reflect the views of the National Science Foundation.

postvictimization experience will differ according to whether the victim was targeted because of their race, ethnicity, sexual orientation, or other social group status, it is also useful to consider the distinctive stereotypes associated with the different social groups. Doing so will permit elucidation of the best practices for counseling and provision of services to hate crime victims.

BIAS CRIME VERSUS NONBIAS CRIME VICTIMIZATION

Victims of hate crimes are targeted because of their perceived membership in a particular group. Although definitions of hate crime vary, most emphasize the motivation of the offender as well as the group status of the victim (Anti-Defamation league of B'nai B'rith, 1994; Hamm, 1994; U.S. Department of Justice, 2004). Both of these elements of a hate crime have implications for the postvictimization experience of victims as well as determining the best strategy for delivery of services to victims (Craig & Sloan, 2003).

Following a hate crime incident, the victim immediately confronts the reality of the offender's hate-filled motives. Although the victim may have been aware of the existence of the sentiment that propelled the offender, the fact of their victimization heightens their awareness. That is, whereas they may have previously known that people like the offender existed, their knowledge and awareness was more vicarious than experiential. After being victimized, they are acutely and painfully familiar with people like the offender and what they represent for people like themselves.

This shift in awareness or consciousness is one way that bias crime victims are distinguished from victims of other similarly egregious crimes (i.e., nonbias crimes). Although it is true that victims of all crime lack a complete understanding of the experience of victimization before it happens, in the case of hate crime, the change in awareness that accompanies their victimization is likely to be profoundly life-altering. Moreover, if the hate crime involves a physical assault and violence, this is even more likely to be the case.

Findings from one study on hate crime victimization in New York City and Baltimore County in the United States provides evidence for the claim that the postvictimization experience for bias crime victims is qualitatively distinct from that of nonbias crime victims (Garofalo, 1997). In that study, the researchers conducted a small telephone survey of victims of bias and nonbias crimes. According to Garofalo (1997), one of the study's authors, "some clear patterns of differential effects emerged" (p. 141). Results of a comparison of 30 bias crime victims to 28 comparison crime victims revealed that the bias crime victims were more likely to rate their crimes as "very serious," report being "frightened" and "very upset" rather than "angry or mad" after the incident, and more likely to say that the incident had a "great deal" of an effect on their lives in the short and long term. These differences in the postvictimization experience of bias crime victims have obvious implications for the types and effectiveness of services that mental health professionals, social workers, and law enforcement personnel can provide.

Another way that bias crime victims may differ from victims of nonbias crimes concerns their likely absence from the web of violence. In many cases, victims of violent crime appear to be at greater risk of subsequent victimization. For example, according to Friedman and Tucker (1997), victims of certain violent crimes may be susceptible to settings, behaviors, and lifestyles that predispose them to repeat violent encounters. This is certainly the case in domestic violence and child abuse incidents, as well as those situations where individuals who observe violence in their homes or neighborhoods may be more prone to behaving violently or ignoring safety precautions.

Hate crime victims have the dubious distinction of having been in the wrong place at the wrong time. More often than not, anyone meeting the criteria of membership in their particular social group (e.g., race, nationality, sexual orientation) would have elicited the offenders' ire. They were singled out simply because they were perceived to be members of the group the offender despises. Because hate crime victims span the gamut in terms of demographic characteristics, they are no more likely than nonvictims to be engaged in subsequent criminal victimization. Thus, their presumed absence from the web of violence may represent an important difference between bias crime victims and nonbias crime victims and have implications for victim assistance programs and service providers.

STEREOTYPES AND PREJUDICE

To be sure, the stereotypes associated with the victims' social status impact the way that victims view their victimization experience, the amount of support received from others, as well as the extent of blame attributed to victims and their offenders. For example, with respect to the latter issue regarding blame, among the findings from earlier research by Craig and Waldo (1996), observers' stereotypes of victims and perpetrators were evident in their attributions of blame. That study revealed that there are different stereotypic perceptions of perpetrators and victims of hate crime, and these differences are likely to be a function of the demographic characteristics of the perceiver. The researchers concluded, among other things, that victims may have different postvictimization experiences depending upon their demographic characteristics, the motives of their perpetrators, and the stereotypic perceptions of immediate others.

Importantly, stereotypes exert an influence at every stage of the hate crime incident. In addition to affecting the blame attributions others make and the support provided them, they are also partly responsible for the actual commission of the hate crime. Stereotypes refer to the beliefs about the characteristics of individuals and groups (Hamilton & Sherman, 1994). These beliefs are often pervasive and resistant to change, and include information about aspects of an individual including their physical appearance, habits, traits, and behaviors (Mackie, Hamilton, Susskind, & Rosselli, 1996).

In general, stereotypes are regarded as functional, and permit individuals to perceive large numbers of stimuli and process infinite amounts of social information (Tajfel, 1969). Stereotypes tend to be activated in situations where one encounters a member of a group about whom they have a stereotype and when no other individuating information about the individual is available (Brewer, 1996). Any observed differences between the individual and the stereotype that might be brought to mind are quickly disregarded in the interest of cognitive economization. Thus, the hate crime offender sees a potential victim first as a representative of a group about which he or she has a stereotype, and ignores any features that would distinguish or individuate the person. That the victim is someone's son, or father, or a recent recipient of a humanitarian award, or is suffering illness, matters little to the offender.

Stereotypes about the different groups to which victims belong are also likely to differ according to a group's perceived *entativity*. This social psychological concept refers to the extent to which the group is seen as having a real existence. Groups differ in the extent to which they are perceived to possess entativity and this difference has implications for how the group is perceived and how others treat its members. A group perceived to be high in entativity would be one that is highly organized, perhaps with an identifiable leader or cause (Hamilton, Sherman, & Lickel, 1998). The groups in which the most frequent hate crime victims are perceived to belong are likely to be viewed by offenders as high in entativity. For example, the stereotype for Arabs or middle Easterners is high entativity. Offenders perceive them to be well organized and ruled by an identifiable leader with goals aimed at the overthrow of the United States.

According to most process models of stereotyping, the stereotype is activated when a person encounters the target of the stereotype. In the case of hate crime, the crime offender encounters a potential victim and the stereotype is activated. The offender (unlike a nonoffender) is likely to have a fully developed repertoire of stereotypes about the potential victim that are accompanied by deep-seated prejudice. The offender then acts on that prejudice and strikes out at the target of those negative stereotypes and prejudice.

DIFFERENCES AMONG HATE CRIME VICTIMS

In considering best practices for helping victims of hate crimes, it is important to recognize that the experience of victimization for hate crime victims will differ depending upon whether they were targeted because of their race, ethnicity, religion, sexual orientation, or other minority social status. Almost all perpetrators of hate crime target their victims because they perceive them to be members of groups for which they have strong negative stereotypes and feelings. Yet, although all victims of hate crime tend to be members of groups that are negatively stigmatized, the experience of being victimized will differ according to whether one is targeted because they appear to be homeless, disabled, black or gay (Cowan & Hodge, 1996).

The theory of integrated threat by Stephan and Stephan (2000) would seem to have particular relevance in considering the unique experiences of the different hate crime victims and likely recommendations for victim services. Although the theory was not formulated with hate crime in mind, because it holds that there are different types of threat that give rise to prejudice it can be useful in understanding the subtleties that are likely to distinguish hate crime victims from each other.

The first type of threat involves perceptions of threat to the well-being of the group. Retrospective accounts of antiblack hate crimes have sometimes revealed this type of a perception among offenders. For example, consider one of the more infamous racist hate crimes, which occurred in Howard Beach, a neighborhood in the Queens borough of New York City. In 1986 three African American men whose car had broken down were attacked and pursued by a racist mob of white youths while searching in vain for a telephone. One of the men, Michael Griffith, who was 23, was beaten, shot, and eventually run down on a busy roadway.

Following the incident, the youths who were interviewed and apprehended boasted of protecting their neighborhood. Ironically, they claimed to feel threatened by the presence of the three African Americans. What is clear is that their assault on the innocent motorists was instigated by their perceptions of threat coupled with the negative stereotypes and racial prejudice that they harbored for African Americans in general.

According to the theory, the second type of threat involves the perception of threat to the perceiver's worldview. An outsider is perceived to threaten the norms, values, and beliefs with which the perceiver identifies. Hate crime offenders who target religious minorities are likely to be motivated by this type of threat. In addition to prescribing acceptable norms, values, and beliefs, religion provides followers with guidelines for behavior. Thus, in many ways it can be regarded as all-encompassing; it provides the worldview. Anyone who openly espouses another religion is suspected to be a potential threat to the worldview. For example, following the 2001 terrorist attacks in the United States, the surge in the numbers of hate-motivated offenses targeting those perceived to be Arab, Muslim, or Middle Eastern is suggestive of this type of perceived threat. Consider the case of homicide involving a white man who murdered an Indian man who upon being apprehended proclaimed, "I'm for America all the way! America all the way!" His remarks suggest he was motivated at least in part by the perception that his victim's very existence somehow posed a threat to him and the security of America (Yang, 2003).

The third threat identified in the theory occurs when people are concerned about the potential negative outcomes resulting from an encounter with members of the negatively stereotyped group. Recent considerations about the utility of pathologizing extreme prejudice suggest the pervasiveness of this perceived threat as well as the likelihood that it will instigate certain types of hate crime (Sullaway, 2004). For example, the term *racial paranoia-induced delusional disorder* has been used to characterize an offender's delusion that members of a victim's group are dangerous and intend to harm the offender (Gerstenfeld, 1992). Current debates about whether pathological bias can and should be a recognized diagnosis within the psychiatric cannon of diagnoses focus on the extent to which treatment and medication is consistent with approaches to other delusional disorders.

Those who target gays and other sexual minorities often claim that feelings of threat instigated their *reactive* aggression. That is, some offenders claim that their interaction with the victim put them (the offender) at risk. Indeed as a defense strategy, antigay hate crime offenders increasingly cite feelings of threat as justification for their assault or criminal offense. Such was the case in the criminal trial of one of the offenders in the Mathew Shepard case involving the 1998 beating and subsequent death of the white, gay college student in Wyoming. The murderer's defense strategy was to argue that he suffered from "gay panic," and merely reacted defensively (Glick, 1959, as cited in Sullaway, 2004).

The fourth and final threat outlined in the integrated threat theory is evoked by the use of stereotypes that suggest negative experiences with members of the stereotyped group. This is perhaps the most general of the threats described by the theory and it may be the culprit in other types of hate crimes targeting the homeless, or the disabled. For most people, interactions with members of these groups are likely to be in some ways strained. This is because of a lack of previous interactions with members of these groups, the extent of negative stereotypes about them, as well as the extent to which social comparison processes lead individuals to clearly see themselves as superior.

These different threat processes are likely to give rise to different hate crime offenses, and have different implications for the postvictimization experience of victims of these crimes. The different implications should inform specific strategies for victim service providers who interact with hate crime victims. For example, consider the case of the African American hate crime victim of the antiblack assault who was targeted because he was perceived as a threat to his offenders' neighborhood. Following the experience, the victim, being overcome with fear and a sense of powerlessness, may curtail his activities by deciding to avoid that neighborhood (and those like it) in the future. This may initially serve as a cautionary strategy, although it is acknowledged that there is the risk that in its extreme the victim might find himself eliminating requisite activities in his quest to avoid that particular neighborhood.

Among the victim service providers, the mental health professional is likely to be especially useful. When interacting with the victim of this particular type of a hate crime, they should recognize the importance of the victim's need to alter existing routines or create new ones at the outset. Mental health professionals should not be judgmental and they should be supportive of decisions made by victims and members of their families. At the same time, if victims make maladaptive choices throughout the postvictimization experience, counselors should then refer them to appropriate resources and suggest alternative options.

This strategy is likely to differ in the case of the victim of a religious hate crime who may have been targeted on a religious holiday, for example. When victims are singled out because they are associated with a religious event, celebration, or holiday, the postvictimization experience may involve activities aimed at creating greater solidarity with members of their religious community as well as engaging in efforts to build bridges with other communities. This is one way that victim service providers can be especially useful. They can assist victims in identifying viable connections with other community-based groups. In this case, a social worker or community activist may be more instrumental than a mental health professional in assisting the hate crime victim.

SHORT-TERM VERSUS LONG-TERM CONSEQUENCES

Importantly, victim service providers and counselors who interact with hate crime victims should be aware of the distinctions between short-term and long-term consequences of the victimization experience (Norris, Kaniasty, & Thompson, 1997). This is because initial reactions to the incident will reflect the state of crisis, but later reactions will be more transient and may require additional types of assistance and support. For example, although the short-term consequences of the hate crime may involve assistance from law enforcement personnel or social workers, the long-term consequences may well involve systematic interaction with a mental health professional in addition to any continuing interactions with police or social workers. The following section describes some ways that the postvictimization experience (including short-term and long-term consequences) for hate crime victims can proceed in such a way as to minimize the deleterious impact on victims.

The short-term consequences of the victimization experience involve any immediate harm or injury sustained as well as any of the accompanying emotional and psychological reactions that occur during the commission of the crime and immediately following it. Once the victim has received medical attention, victim service providers should attend to the victim's crisis state. The victimization experience, particularly when it involves violence, constitutes a significant life crisis for the victim. The perspective of crisis theory can be useful here (Sales, Baum, & Shore, 1984). According to this theory, the victim will experience an immediate and intense negative reaction to the incident and this will be followed by a gradual return to their characteristic way of functioning before the incident. The theory's utility lies in its ability to distinguish between the stress-related symptoms of healthy people in the midst of a crisis from those that indicate an enduring psychopathology.

In the case of hate crime victims, the immediate reactions and their short-term consequences will involve concerns for safety, physical security, and an understanding of what has happened. Victim service providers, which may include law enforcement personnel and social workers, can help victims by insuring their immediate safety and sense of security. In helping them to immediately come to terms with the incident, they can also help them to reestablish a sense of control in their lives. This latter suggestion is likely to involve a more long-term strategy within the postvictimization experience, and has implications for the victim's future coping prospects.

It is useful for mental health professionals to keep in mind that survivors of hate crime often see themselves as deviant because of their victimization. Usually no one else in their social network has had similar experiences. Consequently, there is a tendency for victims to view themselves as deviant in some way from others, and this in turn impacts their self-esteem and overall feelings of self-worth. Indeed, the survivor who sees herself as deviant is more likely to be depressed and to feel powerless.

In addition to any one-on-one counseling that the survivor of a hate crime may receive, peer support groups can also be effective in helping to diminish the feelings of deviancy that survivors report having. Peer support groups offer survivors the opportunity to meet and talk with other victims. Psychological counselors working with survivors of hate crime can refer them to appropriate support groups and encourage them to participate in these groups.

CORRELATES TO VICTIMS' USE OF SERVICES

Whether victims of hate crime will seek and use services following the incident will be determined by a variety of factors including the type of crime and whether it involved violence, the victim's depressive symptomatology, and the extent of their perceived family and friend support. However, because of the paucity of research that has specifically examined predictors of seeking mental health treatment among hate crime victims, what is reviewed here pertains to crime victims in general. For example, research by Norris, Kaniasty, and Thompson (1997) has explored some of the determinants of service use among crime victims in general. They argue that doing so results in useful strategies that increase victims' use of or access to health services.

Their study included a telephone survey of 522 households that were randomly selected and surveyed at three separate times over the course of a year. They focused on the presence of violence in a reported criminal incident, as well as the presence or absence of lasting, enduring psychological symptoms. The longitudinal design permitted examination of the course of recovery as well as the extent of engagement with victim services.

Findings from that study can be useful in coming up with recommendations and strategies for remedying the physical pain and psychological distress of hate crime victimization. Results of their analysis revealed that victims of violent crimes were more likely than victims of property crimes to have had contact with professionals including police, attorneys, doctors, and counselors. Moreover, in the case of mental health services, although victims of violent crime reported more use of these services, they also tended to indicate being less satisfied with them.

Another interesting correlate to mental health service use identified in the Norris and colleagues' (1997) research involved the victim's perceived social support. The more social support the victim reported receiving from family members and friends, the more likely he or she was to seek help from professionals. The researchers note that this particular finding "suggests that responsive social networks facilitate use of services by encouraging and enabling victims to seek the care they need" (p. 156). That is, although it might seem that those lacking informal support networks would seek formal victim services first and foremost, these data suggest that those who actually have informal social support networks will be more likely to seek victim services.

Overall, the two most important factors that were predictive of whether a victim would seek out mental health services were depression and the presence of violence during the commission of the crime. Although victims of violence were clearly the most psychologically distressed, victims of property crime also showed considerable distress. Criminal victimization was associated with depression, anxiety, hostility, lower self-esteem, and a need for both formal and informal social support, among other things.

How can these findings inform recommendations for delivery of service and use by hate crime victims? First, these findings underscore the importance of distinguishing between the different types of hate crime. Not only should the victim service provider(s) consider the specific type of hate motive responsible for the incident (e.g., anti-Semitism vs. heterosexism), they must also keep in mind that a property crime like the spray painting of a swastika on a Jewish synagogue will have unique consequences for its victims. An incident such as this will require interaction between members of the Jewish community and the police and possibly even victims' rights advocates and other community group leaders. It is also the case that the physical and violent assault against a lone gay male by a group of teenage youths will require its own unique proscription, and likely involve multiple victim assistance service providers including the police, social workers, victims' rights advocates and attorneys, and mental health professionals.

What may be most important in any case of hate crime victimization is to ensure provision of the type of support (formal vs. informal) that is most effective in alleviating the negative consequences (psychological, physical, social) of the hate crime. Ideally, an optimal matching model of stress and coping would inform victim service providers (Cutrona, 1990; Cutrona & Russell, 1990; Iwasaki, 2001). According to this model, the demand of a stressor (in this case the experience of hate crime victimization) should correspond to or "match" the function of a coping strategy in order to result in a positive outcome (i.e., reduction in psychological distress and increase in overall well-being). In this model, an event is judged on various dimensions such as controllability, desirability, or life domain in order to determine what kinds of coping resources will be needed to alleviate the victim's distress.

In the case of hate crime victimization, the stressor experienced is uncontrollable, undesirable, and may affect psychological well-being or it may have resulted in physical costs. According to Cutrona and Russell (1990), all criminal victimization is uncontrollable and as such most likely to benefit from emotional support. Although their optimal matching model of stress did not speak specifically to hate crime, it can be useful in helping to delineate specific recommendations for hate crime victims.

By starting with the assumption that all hate crime is uncontrollable by the victim, the hate crime victim service provider recognizes at the outset that some degree of emotional support will be necessary. Drawing from this type of model, the service provider would need to determine the costs to the victim. Was this a property crime or a crime against a person? Both types of crime are likely to involve financial costs. Property crimes will require money to repair or replace what was vandalized or stolen. Crimes against persons may or may not involve violence and whether they do or not they are likely to entail a period of adjustment for the victim, who may be forced to take time off from work, be hospitalized, or find it necessary to relocate. Any one of these adjustments will have financial costs.

Each of the different costs associated with victimization will engender specific types of interactions with the various victim service providers. Victim service providers should recognize that the way victims interact with them will be influenced by the types of needs that they have as well as the victim's perception of the likelihood that the service provider will be able to assist them. For example, whereas law enforcement personnel will gather information from victims in order to apprehend the offender, the mental health professional will extract information and subsequently engage the victim in order to provide a therapeutic intervention for the victim. Figure 9.1 provides a rough outline of potential needs of hate crime victims associated with the requisite victim services providers. This is a useful way of delineating the optimal amount and type of support that corresponds with the stressor of hate crime victimization. Importantly, this is presented against a backdrop of emotional support from friends and family members.

The following section outlines specific ways that service providers, spanning the gamut from police to social workers to mental health professionals, can work effectively to address the needs of victims of hate crime. These strategies are based on the recommendations of governmental agencies, community advocacy groups, and existing research in the area (e.g., Coates & Winston, 1983; Frieze, Hymer, & Greenberg, 1987; Taylor, 1983; Umbreit & Coates, 2000).

SPECIFIC RECOMMENDATIONS FOR VICTIM SERVICE PROVIDERS

Hate Crime Ordinances as Deterrents

In the last decade, local municipal ordinances and college campus speech codes have also been enacted to stem the tide of expression of extreme bigotry and its effects (Delgado & Yun, 1994; Gellman, 1991; Lederer & Delgado, 1995). A majority of states and the District of Columbia have enacted statutes commonly known as hate crime laws. States vary with respect to their actual laws aimed at hate crime and hate speech. Whereas some states create a hate crime offense with its own set of penalties, others impose additional criminal sanctions on a person who commits a crime stemming from bias. For example, some states such as California and Vermont explicitly recognize hate crimes emanating from antigay bigotry, while other states such as Wyoming and Virginia do not. In general, hate crime statutes can address bias violence/intimidation, sexual orientation, gender, institutional vandalism, race, religion, and ethnicity.

Researchers and lawmakers alike contend that the existence of legislation aimed at penalizing hate-motivated criminal behaviors (at both the federal and state levels) serves to not only provide a ready means of punishment, but perhaps more importantly, can serve to deter potential offenders (Garofalo & Martin, 1993; Finn & McNeil, 1987; Jenness & Grattet, 2001; Lawrence, 1999). Legislation that penalizes certain behaviors sends out a strong and clear message that hate-motivated behaviors are wrong, and will not be tolerated. Importantly, it should be noted that although many researchers and representatives of advocacy groups have sought to ensure the enactment of hate crime legislation that either enhances punishment or creates a special crime for a hate-motivated offense (ADL, 2003; Delgado & Stefancic, 1997; *Wisconsin v. Mitchell*, 1993), few comprehensive analyses and discussions of national trends exist.

One exception by Craig-Henderson and Branch (2004) is worth noting here. That study examined the relationship between official reports of hate offenses, and the existence of legislation that penalizes the commission of hate-motivated offenses within each state. They conducted a systematic comparison of the number and type of reported hate offenses within each state to the type of existing legislation in that state, if any, aimed at penalizing hate offenses. Results suggested that the number of reports of hate crime within a state was related to the extent of existing legislation in that state. Moreover, the findings revealed that there were a number of differences among the states in the type and extent of existing legislation penalizing hate crime. For example, as of 2001, California, New Jersey, Rhode Island, Minnesota, and Illinois were the states that had the most extensive legislation penalizing hate crime. Among other things, the authors concluded that it was reassuring that California and New Jersey, two of the three states reporting the greatest number of hate offenses, have extensive legislation penalizing hate crimes. To the extent that such legislation provides a ready means for punishing offenders, it is reasonable to expect that hate crime offenders who are apprehended will be punished.

Law Enforcement Personnel

Law enforcement personnel and other first responders who initially interact with hate crime victims share a special responsibility to report evidence of hate crimes. Thus, municipalities should ensure that their law enforcement personnel follow model policy supported by the International Association of Chiefs of Police (IACP). This policy employs the definition and reporting form developed by the FBI following passage of the 1990 Hate Crimes Statistics Act, which was amended in 1996.

Whether an actual hate crime is recorded as such is very much a matter of the individual law enforcement officer. Like other offenses included in the FBI's Uniform Crime Reporting (UCR) system, hate crimes are voluntarily reported by local jurisdictions. There is evidence that these reports may at times be inaccurate. Results of one study funded by the Bureau of Justice concluded, "a full picture of hate crimes . . . has not yet been captured through official data" (as cited in Wang, 2003, p. 30). The study revealed serious disparities between what police officers believed to be the frequency of hate crime in their jurisdictions and the actual numbers of hate crimes filed in their agencies' reports. More than one-third of the respondents in the study whose agencies failed to submit a report in 1997 believed that their departments had received at least one report of a hate-motivated offense (Wang, 2003). Two years later in 1999, there continued to be many agencies that did not participate in the reporting system (Levinson, 2002).

The Bureau of Justice report offered four categories of recommendations to improve the reporting of hate crimes. Two of those recommendations are particularly relevant to variation among police officers' tendency to identify incidents as hate crimes and include the following: development in police agencies of formal policies for dealing with hate crimes including procedures for investigating, recording, verifying, and reporting; and providing hate crime training to local law enforcement. The FBI recommends that the data collection system include the reporting police officer on the scene making an initial determination that a bias motivation is suspected, and following this, a second officer with more experience in bias crimes should make the final determination of whether a hate crime has actually occurred. Obviously, this assessment must be done in concert with an accurate awareness of the victim's situation.

Social Workers

As professionals aimed at improving people's lives, social workers can play a unique role in the postvictimization experience of hate crime victims. Social workers can specialize in a host of fields including family, child, and school issues, or medical and public health, or mental health and substance abuse. Given the likelihood that crime victims in general who seek professional assistance will at some time in the process interact with a social worker, many representatives of the social work profession see themselves as victims' rights advocates. Consequently, hate crime victims may also avail themselves of such services.

In the case of hate crime, the social worker can help to find resources for the victim. Like other crime victims, the hate crime victim needs to know that he or she is not alone in their experience and that there are others who have been similarly targeted. Social workers can locate peer support groups, and this may be invaluable for certain types of hate crime victims. For example, consider the target of an antigay assault who has not disclosed her sexual identity to many. She may have a particularly difficult time finding out about the existence of a peer support group including others who were targeted because of their perceived sexual orientation. In this case, the social worker can help her to identify an appropriate support group.

Alternatively, consider the case of the hate crime targeting a teenager (which often occurs when hate crimes are school related). Because of their knowledge of existing resources and school-based policies and procedures, social workers are uniquely suited to help the family identify strategies for prosecuting the offender, minimizing disruption to the teen's education, and reducing the like-lihood of future victimization. Indeed, it may well be that some social workers set up resources specifically aimed at ameliorating the effects of hate crime and for some, this may involve the provision of counseling services.

Mental Health Professionals

The long-term consequences of the hate crime for victims may also involve the need for assistance from mental health professionals such as psychologists or psychiatrists. Mental health professionals who conduct postvictimization counseling with victims can provide additional emotional support after the initial crisis period. At its core, the postvictimization counseling should entail the processes of ventilation and validation (Office for Victims of Crime, 2000). Ventilation refers to the process of allowing survivors to retell their story. This may be challenging for victims, but the repetitive process allows the victim to make sense out of the incident and integrate it into his or her life story. Mental health professionals will notice that the initial retelling of the tale is likely to differ from subsequent retelling as the victim becomes more comfortable with psychologically revisiting the incident. As time passes, the victim's memory will change and these changes will be reflected in the different nuances that characterize later descriptions of the incident.

Because the ventilation experience involves the challenge to articulate the incident by finding the right words to describe the victim's feelings, the mental health service provider should recognize that ventilation is often culture-specific. Some cultures may be less likely to express reactions through words, and may typically express reactions through artistic forms, for example. Although in the United States, words tend to be the typical form of expression, because hate crimes target many because of their different nationality, racial, or ethnic status, mental health providers should be prepared for unique cultural expressions during the ventilation process.

In addition, it should be noted that this process of retelling (and reconstructing) the incident reflected in the ventilation experience results in inconsistent information that can seriously undermine an investigation. However, its usefulness lies in its ability to alleviate long-term victim distress (Office for Victims of Crime, 2000). By retelling the incident, the victim integrates the experience into her personal life stories and ultimately gains a cognitive sense of control over the incident. The story of the incident is recorded in the victim's memory and not only includes details about the incident but also includes all of the ensuing experiences (e.g., family support, friends' involvement, legal ramifications, etc.) relating to the incident.

Validation refers to the process through which the mental health professional confirms that the survivor's reaction to his experience is normal and to be expected. It is at this stage that the survivor should be reassured that although the crisis of victimization may have been chaotic, he or she is not crazy because of it. The survivor should be reminded that the reactions of anger, fear, and overwhelming sadness are normal responses to the experience. Periodically using the same phrases the survivor uses in describing his or her experiences can be useful in validating the survivor's feelings.

Attorneys and the Courts

Penalties for hate crime generally assume one of two forms, including those that enhance penalties for certain criminal conduct when it is hate-motivated such that additional criminal sanctions are imposed when a "normal" crime (e.g., an assault) stems from bias or bigotry. The other form that penalties assume occurs when a distinct hate crime offense is created. With respect to the former, when the commission of a given list of offenses (e.g., assault) is motivated by bigotry, that is, the victim is intentionally selected because the perpetrator believes the victim is associated with a particular category, the offense is more heavily punishable. The net effect of this type of a statute is that it punishes ordinarily criminal conduct in the usual way, and adds an additional penalty for the offender's intentional selection of the victim, that is, the offender's hate motive.

The alternative form that penalties take treat the combined effect of the criminal conduct and the bias motive as qualitatively greater than the sum of its parts. According to this approach, the presence of the bias motive makes a qualitative change in the conduct itself so that a completely different action is regarded as having been committed. This new action has different and presumably more far-reaching consequences. This approach to punishment of hate crime offenders regards bias incidents as especially pernicious because they are not limited to the immediate victim's geographic and temporal locale, but instead have implications for nonvictims who share association with the actual victim's social category.

Whether a hate crime victim retains an attorney or interacts with representatives of the courts will depend upon a number of factors including the identification and apprehension of an offender. Furthermore, whether the case involves a criminal or civil suit will also determine the nature and extent of interactions the victim has with the courts. However, what remains constant across all cases is the victim's need for candid, reasonable guidance that inoculates him or her from experiencing what is referred to as "secondary victimization." Although most frequently used to describe the experiences of rape victims who interact with the criminal justice system, it represents an adequate description of the way that many hate crime victims (who are often minority group persons) experience their own pursuit of justice in the courts. Secondary victimization is evident in the apparent absence of sympathy or concern for the victim's plight. In its most benign form, secondary victimization occurs as a result of the inherent difficulties in a system that strives to balance the rights of the victim against the rights of the accused (Symonds, 1980). At its worst, secondary victimization involves prejudicial or hostile skepticism of the victim's claim, and the infliction of deliberate psychological harm upon the victim.

Media and Public Involvement

When incidents occur in communities, they are often fueled by rumors. This has the effect of aggravating the situation, which in turn leads to more widespread community unrest and intergroup conflict. Given its ability to influence public attitudes, the media can play a critical role by disseminating useful and accurate information. Local officials should maintain open channels of communication with the media. One way of accomplishing this is by designating an official point-of-contact or liaison for hate crime information or incidents. A point-of-contact can control the proliferation of rumors immediately following the hate crime.

COMMUNITY RELATIONS SERVICE OF THE U.S. DEPARTMENT OF JUSTICE

The Community Relations Service (CRS) of the U.S. Department of Justice (USDOJ) provides recommendations and offers a number of services for victims and communities that have experienced hate crime. This final section describes some of the strategies and services that the CRS promotes in an effort to defuse hate crime activity. The utility of any one of these recommendations will necessarily depend upon the type of hate crime, victim, and context of the incident.

Mediation and Conciliation

Mediation and conciliation refer to techniques enacted at the community level and that have proven helpful in restoring stability in neighborhoods that have experienced the disorder of hate crime. The techniques involve participation of community leaders and victim representatives. A facilitator who establishes ground rules for participation and communication at the outset of the interaction mediates the interaction between victim groups and offenders.

Training

CRS offers training to members of communities that have experienced hate crime including law enforcement personnel, community leaders, and other volunteers. The training focuses on recognition of a hate crime, mobilization of community support, and identification of victims and witnesses. This type of training can ultimately be useful in educating communities and reducing the likelihood of future hate crime incidents.

Public Awareness and Education

Similar to the formal training services provided, CRS also offers hate crime prevention and education programs for schools, colleges, and community groups. These programs are designed to establish a sense of community across social boundaries and promote mutual respect. The educational programs address existing intergroup conflicts by reducing tension and include students, teachers, administrators, and parents within communities.

School-Based Programs

In addition, there are education and hate crime prevention programs that focus primarily on school settings. Some hate crimes occur in communities that have recently undergone population changes as a result of migration and immigration. Where these trends are most visible is in schools. Consequently, schools settings are often the site where hate crimes occur or where potential victims are targeted. School-based programs attempt to defuse ethnic and racial tensions. As a result of the success of these programs the CRS has expanded training to include "train-the-trainer" programs for local police, security officers, and school officials.

Event Contingency Planning

Most services offered by CRS are reactive and involve attention to the problem of hate crime after a hate crime has occurred. One exception is assistance that CRS can provide in contingency planning in order to ensure that marches, events, and demonstrations transpire in the absence of confrontations. At the request of local officials or event organizers CRS will help communities to successfully prepare for demonstrations and counter-demonstrations.

CONCLUSION

The Federal Bureau of Investigation (FBI) of the U.S. Department of Justice (2007) reported that 7,163 hate crimes, occurred in 2005. Of these incidents, by far the greatest proportion of them was instigated by racial animus (3, 919) and more than a third (37 percent) of these incidents were directed at blacks. Hate crimes target individuals, groups, and property because of race, ethnicity, religion, sexual orientation, gender, and physical and mental disability status. Moreover, victims of hate crime can also include the homeless, migrant workers, immigrants, and refugees. Victims can span the gamut and have little in common with one another other than the misfortune of having elicited a perpetrator's extreme bias.

To the extent that hate crimes continue to occur, victim assistance services must extend to address the needs of all of the different types of hate crime victims. Victim service providers, including mental health professionals and law enforcement personnel among others who assist hate crime victims, have a role to play and represent an important part of the postvictimization coping process. This discussion has focused on the specific ways that members of each of these groups can assist hate crime victims. In addition, the present discussion underscores the need for continued research on the factors associated with victims' use of the different services, as well as the services most useful for specific types of hate crimes.

NOTE

1. Throughout this discussion I will use the terms *hate crime* and *bias crime* interchangeably. Although this is the tendency throughout this area of inquiry and scholarship, it should be noted that not all of these crimes involve the actual emotional state of hate, and in many cases when this emotion is expressed it does not reach the level of illegality required for determination of a hate crime.

REFERENCES

Anti-Defamation League of B'nai B'rith. (1994). *Hate crime laws: A comprehensive guide.* New York: Author.

Brewer, M. B. (1996). When stereotypes lead to stereotyping: the use of stereotypes in person perception. In C. N. Macrae, C. Stangor, & M. Hewstone (Eds.), *Stereotypes and stereotyping* (pp. 254–275). New York: Guilford Press.

Coates, D., & Winston, T. (1983). Counteracting the deviance of depression: Peer support groups for victims. *Journal of Social Issues, 39,* 169–194.

Cowan, G., & Hodge, C. (1996). Judgments of hate speech: The effects of target group, publicness, and behavioral responses of the target. *Journal of Applied Social Psychology, 26,* 355–374.

Craig, K., & Waldo, C. (1996). "So, what's a hate crime anyway?" Young adults' perceptions of hate crimes, victims, and perpetrators. *Law and Human Behavior, 20,* 113–129.

Craig-Henderson, K., & Branch, A. (2004). *Hate crime, ethnic diversity, and legislation.* Unpublished manuscript.

Cutrona, C. (1990). Stress and social support—In search of optimal matching. *Journal of Social and Clinical Psychology, 9,* 3–14.

Cutrona, C., & Russell, D. (1990). Type of social support and specific stress: Toward a theory of optimal matching. In B. R. Saranson, I. G. Saranson, & G. R. Pierce (Eds.), *Social support: An interactional view* (pp. 319–366). New York: Wiley.

Delgado, R., & Yun, D. H. (1994). Pressure valves and bloodied chickens: An analysis of paternalistic objections to hate speech regulation. *California Law Review, 82,* 871–892.

Finn, P., & McNeil, T. (1987). *The response of the criminal justice system to bias crime: An exploratory review.* Contract report submitted to the National Institute of Justice. (Available from ABT Associates, 55 Wheeler St., Cambridge, MA 02138–1168.)

Friedman, L. N., & Tucker, S. B. (1997). Violence prevention through victim assistance. In R. C. Davis, A. J. Lurigio, & W. G. Skogan (Eds.), *Victims of crime* (pp. 183–93). Thousand Oaks, CA: Sage.

Frieze, I., Hymer, S., & Greenberg, M. (1987). Describing the crime victim: Psychological reactions to victimization. *Professional Psychology: Research and Practice, 18*, 299–315.

Garofalo, J. (1997). Hate crime victims in the U.S. In R. C. Davis, A. J. Lurigio, & W. G. Skogan (Eds.), *Victims of crime* (pp. 134–145). Newbury Park, CA: Sage Publications.

Garofalo, J., & Martin, S. (1993). *Bias-motivated crimes: Their characteristics and the law enforcement response.* Final report to the National Institute of Justice. Carbondale: Southern Illinois University, Center for the Study of Crime, Delinquency and Correction.

Gellman, S. (1991). Sticks and stones can put you in jail, but can words increase your sentence? Constitutional and policy dilemmas of ethnic intimidation laws. *UCLA Law Review, 39*, 333–396.

Gerstenfeld, P. B. (1992). Smile when you call me that! The problems with punishing hate motivated behavior. *Behavioral Sciences and the Law, 10*, 259–285.

Hamilton, D. L., & Sherman, J. W. (1994). Stereotypes. In R. S. Wyer, Jr., & T. K. Srull (Eds.), *Handbook of social cognition* (2nd ed., Vol. 2, pp. 1–68). Hillsdale, NJ: Erlbaum.

Hamilton, D. L., Sherman, J. W., & Lickel, B. (1998). Perceiving social groups: The importance of the entativity continuum. In C. Sedikides, J. Schopler, & C. A. Insko (Eds.), *Intergroup cognition and intergroup behavior* (pp. 47–74). Mahwah, NJ: Erlbaum.

Hamm, M. (1994). (Ed.). *Hate crime: International perspectives on causes and control.* Cincinnati: Anderson.

Iwasaki, Y. (2001). Testing an optimal matching hypothesis of stress, coping and health: Leisure and general coping. *Society and Leisure, 24*, 163–203.

Jenness, V., & Grattet, R. (2001). *Making hate a crime: From social movement to law enforcement.* New York: Russell Sage Foundation.

Lawrence, F. (1999). *Punishing hate: Bias crimes under American law.* Cambridge, MA: Harvard University Press.

Lederer, L., & Delgado, R. (Eds.). (1995). *The price we pay: The case against racist speech, hate propaganda, and pornography.* New York: Hill and Wang.

Levinson, D. (Ed.). (2002). *Encyclopedia of crime and punishment* (pp. 822–826). Thousand Oaks, CA: Sage.

Mackie, D. M., Hamilton, D. L., Susskind, J., & Rosselli, F. (1996). Social psychological foundations of stereotype formation. In C. N. Macrae, C. Stangor, & M. Hewstone (Eds.), *Stereotypes and stereotyping* (pp. 41–78). New York: Guilford Press.

Norris, F. H., Kaniasty, K., & Thompson, M. P. (1997). The psychological consequences of crime. In R. C. Davis, A. J. Lurigio, & W. G. Skogan (Eds.), *Victims of crime* (pp. 146–166). Thousand Oaks, CA: Sage.

Office for Victims of Crime. (2000). *Bridging the systems to empower victims: Mental health and victim services training guide.* Washington, DC: U.S. Department of Justice. Retrieved August 23, 2007, http://www.ojp.usdoj.gov/ovc/publications/infores/student/student.pdf

Sales, E., Baum, M., & Shore, B. (1984). Victim readjustment following assault. *Journal of Social Issues, 40*, 117–136.

Stephan, W. G., & Stephan, C. W. (2000). An integrated threat theory. In S. Oskamp (Ed.), *Reducing prejudice and discrimination* (pp. 23–45). Mahwah, NJ: Erlbaum.

Sullaway, M. (2004). Psychological perspectives on hate crime. *Psychology, Public Policy and Law, 10,* 250–292.

Symonds, M. (1980). The "second injury" to victims. In L. Kivens (Ed.), *Evaluation and change: Services for survivors* (pp. 36–38). Minneapolis, MN: Minneapolis Medical Research Foundation.

Tajfel, H. (1969). Cognitive aspects of prejudice. *Journal of Social Issues, 25,* 79–97.

Taylor, S. (1983). Adjustment to threatening events: A theory of cognitive adaptation. *American Psychologist, 38,* 1161–1171.

Umbreit, M., & Coates, R. B. (2000). *Multicultural implications of restorative justice: Potential pitfalls and dangers.* St. Paul, MN: University of Minnesota, Center for Restorative Justice and Peace Making.

U.S. Department of Justice, Federal Bureau of Investigation. (2004). *Hate crime statistics, Annual Report 2003.*Washington, D.C.: Government Printing Office.

U.S. Department of Justice, Federal Bureau of Investigation. (2007). *Hate crimes statistics: 2005.* Washington, DC: U.S. Department of Justice.

Wang, L. (2003). *Hate crimes law.* St. Paul, MN: Thomson/West.

Wisconsin v. Mitchell, 508 U.S. 47 (1993).

Yang, S. (2003, September 30). Man convicted in 9-11 era slaying of Sikh. Associated Press.

CHAPTER 10

HATE ON THE INTERNET LEADS TO HATE CRIME: WHAT IS SOCIETY'S BEST RESPONSE?

Christopher Wolf

Manhasset, New York, is a bedroom community of New York City on the North Shore of Long Island. A 2005 *Wall Street Journal* article ranked it as the best town for raising a family in the New York metropolitan area. John Rocissano is a graduate of the Manhasset High School, someone described by a neighbor as a "good kid." After graduation, Rocissano attended community college and found a job at the local Staples office supply store.

By day, Rocissano helped customers find printer cartridges and copier paper. By night, like many young adults, he used the social networking site, MySpace, to connect online with people sharing his interests. On MySpace, he became a group leader of the National Alliance discussion site.

The name, by itself, does not say much. National Alliance could be a well-intentioned group. But it is not. National Alliance is a neo-Nazi, white supremacist hate group recognized for decades as one of the most formidable white supremacist groups on the country. The founder of the National Alliance is William Pierce, the author of *The Turner Diaries*, a novel calling for the violent overthrow of the federal government and the systematic killing of Jews and nonwhites in order to establish a so-called Aryan society. *The Turner Diaries* is thought to be the inspiration behind Timothy McVeigh's bombing of the federal building in Oklahoma City, which resulted in the deaths of 168 people.

Rocissano also was inspired by the teachings of the National Alliance. On MySpace, he listed *The Turner Diaries* as his favorite book. At first, he merely handed out fliers for the National Alliance, to recruit new members.

But in the late summer of 2007, he and a friend went on a hate crime spree in Manhasset, home to a large Jewish community, including Holocaust survivors. Over Labor Day weekend, the pair painted red swastikas and other graffiti espousing hate on an elementary school, on a school bus in a high school parking lot, at a synagogue (where they also smashed windows), on a home in nearby Roslyn Estates, New York, and on a street sign in a residential neighborhood. Before their violence escalated any further, they were arrested and charged with misdemeanors—first offenses for each. Ironically, in the "About Me" section of his MySpace home page, Rocissano wrote: "Don't judge me until you get to know me."

On MySpace, as well as on the social networking site Facebook.com, there are hundreds of groups featuring the words *Hitler* or *Nazi*, many established to promote neo-Nazism and other anti-Semitic feelings. The "virtual community" of haters no doubt gave Rocissano the feeling that his views were mainstream and acceptable, and that it was okay to act on them.

Had the police searched the computer of the newly apprehended hate criminal, they likely would have seen evidence of visits to the wildly popular YouTube Web site. (Videos on YouTube created more traffic on the Internet in 2006 than existed on the entire Internet in the year 2000. My Space and YouTube, along with Facebook, are "killer aps" on the Internet today, used by millions.)

On YouTube, hundreds of hate videos have been uploaded, including music videos from the neo-Nazi heavy metal band Landser. Images of Hitler and swastikas are staples of Landser's videos. One of their hits is a tribute to Rudolf Hess, a top Nazi deputy of Adolf Hitler.

YouTube features clips from the 1940 anti-Semitic Nazi film *Jud Suess*, made under the supervision of Joseph Goebbels to justify anti-Semitism. It is considered one of the most hateful depictions of Jews on film. Also on YouTube is a video of an April 2006 rally held in Lansing, Michigan, by the National Socialist Movement (NSM), a Minneapolis-based neo-Nazi group. The video shows NSM members, dressed in Nazi regalia, making virulently anti-Semitic statements on the steps of the state capitol. The neo-Nazis cap their comments with "Sieg Heil" salutes.

If offered in an educational context, with explanation of their hateful origins and of how they glorified or played a role in the deaths of millions, perhaps such material would serve history. But they are not offered in that context; they are posted to provoke hate and to recruit haters. Such hate material violates the terms of use on YouTube, which, like the MySpace and Facebook terms of use, prohibit content that is harmful, offensive, or illegal, or that violates the rights or threatens the safety of any person. On MySpace, as well as on Facebook and YouTube, users have the right to report material violating the terms of use. However, such reports often are ignored.

In August 2007, a German government-sponsored Internet watchdog group, Jugendschutz.de, with Google—parent of YouTube—lodged complaints about the Nazi propaganda. The complaints were not responded to, although some of the complained-about videos disappeared. The Central Council of Jews in Germany has threatened legal action against Google, the parent of YouTube, given the German laws against the display of Nazi propaganda.

The MySpace, Facebook, and YouTube materials join the thousands of Web sites that deny the Holocaust and that espouse virulent anti-Semitism; others portray gays and lesbians as subhuman in the guise of promoting so-called family values; and still other Web sites contain racial epithets and caricatures. As new technologies for information become available over the Internet, members of hate groups have proven themselves to be "early adopters." For example, with faster bandwidth, online gaming is popular and hate-filled online games now are available that celebrate in gory detail the random killing of minorities.

The effect of such content on people—especially children—and on society is profoundly troubling. Some call Internet hate speech the "direct marketing" of racism and violence. And as bad as the directly racist and violent Web sites and Internet content may be, perhaps more troubling are the hate sites masquerading as scholarly and reliable sites.

Stormfront, which describes itself as the "White Nationalist Community," hosts a site about Martin Luther King, Jr., that appears to be legitimate but in fact contains racist propaganda. To a schoolchild doing homework research, the site is terribly misleading and has the potential for instilling biased and hateful preconceptions in young minds.

Before the Internet, hate speech largely was available only in plain brown envelopes and down dark alleys, and its reach was limited. Rallies rarely attracted large crowds. Now, on the Internet, hate is on display for all to see, and the potential audience is vast.

The dawn of hate on the Internet has wreaked havoc on American society with a marked increase in hate crimes. Online recruiting has aided many hate groups linked to violence against Jews, African Americans, gays, and lesbians in their efforts to increase their membership. In fact, Don Black, former Grand Dragon of the Ku Klux Klan, noted that, "[A]s far as recruiting, [the Internet has] been the biggest breakthrough I've seen in the 30 years I've been involved in [white nationalism]."

Online hate speech indeed has had pernicious effects, resulting in deaths. In California, Matthew Williams and his brother Tyler were charged with murdering gay couple Gary Matson and Winfield Mowder and helping set fire to three Sacramento-area synagogues. Matthew Williams was an Internet addict. He adopted nearly every radical-right philosophy he came across online, from the antigovernment views of militias to the racist and anti-Semitic beliefs of the Identity movement. He regularly downloaded pages from extremist sites and used printouts of these pages in his frequent attempts to convince his friends to adopt his beliefs. Without question, the easy accessibility to rapidly hateful content inspired Williams to go on his real-world hate rampage.

Benjamin Nathaniel Smith went on a racially motivated shooting spree in Illinois and Indiana targeting Jews, blacks, and Asians. He killed two people and wounded eight. As law enforcement officers prepared to apprehend him, he took his own life. "It wasn't really 'til I got on the Internet, read some literature of these groups that . . . it really all came together," Benjamin Smith told documentary filmmaker Beverly Peterson months before his spree. "It's a slow, gradual process to become racially conscious."

Pittsburgh gunman Richard Baumhammers murdered members of several minorities in April. He was convicted of killing five people, and leaving a sixth paralyzed, and he was sentenced to death. His victims were a Jewish woman, a black man, two Asian Americans, and two Indian men. Before his shooting spree, Baumhammers visited Tom Metzger's WAR Web site. (Metzger later characterized him as "a white man" who "decided to deliver Aryan justice in a down home way.") Baumhammers joined the e-mail mailing list of the hate rock band Aggressive Force, repeatedly visited the popular white supremacist site Stormfront, and downloaded material from hate sites created by members of the neo-Nazi National Alliance. He also hosted his own Web site to further disseminate the teachings of hate and intolerance.

British neo-Nazi David Copeland planted nail bombs in a black neighborhood, an Indian area, and a gay pub in London, killing three and injuring more than a hundred. Copeland later wrote, "I bombed the blacks, Paki's [sic], [and] Degenerates," and he boasted, "I would of [sic] bombed the Jews as well if I got a chance." A court handed Copeland six life sentences for his crimes. He had learned how to build his bombs by visiting a cybercafe, where he downloaded *The Terrorist Handbook* and *How to Make Bombs: Book Two* from the Internet.

The Better than Auschwitz Web site includes pictures of bombing victims and detailed bomb-making instructions. In addition, Better than Auschwitz features instructions for using knives and brass knuckles in fights against minorities, as well as tips for hand-to-hand combat. A "Nigger Baiting Made Easy" section describes "the various methods of selecting muds [sic] and queers, and getting them to fight, or throw the first punch." Such material resembles the instructions the group White Aryan Resistance gave the skinheads of East Side White Pride before their violent rampage in Portland, Oregon, in 1988.

Online, extremists may find guidance not only on how to attack, but also whom to attack. Antigovernment sites frequently post information about judges, law enforcement officers, and other government officials.

An understandable immediate reaction to the hate found on the Internet is, "There ought to be a law." But, in the United States, the First Amendment to the United States Constitution applies with full force to the Internet, the Supreme Court has ruled. And that freedom of expression protection means most speech is permissible unless it threatens imminent violence directed at identifiable victims (or is pornographic or violates intellectual property rights, among other limited categories of prohibited speech.) Of course, hate speech, online or off, can be used as evidence to show a prohibited motivation for a crime. Such evidence can result in an enhanced penalty for physical crime under hate crime laws that exist in many states. (A federal hate crime law is pending in Congress.) But the speech itself is rarely prosecutable.

In Europe, by contrast, there are laws prohibiting online hate speech and images. Why the difference in approach? Although freedom of expression is a valued principle in most modern democracies, it is counterbalanced by the belief that government has a role in protecting its citizens from the effects of hate and intolerance. Nowhere is this belief stronger than in Germany and its neighbors, countries that less than a century ago witnessed how words of hate against Jews and other minorities exploded into the Holocaust, with the attendant murder of more than six million people.

As a result, there are laws in Germany and elsewhere in Europe that prohibit words and images attacking religious, racial, and sexual minorities, and that revive the words and images of the Nazi era. In Germany, *Volksverhetzung* (incitement of hatred against a minority) is a punishable offense under Section 130 of the *Strafgesetzbuch* (Germany's criminal code) and can lead to up to five years of imprisonment. *Volksverhetzung* is punishable in Germany *even if* committed abroad and even if committed by non-German citizens, if the sentiment was made accessible in Germany.

A famous instance of German prosecution of someone whose hate speech was launched from abroad but was available in Germany is Ernst Zundel. Zundel is a Holocaust denier who published "The Hitler We Loved and Why" and "Did Six Million Really Die" while he lived in North America. Zundel was deported from the United States to Canada and onward to Germany, and tried criminally in the state court of Mannheim on outstanding charges of incitement for Holocaust denial dating from the early 1990s, including for materials disseminated over the Internet. On February 15th, 2007, he was convicted and sentenced to the maximum term of five years in prison.

Similarly, an Australian Holocaust denier, Frederick Toben, used his Australia-based Web site to publish his benighted views. Upon visiting Germany, he was arrested, tried, and convicted of violating German law as a result of his Australian-based Web site that was viewable in Germany. The conviction and subsequent jailing made Toben a hero of sorts among Holocaust deniers, so much so that he was a featured speaker at the infamous conference sponsored by the Iranian government on whether the Holocaust really happened. And the convictions did not do much to silence their hate speech. All one need do is insert the names of Toben and Zundel in a Google search bar, and you will find Web sites of supporters paying homage to them as martyrs and republishing their messages.

In addition to national laws like that in Germany used to convict Toben and Zundel, the Council of Europe has included in the Cybercrime Treaty a prohibition against online hate speech. Specifically, the provision bans "any written material, any image or any other representation of ideas or theories, which advocates, promotes or incites hatred, discrimination or violence, against any individual or group of individuals, based on race, color, descent or national or ethnic origin, as well as religion if used as pretext for any of these factors." It also outlaws sites that deny, minimize, approve, or justify crimes against humanity, particularly the Holocaust.

The treaty is beginning to be implemented through legislation among European member countries. The United States is a signatory to the Cybercrime Treaty but did not sign the protocol on online hate speech, in light of its invalidity domestically under the First Amendment. And the European Union recently passed legislation extending to the Internet its broadcast rules, which restrict hateful and other content deemed inappropriate.

There is a fundamental difference in approach in the United States to hate speech. The framework of the First Amendment presupposes that just as hate speech is permissible, so too is speech intended to counter and negate such hate speech. Simply put, for every hurtful lie told about a group of people, someone can tell the truth about the falsity of stereotypes and about how important it is to judge people as individuals. But in the Internet era, it appears there are more people interested in spewing hate than in countering it. On the social networking sites and on YouTube, inflammatory, hate-filled content overwhelms the limited efforts to promote tolerance and to teach diversity. And, as we have seen, hate speech inspires violence.

So, given the link between hate speech and violence, how do we draw the line between permissible speech protected by the First Amendment and criminal conduct? Historically, American lawmakers have generally taken a hands-off approach to hate on the Internet, recognizing the broad First Amendment protections. Internet legislation largely has focused on copyright and trademark violations. (Those are the laws focused on domain names and illegal downloading of music.) In terms of objectionable content, Congress has attempted to limit sexually explicit materials deemed harmful to minors, but much of that legislation has been struck down as overly broad and violative of Constitutional free speech protections. Hate speech per se has not been a focus of Internet-era legislation.

Still, pre-Internet era laws prohibiting obscene materials, threats of imminent violence, and violations of civil rights have been applied to the Internet. Judges have struggled over the electronic dissemination of hate speech because although it is offensive and hurtful, the First Amendment does protect such expression. When speech, however, contains a direct, credible threat against an identifiable individual, organization, or institution, it crosses the line to criminal conduct. And although criminal cases concerning hate speech on the Internet are few in number, there are lessons from the early successful prosecutions of hate speech in the United States.

All of the cases build on the foundation built by the courts in non-Internet cases, where they have been reluctant to draw a line for expressions of hate speech. The most famous example is the historic case in Skokie, Illinois, which allowed a Nazi parade to march through the streets of the predominantly Jewish town. The National Socialist Party of America told the village of Skokie that demonstrators would wear German Nazi Party uniforms and carry signs with the message "White Free Speech." The Village of Skokie filed suit to stop the march, and the case worked its way up to the Supreme Court, which refused to grant an injunction to stop the parade. The Court did not say the Nazis had a constitutional right to march, but it did say the Nazis had a constitutional right to be free of "prior restraints" unless special procedural safeguards accompanied the prior restraints. The Village of Skokie passed ordinances prohibiting dissemination of hate materials, and prohibiting marches by political parties in military-style uniform. The Nazi party sued again, and the courts found the ordinances unconstitutional. The rally was finally held; 25 Nazi demonstrators were protected by 400 police.

The U.S. Supreme Court later confirmed its reluctance in permitting regulation of hate speech when it struck down a Minnesota city ordinance banning speech that "arouses anger, alarm, or resentment in others on the basis of race, color, creed, religion, or gender." The Supreme Court established a clear rule that a government cannot impose special prohibitions on those who express disfavored views.

The leading case that sought to establish the line with respect to hate speech *online* involved the American Coalition of Life Activists (the ACLA) and its anti-abortion site known as "The Nuremberg Files." The site was essentially a hit list, targeting abortion providers with intention to inspire attacks against them. The ACLA Web site offered extensive personal information about abortion providers: pictures; addresses and phone numbers; license-plate numbers; Social Security numbers; names and birth dates of spouses and children. Viewers were exhorted to send photos, videotapes, and data on "the abortionist, their car, their house, friends, and anything else of interest."

The ACLA Web site said that the information garnered would be used to prosecute abortion providers when abortion becomes illegal, comparing the doctors to Nazi leaders who were prosecuted after the Second World War. The list of abortion providers at "The Nuremberg Files" was effectively a list of targets for assassination. Names listed in plain black lettering were of doctors still "working"; those printed in greyed-out letters were "wounded"; and those names that were crossed out indicated doctors who had been murdered.

The "Nuremberg Files" trial court wrestled with the issue of whether the Web site constituted protected speech under the First Amendment or qualified as a true threat. At trial the jury found that the ACLA Web site was a threat to plaintiffs and ordered the Web site owners and operators to pay plaintiffs over $100 million in damages. The court then issued a permanent injunction to prevent the defendants from providing additional information to the "Nuremberg Files" Web site.

The appellate court at first unanimously *reversed* the trial court's decision, holding that the defendants' Web site was a lawful expression of views protected by the First Amendment. The court concluded that "unless [defendants] threatened that its members would themselves assault the doctors, the First Amendment protects its speech." However, the court of appeals later decided to rehear the case en banc and in an 8 to 3 decision held that the Web site indeed constituted a true threat of force and was *not* protected by the First Amendment.

Thus the appellate ruling found that a true threat, that is, one where a reasonable person fears physical violence, is unprotected under the First Amendment. Thus, after the "Nuremberg Files" case, it is clear that hateful content, when it knowingly and intentionally communicates a credible threat, will not be protected.

The few other cases involving hate speech on the Internet in the United States have also wrestled with the issue of where to draw the line. The case of *United States v. Machado* was one of the first examples of successful prosecution of hate online. Richard Machado, a 21-year-old expelled college student, sent a threatening e-mail message to 60 Asian students: "I personally will make it my life career [*sic*] to find and kill everyone one [*sic*] of you personally. OK?????? That's how determined I am." Machado's first trial ended in a hung jury. A trial in 1998 resulted in Machado's conviction for interference with federally protected activities in violation of a federal statute. He was sentenced to a year in jail and a year of supervised release. The conviction was upheld on appeal. That precedent, and similar ones, make clear that threats like Machado's, should they appear on a MySpace homepage or on Facebook, or if they were to be contained in a video uploaded to YouTube, would likely subject the person creating such content to legal liability.

As the *Nuremberg Files* and *Machado* cases demonstrate, hate speech *will* be prosecuted and enjoined in the United States if a credible threat to an individual or group exists. And, as noted, enhanced penalties may result from the evidence of hateful motivation shown by hate speech. But, by and large, Internet hate speech legally is uncontrolled in the United States.

What does that mean for the Internet worldwide? We have seen that other countries—like Germany—criminalize Internet hate speech and issue orders requiring people to take down Web pages and video that would be illegal in the United States. Indeed, people have been arrested and jailed because of their online content. Does that mean that the laws in Europe result in a cleaning up of the Internet? The answer is no.

The borderless nature of the Internet means that if placing certain content on the Internet is illegal in one place, all one needs to do is place the prohibited content on the Internet in a jurisdiction where it is legal. That means the United States, which is the most permissive nation in the world when it comes to allowable speech, can serve as host to hate-filled content that is illegal elsewhere. Once launched from the United States, it is viewable worldwide, except in certain situations where there is massive censorship blocking incoming Internet content, such as China. And one need not be physically present in the United States to launch content from an Internet server here. Telecommunication lines make remote Internet hosting simple from someone overseas.

So laws addressed at Internet hate, even though understandable in light of a nation's history, are perhaps the least effective way to deal with the problem. There may be symbolic value in prosecuting hate speech online, to show that a country will not sit idly by and allow speech that is contrary to its values of tolerance and personal respect in light of its history, such as in Germany. But the reflexive use of the law as the tool of first resort to deal with online hate speech threatens to weaken respect for the law if such attempted law enforcement fails to stop the content from appearing online, as most often will be the case since it can be reposted in the United States once taken down abroad, or if it is used to deal with minor violations.

A well-known case brought against Yahoo! to enforce the French law that prohibits the selling or display of neo-Nazi memorabilia in the end trivialized the speech codes directed at Holocaust deniers. An extraordinary amount of time and legal resources were used to combat the online auction sales of swastika cufflinks—time and money that could have been spent focusing on the larger problem of hate on the Internet.

In 2000, the Paris-based International League against Racism and Anti-Semitism sued Yahoo! in France to stop sales of Nazi paraphernalia to French citizens on its U.S.-based auction site. French law prohibits the sale or exhibition of objects associated with racism. A French court agreed with the International League and required Yahoo! to make it impossible for French citizens to connect to a Yahoo! Web site with messages relating to Nazi objects.

The decision of the French court was roundly criticized for failing to recognize the reality of the Internet—that content originating in the United States should not be subject to every nation's laws just because the content is visible worldwide on the Internet. Under such a scenario, an author would have to learn the laws of every country in the world before posting content, for fear of liability. That situation would thwart the purposes of the Internet—unfettered worldwide communication. Critics pointed to repressive regimes, like China. If all Internet content, no matter where hosted, had to comply with Chinese law, what would that mean for the free expression of ideas?

In the situation in France, Yahoo! sought help from a United States court to thwart the French judgment and in November 2001, a federal district judge ruled that "although France has the sovereign right to regulate what speech is permissible in France, this court may not enforce a foreign order that violates the protections of the United States Constitution." That order was reversed on technical grounds of ripeness and personal jurisdiction, without the court addressing the First Amendment issue. While Yahoo! voluntarily removed the offending items from its Web site to end the case, the case stands as a monument to the frivolous use of law to regulate online speech.

The law is but one tool in the fight against online hate. Indeed perhaps the best antidote to hate speech is counter-speech—exposing hate speech for its deceitful and false content, setting the record straight, and promoting the values of tolerance and diversity. To paraphrase U.S. Supreme Court Justice Brandeis, sunlight is still the best disinfectant—it is always better to expose hate to the light of day than to let it fester in the darkness. The best answer to bad speech is more speech. Regrettably, it is not fashionable to promote tolerance and diversity, and to counter hate speech, on the Internet. Hate sites far outnumber sites with messages to counter hate speech.

So what are other possible antidotes to hate speech online? The voluntary cooperation of the Internet community—internet service providers (ISPs) and others—to join in the campaign against hate speech is urgently needed. If more ISPs, in the United States especially, block content, it will at least be more difficult for haters to gain access through respectable hosts. Section 230 of the Telecommunications Act of 1996 specifically states that ISPs will not be held liable on account of "any action voluntarily taken in good faith to restrict access to or availability of material that the provider or user considers to be obscene, lewd, lascivious, filthy, excessively violent, harassing, or otherwise objectionable, whether or not such material is constitutionally protected." That means that ISPs can enforce their terms of service prohibiting offensive material; they can respond to complaints and act on them by editing out hate speech, without fear of liability. The latest social networking and video sites go to great pains to eliminate obscene (but not legally pornographic) content because of the anticipated public outcry over the appearance of such material. That is why YouTube's videos all are G rated. A similar effort could help eliminate hate content, but it appears that public demand for such editing is needed to prompt adequate attention.

But in the era of search engines as the primary portals for Internet users, cooperation from the Googles of the world is an even more important goal. The experience with Google concerning the hate site "Jew Watch" shows how search engine companies can help. When entering the search term *Jew*, the top result in Google was the hate site "Jew Watch." The high ranking of Jew Watch in response to a search inquiry was not due to a conscious choice by Google, but was solely a result of an automated system of ranking. In response to contacts from the Anti-Defamation League, Google placed text on its site that apologized for the ranking, and gave users a clear explanation of how search results are obtained, to refute the impression that Jew Watch was a reliable source of information.

The International Network Against Cyber-Hate (INACH), a coalition of national organizations fighting hate and discrimination has reported that over a recent four-year period, it received complaints on fifteen thousand cases of online hate. By forwarding the complaints to ISPs and search engines, more than five thousand hate sites, discussion threads, videos, and music files were removed. Still, requests for removal frequently are not acted upon, as evidenced by the recent case of Germany's Jugendschutz.de complaining to YouTube but receiving no response.

For the time being, YouTube is the single major video-sharing portal. So its decisions on what content appears do make a difference. But where there are multiple outlets for content, as is the norm on the Web, the effectiveness of the take-down remedy is limited. For example, a subscriber to an ISP who loses his or her account for violating that ISP's regulations against hate speech may resume propagating hate by subsequently signing up with any of the dozens of more permissive ISPs in the marketplace.

Another group that can help in the fight against online hate speech is that of schools and universities, where many people obtain Internet access both for hosting and viewing. Because private educational institutions are not agents of the government, they may forbid users from engaging in offensive speech using university equipment or university services. Public schools and universities, as agents of the government, must follow the First Amendment's prohibition against speech restrictions based on content or viewpoint.

Nonetheless, public universities may promulgate content-neutral regulations that effectively prevent the use of school facilities or services by extremists. For example, a university may limit use of its computers and server to academic activities only. This would likely prevent a student from creating a racist Web site for propaganda purposes or from sending racist e-mail from his student e-mail account. One such policy—at the University of Illinois at Champaign-Urbana—stipulates that its computer services are "provided in support of the educational, research and public service missions of the University and its use must be limited to those purposes."

Universities depend on an atmosphere of academic freedom and uninhibited expression. Any decision to limit speech on a university campus—even speech in cyberspace—will inevitably affect this ideal. College administrators should confer with representatives from both the faculty and student body when implementing such policies. Public schools receiving E-Rate funding from the federal government must, as a matter of law, have filters to block sites with indecent material; hate speech typically has not been a focus of the filtering efforts and perhaps the time has come to consider that.

The problem of hate speech on the Internet is not one that is easily solved. The law has a limited role to play, especially in light of the permissive rules in the United States that allow hate speech to be launched for viewing worldwide. The ISP and search engine operators could, if they wished, play a greater role in controlling hate speech, but even their efforts, unless coordinated, may have limited impact. Thus, Justice Brandeis's remedy of *more* and truthful speech to counter the harmful effects of hate speech may, in the end, be the most enduring solution. Just as words do motivate people to act, and in the context of hate speech, to act criminally, perhaps words of tolerance and understanding will motivate people to control their basest instincts.

CHAPTER 11

TAKING ON HATE:
ONE NGO'S STRATEGIES

Heidi Beirich and Mark Potok

Three years after the civil rights movement came to a bitter end with the 1968 assassination of Martin Luther King, Jr., two white lawyers in Alabama formed a nonprofit organization to take on the legacy of racism in America. Though initially a small and money-strapped group, the Southern Poverty Law Center (SPLC) would grow over the next four decades into a power-house foe of race-based hatred.

Based in the state capital of Montgomery, the SPLC spent its early years filing more or less traditional civil rights lawsuits—important cases that desegregated the all-white Alabama State Highway Patrol, ended the in-voluntary sterilization of many mentally challenged young black girls, and mandated equal benefits for American servicewomen, among other things. In the early 1980s, it began filing the lawsuits against white supremacist groups that more than any other venture would make it nationally known, especially after a retaliatory 1983 Ku Klux Klan firebomb attack. It launched Teaching Tolerance, an educational project meant to provide America's schoolchildren with high-quality multicultural teaching materials. And it kicked off Klanwatch, a program later renamed the Intelligence Project, to monitor and investigate the activities of extreme-right-wing hate groups. Klanwatch produced a newsletter that would eventually grow into a major investigative magazine.

Over the years, the SPLC developed a reputation for excellence in its legal work, its investigative and research capabilities, and the publications it pro-duced to help educate the public. Many of its lawsuits produced hard evi-dence of criminality that led to criminal convictions in cases authorities had abandoned earlier. In the fall of 1994, its letter warning the U.S. attorney general that the militia movement's mix of guns and extremist antigovernment ideology was creating a "recipe for disaster" was sent just six months before the 1995 bombing of the Alfred P. Murrah Federal Building in Oklahoma City left 168 people, including 19 children, dead. Worrying evidence of the SPLC's effectiveness came in the form of the 30 white supremacists sentenced to federal prison over the years in various attempts to destroy the SPLC's building or assassinate one of its two founders, Morris Dees and Joseph Levin.

In many ways, the SPLC's lawsuits against hate groups—judgments had been reached against 46 individuals and 9 major white supremacist groups as of this writing—have been its key line of attack for most of its history. The judgments bankrupted some of the most important hate groups of our times and also had a kind of demonstration effect, holding racist violence in check because extremists feared that they, too, could be ruined financially. But as the decades have passed, extremist leaders have grown increasingly savvy about the kinds of actions that could land them on the wrong side of such a lawsuit. As a result, the Intelligence Project has turned more and more to new antihate strategies, many of them dependent on the department's award-winning investigative magazine, the *Intelligence Report.*

What follows is a look at key strategies and tactics employed by the SPLC, especially in its Intelligence Project, in its work to hobble and destroy hate groups in America. After an initial section summarizing some of the lawsuits that have been among SPLC's best-known work, we look in some more depth at more recent tactics and strategies, with an emphasis on the public information aspects of our work.

THE CASES

United Klans of America

In 1981, a 19-year-old black man named Michael Donald was on his way to a store in Mobile, Alabama, when two members of the United Klans of America (UKA)—the Klan group responsible for the worst violence against the civil rights movement—abducted him, beat him badly, cut his throat, and hung his body from a tree. The two Klansmen, who had apparently intended to terrorize South Alabama blacks with their attack, were arrested and convicted of murder. But SPLC investigators, looking into the case, also found evidence to support a civil suit alleging conspiracy.

In the end, the SPLC won a $7 million judgment for Donald's mother, Beulah Mae Donald, who wound up with title to the UKA's headquarters building. The UKA had no other substantial assets and never came close to satisfying the entire judgment. But it was wiped out by the case, and its officials promised never to re-form the group. Evidence from the case also resulted in two additional Klansmen being convicted of criminal charges. As in all the cases it handles, the SPLC accepted no attorney's fees and turned over all proceeds to the plaintiff. It was the first real test of the "vicarious liability" theory that the SPLC was pioneering.

The basic goal of these lawsuits is to hold the leaders of hate groups that preach violence responsible for the criminal violence of their followers. We aim to bankrupt the organizations and individuals civilly responsible for the crimes (our suits are typically filed only after any criminal case is completed). And we also seek to use the suits to separate the foot soldiers from the leaders, whose charisma and relative intelligence make them harder to replace than their followers. Some SPLC suits have resulted in the loss of key extremist assets, such as paramilitary training grounds and compounds used to host major gatherings of the radical right. Most of them have helped stop leaders from preaching violence to susceptible youths.

As a general matter, the SPLC's cases depend on careful investigation. That is partly because discovery, the process of obtaining information from an opposing party in a lawsuit, has extremely limited value when dealing with hate groups—after all, the groups rarely keep documentary records related to crimes their members commit or their group policies. Interrogatories are also only rarely useful because defendants will hardly ever admit to past attacks. To compensate for these weaknesses, Klanwatch (known as the Intelligence Project after 1998, when the name was changed to reflect the project's broadened scope) must do extensive detective work. Typically, this has taken the form of working hard to find former insiders willing to testify and also carefully collecting data over decades that may one day be useful in a lawsuit. To this end, the Intelligence Project has developed a massive database on extremists with information dating to the early 1980s.

Each case presented a different set of facts and, therefore, required somewhat different courtroom strategies. Here are descriptions of a few key lawsuits.

White Aryan Resistance

In 1988, neo-Nazi White Aryan Resistance (WAR) leader Tom Metzger and his son John sent their best recruiter from their Southern California base to Portland, Oregon, to help organize a racist skinhead gang there as part of an effort to kick-start a white supremacist revolution. After being trained in WAR's methods, the gang, East Side White Pride, beat an Ethiopian graduate student to death with baseball bats. Metzger, who had not known of the attack until afterward, responded by praising the skinheads for doing their "civic duty."

Utilizing Oregon's wrongful death statute and traditional principles of vicarious liability—attributing fault to persons who do not directly cause harm to a victim—SPLC lawyers focused in on the link between the WAR recruiter, Dave Mazzella, and the Metzgers. They established their preexisting relationship (WAR had recruited Mazzella at age 16 and trained him to lead others in perpetrating racial violence) and showed that Mazzella had come to Portland with an introductory letter from the Metzgers. And they argued the Metzgers' leadership of WAR and WAR Youth, headed by John Metzger, placed them in authority over the Portland skins—similar to the close relationship of an organized crime boss to his followers.

In October 1990, after an extended trial, a jury agreed and awarded $12.5 million to the family of the victim, Mulugeta Seraw. In 1994, the Supreme Court declined to hear Metzger's appeal and SPLC attorneys began distributing funds that were collected from the sale of WAR assets to Seraw's surviving young son.

Knights of the Ku Klux Klan

In 1981, Texas Klansmen, enraged by the success of immigrant Vietnamese shrimpers in Galveston Bay, tried to destroy their livelihoods by burning their boats and threatening their lives. Armed Klansmen patrolled the bay and practiced guerrilla tactics, including burning boats, at secret paramilitary training camps. The SPLC convinced the fishermen to sue the Klan in a case that ended its campaign of terror and shut down its paramilitary camps.

White Patriot Party

In the mid-1980s, the White Patriot Party, with more than 1,000 members, was the South's most militant Klan group, holding public rallies almost every week. An SPLC investigation found that the group was using U.S. military personnel to train recruits and had acquired stolen military weapons. After SPLC filed a lawsuit against the group, a jury found its leaders had illegally operated a paramilitary army and forced the party to disband. Several members were later convicted of attempting to blow up SPLC headquarters in retaliation.

Southern White Knights

On the 1987 anniversary of Martin Luther King, Jr.'s, birth, an interracial antiracist group marching in protest in Forsyth County, Georgia, was attacked by Klansmen throwing rocks and bottles. SPLC attorneys sued the Southern White Knights of the Ku Klux Klan to vindicate the marchers' rights and, in late 1988, a jury awarded the plaintiffs a judgment of nearly $1 million. To make sure the Klan felt the financial pain of the verdict, the attorneys were obliged to trace its assets over a five-year period. Ultimately, the group was forced to disband to meet the judgment's requirements, giving its office equipment to the NAACP.

Church of the Creator

On May 17, 1991, a member of the neo-Nazi Church of the Creator (COTC) murdered Harold Mansfield, a black sailor who had served in the Gulf War, in a Florida parking lot. After SPLC investigators documented the group's violent history, a suit was brought that resulted in a $1 million default judgment. Prior to completion of the case, COTC transferred title to its headquarters property in North Carolina to William Pierce, who headed the notorious neo-Nazi National Alliance group. In 1995, the SPLC sued Pierce on behalf of the family of Mansfield, winning an $85,000 judgment because of the fraudulent transfer.

Christian Knights

In the largest judgment ever awarded against a hate group, a South Carolina jury in 1998 ordered the Christian Knights of the Ku Klux Klan, its state leader, and four other Klansmen to pay $37.8 million for their roles in a conspiracy to burn a black church. Although a judge later reduced that award to $21.5 million—still vastly more than the group had in assets—the verdict forced the group to give up its headquarters. Within years, it had disappeared.

Aryan Nations

In 1998, security guards at the compound of the Aryan Nations, an infamous neo-Nazi group in Idaho, chased and shot at a woman and her son, whose car's backfiring they had apparently mistaken for an attack. The SPLC sued on behalf of Victoria and Jason Keenan and, in 2000, a jury ruled that Aryan Nations boss Richard Butler and his organization were grossly negligent in choosing and supervising their armed guards. The Keenans were awarded a $6.3 million judgment that ultimately forced Butler to sell the 20-acre compound that had long served as a venue for annual Aryan World Congresses. The Keenans later sold the compound to a philanthropist who allowed firefighters to burn down its buildings, including an infamous guard tower with a swastika flag, in a training exercise.

Ranch Rescue

In 2003, the SPLC sued a vigilante group called Ranch Rescue that had made it its business to patrol private property on the U.S.-Mexico border to deter undocumented immigrants. Representing six plaintiffs from Mexico and El Salvador, the suit accused Texas rancher Joseph Sutton and heavily armed members of Ranch Rescue clothed in camouflage uniforms of accosting the migrants and abusing them physically and emotionally. In the end, Sutton's insurance carrier settled the claim against him while a Ranch Rescue member, Casey Nethercott, was forced to give up a paramilitary training compound he had set up on a piece of land on the Arizona-Mexico border to settle the $350,000 assessed against him.

INFORMATION, EDUCATION, AND EXPOSURE

Over the decades, the SPLC's Intelligence Project has developed a series of other methods of attacking the extreme right, beyond SPLC's lawsuits. One of the most important has been the annual publication of a list of all hate groups operating in America, along with a map depicting their types, numbers, and locations.

The hate group list today reflects the broad scope of the SPLC's coverage of the radical right—it includes subsections devoted to Ku Klux Klan, neo-Nazi, white nationalist, racist skinhead, Christian Identity (this refers to a bizarre, racist, and particularly anti-Semitic theology popular among extremists), neo-Confederate, black separatist, antigay, anti-immigrant, Holocaust denial, racist music, "radical traditionalist Catholic" (an anti-Semitic variant of Catholic theology rejected by the Vatican), and other groups. Also published annually is a categorized list of U.S.-based hate Web sites. These lists are the most comprehensive available and have proven to be extremely useful to law enforcement officers, journalists, scholars, human rights activists, and others.

The Intelligence Project also trains law enforcement officers, typically detectives and federal agents rather than street-level patrol officers, in hate and bias crimes, and also in domestic terrorism. Its instructors, who are certified by the federal government, deliver this training, normally tailored to a specific state or region of the country, to about 8,000 law enforcement officers a year.

In addition, Intelligence Project staffers offer direct help to law enforcement—typically in the form of background political or criminal information about suspects and their groups—in developing and prosecuting criminal cases against extremists.

Overall, the department's most important strategy has been the provision to the public of information about hate groups and their members. It has sought to wreck these groups using such information in exposés (more below); to work with reporters covering them by providing background and investigative information; to create a firewall between extremist ideology and the mainstream by exposing the radical right's attempts at infiltration;

to track specific dangerous individuals and their groups; and to monitor trends and other developments on the racist right.

This information is provided to the public in the form of several vehicles. Hatewatch, a blog started in 2007, carries breaking news and other short items. Two electronic newsletters, one on hate groups in general and another on anti-immigrant groups, provide weekly synopses of mainstream press reports. But most important is the department's magazine, the *Intelligence Report*, which is our primary means of communicating such information and has become the nation's preeminent periodical on the radical right. The quarterly is sent to more than 300,000 people, including 80,000 law enforcement officers, plus thousands of journalists and scholars. The magazine has won several national design and journalism awards, including a 2007 prize from the prestigious *Utne Reader* Independent Press Awards for best publication in America in the competition's "In-Depth/Investigative Reporting" category.

The *Intelligence Report*

In an era when newspapers and broadcast media are downsizing news staffs and shrinking or eliminating their investigative teams, the *Intelligence Report* has an unexpectedly important role to fulfill. It is highly specialized in the radical right—a focus virtually unheard of on the staffs of major news organizations—and, because it does not depend for income on advertisers but rather on donors, it can undertake the lengthy and expensive investigations that most news operations avoid.

The *Report* is also a form of what is often called the "new journalism." It employs the techniques and forms and values of serious journalism, but uses them to support a specific agenda—the attempt to roll back racist hate groups and their ideologies and, more specifically, to prevent their poisoning of mainstream political discourse in America. Unlike the traditional "Fourth Estate," which typically sees its primary role as defending the citizenry from abuses by the government, the *Report* attempts to protect civil society from insidious and antidemocratic activists.

Essential to the mission of the *Report*, and the Intelligence Project that produces it, is that it build and maintain credibility among serious journalists as a trustworthy and accurate publication. That is because the *Intelligence Report* does not seek to compete with other publications—for this reason, it has never been sold on newsstands—and instead hopes other journalists will use it as a source. The idea is that mainstream journalists will use our investigative work and build on it. One result of this is that department staff are quoted often in the mainstream press, allowing our staffers to impart important information to an audience much wider than that of the *Report*.

How precisely does the Intelligence Project use information to attack hate groups? The best way to communicate this is through examples. Often, a relatively simple journalistic finding—coupled with effectively making that information public—can have the result of destroying or crippling a group with little further work. In other cases, such findings must be accompanied by community outreach, media campaigns, and other efforts.

The work can be remarkably straightforward. In 1999, for example, Intelligence Project staffers began to look into a group called Knights of Freedom, a neo-Nazi organization organized over the Internet by a student operating out of his dormitory room at Wofford College, in Spartanburg, South Carolina. The student, a sophomore named Davis Wolfgang Hawke, was selling Hitlerian paraphernalia and boasting to the world that he intended to lead a revolutionary takeover of the country.

Within days of beginning its investigation, a remarkable discovery was made: The Germanic-sounding Hawke had changed his name just after leaving home for college—from Andy Greenbaum, son of Hyman Greenbaum. Hawke's father, much to his son's dismay, was Jewish. This fact was communicated first to a newspaper in Spartanburg and then to the *Boston Globe*, whose readership included the suburb where Hawke grew up. The resulting front-page splash about a young neo-Nazi leader with a Jewish father provoked a firestorm on the radical right, where a boycott of Hawke's group—motto: "No Kosher Nazis!"—drove the Knights of Freedom into oblivion and forever discredited its mortally embarrassed führer (SPLC, 1999a).

Years later, Hawke would reappear briefly in the news. But he was no longer planning to take over America and "make the Final Solution a reality." Hawke had become one of the largest salesmen of penis-enlargement pills on the Internet and was being sought to satisfy a huge civil judgment against him for spamming (Moser, 2003).

Another example of rapid work in battling hate groups came in 2003, when staffers were researching public records on one Vince Breeding, whose real name is Bruce Alan Breeding, for a profile of leading racist activists. Breeding was a former member of the neo-Nazi National Alliance who was then very close to former Klan leader David Duke. Breeding had helped Duke create his latest group and, when his mentor went to federal prison on tax and mail fraud charges in 2003, he moved into Duke's house and took the reins of that organization until Duke's release.

The records revealed something unexpected. In late 2002, it turned out, Breeding had set up a New Orleans–based porn Web site, xsitenola.com, and a porn magazine, *Xsite*. Remarkably for a white supremacist and avowed savior of the white race, the smut peddled by Breeding included mother-daughter sex, "slave girls for voyeurs," and—in the most damaging revelation by far—racy ads for nonwhite women (specifically, "Ebony Escorts, Beautiful Women of Color, 24–7"). The story that the *Intelligence Report* ran included the views of movement heavyweights like National Alliance leader William Pierce, who blamed porn on "the Jews" (Beirich & Moser, 2003).

The story was explosive. Shortly after its publication, Breeding said he was leaving the white supremacist movement, later buying a strip club in Ascension, Louisiana. "I like naked women," he eventually told the *Report*. "That's what I do now" (SPLC 2004a).

In 2003, the same year that Breeding quit the movement, a neo-Nazi activist named Anthony Pierpont was making a name for himself in white supremacist circles. He had built up a major hate music operation, Panzerfaust Records (the name is taken from that of a Nazi antitank weapon that translates as "armored fist") that was a widely respected and major player on the radical right. He was close to the extremely violent racist skinhead group, the Hammerskins, and regularly wrote about the "hatecore" music scene in *Hammerskin Press*. Then, in early 2004, he made national news with his provocatively titled "Operation Schoolyard"—an effort, modeled on one already undertaken by neo-Nazis in Germany, to distribute a free hate music sampler to 100,000 American middle and high school students (Beirich & Potok, 2003).

Pierpont's efforts were worrying. He was getting enormous amounts of press and drawing the attention of many young Americans—youngsters for whom the racist music scene is the primary gateway into the world of white supremacy.

But they wouldn't last long. First, Pierpont's partner at Panzerfaust, a well-known activist named Bryant Cecchini (alias Byron Calvert), found Pierpont's birth certificate, showing that his mother was Mexican. (Pierpont had long been rumored to be less than fully "Aryan," but this had never been proven.) The *Report* found Cecchini's posting and worked to widely publicize it, knowing it would likely have a devastating effect on Pierpont's standing. And the *Report* raised the ante, publishing photos obtained from sources that showed Pierpont in a California prison yard, posing with friends while serving time for drug offenses in the 1990s. To the shock of many of Pierpont's racist colleagues, his prison buddies had clearly been Latinos (SPLC, 2005b).

That, plus the revelation that Pierpont had gone on an Asian sex tour (an unacceptable transgression for those opposed to race mixers), ruined Panzerfaust Records. Cecchini quit as his partner, the label found its customers had disappeared, and reporters who had been talking to Pierpont days earlier could no longer find him at all. Pierpont resurfaced in 2006, but only to put up a Web site saying he was having a ball and attacking "white trash hypocrites and alcoholic Internet activists" (Zaitchik, 2006).

The Pierpont case reflected a change in the way the *Intelligence Report* can sometimes affect the world. In the past, the magazine went only to law enforcement officers and others interested in battling white supremacy. But since the Southern Poverty Law Center began posting the magazine on the Internet in its entirety, the publication has drawn an unexpected audience—members of the radical right who have no other publication that so closely tracks their movements. That has given *Intelligence Report* the power to sometimes directly affect white supremacist activists like Pierpont. It has also provided a tool that is useful in SPLC's longer, more difficult campaigns.

The Intelligence Project's magazine, and to a lesser extent its blog, commonly carry short, hard hits, such as those described above. But there are many occasions when it can take years, and carefully engineered approaches, to weaken or destroy a hate group. These cases typically involve extended investigative efforts, close work with print and broadcast media reporters, and other labors. What follows are detailed accounts of four major antihate campaigns carried out by the Intelligence Project.

DRAWING A BRIGHT LINE

In the late 1990s, a group called the Council of Conservative Citizens (CCC), based in St. Louis but with the bulk of its strength in the Deep South, claimed 34 Mississippi state legislators as members and a number of leading national politicians as endorsers. Backed by plaudits from the likes of then-Senate Majority Leader Trent Lott (R-Miss.), the CCC's leaders had managed to convince most people that theirs was a conservative, but still respectable and mainstream, organization.

It wasn't true. Although the CCC did have remarkable pull among some politicians, judges, and other leaders, it in fact embraced white supremacist ideology and, it turned out, was directly descended from the old White Citizens Councils, formed to resist the desegregation of the South. (Thurgood Marshall, who would later become the first black U.S. Supreme Court justice, famously referred to the old councils as "the uptown Klan.") The *Intelligence Report*, knowing some of these facts but not others, undertook a major investigation of the CCC—a group that claimed 15,000 members, vastly more than other U.S. hate groups. In the end, the *Report* was able to clearly show the racist underpinnings of the group (SPLC, 1999b). Based on the magazine's late 1998 findings, the SPLC added the CCC to its hate group list.

Now the SPLC's job, common in such cases, was to make its description of the CCC stick. The CCC's leader, Gordon Lee Baum, didn't help himself much when he went on National Public Radio to debate the editor of the *Intelligence Report* and spent much of a half-hour show fretting about white women and black men. But the story was released amid the Monica Lewinsky scandal and in the run-up to Christmas—an extremely difficult news environment, to say the least.

As a result, despite a story in *The Washington Post*, the *Report*'s investigation of the CCC seemed to disappear from the public eye. Largely ignored by news reporters, SPLC staffers now turned to opinion columnists. Remarkably, after a few major columnists wrote about the CCC, newspapers began to report on the SPLC's findings. After a column on the *New York Times* op-ed page appeared on the matter, a major story ran in that newspaper's columns. At that point, news reporters all over the United States noticed the controversy and wrote stories of their own. As reporters did their own research into the group, they found what the *Report* had. As a result, most of the media came to routinely describe the CCC as a racist group.

The SPLC's public relations battle, in other words, had been won.

The confrontation with the CCC was very much a part of the *Report*'s "bright line" strategy—our attempt to draw a clear line separating groups and individuals engaging in the legitimate democratic process from those who seek merely to inject racist ideas into the debate. The theory is that publicly identifying noxious groups will dramatically weaken their ability to distort the American political process.

By mid-2000, the *Intelligence Report* article had seriously weakened the CCC, driving away such national politicians as Lott. Key officials including the head of the Republican National Committee denounced the group. But other politicians, especially in Mississippi, continued to attend the group's meetings and in other ways legitimize it. As a result, in 2004, the magazine ran a second major investigative story on the CCC. This one entailed compiling and publicizing a list of all state and national politicians who had courted votes at CCC meetings between 2000 and 2004 (Beirich & Moser, 2004).

It turned out that at least 38 state and federal officials, most of them in Mississippi and most Republicans, continued to pander to the CCC. The *Report* sought an explanation from every one of them, and published their responses. Several, such as Mississippi State Representative Jim Ellington, claimed that they had spoken at CCC meetings in response to an invitation and had no idea what the group was about.

The upshot was that newspapers across the South reported the SPLC findings, sharply embarrassing a number of politicians. Since that occurred in 2004, the CCC has had no major politicians participate in its activities. The SPLC campaign—meant to inoculate the public against the CCC and its ideology—had worked.

STOPPING THE FUNDING OF INTERNATIONAL HATE

The investigations of the CCC also led to a related probe that eventually became one of the Intelligence Project's most successful attacks on a hate group, resulting in the group's complete dissolution and the deportation of its leader.

In 1998, while pulling together the CCC report, a staff writer attended and wrote about a CCC gathering just outside Washington, D.C. Describing the proceedings, she reported that the chapter leader was a man who identified himself as Mark Cerr but was actually Mark Cotterill, a Briton who'd worked with key U.K. racist groups (SPLC, 1999c). Although he had no work permit, Cotterill had come to the United States in 1995 and begun working with such extremists as long-time anti-Semite Willis Carto. Over the years, Cotterill managed to make contact with most American radical right leaders, including William Pierce, the National Alliance chieftain who was then probably the country's most important white supremacist. He developed a friendship with former Klan leader David Duke. And he managed to become the CCC's national youth organizer—until his past was exposed by the SPLC. At that point, Cotterill resigned, presumably to save the CCC embarrassment.

But his activism continued. Immediately after resigning from the CCC, which was trying hard to maintain its claim to be a mainstream group, Cotterill founded a group called the American Friends of the British National Party (AFBNP) to support the party of which he himself was an official, the British National Party (BNP). The BNP has for most of its history restricted its membership to whites; its leader, Nick Griffin, was a former member of Britain's neo-Nazi National Front, a founder of the neofascist International Third Position (SPLC, 2000), and a Holocaust denier; in 1999, a former BNP member, David Copeland, killed three people in London and injured more than 100 others in a bombing campaign against blacks, Muslims, and gays; and at one point, the party distributed lists of people supposedly involved in a Jewish conspiracy. Cotterill was a long-time ally and friend of Griffin's.

Cotterill put up a Web site for the AFBNP in 1999 that caught SPLC staffers' attention because of its elaborate descriptions and photographs of well-attended meetings featuring prominent American racists like Duke. In the summer 1999 issue of *Heritage and Destiny*, AFBNP's publication, Cotterill explained that the publicly owned British Broadcasting Corporation had recently raised the minimum number of districts in which parties must run candidates in order to receive free air time. "The new conditions mean that the BNP must redouble its efforts, particularly with regard to fundraising," wrote Cotterill. "To help the BNP reach its target, an American support group for the party has been set up. 'American Friends of the BNP' was formed in January by a number of expatriate Britons." (Cotterill later said that one of the inspirations for the AFBNP was Noraid, which has reportedly raised millions of dollars from Irish Americans for the Republican cause in Northern Ireland.)

The Intelligence Project was concerned. Not only did money raised from Americans seem to be significantly raising a racist British party's electoral chances, but Cotterill's AFBNP fundraising meetings were clearly serving to bring together the often fractious groups that make up the American radical right. The danger of a viable alliance emerging out of the AFBNP events seemed increasingly real.

Staffers began collecting all AFBNP printed materials and, what would turn out to be most important, videotapes of the group's fundraising events, most held in the Washington, D.C., area. One staffer began to attend the AFBNP meetings, which were open to the public and mostly held in local hotel conference halls. It was soon learned that Cotterill, who operated out of a small apartment in Falls Church, Virginia, was regularly bringing in speakers from foreign racist groups including the BNP, Germany's neo-Nazi National Democratic Party, and the Danish Racial Nationalist Movement, among others. He also met privately in the United States with leaders of France's xenophobic Front National. All these contacts between top European and U.S. extremist leaders helped radical-right groups see eye to eye on issues as narrow as NATO's alleged injustices in quelling ethnic conflict in the former Yugoslavia and as broad as the building up of a new pan-Aryan internationalism.

A special Cotterill talent was the employment of what the British call "entryism" into the mainstream—an uncommon strategy for American extremists, who have more often than not rejected working within the system. During the 2000 presidential race, the AFBNP nearly succeeded in its explicit strategy to infiltrate and hijack several state chapters of the Reform Party, which was already heading to the far right under presidential candidate Pat Buchanan. Cotterill even worked in the Reform Party's campaign headquarters in Virginia. Though Cotterill never did win acceptance in the mainstream and the Reform Party collapsed after the presence of radical racists in its ranks was exposed in 2000, he did significantly help to bridge differences between key groups and individuals on both sides of the ocean.

The SPLC investigation ultimately found that since the AFBNP's founding it had held at least 19 meetings, attended by an average of 80 to 100 people who paid $10 to attend and then donated an average of $10 more. In addition, investigators personally saw or were told of very large checks— including one for $16,000 and another for $10,000— destined for the BNP. Overall, the SPLC concluded, Cotterill had managed to raise at least $85,000 for the BNP, and very likely much more.

From the perspective of the SPLC, this activity cried out for a counterattack. A promising avenue soon appeared when staffers realized that AFBNP's raising of money was an apparent felony violation of federal law. The U.S. Foreign Agents Registration Act (FARA) of 1938—passed by Congress just before World War II to keep tabs on the large number of German Nazi Party propagandists operating in the United States—specifies that any "agent" or "representative" of a "foreign political party" who "solicits . . . money or other things of value" for that foreign party must register with the Department of Justice and provide detailed records of income and expenses (U.S. Department of Justice, 2008). Penalties for noncompliance are five years in prison and a fine of $10,000. It seemed obvious that Cotterill, who was listed by the

BNP as a "Key Party Official," had committed multiple felonies by violating the FARA act.

Shortly before the *Intelligence Report* carrying a major piece on Cotterill and the AFBNP was released in late 2001 (SPLC, 2001b), though pure serendipity, a CNN European correspondent who had been looking into BNP fundraising called SPLC. As a result, CNN and SPLC collaborated on a lengthy CNN report that detailed and expanded the *Report*'s findings. The story, which later ran on CNN and CNN International, included a lengthy section suggesting that the AFBNP had violated the FARA Act. It also reported that the BNP might have violated British electoral laws that sharply limited how much money could be raised overseas. It relied heavily on videotapes of the AFBNP meetings that had earlier been collected by the Intelligence Project.

The story, lifted up by this serious and detailed CNN coverage, hit like a bomb. Cotterill sent out an e-mail to his supporters saying he was shutting down AFBNP. Remarkably, the Department of Justice's FARA office declined to pursue the case, ruling instead that Cotterill could retroactively legalize AFBNP's activities by providing back records despite the clear evidence of his criminal behavior (SPLC, 2002b).

But that didn't save Mark Cotterill. In 2002, Immigration and Naturalization Service (INS) officials began investigating Cotterill based mainly on the August 2001 exposé in the *Report*. In March 2002, Cotterill flew to England to attend his mother's funeral. Upon his return, he was met at Washington's Dulles Airport by INS agents who told him he was inadmissible because he had been unlawfully present in the United States for more than a year. When Cotterill told officials that he would appeal, he was allowed to reenter the country and retain a lawyer. At a September 2002 deportation hearing, INS officials presented evidence, including that compiled by the *Report*, proving that Cotterill was in the United States for political reasons and had lied about that when he initially entered the country. Seven years after moving to the United States in November 2002, Cotterill was flown back to England (SPLC, 2002f). He was prohibited from returning to the United States for another 10 years.

TAKING DOWN THE NATIONAL ALLIANCE

For some three decades, the most important hate group in America—and a particular nemesis of SPLC—was the National Alliance, a major neo-Nazi group that was headquartered at a rural hilltop compound near Mill Point, West Virginia. The Alliance was for much of its life the best-organized hate group in America. Founded and long led by William Pierce, a one-time university physics professor, the group peaked in the 1990s, when it perfected a remarkably successful business model and Pierce's ideological influence stretched across much of the Western hemisphere. Over the years, it produced huge amounts of very effective propaganda such as Pierce's novel *The Turner Diaries* (MacDonald, 1978), which inspired numerous acts of terror, including the 1995 bombing of the Oklahoma City federal building. The Alliance, which mentions in its platform statement the "temporary unpleasantness" that will follow its accession to power, is explicitly genocidal in intent: Pierce once described how he hoped to lock Jews, "race traitors" and other enemies of the "Aryan" race into cattle cars and send them to the bottom of abandoned coal mines (Lee, 2002). It has produced a large number of extremist assassins, bank robbers, and bombers. And it was for a time the leading player in the white power music business, running a label called Resistance Records that sold its racist products across America and Europe (SPLC, 2002c).

A native of Atlanta, William Luther Pierce became an assistant professor of physics at Oregon State University in 1962, joining the rabidly anticommunist and segregationist John Birch Society during his three years there. Ultimately, disgusted by race-mixing (interracial couples) and the liberal atmosphere, Pierce left academia and began to make contact with such radical groups as the American Nazi Party. During a run by Alabama segregationist George Wallace for the presidency, Pierce became involved in a Wallace youth support group called the National Youth Alliance. In 1974, the group began to fall apart and Pierce gained control of its remnants, renaming the group the National Alliance. A year later, Pierce serialized *The Turner Diaries* in *Attack!*, a publication he had started while he was with the National Socialist White People's Party. The manuscript, which would be published as a book in 1978 under the pseudonym of Andrew MacDonald, described a future race war in which Jews and others are slaughtered by the thousands, with its hero at one point promising to go "to the uttermost ends of the earth to hunt down the last of Satan's spawn"—Jews, that is (MacDonald, 1978). Along with others of Pierce's writings, *The Turner Diaries* became one of the most important pieces of extremist literature ever written in America. Finally, in 1985, Pierce moved the group from the Washington, D.C., area to a 346-acre piece of land in Pocahontas County, West Virginia, where its remnants are to this day.

The alliance was a highly important group on the radical right. That is largely because Pierce was an unusual intellectual in that world, and served to interpret key events for his many less educated admirers. But it also produced a large number of violent criminals. In 1983, for instance, its Pacific Northwest coordinator, Robert Mathews, broke away to form a terrorist group that was called "The Order" and was clearly patterned on "The Organization" described in *The Turner Diaries*. The Order, made up of more than 20 men, carried out a series of murders and armored car heists before Mathews was killed in a 1984 shootout with the FBI (SPLC, 2002d). Eleven years later, when the Oklahoma City bomber was arrested after that mass murder, he was carrying pages photocopied from the novel—apparently to explain his motivation for the bombing in the event he was killed. Alliance members have also participated in bank robberies, shootouts with police officers, bombings, and other attacks.

For all these reasons, the Intelligence Project had long monitored the Alliance extremely closely. In 1995, as mentioned earlier, SPLC lawyers successfully sued Pierce for his fraudulent acceptance of land that was once owned by the Church of the Creator. Many *Report* stories detailed criminal and other matters over the years (SPLC, 2002d). But none of this seemed to slow down the National Alliance effectively.

Instead, it grew rapidly. In 1992, the Alliance had just three chapters. By 1997, after years of careful recruiting, the group had grown to 22 units. Two years later, it boasted of chapters in 11 South American and European countries, and *The Turner Diaries* was being translated and made available free in half a dozen languages. By 2002, the Alliance had 1,400 members in 51 U.S. units. It was also profitable, thanks to the business model Pierce devised. The Alliance had for years derived its income mainly from members, who paid at least $10 a month in dues, and sales from its National Vanguard Books division. Then, in 1999, Pierce added a key component—Resistance Records, an ailing racist music label started by other racists. Pierce paid some $250,000 for the company, which he quickly built up with the addition of a warehouse on the West Virginia compound and a slick advertising campaign. By 2002, the National Alliance was grossing a total of almost $1 million from all these sources, allowing Pierce to pay salaries to 17 full-time national staff members—an accomplishment unmatched by any other hate group since the 1920s Klan (SPLC, 2006).

But it was always Pierce himself who was the Alliance's chief asset. So when Pierce died unexpectedly at age 68 of kidney failure and cancer, it seemed to open up a whole range of possibilities. These were undoubtedly helped by Pierce's choice of a successor—Cleveland unit leader Erich Gliebe, a hard-edged and humorless man who had helped Pierce make Resistance Records profitable. Gliebe, who had boxed professionally as the "Aryan Barbarian," faced an uphill battle keeping the group together that had been built up mainly around the personality of Pierce.

Within two months of Pierce's death, the Intelligence Project obtained a videotape of his last, secret speech, given in April 2002 at one of his semiannual leadership conferences at the West Virginia compound. As SPLC staffers saw immediately, it contained a bombshell—a Pierce harangue against members of other groups on the radical right, men and women who Pierce sneeringly described as "freak and weaklings" and "human defectives." A short time later, details of the speech were published in an *Intelligence Report* cover story (SPLC, 2002e). The result, which came as hate group members began to read the story on the SPLC Web site, was a virtual firestorm. Skinheads and others who had been Resistance's primary customers were furious, starting a boycott of the label and denouncing the man who had pilloried them as fools. A major split, largely provoked by these events, began to seriously weaken the Alliance. Gliebe counterattacked by claiming that the account of the Pierce speech was an "SPLC disinformation effort," but too many people—about 80 in total—had heard Pierce's speech and knew the article was accurate. Several other articles reinforced the original SPLC claim. In addition, the *Report* published follow-up stories that severely embarrassed the Alliance, including the news that a Resistance calendar meant to highlight Aryan female beauty in fact featured a bevy of strippers from an all-nude men's club patronized by Gliebe, and revelations of wasted money and political infighting within the group (Potok, 2003a). By late 2003, the Alliance's membership had fallen from a high of 1,200 to about 800. In the next three years it would plunge to around 100, as Gliebe's leadership continued to harm the group. He did not help matters by marrying a former stripper and two-time *Playboy* model.

Between these kinds of revelations and swelling resentment against Gliebe and second-in-command Shaun Walker because of their dictatorial management style, the Alliance lost most of its key activists and unit leaders. Resistance Records and National Vanguard Books became unprofitable. In a desperate bid to keep the group alive, Walker replaced Gliebe as chairman in early 2005, with Gliebe relegated to running Resistance. But by spring of that year, the group was down to under 200 members and had lost almost all its prestige. When Walker was convicted in 2007 of federal conspiracy charges for leading racially motivated beatings at two bars in Salt Lake City, Gliebe was returned to the chairmanship (Holthouse & Potok, 2008). But by that time, the National Alliance had lapsed into insignificance, a faint shadow of its former self.

COUNTERING NATIVIST EXTREMISM

At the end of the twentieth century and the beginning of the twenty-first, it became increasingly clear that the United States, as it had repeatedly in the past, was seeing the development of a xenophobic and often racist anti-immigration movement. The Intelligence Project ended up concentrating for nearly a decade on this problem, which was accompanied by an apparent rise in nativist anti-Latino violence (Mock, 2007).

The origins of the Intelligence Project's work in this area date back to late 1998 when a small gathering in Cullman, Alabama, drew the attention of staffers. At a protest that featured the burning of Mexican and United Nations flags and the arrest of a former state Klan official, a leader of the allegedly more mainstream anti-immigration movement was spotted. A brief item in the *Intelligence Report* noted the presence of Glenn Spencer, a leading activist behind California's controversial anti-immigrant Proposition 187. The *Report* article was headlined "Right Meets Far Right" (SPLC, 1998).

That small item became the starting point for a series of investigative forays into the world of American anti-immigration groups. Over the following years, the *Report* would document and publish extensive evidence on the cross-pollination of white supremacist hate groups and the larger immigration-restriction movement (SPLC, 2001a). By 2005, staffers had exposed a number of racist elements in the movement; written an exposé on the little-known fact that one man—anti-immigrant impresario John Tanton—was behind nearly every anti-immigration group of note (SPLC, 2002a); and become a key player in exposing and then campaigning against the attempted takeover of a key environmentalist group, the Sierra Club, by anti-immigration zealots (SPLC, 2004c). From 2005 to 2007, staffers worked to expose racist elements in vigilante Minuteman and related groups that were popping up around the country with staggering regularity (SPLC, 2005a).

After the 1998 flag burning, a second event, in early 2000, seemed to confirm that the hard edge of the nativist movement was growing and was increasingly coming to embrace open racism. That May, a major gathering of anti-immigration activists was held in Sierra Vista, Arizona, to celebrate two ranchers—Roger and Donald Barnett—who were boasting of rounding up thousands of border-crossing migrants at gunpoint on their ranch and handing them over to the authorities. The brothers drew national publicity as they complained about undocumented workers crossing their land, and even took reporters from around the world on weekend missions to hunt their human prey. Roger Barnett claimed in 2007 to have captured more than 10,000 people who crossed his land, and upbeat publicity about his personal crusade helped inspire other self-appointed groups of border watchers like the Minutemen. (The SPLC would help fund a lawsuit in 2006 against the Barnett brothers for terrorizing a Latino family of U.S. citizens at gunpoint. The civil trial ended in a judgment of nearly $100,000 against Roger Barnett [Buchanan, 2006].)

More than 250 people showed up in a Sierra Vista motel conference room to listen to Barbara Coe, head of the hate group California Coalition for Immigration Reform and another key Proposition 187 supporter, rail against "alien savages." Coe told her audience that every would-be immigrant caught at the border would be "one less illegal alien bringing in communicable diseases, one less illegal alien smuggling deadly drugs, one less illegal alien gang member to rob, rape and murder innocent U.S. citizens" (SPLC, 2001a). Adding his voice to Coe's, Spencer showed his vitriolic videotape, "Immigration: Threatening the Bonds of Our Union," which outlined an imaginary Latino conspiracy to reconquer the Southwest for Mexico (SPLC, 2001a). Spencer and Coe weren't the only hard-liners there. Others included members of former Klan leader David Duke's group, and unrobed members of the Knights of the Ku Klux Klan. Klan fliers were placed on cars outside the event, just in case any of the participants hadn't yet realized the high interest being evinced in the gathering by openly racist groups (SPLC, 2001a).

The events in Cullman and Sierra Vista seemed to be part of a pattern, and the Intelligence Project began an investigation of possible links between hate groups and the anti-immigration movement. A photo in SPLC files showed Coe had participated in the Cullman rally along with Spencer and unrobed former Klan leader William Burchfield. A search of the newsletter of the white supremacist CCC revealed that it had actually sponsored the event. And the newsletter disclosed something even more revealing: Rick Oltman, west coast representative of the supposedly "mainstream" Federation for American Immigration Reform (FAIR), had also attended.

It was the beginning of a major project. Over the following years, every *Intelligence Report* staffer would be involved in a series of reports exposing the increasingly violent and racist aspects of the anti-immigration movement. Ultimately, our research revealed a tight-knit and interlocking network tying the CCC to several prominent anti-immigration activists going all the way back to the early 1990s (SPLC, 2001a). Emblematic of this relationship was a panel held at a 1999 CCC conference that featured Spencer and the leaders of three other well-known anti-immigration organizations: Wayne Lutton of The Social Contract Press; John Vinson of the American Immigration Control Foundation; and Virginia Abernethy of Population-Environment Balance. Not long after, Abernethy and Lutton joined the editorial advisory board of *Citizens Informer*, the racist tabloid published by the CCC that from that point on began to concentrate heavily on the evils of nonwhite immigration. This research ultimately led to the *Report's* first major story, published in 1999, on what was then still a nascent movement. It also led SPLC to list in 2001 as hate groups three nativist groups that employed particularly racist rhetoric: Spencer's American Patrol, Vinson's American Immigration Control Foundation, and The Social Contract Press, run by Lutton and Tanton. The next year, Coe's California Coalition for Immigration Reform would also be added to the hate group list.

In early 2002, the *Report* expanded its research into the anti-immigration movement. For four months, a staffer teased out the financing and connections between the leading anti-immigration organizations in the United States. What tax records revealed was something quite remarkable—the American anti-immigration movement was largely the creation of one man, a Michigan ophthalmologist named John Tanton, whom the 2002 *Report* cover story would dub "The Puppeteer" (SPLC, 2002a). The fact that one man was so central to this movement was interesting, but Tanton's history of bigotry toward Latinos and his close associations with white supremacist activists

were critical to the research—and showed that most modern immigration
restriction groups had been founded or fostered by a man with racist views.

Interestingly, Tanton came to immigration issues from the left. A Sierra
Club activist from the late 1960s, Tanton was highly concerned with population growth in the United States and, for a time, headed the Sierra Club's
Population Committee. By the late 1970s, Tanton had decided immigration
was the real cause of most environmental degradation. He also became concerned about its effects on our civilization. Tanton has openly said that one of
his main inspirations for taking on immigration was *The Camp of the Saints*,
a racist French novel that lays out a lurid vision of dark-skinned Third
World hordes destroying European civilization (Raspail, 1994). To this day,
Tanton's Social Contract Press sells the book, calling it "gripping." In fact,
the 1994 edition of the book published by Tanton carried a special after-
word from author Jean Raspail claiming that the "proliferation of other races
dooms our race . . . to extinction." Tanton clearly embraced Raspail's view of
the deadly threat to white civilization. When it was published, Tanton wrote
that he was "honored" to republish the Frenchman's race war novel. "We are
indebted to Jean Raspail for his insights into the human condition," Tanton
said, "and for being 20 years ahead of his time. History will judge him more
kindly than have some of his contemporaries" (Potok, 2003b).

In the late 1970s, research showed, Tanton had begun to build a multior-
ganizational anti-immigration movement. He laid out his strategy in 1986
in secret memos that proposed, among other things, the creation of multiple
think tanks to focus on the negative effects of immigration and a possible
anti-immigration takeover of the Sierra Club. Unfortunately for Tanton,
his memos were also marked by anti-Latino bigotry, something made public
when they were leaked to the *Arizona Republic* in 1988 (Tanton, 1986). Several prominent persons, including newsman Walter Cronkite and conservative Republican Linda Chavez, left their positions at Tanton's U.S. English
as a result of the disclosures. Tanton, too, quit as the group's chairman. But
the negative publicity didn't deter Tanton's ambitious work in organizing a
crackdown on immigration. Between 1980 and 2002, Tanton had a hand
in either the founding or the funding of 13 anti-immigration groups, many
of them well known. And staffers found that many of these organizations
inflated membership numbers and nearly all relied on a very narrow donor
base, most notably the far-right financier, Richard Mellon Scaife. They
also found that Tanton employed and shared his office in Michigan with
racist activist Wayne Lutton, with whom he had worked since the early
1990s. Lutton was a longtime member of the CCC editorial board and also
was an adviser to another white supremacist publication, *The Occidental
Quarterly*.

Another battle in this long campaign broke out in 2003, when an Intelligence Project staffer noticed a small ad in *The Social Contract*, the journal

produced by the publishing house run by Tanton. The ad suggested readers join the Sierra Club, the largest environmentalist group in America, in
time to vote early the next year in the group's board elections. Tanton had
written in 1986 of taking over the Sierra Club in a bid to demonstrate that
opposition to immigration came from the left as well as the right, and it
seemed that just such an attempt was under way. It wouldn't be the first
time. In 1998, a Tanton ally, a group then called Sierrans for U.S. Population
Stabilization (SUSPS), had pushed a club resolution calling for closing down
the borders in order to maintain an unsullied environment. Amid much talk
of "the greening of hate," that had been voted down by a margin of 60 to 40
percent.

That 1998 loss didn't stop SUSPS. Instead of pushing further initiatives,
SUSPS began putting its supporters up for the Sierra Club board. By 2003,
they had been so successful in this strategy that three men linked to Tanton
and backed by SUSPS were running for the club's board in the hopes of winning a majority that could change the club's long-held position of neutrality
on immigration.

Drastic measures were called for, and the Intelligence Project responded,
sending an October 2003 letter to Sierra Club President Larry Fahn warning
that the club faced a "hostile takeover" attempt by nativists (Potok, 2003b).
Pushing for more publicity on the SUSPS campaign, the *Report* published the
letter to Fahn and also an interview with a club board director discussing the
past and present takeover attempts. Several major newspaper stories detailed
the SPLC's opposition to the three SUSPS candidates. But staffers worried
that that might not be enough to reach most of the club's 750,000 members.
As a result, a decision was made to ask Morris Dees, the well-known co-
founder of SPLC, to run for the club's board as a way of bringing additional
attention to the purported takeover attempt. Dees only ran so that he could
produce a candidate's statement that would go out to all club members suggesting that they not vote for the three SUSPS candidates. His ballot statement read: "I am not asking that you vote for me. Instead, I am running to
urge that you vote against the 'greening of hate' and against those candidates
backed by SUSPS. Please save the Sierra Club from a takeover by the radical
right" (Dees, 2004). Dees also asked that members not vote for him as he was
running only to publicize the takeover attempt.

After the SPLC letter arrived, a group of Sierra Club members formed
their own group, Groundswell Sierra, to oppose the three nativist candidates.
Using SPLC research, it waged a publicity campaign that was highly effective, endorsing a slate of candidates who believed the club should focus on
the environment alone. And 13 former club presidents signed an open letter
denouncing the takeover attempt.

In the end, 171,000 members of the club voted—the highest total in the
group's history—and the three SUSPS candidates were defeated by margins

of 10 to 1, despite the fact that at least some of them had been expected to win (SPLC, 2004a).

The battle with immigration extremists continued in the years that followed, as vigilante groups exploded across the country and many news commentators and talk radio hosts participated in the spreading of false and defamatory propaganda about immigrants (Beirich, 2007a, 2007b). The Intelligence Project published dozens of important stories detailing the falsity of many of these accusations and the role played by politicians and pundits in helping to spread this propaganda (Beirich & Potok, 2005). In 2007, SPLC staffers would engage in a lengthy battle with CNN anchor Lou Dobbs over his repeated promotion of falsehoods about immigrants and his popularizing of nativist extremists (SPLC, 2007).

CONCLUSION

The Southern Poverty Law Center's Intelligence Project does not merely seek to monitor hate groups or document their activities for future historians—it actively seeks to destroy or incapacitate these groups. Over the years, it has fleshed out several major new strategies, and hundreds of more detailed tactics, that inform its work against these organizations. As lawsuits have become less effective, Intelligence Project staffers have increasingly concentrated on using the tools of public awareness—tools that have turned out to be surprisingly effective, probably largely because the Intelligence Project's magazine, the *Intelligence Report*, has won such widespread respect. As a result, using facts and a carefully cultivated level of credibility, the SPLC has been able to reduce significantly the impact of racial hatred on American society.

REFERENCES

Beirich, H. (2007a, Summer). The paranoid style redux. *Intelligence Report*, 126. Retrieved September 22, 2008, from http://www.splcenter.org/intel/intelreport/article.jsp?aid=797

Beirich, H. (2007b, Summer). Getting immigration facts straight. *Intelligence Report*, 126. Retrieved September 22, 2008, from http://www.splcenter.org/intel/intelreport/article.jsp?aid=797

Beirich, H., & Moser, B. (2003, Fall). Monkey business. *Intelligence Report*, 111. Retrieved September 22, 2008, from http://www.splcenter.org/intel/intelreport/article.jsp?aid=113

Beirich, H., & Moser, B. (2004, Fall). Communing with the council. *Intelligence Report*, 115. Retrieved September 22, 2008, from http://www.splcenter.org/intel/intelreport/article.jsp?aid=487

Beirich, H., & Potok, M. (2003, Fall). 40 to watch. *Intelligence Report*, 111. Retrieved September 22, 2008, from http://www.splcenter.org/intel/intelreport/article.jsp?pid=213

Beirich, H., & Potok, M. (2005, Winter). Broken record. *Intelligence Report*, 120. Retrieved September 22, 2008, from http://www.splcenter.org/intel/intelreport/article.jsp?aid=589

Buchanan, S. (2006, November 27). Border vigilante ordered to pay damages in SPLC-sponsored suit. Retrieved September 22, 2008, from http://www.splcenter.org/intel/news/item.jsp?aid=93

Dees, M. (2004, January 22). Morris Dees' Sierra Club candidate statement seeks tolerance. Retrieved September 22, 2008, from http://www.splcenter.org/news/item.jsp?aid=47

Holthouse, D., & Potok, M. (2008, Spring). The year in hate. *Intelligence Report*, 129. Retrieved September 22, 2008, from http://www.splcenter.org/intel/intelre port/article.jsp?aid=886

Lee, M. A. (2002, Fall). Sympathy for the devil. Intelligence Report, 107. Retrieved September 22, 2008 from http://www.splcenter.org/intel/intelreport/article.jsp?aid=31

MacDonald, A. (1978). *The Turner Diaries*. Mill Point, WV: National Vanguard Books.

Mock, B. (2007, Winter). Immigration backlash. *Intelligence Report*, 128. Retrieved September 22, 2008, from http://www.splcenter.org/intel/intelreport/article.jsp?aid=845

Moser, B. (2003, Fall). Return of the 'Kosher Nazi.' *Intelligence Report*, 111. Retrieved September 22, 2008, from http://www.splcenter.org/intel/intelreport/article.jsp?aid=121

Potok, M. (2003a, Fall). Against the wall. *Intelligence Report*, 111. Retrieved September 22, 2008, from http://www.splcenter.org/intel/intelreport/article.jsp?aid=114

Potok, M. (2003b, October 21). Letter to the Sierra Club. Retrieved September 22, 2008, from http://www.splcenter.org/images/dynamic/main/Potok_Sierra_letter.pdf

Raspail, Jean. (1994). *Camp of the saints*. Petoskey, MI: The Social Contract Press.

Southern Poverty Law Center. (1998, Winter). Right meets far right. *Intelligence Report*, 89. Retrieved September 22, 2008, from http://www.splcenter.org/intel/in telreport/article.jsp?aid=463

Southern Poverty Law Center. (1999a, Spring). Knight of freedom. *Intelligence Report*, 94. Retrieved September 22, 2008, from http://www.splcenter.org/intel/intelre port/article.jsp?aid=344

Southern Poverty Law Center. (1999b, Winter). Sharks in the mainstream. *Intelligence Report*, 93. Retrieved September 22, 2008, from http://www.splcenter.org/intel/intelreport/article.jsp?aid=360

Southern Poverty Law Center. (1999c, Winter). Counsel of citizens. *Intelligence Report*, 93. Retrieved September 22, 2008, from http://www.splcenter.org/intel/in telreport/article.jsp?sid=237

Southern Poverty Law Center. (2000, Winter). Neofascism, European style. *Intelligence Report*, 97. Retrieved September 22, 2008, from http://www.splcenter.org/intel/intelreport/article.jsp?sid=207

Southern Poverty Law Center. (2001a, Spring). "Blood on the border." *Intelligence Report*, 101. Retrieved September 22, 2008, from http://www.splcenter.org/intel/intelreport/article.jsp?aid=230

Southern Poverty Law Center. (2001b, Fall). Hands across the water. *Intelligence Report*, 103. Retrieved September 22, 2008, from http://www.splcenter.org/intel/intelreport/article.jsp?aid=177

Southern Poverty Law Center. (2002a, Summer). The puppeteer. *Intelligence Report*, 106. Retrieved September 22, 2008, from http://www.splcenter.org/intel/intel report/article.jsp?aid=93

Southern Poverty Law Center. (2002b, Fall). Dangerous liaisons. *Intelligence Report*, 107. Retrieved September 22, 2008, from http://www.splcenter.org/intel/intel report/article.jsp?aid=34

Southern Poverty Law Center. (2002c, Fall). William Pierce: a political history. *Intelligence Report*, 107. Retrieved September 22, 2008, from http://www.splcenter. org/intel/intelreport/article.jsp?aid=35

Southern Poverty Law Center. (2002d, Fall). The alliance and the law. *Intelligence Report*, 107. Retrieved September 22, 2008, from http://www.splcenter.org/intel/ intelreport/article.jsp?aid=36

Southern Poverty Law Center. (2002e, Fall). Facing the future. *Intelligence Report*, 107. Retrieved September 22, 2008, from http://www.splcenter.org/intel/intel report/article.jsp?aid=43

Southern Poverty Law Center. (2002f, Winter). U.S. boots Brit. *Intelligence Report*, 108. Retrieved September 22, 2008, from http://www.splcenter.org/intel/intel report/article.jsp?aid=80

Southern Poverty Law Center. (2004a, April 21). Anti-immigration candidates rejected in Sierra Club election. Retrieved September 22, 2008, from http://www. splcenter.org/news/item.jsp?aid=61

Southern Poverty Law Center. (2004b, Spring). EURO chief's final answer: pornography trumps Aryanism. *Intelligence Report*, 113. Retrieved September 22, 2008, from http://www.splcenter.org/intel/intelreport/article.jsp?aid=384

Southern Poverty Law Center. (2004c, Spring). "Hostile takeover." *Intelligence Report*, 113. Retrieved September 22, 2008, from http://www.splcenter.org/intel/intel report/article.jsp?aid=384

Southern Poverty Law Center. (2005a, April 22). Nazis, racists join Minuteman Project. Retrieved September 22, 2008, from http://www.splcenter.org/intel/news/ item.jsp?aid=13

Southern Poverty Law Center. (2005b, January 28). Panzerfaust collapses amid accusations against founder. Retrieved September 22, 2008, from http://www.splcen ter.org/intel/news/item.jsp?aid=9

Southern Poverty Law Center. (2006, Spring). White noise. *Intelligence Report*, 121. Retrieved September 22, 2008, from http://www.splcenter.org/intel/intelre port/ article.jsp?pid=1053

Southern Poverty Law Center. (2007, May 9). Center urges CNN to retract false reporting by Lou Dobbs. Retrieved September 22, 2008, from http://www.splcen ter.org/news/item.jsp?aid=254

Tanton, John. (1986). Memo to WITAN IV Attendees. Retrieved September 22, 2008, from http://www.splcenter.org/intel/intelreport/article.jsp?sid=125

U.S. Department of Justice. (2008). "FARA FAQS." Retrieved September 22, 2008, from http://www.usdoj.gov/criminal/fara/links/faq.html

Zaitchik, A. (2006, Winter). The best revenge. *Intelligence Report*, 124. Retrieved September 22, 2008, from http://www.splcenter.org/intel/intelreport/article. jsp?aid=732

ABOUT THE EDITOR
AND CONTRIBUTORS

Frederick M. Lawrence is the dean and Robert Kramer Research Professor of Law at the George Washington University Law School. He is the author of *Punishing Hate: Bias Crimes Under American Law*, which examines bias-motivated violence and how the United States deals with such crimes. He has written widely in the areas of civil rights crimes and free expression. Dean Lawrence began his legal career in 1980 as clerk to Judge Amalya L. Kearse of the U.S. Court of Appeals for the Second Circuit. Later, he was named an assistant U.S. attorney for the Southern District of New York, where he became chief of the office's civil rights unit. In 1988 he joined the faculty of Boston University School of Law, where he served until 2005, when he became dean at George Washington University. Dean Lawrence has been a senior visiting research fellow with the University College London Faculty of Law and has studied bias crimes law in the United Kingdom through a Ford Foundation grant. Dean Lawrence has coauthored a number of Supreme Court amicus curiae briefs, including the brief on behalf of the Anti-Defamation League, People for the American Way, and a wide range of other civil rights groups in *Virginia v. Black* (2003), concerning the constitutionality of the Virginia cross-burning statutes.

Heidi Beirich is the director of research and special projects for the Southern Poverty Law Center's Intelligence Project.

Jeannine Bell is professor of Law and the Charles Whistler Faculty Fellow at the University of Indian School of Law—Bloomington. Professor

Bell has written extensively on hate crime and criminal justice issues, and is the author of *Policing Hatred: Law Enforcement, Civil Rights, and Hate Crime* (2002) which is an ethnography of a police hate crime unit, and *Police and Policing Law* (2006), an edited collection that explores law and society scholarship on the police. Her scholarship has appeared in the *Harvard Civil Rights-Civil Liberties Law Review*, the *Rutgers Race & the Law Review*, *Punishment and Society*, and the *Michigan Journal of Race and Law*. An associate editor of the *Law and Society Review*, Bell has served as a trustee of the Law and Society Association and as a member of the American Political Association's Presidential Taskforce on Political Violence and Terrorism. Her current research focuses on the impact of hate crime on housing segregation.

Susie Bennett, MA, MS, is a research associate at West Virginia University. Her graduate work was completed at Northeastern University and the University of California, Irvine. Ms. Bennett's current research focuses on inner city gangs, hate crimes, and community policing.

Richard W. Cole, Esq., Civil Rights and Safe Schools Consultant, is a nationally known civil rights attorney from Boston, Massachusetts. He is a former assistant attorney general and Civil Rights Division chief at the Massachusetts Office of Attorney General, with 16 years of experience supervising the enforcement of Massachusetts' civil rights injunction law used to address hate crimes in schools, communities, and cyberspace. For many years Richard led a 100-member statewide Hate Crimes Task Force of law enforcement and community leaders to combat hate crimes in Massachusetts. Richard was national cochair, and a primary author and editor of, the U.S. Department of Justice's publication of three hate crime training modules currently used to train state and local law enforcement throughout the United States on hate crime response, investigation, and enforcement.

Kellina Craig-Henderson is a social psychologist whose research interests and activities have focused on interpersonal and intergroup conflict within dyads, small groups, and organizations; as well as the correlates of aggression at each of the preceding levels of analysis. Dr. Craig-Henderson has published numerous reports of empirical research, and the National Science Foundation, the Ford Foundation, and the American Psychological Association have provided support for her work. She has presented findings from her research activities at a variety of regional, national, and international research and pedagogical meetings. She is currently serving as a program director at the National Science Foundation in the Social Psychology program within the Behavioral and Cognitive Sciences division of the Social,

Behavioral, and Economic Sciences directorate, and retains an affiliation with the Department of Psychology at Howard University at the rank of Full Professor.

Richard A. Devine was elected Cook County State's Attorney in November, 1996. He was reelected to a third term in November, 2004. Mr. Devine is a cum laude graduate of Loyola University and Northwestern University School of Law, where he was the managing editor of the *Northwestern Law Review*. He has argued cases before the Illinois Appellate Court, the Illinois Supreme Court, the Seventh Circuit Court of Appeals, and twice before the U.S. Supreme Court. He has been a trial lawyer handling both civil and criminal cases for more than 35 years. Under Mr. Devine the Cook County State's Attorney's Office has been a leader in the development of hate crime legislation and prosecution of hate crime cases.

Steven M. Freeman is the legal affairs director for the Anti-Defamation League. He and coauthor Michael Lieberman have written widely about the impact of hate crimes and have been actively involved in efforts to secure the enactment and to defend the constitutionality of federal and state hate crime laws.

Lindsay J. Friedman is the director of the A WORLD OF DIFFER-ENCE® Institute. She is also senior associate education director at the Anti-Defamation League, where she oversees the development and dissemination of multifaceted antibias and diversity education resources and training models throughout the United States and internationally. She has written numerous antibias manuals for teachers and students, and has contributed to several reports and articles as well as coauthored a chapter on the institute's work for *Education Programs for Improving Intergroup Relations* (2004).

Paul Goldenberg is the former chief of the Office of Bias Crime and Community relations for the New Jersey State Attorney General's Office, the nation's first statewide hate crimes initiative. He currently oversees the OSCE (Office for Security and Cooperation in Europe) police training and assessment initiative focusing specifically on hate crime investigation and response.

Esther Hurh is director of the Training and Curriculum Department in the Education Division of the Anti-Defamation League. She has developed numerous training and curriculum materials regarding bias and discrimination, and presented extensively on these issues in the school and community settings, both domestically and internationally.

Cynthia Lee is a professor of law at the George Washington University Law School where she teaches criminal law, criminal procedure, adjudicatory criminal procedure, and professional responsibility. Professor Lee has published two books and numerous law review articles. Her book *Murder and the Reasonable Man: Passion and Fear in the Criminal Courtroom* (2003) received an honorable mention from the Gustavus Myers Book Awards in 2004. Professor Lee is currently serving as chair of the AALS Criminal Justice Section. She is also a member of the American Law Institute.

Michael Lieberman is the Washington counsel for the Anti-Defamation League. He and coauthor Steve Freeman have written widely about the impact of hate crimes and have been actively involved in efforts to secure the enactment and to defend the constitutionality of federal and state hate crimes laws.

Nicole Manganelli is the assistant director of the Center for the Prevention of Hate Violence. She has conducted hundreds of bias prevention workshops for faculty and students in schools across the United States and in the United Kingdom. She also developed the center's antibias curriculum for elementary school students and has engaged in focus group research on bias in K-12 schools.

James J. Nolan, PhD, is an associate professor of sociology and criminology at West Virginia University. His research and teaching focuses on group relations, crime, and social control. A former police officer and FBI official, Dr. Nolan earned a PhD at Temple University.

Robin Parker is the executive director of the Beyond Diversity Resource Center and is a coauthor of *The Great White Elephant* (2007), and *The Anti-Racist Cookbook* (2005). He previously worked as a deputy attorney general and chief of the New Jersey Office of Bias Crime and Community Relations. For his work in human relations and training he has received numerous awards including the A WORLD OF DIFFERENCE® Award from the ADL, and the Rachel Davis Dubois Award from the International Institute.

Mark Potok is the director of the Intelligence Project of the Southern Poverty Law Center.

Alan J. Spellberg is a deputy supervisor of the Criminal Appeals Division of the Cook County State's Attorney's Office in Chicago, Illinois. In 1999, he was appointed to the Illinois Commission on Discrimination and Hate Crime, and served as the chair of the Subcommittee on Youth until 2003. A prosecutor since 1994, he has been recognized for his work by both the National District Attorneys Association and the Illinois Prosecutor's Bar Association.

Stephen Wessler is the Executive Director of the Center for the Prevention of Hate Violence. He has written several publications on issues of bias and discrimination including *The Respectful School: How Educators and Students Can Conquer Hate and Harassment* (2003); "Sticks and Stones," published in *Educational Leadership* 88, no. 4 (December-January 2001–2002); "It's Hard to Learn When You're Scared," published in *Educational Leadership* 61, no. 1 (2003); and several other articles, chapters, reports, and monographs.

Christopher Wolf is a litigation partner specializing in Internet and Privacy Law at the law firm of Proskauer Rose LLP. He serves as chair of the Internet Task Force of the Anti-Defamation League and of the International Network Against Cyber-Hate (INACH).

INDEX